DEPARTURE FOR THE SOUTH

Zong Pu

ABOUT THE AUTHOR

Zong Pu, formerly known as Feng Zhongpu (1928-), is the daughter of the famous Chinese philosopher Feng Youlan (1895-1990). She graduated from the Foreign Language Department of Tsinghua University and retired from the Institute of Foreign Literature at the Chinese Academy of Social Sciences. Her work is not only deeply rooted in traditional Chinese culture but is also inspired by prolonged exposure to, and immersion in, foreign cultures. Imbued with the spiritual connotations of oriental tradition, philosophy and culture combined with western humanistic ideology, her work embodies a unique artistic temperament and an elegant style. Her main body of work includes the following:

Prose/Essays - '*West Lake Essay*' (西湖漫笔); '*The Cascading Snowfield*' (奔落的雪原) – a travelogue about a visit to Niagara Falls; '*Flower Festival Commemoration*' (花朝节的纪念); '*Broken Memories of Three Pines Hall*' (三松堂的断忆); and '*Tears Shed for My Little Brother*' (哭小弟).

Novels - '*Red Beans*' (红豆); '*Lulu*' (鲁鲁); '*The Everlasting Rock*' (三生石); and '*The Bright Passage of the Four Seasons*' (四季流光).

Fairy tales - '*Searching for the Moon*' (寻月记); '*Flower Talk*' (花的话); '*The Story of the Fringed-Fin Fish*' (总鳍鱼的故事); and '*Taotao the Little Novice Monk*' (小沙弥陶陶).

A multi-volume series of novels under the series title '*Wild Gourd Overture*' (野葫芦引), comprising the individual titles '*Departure for the South*' (南渡记); '*Eastern Concealment*' (东藏记); '*Western Expedition*' (西征记); '*Return to the North*' (北归记) and '*Wild Gourd Finale*' (接引葫芦); among which '*Eastern Concealment*' won the 6th Mao Dun Literature Prize in 2005, one of the most prestigious literature prizes in China.

Other Awards - Her short story '*Dream of Cello Strings*' (弦上的梦) won the National Outstanding Short Story Award; her novella '*The Everlasting Rock*' (三生石) won the Outstanding Novella Award; her essays entitled '*A Collection of Lilac Knots*' (丁香结) won the Outstanding Prose Prize; and her fairy tale '*The Story of the Fringed-Fin Fish*' (总鳍鱼的故事) won the Outstanding Fairy Tale Award. Many of her novels, fairy tales and collections of prose and essays have been translated into different languages.

Published by
ACA Publishing Ltd.
University House
11-13 Lower Grosvenor Place
London SW1W 0EX, UK
Tel: +44 (0)20 7834 7676
Fax: +44 (0)20 7973 0076
E-mail: info@alaincharlesasia.com
Web:www.alaincharlesasia.com
Beijing Office
Tel: +86(0)10 8472 1250
Fax: +86(0)10 5885 0639

Author: Zong Pu
Translator: Wen Lingxia
Editors: Martin Savery and Elena Stephenson

Published by ACA Publishing Ltd in association
with the People's Literature Publishing House

© 2016, by People's Literature Publishing House, Beijing, China
ALL RIGHTS RESERVED. NO PART OF THIS
PUBLICATION MAY BE REPRODUCED IN MATERIAL FORM,
BY ANY MEANS, WHETHER GRAPHIC,
ELECTRONIC, MECHANICAL OR OTHER, INCLUDING
PHOTOCOPYING OR INFORMATION STORAGE, IN WHOLE OR IN PART, AND
MAY NOT BE USED TO PREPARE
OTHER PUBLICATIONS WITHOUT WRITTEN
PERMISSION FROM THE PUBLISHER.

The greatest care has been taken to ensure accuracy but the
publisher can accept no responsibility for errors or omissions, or
for any liability occasioned by relying on its content.

ISBN 978-1-910760-34-5

A catalogue record for *Departure for the South* is available from the
National Bibliographic Service of the British Library.

EXPLANATORY NOTE TO THE SERIES TITLE

The bottle gourd is an ordinary plant. But this name conjures up a lot of associations in Chinese minds and can be enriched to build a whole world around gourds. A common linked meaning, of course, is the wide variety of medicines sold in various containers made of gourds. That no one could see through the gourd containers or know what medical ingredients were inside has shrouded them in mystery.

Gourds often used to contain wine came to be known as wine gourds. During Lin Chong's* exile at the army supply depot, he took a wine gourd into the field to get wine, and the wine sellers first recognised his gourd and that there could be a world of wine in the gourd.

Gourds are also used as urinals to hold children's urine, which is related to the growth of life. At the end of the first chapter of *'Departure for the South'*, in 'The Heart of the Wild Bottle Gourds' I was writing about urine gourds. Even the story of *'Dream of the Red Chamber'*** starts from the myth of the Mother Goddess Nüwa fixing the broken sky, and then enters the real world from a house near the Gourd Temple.

The boundless universe can be hidden in a bottle gourd, as well as traces of history and the lives of people from many different backgrounds. But compared to the magnificence of the real world, what I have recorded in these books can only be considered as an overture at the start of a symphony. Hence the title for this series of novels: '*Wild Gourd Overture*'.

* *a fictional character in one of China's great classical novels 'The Water Margin'*

** *arguably the greatest classical Chinese novel of all time, written by Cao Xueqin*

Foreword

'The Thunder Storm'

A century full of shame and humiliation
Forged by truces and treaties.
The neverending flames of war burnt the night,
Blazing bright as daylight.
Thousands upon thousands of lives snuffed out
Like the seeds of dandelions dissipated in the wind.
Countless patriotic hearts rallied to the cause
Singing so sweetly that the passing clouds stopped to listen.
Knights in their shining armour inside
And outside the Great Wall
Were seen no more.
Rumbling in their ears instead
Was the piercing roar of gunfire on Marco Polo bridge.

'Tears Fell on 'Square Teakettle''

People shed tears and blood,
Tinting the rivers of bitter woe and lamentation red.
All faded and fell!
People forced to leave their homes,
Condemned to live in exile.
Lives hanging on the muzzles of guns,
Struggling to survive forests of bayonets.
Alive but already having bidden farewell to life,
Leaving behind their noble spirits,
Imperishable in the river of time.
Books discarded,
Sweet ink spilt.
Farewell to the zither room,
When the zither was smashed.
What would that matter if all were fighting for the cause?
How many tears shed!
What would those tiny fireflies matter?

'Meeting in the City of Eternal Spring'

We took refuge in the beautiful city.
Our hearts ached over the remnants of territory.
When would they come to an end,
All those piercing air-raid sirens?
When would we have a decent meal
Instead of beetroot stew?
When would our rice be free of worms or grit?

But the camellia bloomed still,
Pink like the flush on children's faces,
And the winter-sweet flowers bloomed like they did years ago.
The dim flickering light from the oil lamp
Warmed up the shabby home,
The passionate talk about revitalizing the nation
Warmed desperate hearts.
Many of them will be remembered by history.
The tumbling river roaring to the east without turning back,
But not the heartbroken wails of sorrow far and wide.

"Waiting for the Souls to Return"

Bad times bred bad things.
At the front, soldiers died in their thousands.
In the rear, speculators closed their dirty deals.
In the fancy houses in town, chrysanthemums
Bloomed with unbridled joy.
The countryside stricken with floods and droughts in turn,
Troops forcibly recruited from among
The few indignant remaining villagers.
The powerful enemy pressuring our border.
Were we going to lose that frontier city?
Any scholar would trade his precious pen for a sharp sword!
How noble their spirit!
How courageous their spirit to fight the god of death!
How could they tear away the shadow of war overhead?
Gone was their youth.
Gone were the good old times.
When would it be time to go home?

'BROKEN HOMECOMING DREAMS'

Eight years ticked by, longing to go home every night.
The time finally came like a bolt out of the blue.
My heart missed a beat upon thinking of seeing the old place.
Could things have remained the same?
We fought our way back and regained our territory.
How glorious the moment when the enemy surrendered!
How gracious we were standing on our own land!
Who could have foreseen the separation
Between the living and the dead,
The eternal pounding of the parting
Between wife and husband?
What sorrow afflicts the love-stricken heart?
How could one survive for the rest of one's life?
How much more suffering would they have to endure
Till they met each other on the river of woe?

'IN ANTICIPATION OF PEACE'

The sun rose red in the east.
Everyone yearned for the warm fine days of spring,
For a time of blissful happiness.
Who could tell reality from hallucination,
Glory from humiliation,
Passion from indifference,
Good luck from bad?
Story or history?
Readers can judge for themselves.
What was it in those mysterious bottle gourds?
Could it be just visions and dreams?

Chief Characters in the Novel and Their Relationships

Lü Qingfei: Father of Suchu, Jiangchu and Bichu
Zhao Lianxiu: second wife of Lü Qingfei
Meng Fuzhi: professor, History Department, Minglun University
Lü Bichu: Wife of Meng Fuzhi, the third daughter of Lü Qingfei
Earl (aka Meng Liji): eldest daughter of Meng Fuzhi
May (aka Meng Lingji): second daughter of Meng Fuzhi
Kiddo (aka Meng Heji): son of Meng Fuzhi, the youngest
Lü Jiangchu: second daughter of Lü Qingfei
Tantai Mian: husband of Lü Jiangchu, Vice Manager General, North China Power Company
Tantai Xuan: daughter of Lü Jiangchu
Tantai Wei: son of Lü Jiangchu
Wei Feng: nephew of Meng Fuzhi, lecturer at Minglun University
Ling Xueyan: wife of Wei Feng
Ling Jingyao: father of Ling Xueyan
Yue Hengfen: mother of Ling Xueyan
Miao Donghui: uncle of Yue Hengfen,
Zhuang Youchen: professor, Department of Physics, Minglun University
Della: wife of Zhuang Youchen, English
Zhuang Wuyin: son of Zhuang Youchen
Zhuang Wucai: daughter of Zhuang Youchen
Lü Guitang: grandnephew directly linked to Lü Qingfei
Lü Xiangge: daughter of Lü Guitang
Li Yuming: lecturer, Minglun University, best friend of Wei Feng and Ling Xueyan
Thunderhand (Zhang Xinlei): friend of Earl, second-year undergraduate, Minglun University
Paul McAllen : official at the American embassy
Li Lian: lecturer, Chinese Department, Minglun University
Jin Shizhen: wife of Li Lian
Li Zhiqin, Li Zhiwei: daughters of Li Lian

CHAPTER I

PART 1

Beiping (modern-day Beijing) languished in the heat of an extraordinary summer. It wasn't yet the height of the season, but already thermometers across the city had climbed to about 100°F. Even before the sun had fully risen in the sky, the people of Beiping were wiping the sweat from their brows, their clothes beginning to stick. The cool from the previous night didn't help, the dawn dew evaporating with the sun's first rays. Flowers wilted, grass scorched, and trees bowed under the ferocity of the heat, the leaves drooping. As the clock hit noon, the sun burned all the brighter, searing the earth below like an inferno, roasting the city with its relentless heat, showing no mercy to those below. Not a breath of wind could escape the intensity. Even Jingshan mountain, covered with an oasis of lush, green trees, looked glaring white in the heat of the day, and the surface of the Beihai and Zhongnanhai lakes rippled like a mirage, the sun evaporating the water, sucking it upwards. From the steam rising, it was clear there was no hint of coolness left in the body of water to give relief to those who might have taken a dip.

Whether it was a vision seen in the ripple of hot, biting air, the city folk could not be sure, but something terrifying seemed to be approaching in the summer heat. It was unsettling, and nothing could be done to ease the fear.

It was hard to describe the feeling the people of Beiping were experiencing, but it was not unique, or even rare, for the city during the 1930s. It was a feeling they knew well.

In the aftermath of the Japanese invasion of northeast China, a palpable sense of danger enveloped the land. All of China was in danger, and impending doom loomed over the nation, drawing closer with every passing day.

Hoping to halt its approach, the government signed the Tanggu Truce[1], agreeing to the boundaries already demarcated by the Great Wall, drawing a much-needed, understood line between the Japanese army and the Republic of China. Later, another agreement of this kind was signed between the two, the He-Umezu Agreement[2], resulting in the Chinese army stationed in Hebei province being recalled.

From then on, fighting the Japanese openly was forbidden, while a political desire for the 'North China Autonomy Movement' had come to the forefront of the Japanese mindset, perpetuated by their Chinese lackeys. They had big ideas, with ambitions to bring five north China provinces under the rule of the Japanese.

It wasn't just the summer heat the people of Beiping had to contend with, as the political landscape began to change over the following years. Newspaper headlines like 'Strange Spy Planes Spotted over Bailing Temple[3]' didn't alarm people like they used to. It had become the norm. People had even grown

---

[1] The Tanggu Truce, sometimes called the Tangku Truce (塘沽协定 *tanggu xieding*), was a cease-fire signed between the Republic of China and the Empire of Japan in Tanggu district, Tianjin on 31 May 1933, formally ending the Japanese invasion of Manchuria, which had begun two years earlier.

[2] The He-Umezu Agreement (梅津・何応欽協定 *Umezu-Ka Okin Kyōtei* in Japanese) was a secret agreement between the Empire of Japan and the Republic of China concluded on 10 June 1935, two years prior to the outbreak of general hostilities in the Second Sino-Japanese War.)

used to the presence of the Japanese, now daring to stare at the cocky Japanese soldiers marching along the street, though they only chanced it for a couple of minutes, even then.

Day to day life resumed and people got on with it, as they always had, trying to enjoy the lifestyle Beiping had to offer. In the evening, some city folk went to the Peking Opera, to sample the delights of performances from the Tan School or Ma School[4]. During the day, cigarette-stall owners hung their bird cages from the trees all around, keeping the beautiful birds within easy reach to pet and show to passers-by. On their way to school, high-spirited students sped along on their bicycles, their perpetual enthusiasm infectious, undampened by any of the things going on around them.

Like clockwork, the sun rose each morning from the east of the No. 4 East Archway and set to the west of the No. 4 West Archway. The ancient archways had endured more than even the oldest Beiping residents, and they were still standing, defiant and proud. Not once, in their entire history, had they succumbed to fire or anything else, for that matter.

Along the Green Dyke in the Lake of Ten Temples, the farmers set up their wares, offering fresh lotus roots, fresh water-chestnuts, fresh gorgon fruits, anything you could possibly want. However, there was something stirring in the midst of such peace. It was like inviting a stranger into your home, tolerating their presence, trying to act normal, but never fully being able to relax until they had gone again.

---

[3] Bailing Temple: a transliteration of Mongolian, 'Guangfu Temple' in Chinese, located in Baotou city, Inner Mongolia autonomous region, is a Tibetan Buddhist temple.

[4] The Tan School: the earliest creation of Peking Opera genre. It was founded by famous *laosheng*, an elderly male role, Tan Xinpei. This school is known for its simple but elegant singing style. The Ma School: founded by Ma Lianliang, a pupil of Tan. Ma was popular for decades in the 20th century. This school was noted for its unique style and emphasis on the artistic beauty of a performance.

People got on with their lives, as if they couldn't feel anything strange in the air, choosing to ignore it instead. They engaged in small talk, their idle chat often turning to the weather.

"This is a wicked summer! I'm telling you," they'd say, although if truth be told, it might well have been as hot as this last summer, they had simply forgotten.

It was all the common folk could think about - the small things. What might happen tomorrow, or next week, or even in the next minute, was beyond their reckoning. It was too far ahead.

It was just after two in the afternoon when a black car appeared.

From Xizhimen gate, across Gaoliang bridge, there was a gravel road that extended from west to north. The sun's heat baked the road, and the heat rising up was hot enough to pierce any flimsy shoe, made of cotton. It was a long, straight road, with few corners, and it was like entering another world, as you took Xizhimen gate and passed some squat civilian houses, getting out of the city and into the countryside. On the horizon, rolling fields of green stretched away as far as the eye could see, and Xishan (West mountain) rose up more prominently than ever, highlighted by the blazing sun, though at times it seemed to fade into the glare of the bright light, only to reappear again through the heat haze.

Tall trees lined both sides of the road, their branches drooping over, the ferocious heat forcing them into submission. It was along this road that the black car traveled, whooshing past the snail-like vehicles that hogged the quiet lane. One slow horse and cart, and a couple of jinrikishas, pulled by weary drivers, were no match for a car of such speed and power, as it headed north.

In the car were two gentlemen, both in their 40s. The first, wearing a pair of black-framed glasses with thick lenses, was Professor Meng Fuzhi, from the history department of Minglun University, his skin much darker than his companion's. The second was Professor Zhuang Youchen from the physics department, who had fair skin and wore a traditional light-grey silk gown. They had just left a lunch in the city, and it appeared to have made Mr Meng look somewhat sulky, though his companion, Mr Zhuang, looked to be in remarkably high spirits.

"The Lushan Conference presided over by Chiang Kai-shek has invited many prestigious people," Youchen began. Such gatherings never lost their excitement with him. Although the conference had been in the papers for a couple of days, it was still fresh news for him. The conference, divided into three phases, invited many noted scholars to participate, aiming to analyse the current situation and offer corresponding strategies.

Staring at the quickly shortening blinding white road ahead, Meng Fuzhi replied rather absent-mindedly: "What kind of problems can the talks solve?"

"You are invited for the third phase. You are going, aren't you?" Youchen asked, his small head and narrow, crystal-clear eyes making him look very innocent.

Meng Fuzhi turned to Youchen and smiled: "Yes, I am. But I'm not optimistic about the outcome. President Yang and Qin from our university have already arrived in Nanjing. They might be in Lushan now."

"Talking always helps," Youchen said, optimistically.

"Our nation has been poor and weak for so long. We need change. Complete change." Fuzhi said. "Have you heard of that nursery rhyme?" With these words, his mind went back to the lunch where his brother-in-law Tantai Mian recited the nursery rhyme to him. Tantai Mian was the vice general manager of the North China Power Company. He had attained his degree in Germany and was quite well recognised in business circles. He mentioned that, during his visit to the Lower Garden Coal Mine, Shijiazhuang, Hebei province, he came across a nursery rhyme that was very popular among the miners' kids:

> *'To the South, further south,*
> *No one came back north;*
> *Bloody wind,*
> *Reign of terror,*
> *The scorching sun in May.'*

Those at the lunch had agreed it actually sounded like the first half of some Song dynasty lyrics in the 'silk-washing stream' style, and Meng Fuzhi said nursery rhymes always mirrored people's minds, bearing a certain prophecy. He then echoed two of the last three lines of the rhyme: '*Bloody wind, reign of terror, the scorching sun in May.*' The tension in the air became palpable, growing heavy with poignancy. Two gentlemen were trying to reach some dishes, but hearing these words, their ebony chopsticks hovered for a second over the table.

"Nursery rhymes are made up," Youchen continued. "Before Li Yuan, the founding emperor of the Tang dynasty, planned to overthrow the Sui dynasty and establish his own, he conceived the myth of 'imperial destiny'[5]. The slate with

---

[5] Before Li Yuan (李渊) took over the Sui dynasty and established the Tang dynasty, he spread a made-up prophecy in nursery rhymes that someone from the Li family was destined to be the emperor. The first two lines go like this: '*The 18th son from the East Sea, is going to be your best king.*' The Chinese character for Li is 李, which is composed of three elements: 十 *shi* (ten), 八 *ba* (eight), and 子 *zi* (son).

the inscription of the prophecy that he was destined to be the rightful ruler was, of course, buried in front of the Hall of Loyalty beforehand."

"What do those lines mean?" Meng Fuzhi asked, more to himself than his companion. "Our nation has been suffering through bloody winds and a reign of terror for almost a century – there is already no escape."

"Are you implying – war?" Youchen wondered, straightening up anxiously.

Meng Fuzhi said nothing for a moment, lost in thought. Finally, he spoke: "The government is still sticking to its appeasement policy. Our chats over lunch today showed our preference for war, but there was a lot of caution in saying so. Did you notice that?"

Youchen's eyes widened, as he racked his brain, reflecting very seriously on whether or not he had seen it.

The gleaming road was looking shorter and shorter, curving ahead of them into the countryside. The car turned off the tree-lined road, heading through a small town. The gate of Minglun University popped into view.

When the car passed, the campus guards, dressed smartly in uniform at the gate, stood to attention and saluted. Meng Fuzhi waved at them. The campus looked like another world. Tall thick trees towered over it, blocking out the heat from the sun, and the noise and chaos from beyond the campus walls. The campus itself was engulfed in green; everywhere you looked, vivid nature peppered the scenery, and the blazing heat was noticeably subdued upon entering the gate, like stepping through a portal into another realm.

"Take Mr Zhuang home first, please," Meng Fuzhi told the driver, Old Song.

Crossing a babbling river, the car halted in front of a Chinese house. Before getting out, Youchen stated solemnly: "Someone was not that cautious. I did notice that. Did you?" Without waiting for the answer, he continued: "That 'someone' was you."

Meng Fuzhi did not reply, as both of them raised their arms a little, bidding each other goodbye. With that, the car turned around and crossed the river again, going into the depths of the campus.

"What did I say?" Meng Fuzhi wondered to himself. As a cautious person, he had a habit of reflecting on the things he had done. He once mentioned: "It would be too time-consuming to indulge in self-reflection three times a day[6], but I guess I can manage at least once a day." He hadn't been dwelling upon his thoughts for long, when he figured out what he had said during the meal time, that he had spoken without due caution: "What brought our nation to such a plight are two things. The longstanding one is for sure the corruption of the Qing dynasty, but the more recent one needs clarification. Our nation has never been short of people with insight and lofty ideas, then why have we failed in so many tasks? One key reason lies in the fact that we are not united." He then recalled how he had talked about the impracticality of turning Beiping into an international city of culture. Such a thought emerged a couple of years ago, with the intention of transforming Beiping into a borderless city, and north China into a separate special region. Meng Fuzhi then pointed out the special separation of north China was nothing but an extension of the 'North China Autonomy

---

[6] Meng Fuzhi was quoting from Master Zeng, one of Confucius' favourite disciples, who once said: "吾日三省吾身，为人谋而不忠乎？与朋友交而不信乎？传不习乎？" ("I engage in self-reflection three times a day. In counseling others, am I sincere? In communicating with friends, am I trustworthy? In learning, am I proficient?")

Movement' manipulated by the Japanese government. "Autonomy or self-government, all automatically go to others in the end." What he had said next, he supposed might have been what Youchen had labeled as 'not so cautious': "We might learn something from the successful revolution of the Soviet Union. Does socialism have more respect for its talented people? Is it better at motivating individuals and uniting them?" Now that he thought about it, he recalled that his talk had been interrupted by a cough from Qian Jingming, a lecturer from the Chinese department, who didn't seem to agree. Xiao Cheng, a professor from the biology department, quickly directed the conversation to a few very general current issues. Not unlike the common folk of Beiping, he was more concerned with small talk than big issues, to divert attention away from anything potentially incendiary.

"Xiao Cheng is even more cautious than I am!" Meng Fuzhi thought. The car traveled down a road shaded with two regimented lines of Chinese Scholar trees on each side and, having passed several antique Chinese-style buildings, the car stopped in front of the gate of the Meng residence. Meng Fuzhi opened the door and got out. Before he left, he told Old Song: "Pick me up at three tomorrow afternoon. I'm going to the Euro-US Alumni Association."

Old Song gave a respectful "yes", and didn't move the car until he had lost sight of Mr Meng, as was his way.

It was quiet inside the residence. The entrance was small but cozy with light-yellow gauze screens on the windows that gave the place a pleasant glow. On the top of the doorframe of the hallway leading to the living room hung a delicate board with two Chinese characters in the style of large seal scripts saying: 'Square Teakettle'. It was thought that this was the original name of the house, after lengthy research into its meaning. Not very far away from the Meng residence was the university president's residence, which had a similar board with inscriptions meaning 'Round Rice-Steamer'. Every time, without exception, when Meng Fuzhi came back home, he felt a palpable sense of safety upon entering the gate. It was good to be home, and he thought of only one thing, his one constant – the radiant face, with a gentle smile, and that innocent voice calling "daddy" would be waiting for him, ready to greet him. Were they already up from their naps? He hoped so.

He moved from the front of the house, walking down into the hallway which had a bay window facing out into the garden. The window was shaped like a half dome, protruding from the wall toward the garden, and under the half dome of the window lay a long wooden bench attached to the wall. The children never got tired of clambering all over that bench, their laughter echoing down the halls. Today, however, rather unexpectedly, Meng Fuzhi found someone sitting on it, with his head drooped low on his small chest.

"Kiddo! Why aren't you taking your nap?" It was something of a shock to see his youngest son at this time of the day, in the garden.

Kiddo didn't jump to his feet or run to greet his father, as he usually would on hearing his father's voice. Instead, he slowly put down what he had been fiddling with, and raised his head so he could look his father in the eye. His face carried a deep solemnity rarely seen on the features of a six-year-old. The boy paused for a second and then, as if he had finally decided against staying put, ran to his father. Grabbing his father's hand, he looked up again into his father's eyes, and asked: "Daddy, when was Jesus born?"

In all honesty, Meng Fuzhi didn't spend much time talking with the children, but even with the limited time they spent together, Kiddo would bombard him with different questions at every opportunity. Sometimes, it made Meng Fuzhi feel quite embarrassed, when a professor like him failed to provide satisfactory answers to most of the questions from his six-year old. But today, he was at ease with this question. It was one he knew the answer to, and he immediately provided it with a small sense of satisfaction: "Today is 7 July 1937, so Jesus was born 1,937 years ago since the solar calendar takes the year of Jesus' birth as the first year."

"Why did people pick Jesus' birthday as the beginning? Why not your birthday, or mum's birthday? Or elder sister's, or May's?"

"Because... because Jesus was a great man," answered Fuzhi, feeling the familiar sensation of uncertainty creeping up on him. He felt suddenly trapped, knowing his son would continue to bombard him with questions, yet knowing it would be impossible for him to tell his son, in a few words, why Jesus was great. "Well, he loved people. He was always ready to help – what were you playing with just now?"

Hoping he could distract Kiddo from his line of questioning, they went back to where Kiddo had been sitting. Kiddo picked up a wooden cross he had left behind on the bench and gave it to his father. The cross had an intricately-carved crucifix, and then it slowly began to dawn on Fuzhi what had prompted Kiddo's question.

"May took it from sister's room."

Kiddo's sister, Meng Liji, nicknamed Earl, was the eldest daughter of Fuzhi. She was graduating from a private Catholic high school this year and was applying for a college.

"That was why people killed him by nailing him to a cross

because Jesus loved people and helped them?" Kiddo asked, his curious eyes still looking up at his father.

"Those… those were definitely bad people," Fuzhi replied, though he found himself unwilling to say more. Seemingly from nowhere, he had begun to grow impatient. He gave the wooden cross back to Kiddo, who sensed the impatience, pondering whether it was because his father was tired at the end of the day. The boy grew silent, not wanting to aggravate his father's impatience. Holding the cross, he followed his father into the master bedroom.

The room was bathed in iridescent colours. The bed and the floor were covered with shiny paper rings, brightly coloured, that were glued up into chains. They looked like rivers of rainbows, flowing in all directions. Fuzhi's wife, Lü Bichu and his 10-year-old daughter May (Meng Lingji) were busy gluing the loose rings.

"Watch out! Don't step on any of those!" they warned the two newcomers, smiling. Kiddo picked up a golden chain and a red chain, and shouted: "I can glue, too!"

"Run along! We are already done here," his mother said, stopping him.

"Is this for Wei Feng's wedding tomorrow?" asked Fuzhi, taking off his gown. May took it immediately and put it on a chair. His wife stood up, still smiling. She took the gown from the chair and hung it up, before heading into the bathroom. When she came out, she handed a cool, wet face-towel to her husband for him to freshen up. Her facial expression calming him, she said: "We don't need to worry about the wedding. It's just that the bridal room is a little bit dull, I think, so some colourful chains of rings might be just the right addition. The room will be brightened up considerably! We have made enough." With those words, she took the cross from Kiddo and inspected it closely: "This belongs to Earl. Why did you take it? Your sister will surely be upset when she finds out."

"I took it," May admitted without delay. "We'll put it back now." Their sister was easily offended, and no one wanted to offend her.

"Let's clean up here first," their mother insisted. Kiddo grinned, joining the clean-up. The mood was instantly brighter, as they all talked and laughed. It was hard to figure out what they were talking about, or why they were laughing, but the sight of them had a strange, calming effect. Sitting comfortably in his wicker chair, Fuzhi murmured to himself: "If the nest is overturned, could the eggs remain intact?"

"What did you say?" Bichu turned to him. She had gathered up the colorful paper chains into one bundle and put it into the closet. Without waiting for the answer, she continued: "How are things now? Anything in the news?"

"The encroachment policy is as obvious as head lice on a monk's head. Their ambition has gone wild. It's impossible to satisfy their appetite. Appeasement only leads to death," he answered. Realising that there were three very similar-looking, stunned faces staring at him, he laughed, more at himself than anyone else: "Well, it won't immediately hit Beiping." The words were supposed to ease their worried faces and, as he spoke them, he stood up and headed for his home office, a strictly restricted area in the house off limits to the children. It was his private sanctuary, with rows upon rows of bookcases occupying more than half of the room. A large desk stood next to the window, filled to the brim with manuscripts. This desk was the Forbidden City in the room; even Bichu did not have access to it. As Fuzhi always said: "Although the room looks like a mess, it's an orderly mess. If that order is interfered with, it would turn into a real mess." Behind the swivelling armchair was a wall with a giant pair of couplets. Each character from the couplets, covering almost one square foot, was a genuine rubbing from the original inscriptions of Sutra Vajra in the Inscription Valley of Mount Tai in Shandong province. On the left was '*no me no you*', and on the right '*see heaven see truth*'. Standing among the manuscripts was a table lamp with a green glass lampshade framed with copper lines. The body of the lamp was covered with tiny inscriptions in small seal style. On closer inspection, one could see it was a complete copy of the 5,000-character book *Tao Te Ching* by Lao Tzu[7].

In front of the chair was a small rectangular table crowded with several calligraphy inkstones in assorted shapes and sizes. Some were encased in painted boxes made of ordinary wood, some in boxes made of mahogany. The one named 'the Ink Sea' was carved out of a rectangular stone, and at each corner of the stone stood a bridge, all clustered around a circular concave centre where the ink was contained. Another inkstone looked just like a big brick, simple in looks but smooth to the touch. It was a genuine Han dynasty[8] antique. Both inkstones were Fuzhi's prized possessions, but his eyes were not drawn to them as they usually were. Instead, he found himself fixated by the couplets on the wall, simply staring at those big characters in total silence. A long while later, he suddenly turned from the couplets, their hypnotic spell over him broken, and sat down at his desk. He swept all

---

[7] *Tao Te Ching*: (道德经 *daode jing*) written by Lao Tzu (老子) is one of the great Chinese classical texts. As a major founding source for both philosophical and religious Taoism, this book has had a far-reaching influence on Legalism, Confucianism and Chinese Buddhism.

[8] The Han dynasty: (漢朝 *han chao*) was the second imperial dynasty of China (206BC-220AD), preceded by the Qin dynasty (221-206BC) and succeeded by the Three Kingdoms period (220-280AD). Spanning over four centuries, the Han period is considered a golden era in Chinese history.

the manuscripts out of the way, ignoring the way they creased, twisted or crumpled up as he did so, and immersed himself in the task of writing his book – *Exploring Chinese History*.

May and Kiddo horsed around in their parents' room for some time until Amah Zhao came in and told Bichu that Chef Chai wanted to know whether he should plant those 'bleeding hearts' he had taken from President Qin's family garden, along the border of the flowerbed in their own garden. Chef Chai's name was Chai Fali, and he was the cook and the gardener for the Meng family. They treasured him, knowing Chef Chai had good taste when it came to both cooking and gardening, making the kitchen smell good and the garden look beautiful. Bichu told Amah Zhao she would go and have a look. Amah Zhao smiled and reminded her: "The sun is still high in the sky. The ground is scorching hot. How about my lady going after dinner?"

"Tell him to plant along the border of the flower bed then," Bichu said, after thinking for a while, "and when you are done, please come to help me arrange the kids' outfits. May's is ready, but Kiddo's shorts need new buttons."

"Miss Earl is not going?" Amah Zhao asked, tidying as she went.

"She's busy," Bichu answered. "She's busy even after the graduation exams," she sighed, furrowing her eyebrows in thought. Turning around, she saw May and her little brother absorbed in reading *Grimm's Fairy Tales*, and a warm smile of contentment emerged at the corners of her mouth upon seeing the two small heads knitted together over the book. Their dark hair was shiny like silk, gleaming in the sunshine that glanced in. "Has grandfather got up from his nap?"

"He has just now. He's doing his brush-writing," Amah Zhao answered, with a forced smile. "I'm going to tell Chef Chai how to plant the flowers. I'll be right back." With a quick nod, she excused herself to deal with the tasks at hand. The flowers could not wait.

"Let's go and see grandpa," Kiddo said, raising his head from the book. His grandpa, Lü Qingfei, lived in town and was a 'neighbour' of his second daughter Jiangchu. He paid regular visits to his youngest daughter Bichu and would spend a couple of weeks at a time with the family. The two lovely children, especially Kiddo, were his reason to visit, and they loved to see him too.

"You go first. I'll be a while," May was still reading the story, her eyes transfixed, a look of consternation on her sweet face. She was so worried about the fate of the young hero in the book that she wished she could jump into the book to help, and could do nothing but read on, hoping for the best.

"Grandpa says we can go to his room. We can go every afternoon." Kiddo ran to his mother and leaned on her, as Bichu lovingly patted him on the head: "There's prepared litchi in the fridge. You go and help yourself. Grandfather will come out of his room when he gets tired of writing."

"May, do you want some litchi?" Kiddo asked. May didn't raise her head from her book, she didn't even hear Kiddo, she was so engrossed in what she was reading. He ran to her impatiently and covered the pages she found so exciting with his hands. May pushed him away, irritated by the rude interruption, and said: "No! No! I don't want any." Kiddo ran away, laughing. Although he loved his sister, he did so like to tease her.

Meanwhile, Bichu took a pair of copper paperweights from her dressing table. On the front sides of the paper weights were the third and fourth lines from a poem by Tang dynasty poet Wang Wei – *'The bright moonlight beamed through the pine trees,'* and *'the crystal-clear spring water dashed against the big rocks'*. The backs were painted with elegant patterns of pine trees and cranes, symbols of happiness and longevity that always brought Bichu pleasure. Carefully, she put them into the centre of a padded carton; these were to be wedding presents from her father Mr Lü Qingfei to the new Wei couple. Wei Feng was the son of Fuzhi's female cousin from his father's side. A very close relative. Feng, who admired Mr Lü very much, had invited Mr Lü a couple of times to attend his wedding, but Mr Lü only sent his presents and best wishes. After reaching his 70s, he no longer attended such festivities, though he looked fairly hale and hearty for his age. As an excuse for his absence, he would always say: "Being old is quite annoying. I'd like to spare those who are not."

The phone beside the door began to ring. May rushed to answer it, the book still clutched in her hand: "Aunt Jiangchu? It's me, May…. I'm reading my *Grimm's Fairy Tales*. Yes, mum's coming." Bichu took the phone May handed to her: "Sis Jiangchu? Ah yes, father is going back to town tomorrow and will stay there for a couple of days. We'll go with him. Mian is coming to pick him up? Does he have some business to deal with here? Alright. Yes, I know. The kids have been nagging me to take them to town once school stopped for the summer vacation. But tomorrow is not the day. After Wei Feng's wedding, I need to come back and entertain the remaining guests. The bride's room is set in the Hall of Leaning-Against-the-Clouds, the bachelor's apartment building. Everything has been arranged. Yes, we'll go into town in a few days. Wei wants to talk to May? Sure." May had stuck around, leaning against a small desk, reading her book – it was just reaching a juicy bit. She took the phone from her mother, with her eyes still glued to the page: "Cousin Wei, what are you doing right now?"

Tantai Wei, on the other end of the line, answered: "I finished the first draft of my map of China. It looks like a begonia leaf, but I don't want to colour it green like a begonia leaf."

"I drew one myself. I coloured it red, like a maple leaf," May said, matter-of-factly.

"I don't want red, either. It doesn't match, and there are many worms on the leaf," Wei wailed, complaining as if there really were worms wriggling about on his drawing.

May put down her book, surprised. "Those are the foreign army camps. I know they are. Cousin Wei, have you read '*Copper Drum*'? You hit the drum, and an army of soldiers comes out."

Wei laughed out loud on the other end: "It's not that simple! I'll mark out where those worm camps are and show you when you come." He then drifted off thoughtfully, speaking more to himself than to May: "Maybe I can use different colours to colour the provinces."

"Are you going to Cousin Feng's wedding tomorrow?" May asked, regaining Wei's attention.

"Mum and dad won't be going, they're busy, but mum said me and Xuan can go," Wei replied, with a note of excitement. He always addressed his elder sister Tantai Xuan by her name instead of the usual 'sister', just the way Kiddo addressed his second elder sister as May.

"May, you are one of the flower girls and you are going to hold the bride's train! You cannot fool around like the others," Bichu reminded May, her voice echoing from her room. "Wei can come and stay with us for a couple of days, if he likes."

Wei knew that, tomorrow, May and Wucai, from the Zhuang family, would hold the bride's train together, and curiosity prompted him to ask: "Is Wuyin going to town, too?"

May shrugged, although she knew Wei couldn't see her. "I don't know. I haven't seen him around recently." Wuyin and Wucai were Zhuang Youchen's twins. Wuyin, the brother, went to the same middle school as Wei, and the pair of them, with May and Kiddo, had always been very good friends.

They talked for a short while longer, not saying much of importance, but they eventually agreed that Wei should come to stay with the Meng family. He yelled something away from the phone at someone May couldn't hear, only to return to the call excitedly to say that his mother, Jiangchu, had given her permission.

"Hold on! Hold on! One more thing! Are the fireflies already around?" Wei asked, just as May threatened to hang up. When summer came, the creek flowing by the Meng residence always teemed with fireflies that twinkled like stars against the black velvet of the evening sky. The kids loved to watch the bobbing, glowing lights and let their imagination twinkle with the flies, into the night.

"Cousin Wei, you are so sweet to think about those fireflies!" May said, smiling.

"Ask him whether his elder sister Xuan is coming," Bichu added, poking her head around the door.

Wei, overhearing Bichu's words, told May that Xuan was not at home. "I'm coming for the fireflies," he said solemnly, before hanging up the phone.

May put down the phone too, and went to the bay window. Opening her book on her lap, she sat down on the bench, the nearest thing available to sit on, and swiftly picked up where she had left off before the phone call had interrupted her reading.

Kiddo, meanwhile, was in his grandfather's room. Both were enjoying themselves immeasurably, sharing the cool litchi, before falling into their usual routine of grandfather and grandson. First, they took turns to write Chinese characters with a brush, and when one finished writing a row, the other took over and wrote another row. It was more like a game for them, and one they loved to play. When they were done with their writing, they started carving characters on soap bars, and when they were done with the carving, they discussed which character was nicely carved, and which was not. It was a routine they both looked forward to.

Grandpa Lü's morning routines remained exactly the same wherever he was – he would do only two things in turn, read newspapers and chant sutras, or vice versa. Wherever he went, he took with him a small copper Ming dynasty incense burner, although it weighed over 2 kilos and was a hefty thing to carry around. Regardless of his location, he would keep a full burner of fragrant incense burning all morning, and although he led a very austere life, when it came to the type of scent rising from the burner, he was very picky. The lilac scent from Yunnan province in southwest China was his favourite. Other types of scent made him feel light-headed, and he'd grown so used to the lilac scent that, without it, he felt light-headed, too. The sutra he would chant was the Heart Sutra, and he would chant it loudly 10 times, from the very beginning '*Avalokita, the Holy Lord and Bodhisattva, was moving in the deep course of the Wisdom which has gone beyond*' until the very end '*Oh what an awakening, all-hail!*' Once that was done, he would switch to quietly chanting other sutras. He would chant for a while before he read the day's newspaper, and if the paper was not available, he would ask whether the paper had arrived and why it hadn't been delivered to his room. After lunch, he was prone to very long afternoon naps. When he got up from one of these naps, if his grandchildren were available, he would devote his time to them. In town, he would play with Wei; in the countryside, he would play with Kiddo. For his own offspring, he had only three daughters. No son. As time had worn on, and he had reached old age, he felt very blessed that he had been given the opportunity to spend time with his grandchildren. Not everyone was so lucky.

On this occasion, both grandfather and grandchild were satisfied with the quality of the soap bars. Kiddo had finished carving the character '*May*' and was working on three characters that depicted his name, '*meng he ji*'. His grandfather was working on a large soap bar, about the size of a book, which had been moulded by melting several regular-size soap bars into a larger one. He was on four characters '*huan wo he shan*', meaning 'to recover our lost territory'. He wasn't happy with the first carving, so he did it again, ever the perfectionist. On the third try, he finally put the seal ink onto the carving and printed out the characters on a piece of paper. Looking at them closely, he studied the printed characters with a critical eye, and asked Kiddo to tell him which strokes he thought weren't good enough. Kiddo looked over the work, and announced that he couldn't find any problems: "You always do better than me."

"Look at '*huan*' (还). The stroke showing the 'walking part' on the outside. It's not good – it's a difficult stroke, though. The last stroke of '*wo*' (我, meaning 'I') on the right is not good either. Look, the right part is '*ge*' (戈), a dagger-ax. Only when '*wo*' (我) can protect itself, can it be called '*wo*' (我)."

Kiddo looked at his grandfather with a bewildered expression.

"Now, let's look at yours."

The three characters '*meng he ji* (孟合己)' were printed in

red seal ink on the paper. Kiddo was thrilled upon seeing the red characters, and he yelled and applauded excitedly.

"Meng Heji, that's me!"

"Indeed it is you, Kiddo!" his grandfather laughed. "But, look. '*Meng*' is not good," he said, before deftly cutting off a layer from the bars to remove the defective carvings. "Let's do it again, my friend." 'My friend' was the old man's pet phrase, but he saved it only for the ones he loved.

The two resumed their carving activities in a companionable silence.

Mr Lü Qingfei was born into a noble family in Anhui province, eastern China. In his teens, he participated in the Imperial Civil Examination in the Qing dynasty and was a successful candidate for a position similar to that of a master's degree. Later, in his 20s, he joined Sun Yat-sen's alliance for democracy, feeling the need for adventure and to do his duty, and broke into the county prison to save a comrade of his. Sadly, that was how he lost his scholarly title. When the Republic of China was founded, he was elected as a member of parliament. In his 40s, the devastating loss of his wife, combined with the country going from bad to worse, brought to an end the youthful ambitions he had once harboured. No longer seeking those avenues that had sculpted his formative years, he sold his farm and land, and moved to live in the town, to be closer to his two daughters there.

"Master Lü, dinner is ready," Amah Zhao informed him, respectfully, with a raised voice at the door of the room. She didn't enter until called. Grandpa Lü had his breakfast and lunch alone in his room, but he would have dinner with the rest of the family in the dining room, chatting a little bit over the meal, going over the events of the day in the household.

Upon Amah Zhao's words, Kiddo leaped up from his small

stool. His grandfather got up a little more slowly, his bones creaking, as he and his grandchild went together to the dining room, where the Meng couple were waiting. Grandpa Lü took the seat of honour, with the Meng couple sitting either side of him. May sat next to her mother, Bichu, but the seat beside her father, Fuzhi, was still not occupied.

"Where is Miss Earl?" frowned Bichu. Earl walked in at the end of her mother's question. Earl was a young girl in the flower of her youth, and she was proving to be quite a beauty. Her slender figure was wrapped in a bluish, moon-white *qipao* (a cheongsam or mandarin gown – a long figure-hugging dress with a high neck and slit skirt) made of fine woven cotton. There was a confidence in her gait, and with her white dress-socks and white flat shoes, she was quite the 1937 Beijing college girl, following the fashion of the day. The smile on her face was radiant, but her sharp chin seemed too sharp to hold that smile.

"Where have you been? You haven't been home all day," Bichu asked amiably.

"At one of my classmate's."

"Were you reviewing your lessons?" Fuzhi asked, in the same amiable manner as his wife.

"A little," answered Earl, rather reluctantly.

Kiddo was sitting in his baby chair – a tall chair with a board set in front of him for putting his dishes on. He had been asking to sit at the table for ages because, after this summer vacation, he would be enrolled as an elementary school student. In keeping with this new status, he felt it was only right that he should be promoted to sit at the table, like the others. He had been lingering around the seat between Earl and May, and was keen to make a move towards it. "I can engrave seals now," he said, bargaining with the progress he had achieved, hoping it would make him seem grown-up enough to join the others.

"I didn't tell the servants to set up your seat," Bichu said good-temperedly. "Let's do it tomorrow, shall we?"

"How about the day after tomorrow? I'd like to start the day after tomorrow," Kiddo calculated. Tomorrow, he knew they would be going into town and wouldn't have dinner at home. For the very first day of his official sitting at the table, to skip one meal would feel like a huge loss. "When Cousin Wei comes, I'll sit beside him then," he said, the date of his promotion confirmed. As he said so, he climbed up into his baby chair for what he hoped would be the last time.

In front of him, Grandpa Lü had a small, brown, fine clay pot made in Yixing, Wuxi city, Zhejiang province, a town renowned for its clay artifacts. It looked more like a big bowl with a handle and a lid. Bichu took the lid off and the room was instantly filled with the sweet smell from the pot that tantalised the taste buds. Inside the pot was delicious porridge, stewed with dried lily bud slices, red Chinese jujube, sticky rice, and a Qinghai province specialty, the longevity fruit. In keeping with tradition, after Grandpa Lü had taken a spoon of porridge, the rest of the family began to eat.

"Tomorrow evening when Cousin Wei arrives, we are going to watch the fireflies by the lotus pond. He asked about the fireflies today," May said, with a mouthful of rice.

"Don't talk while you're eating," said Earl, darting a severe glance at her.

May's dark, shining eyes surveyed all the people sitting around the table, ignoring Earl as she decided who to direct her attention to. Finally, she settled on her grandfather. Taking another bite of rice, she went on: "The fireflies there are quite like those by the creek…"

"I told you not to talk while you're eating!" Earl snapped.

"You are eating and talking at the same time, too!" May retorted. Earl put down her chopsticks at once.

"Your sister is right, May. Both of you just eat," Bichu interposed gently, her eyes on both her daughters, warning them despite her pleasant demeanour. In the Meng family, it was a respected tradition that the younger ones should always respect their elders, much as May resented it.

Earl and May shared similar delicate facial features and profiles. Their eyes were similar in their shiny darkness, but different in their content. The elder sister, Earl's, were filled with adolescent confusion and nebulousness, while the younger sister, May's, were filled with childlike innocence and simplicity. The one thing that told their two faces apart, however, was the expression they exuded, which had nothing to do with their age difference. Wei Feng once commented that the elder sister might taste sour mixed with some hot spices, while the younger sister would taste sweet with a bitter after-taste. "What do I taste like?" Kiddo blurted out, but Wei Feng had run out of ideas. As a consolation prize, he held Kiddo up high in the air.

"You taste delicious and are full of flavour," Wei Feng answered, making everyone burst out laughing.

"It's hot these days. Why does father want to go back to town tomorrow?" Fuzhi asked. A small Persian kitten jumped up into his lap, looking for a comfortable spot. It turned around twice, patting its paws against Fuzhi's leg, before finally sitting down, its eyes looking up expectantly at the people at the table. The beautiful kitten was a pedigree species from Shandong province, and was covered in snow-white fur, with a striking black spot on the top of its head and another on the tip of its tail. Its pedigree document referred to the cat as 'whipping an embroidered ball'. It was a rare one.

Grandpa Lü took a serving of tantalising food from a dish in front of him with his chopsticks. His dishes were put onto small plates, and there were several slices of fresh ham, some tender soybean sprouts, and a small bowl of scrambled eggs with chopped tomato, laid out before his eager eyes. The dishes were simple but cooked with care.

"Father said he'll stay for a couple of days before he comes back again to stay with us," Bichu said, answering for her father.

After a while, the old man put down his spoon and chopsticks, and looked across the table at Fuzhi. "How's the situation?" he asked solemnly; it was the same question he asked every day, these days.

"I attended a lunch in town earlier today. Some mentioned that the Japanese are deploying armies to Fengtai," Fuzhi said, with a touch of reluctance.

"Fengtai is only 15 miles from Beiping city, but the Japanese have been persistent in stationing their armies there. It has been three years," the old man turned to Earl and May. "They want to turn Beiping into another Shenyang[9]. Since I was 18, I have been dedicated to revolution and reform. Now the Qing dynasty has been overthrown, but the country is still a mess. I have been keeping myself busy for my whole life, in vain." A look of sad disappointment passed across the old man's face. Trying to distract himself, the old man attempted to take a spoonful of porridge, but he put it down shortly after, muttering to himself: "I'm ashamed of myself!" The

---

[9] Shenyang: (沈阳) the provincial capital of Liaoning province, closely linked with the Mukden Incident. The Mukden Incident, or Manchurian Incident, was an event engineered by the Japanese military as a pretext for the Japanese invasion of the northeastern part of China known as Manchuria in 1931.

food seemed to have lost its appeal, growing bitter in the old man's mouth as his memories flooded back.

"You are always the first to worry about people's woes," said Earl, ironically.

"Father, you have struggled through all these years, and have tried your best. Now it's time for you to let go," Bichu said, casting a sharp glance over at Earl.

"I was informed that, next week, some famous performers of the Kun Opera are coming to perform in the university auditorium. It is said they were keen fans before they became star performers. It's set to be a very rare performance," Fuzhi said. "Father, you have to come. The lotus will be in full bloom at that time, too." While he was talking, he held his chopsticks in the air, punctuating his words with them as he paused to select each dish he fancied. The kitten stared hungrily at the dish, studying it for a moment before it sprang up and snatched at the food with its paw. As the dish fell to the ground with a clatter, the kitten lept from Fuzhi's lap, landing softly beside the spilled food, sniffing at it with interest. The table went silent, all of them stunned at the kitten's sudden move. A moment later, they burst into laughter, as Amah Zhao hastened to clean up the mess.

"Have you fed the cats?" asked Bichu, wiping happy tears from her eyes. The Meng family was much more tolerant of their cats and dogs than their children.

"I have fed them but they didn't finish it," Amah Zhao answered, smiling, as she took the kitten away, where it wouldn't have the chance to knock over any more dishes.

A short while later, they finished dinner and began to enjoy some watermelon, to refresh their palates after the intense flavours of their meal. Just then, the doorbell rang. Putting down her melon, May ran to answer it, her hands still sticky with juice. Opening the gate, she was half-surprised to see a beanpole of a young man standing there, waiting patiently.

"Excuse me. Is Miss Meng Liji at home?" he asked politely, pushing up his glasses with one finger.

"Sister, it's for you," May called, turning from the gate. She knew this young man. He was Zhang Xinlei, a sophomore in the economics department. His name sounded exactly like 'Thunderhand' (literally 'thunder in the palm of the hand'). May let him in, informing her sister who had come to visit. As a family rule, children in the Meng family were not allowed to eavesdrop on adults' conversations, but she could just about overhear her sister saying: "Zhang Xinlei, you came?" There was a questioning tone in her voice that indicated her true meaning of "what are you up to?"

May didn't linger any longer, as she headed back to the dining room. It was much the same, although grandfather and father were in the middle of a heated discussion, and Kiddo had got down from his baby chair.

"Shall we go and play outside?" Kiddo asked May.

"Mum, can we go and play outside?" May asked Bichu, who was tidying up food in the pantry, the last hint of a bronzed sunset glowing through the screen windows. "The fireflies are about to fly," May added.

"Just don't go too far. And remember: you can watch, but you can't chase or try to catch those bugs," Bichu demanded. The two kids said yes, their faces a picture of glee, as they ran out of the door in high spirits. The fireflies were a real treat.

In front of the back gate of the Meng residence meandered a creek, which flowed down from Jade Spring mountain and rippled through the campus. The section around the Meng residence was a tributary from that same creek, and the crystal-clear water nourished the wild artemisia along the banks. These plants were taller than Kiddo, and a barely discernible path through the wild flowers led to a small stone bridge that looked as if it had been plucked from a fairytale. Beyond the far bank stood a hill, behind which was the girl students' dormitory building. The sun was just setting behind the building, bathing its roof in an amber afterglow.

The two kids sat at their favourite spot – a square piece of slate lying abandoned at one end of the stone bridge. People said the slate was from Yuanming Yuan[10], the old Summer Palace, but the two children just knew it got warm in the sun, and gave the best view of the fireflies. They sat for a while, waiting. In the distance, the bronze glow grew dimmer by the minute, as twilight hung over the tall wild grass, shrouding the world in a strange, dusky purple. The children watched the grass carefully, and noticed that the thin darkness of approaching night was mixing into the thick grass. The show was about to begin.

"I've spotted one over there," said Kiddo, standing up excitedly, teetering close to the edge of the bank. May dragged him back just in time – they had both fallen into the creek countless times when chasing after fireflies, and returned to the house dripping wet, to their mother's chagrin. "I've found one here," May shouted. A little dot of light was dashing toward them from the opposite side of the river, and another twinkling spot of light was sliding away from them.

---

[10] Yuanming Yuan: also known as the Old Summer Palace (圆明园; literally meaning "Gardens of Perfect Brightness"), was a complex of palaces and gardens in present-day Haidian district, Beijing. It is located 8km northwest of the walls of the former Imperial City section of Beiping. In 1860, during the Second Opium War, as the Anglo-French expeditionary force relentlessly approached Beiping. two British envoys, a journalist for *The Times* and a small escort of British and Indian troops were sent to meet Prince Yi under a flag of truce to negotiate a Qing surrender. Meanwhile, the French and British troops reached the palace and conducted extensive looting and destruction.

It was like seeing a magical realm, watching the glow of unseen fairies dancing. Just then, something popped out from behind the hill on the opposite bank. Whatever it was, it was speeding towards them. As the figure came closer, the children saw it was a young man on a bicycle, whizzing over the bridge. He came skidding to a halt right beside them. "Cousin Zhuang!" May and Kiddo cried, addressing the newcomer with gleeful smiles. Zhuang Wuyin sat on his bike with his feet on the ground. He had a long, slim figure, and long, narrow eyes and eyebrows, just like his father Zhuang Youchen. What distinguished him from his father was a slight trace of sadness in his eyes, rarely found in people of his age. It made him look like he was always musing over something, always buried deep in thought, although such a trace of sadness made him stand out from the crowd. There was something special about Zhuang Wuyin.

"Here you are! Again! You two great dreamers!" Wuyin exclaimed. "What have those fireflies told you?"

"Wei asked whether you are going to town tomorrow," May said eagerly.

"For the wedding? No, I'm not. It's girls' stuff," Wuyin answered, rather absent-mindedly. He was too absorbed in the mystical world of the fireflies, laying on their performance just up ahead.

As they watched, more and more specks of glowing light rose up from the grass, like sparks flung from a raging fire. Through the grass, the rippling water of the creek mirrored the glimmering lights that were reflected in the six shining eyes. They watched and watched in total silence, transfixed by the luminescent ballet.

"Miss May," Amah Zhao said, coming out of the house, toward where the children sat. She had been instructed that she could address May by her name, but she always went with 'Miss May' as a matter of habit. She saw the lean young man who had joined the children, and gave a surprised cry: "Master Zhuang is here, too! Miss May, madam is asking you two to come back."

"Many more still haven't come out yet," said May.

"A big one over there!" Kiddo pointed up to the creek. True enough, a big dot of light danced over the water, leaving a glowing trail on the rippling surface. Was that the light from the fairy? Or was it the fairy itself?

"Come again tomorrow when Master Wei is here. You can hang out together then."

"Tantai Wei is coming tomorrow? I'll come again then!" Wuyin said.

"Remember to invite Cousin Xuan to come along!" Kiddo reminded him.

"Alright! Alright!" Amah Zhao answered for Wuyin, as Wuyin kicked his feet against the ground to get the bike going, before both bike and rider glided off into the twilight.

"See you tomorrow!" The two kids stood up obediently and waved goodbye to the quickly disappearing figure on the bike. Knowing they would get to see no more fireflies that night, they started running back home. In the hallway, they overheard their elder sister telling their mother that she was not going to Cousin Wei Feng's wedding, saying she had to attend a concert held by the nearby Catholic university with her classmate Wu Jiaxin, and her friend Zhang Xinlei. She was telling her mother she planned to ride her bike there, so it wouldn't be a hassle for anyone.

"We are having a dance meeting tomorrow," said May, swelling with pride that was difficult for her to hide. The special dancers were going to play the part of fireflies and the white blooming lotuses in the pond, her favourites, and the spectators would be Cousin Tantai Wei, the son and daughter from the Zhuang family, and Kiddo and May.

It was the most silent and sweet night, with much to look forward to. Everyone in the Meng residence went to sleep like the rest of Beiping city, their hearts full of hopeful, pleasant expectations for the following day.

PART 2

Early next morning, together with the rising summer sun, the iceman arrived at the Meng residence. His ice was taken from the frozen lakes or rivers of the previous winter and stored in underground ice cellars until the next summer. He then delivered the chunks of ice to his customers. The ice was kept in a wagon pulled by a donkey. Through the thick cover of tarpauline and cotton-padded quilts, a cold steam sizzled out. The donkey and the wagon went from door to door, accompanied by a trail of misty fluffy cloud. The iceman first moved the block of ice secured with ropes made of reeds out of the carefully covered wagon to the outside of the residence with a pair of iron tongs, and then took it to the Meng family's fridge. He would try to dry his hand on his already soaked apron before he exchanged greetings with Old Chef Chai or Amah Li. Then he would go back to his wagon and drive away, leaving behind the whooshing sound of his whips. On the iceman's heels was the milkman. Then came the vegetable man, an employee from a restaurant named Ruyi, the chief fresh vegetable supplier for most of the families living on campus. Even during those periods of short supply, they could always manage to rustle up some fresh ripe tomatoes, green beans and tender cabbage heads. Green leafy vegetables from the south, like charlocks and choy sum, were also included in their delivery. When May and Kiddo played House, they would include ordering some items from Ruyi restaurant, like the adults did.

They then had breakfast. Things seemed to be quite normal. Bichu, followed by May, Kiddo, and a younger servant Amah Li, went to the bachelor's apartment building Leaning-Against-the-Clouds to add some decoration to the bridal room. The apartment building was an old-fashioned one with courtyards. It offered at least 100 rooms around the yards for bachelor staff and faculty members. Wei Feng's room, the bridal room, was behind a full-moon shaped gate, in the depths of patches of woods and flowers. The room was already a conglomeration of beauty and delicacy. The plan was for Wei to take his new wife back here after the wedding ceremony. Since Wei Feng had been in town for the past few days, Bichu wanted to make sure things were perfect, so here she was.

"Don't!" Bichu told the two kids before they opened the door. "Just don't touch anything." Everything was in place. The bed had been made by the bride Ling Xueyan's mother two days ago. The embroidered silk bedcover was free of a single crease. The light pink gauze curtains shone with the green shade cast from the outside. The kids tiptoed, tagging along with their mother, as if they were walking on sacred soil.

As Bichu had instructed, the colourful paper chains had been hung up in the room, immediately adding a livelier atmosphere to it. "What a beautiful room!" exclaimed Amah Li.

Taking another look around, Bichu noticed a small, round table under the glass window, devoid of any decoration. Dissatisfied with the way it looked, she made a mental note to ask Amah Zhao to put a snack dish on it later. With that one vacant space sorted, she finally felt pleased with the way things looked – everything was impeccable and perfect for a bride. Turning, she called to the two children, who were holding onto the edge of the windowsill, teetering on the tips of their toes, desperate to get a glimpse of the outside world.

"I'm done here, we should be getting back," she announced, heading towards the door.

As they walked out, they were met with the surprising figure of Wei Feng, hurrying through the full-moon shaped gate toward them. He looked to be in quite a hurry.

"Cousin Feng!" The two kids called, with a cry of delight.

Wei Feng was a handsome, graceful young man with bright sparkling eyes, his lean figure dressed in a flattering white silk shirt, paired with light grey suit trousers. Draped across his arm was a silver-grey yarn gown, the ends flapping as he ran.

"What are you doing back so soon?" Bichu asked in a surprised tone.

"Last night, the Japanese soldiers tried to pick a fight. They tried to attack Wanping fort[11]," he explained, slightly out of breath.

Bichu remained silent as she anxiously absorbed the news. It wasn't good, and her anxiety was contagious, affecting the children as well. Letting the words sink in, Kiddo reached up and grabbed at a corner of his mother's blouse, while May immediately put herself between her brother and anyone that might want to do him harm, protecting him from the unseen invaders.

---

[11] Wanping fort, also known as Wanping castle (宛平城 *wanping cheng*), is a Ming dynasty fortress or 'walled city' in Beijing. It was erected in 1638–1640 to defend Beijing against Li Zicheng and the peasant uprising. In Chinese, the fort is sometimes called Wanping city, and from the beginning, it functioned as a military fort.

"The 29th infantry unit defended the city heroically," said Wei Feng, forcing himself to speak calmly, though inside he was raging. "I need to do something to help," he added. It was clear he'd already made up his mind – he was ready to leave, to do just that, to help fight for the cause.

"What about the wedding?" Bichu felt compelled to ask, trying to keep the stern note from her voice. "It's this afternoon, remember?"

"We'll stick to the plan. I'll manage to get back to town in time, don't worry," Wei Feng replied, pushing through into the room beyond before he had even finished his sentence.

"Don't mess things up," said Bichu, suddenly nervous about her beautiful display being ruined.

"I know."

It wasn't clear what he was doing in the room, seeing as he had no pressing purpose there, but Bichu was certain he wouldn't even notice all the hard work she had put in to make the place beautiful. Her impeccable arrangements would go unappreciated, she thought, sighing softly, as she took her children by the hand and left, leaving Wei Feng to whatever it was he was up to.

They arrived home to find Fuzhi deep in conversation on the phone. Although it was rude to eavesdrop, the family couldn't help but overhear him mentioning the words Marco Polo bridge[12] a couple of times, his loud voice echoing through the house. They quickly let him be, hurrying toward the living room, to give him the peace and quiet he needed.

There was a click as he put the phone down, followed

---

[12] The Marco Polo bridge or Lugouqiao bridge, is a stone bridge located 15km southwest of Beijing city centre in the Fengtai district. It bridges the Yongding river, a major tributary of the Haihe river. Situated at the eastern end of the bridge is Wanping fort, a historic 17th-century fortress, which now houses the Museum of the War of Chinese People's Resistance Against Japanese Aggression.

swiftly by his appearance at the living room door. He looked weary, as he announced what he'd heard: "I just got off the phone with Professor Xiao. There has been an incident… the Japanese army stationed at Marco Polo bridge – they were looking for any excuse to attack. By all accounts, they claimed that one of their soldiers was missing and that they had to go into the city to find him. A likely story! Anyway… they opened fire on our army."

Bichu nodded sadly. "Wei Feng told us what had happened just now. We bumped into him hurrying back – he said he had something to take care of, but he promised the wedding would go ahead as scheduled."

Fuzhi sighed, sitting down in one of the living room chairs. "I truly hope it will go ahead as scheduled."

"I have to tell father about this," said Bichu, rising from her seat. She excused herself quietly, before heading up the stairs to the old man's room, to relay all she'd heard. Fuzhi followed her reluctantly, wondering how the old man would take it.

With his poor hearing, the old man didn't really understand what was going on at first, peppering Bichu's words with casual noises of agreement, though he hadn't the slightest clue what he was agreeing with. However, Bichu was persistent, repeating the words over and over until the news finally sank in. She knew he'd understood when she saw the change on his face, as it clicked. He paused in his task, his expression thoughtful, before his eyes lit up and he cried out animatedly: "Engaged in combat! Good! Don't know how long it will last this time, mind you."

"They always fight and then talk," Fuzhi said.

"The sacrifice of lives is the only way to protect our

homes," the old man said. "It's a good sign that they are engaged in fighting. It's a positive move, you mark my words. At the very least, it won't be like what happened to the three provinces in northeast China, where 10,000 troops literally just handed over our territory without a fight at all. At least there's some fighting spirit here this time!"

"If we are at war again, we will have to put up with a lot, father. I'm worried about you," said Bichu.

The old man looked at her rather harshly: "You'll have a lot more to worry about than me."

"The university is prepared," said Fuzhi, cutting in. "A temporary campus has been set up in Changsha city, Hunan province. Some books and laboratory facilities have already been transported there." His words were cut short as he heard the happy sound of the two children twittering from the backyard, the noise filtering in through the window; they were talking and laughing, as if nothing were the matter. The blissful ignorance of childhood. Puzzled, Fuzhi glanced at his wife for an explanation.

"Peddler Guangdong is probably here. I'll go down and check," said Bichu, leaving the room, and leaving Fuzhi and the old man alone to discuss past wars and future battles. Heading out to the garden, she could see the two children standing in front of two wagon-loads of goods, happily talking to the owner.

The peddler, known to the locals as Peddler Guangdong, was actually a genuine Beiping native, who had nothing at all to do with Guangdong province. He'd garnered the title because of the wares he sold – mostly refreshments and snacks from the south of the country, which he stored in two containers decorated with delicate, flowing designs of exquisite beauty. The first container was round, and looked like a traditional food box, rising up in several elegantly designed layers. Every level was filled to the brim with delicious food, to stimulate the taste buds. The other one was rectangular in shape, and equally beautiful, equipped with rows of small glass boxes that one could peer into, to see the various delicate pastries and light refreshments within, brought from the famous Paddy-Sweet Cottage Bakery[13]. There were duck eggs preserved in rice wine, and fried spicy water-beetles, among other tasty treats, but what May and Kiddo loved most were the egg crackers the peddler brought, baked to a delicious golden brown. Each piece was curved up at the edges, reminding the children of roof tiles, though infinitely tastier – it was this resemblance that gave the snacks their nickname of 'tiles'. The children always pleaded for a bite of these tasty morsels, and Bichu would always buy a tile or two for the children every time Peddler Guangdong called.

"Madam, you are here! The goods today are very fresh. I packed them up as soon as they came in on the delivery truck, and headed to you immediately," said Peddler Guangdong, smiling. He looked the same as always, but it was clear he had just shaved his head, the smooth scalp looking a shiny bluish-white, a few beads of sweat trickling down prompted by the insipid heat. There was a purple birthmark beside his left eyebrow and a clean white towel on his shoulder, making him look very neat and proper, and ready to serve his customers. Although he too had heard about the onset of war, it was easy to ignore this far away from the action – to him, it felt a world away, especially at the campus, which already seemed so otherworldly compared to the hot, sticky city. Besides, his two loads of goods were his world; there was nothing beyond his daily duty.

---

[13] Paddy-Sweet Cottage Bakery: (稻香村 *daoxiangcun*) is a legendary bakery in Beijing selling authentic Beijing pastries.

"The children can have whatever they like," smiled Bichu, striding down the steps toward the peddler. In one of the containers, she noticed the walnut pastry her father liked, as she was picking two snacks for Earl. Still uncertain as to whether he was staying past that afternoon, she paused, deciding to buy it next time instead. Next time! Her heart gave an extra beat, at the thought that there might not be a next time.

"What is going to happen next time?" She couldn't help thinking: "Maybe they could wait for a couple of years before they start the war, when Kiddo is older," she wondered, but immediately stopped, chastising herself. "No, that is no good! That's a woman's way of looking at things!"

May and her younger brother were discussing what they should pick for their cousin Tantai Wei. It was a hard decision for such young minds, and they talked for a while before deciding that their favourites, the tiles, were the best choice. Peddler Guangdong made small talk with Bichu as he packed up the items and took the money, before handing over the tantalising parcels. A smile never left his face; he was of a perpetually cheerful disposition, happy in the life he led. To his mind, there was nothing to be sad about, not even the far-off echo of war. Chef Chai came out of the Meng residence to invite the peddler to have tea in the servants' quarters, his intentions pure. Where others might have invited him in to have more commission on the peddler's sales, Chef Chai was not so shallow; he had an appreciation for Peddler Guangdong's tastes, which went beyond satisfying the stomach and having fun. In truth, they got on well, sharing a lot in common, and he enjoyed the peddler's company immeasurably. Besides, even if Chef Chai had had his eye on something more business-minded, commission followed a strict set of rules and proportions that weren't easy to overcome. It was easier just to call the peddler in for a convivial chat. Sometimes, as well as the talk and tea, Chef Chai bought two pieces of *mung* bean cake stuffed with mashed jujube, for himself and his imaginary son.

Satisfied with their treats, the two children went back inside and headed up to their room. May picked up a rather ragged doll that had been sitting on the table, and pulled it into her arms, clutching it tightly. It was 'Little Pitiful', a hand-me-down from Earl, but it was no less loved for being second-hand. The doll had long been May's favourite toy, there to comfort her, and to be comforted by her: "Don't be scared! You have me," she said, but it didn't seem enough. Looking thoughtful, she tried to come up with some more comforting words, but try as she might, what came out in the end was exactly the same: "Don't be scared! You have me."

"What is war?" Kiddo asked, thoughtfully. It was clear the word had been playing on the young boy's mind, after hearing it so many times of late.

May, holding her doll in her arms, didn't hear him at first. She was staring out of the window at the garden below, thick with green vegetation and blossoming flowers. A flowerbed along the edge of the grass was planted with cosmos, a plant with long, thin stems and big flower heads on top, which made them appear rather delicate and lonely if grown individually. Here, however, they were growing in big clusters, making them appear bold and loud, flourishing with such wild abandon that it looked like nothing would ever be able to hold back their onslaught, as they approached the emerald green of the lawn.

"I must take one more look at those flowers," May said to herself, turning over her shoulder to look at her brother. "War means war," she explained, finally answering Kiddo's question. He frowned, his eyes blank. Seeing that he clearly didn't get it, she continued: "If we are at war, all these flowers will be gone. So, we need to take one more look."

"I don't like wars," Kiddo said glumly, picking at a thread of the rug beneath him.

"I don't either," said May, as she put the doll on the window sill and let the ragged girl have one more look at her and the blooming flowers outside.

Throughout that afternoon, the phone in the Meng residence rang off the hook, and visitors kept streaming in. Where their morning had been quiet, the afternoon was chaos. At about two o'clock, Tantai Mian came to pick up his father-in-law, Mr Lü Qingfei, though with his arrival came more bad news. Standing in the hallway, waiting for his father-in-law, he informed the household that the Japanese had demanded that the Kuomintang (KMT) army evacuate the Marco Polo bridge. He explained that the demand was, of course, rejected, so the Japanese army launched another attack, meaning they were again engaged in a fire-fight. There was excitement in his voice too, as he relayed the information, noting with a sense of pride that, if our troops fought back, they had a chance of winning. He reasoned that the thing people worried about most was no fighting at all. A cold war was an anxious war, with everyone waiting for a first strike. With the first strike already landed, Mian was convinced it was best for the future of the nation.

He had just come to the end of his excited thoughts, when Mr Lü came down, announcing that he would be taking the big soap-bar carved with the four characters '*huan wo he shan*'. Although he would be back again in a couple of days, he wanted to take it with him because the carvings needed fine adjustments, that he was keen to get done in his own time, when he had the luxury of peace and quiet. Following his son-in-law through the house, he got into the waiting car that was parked nearby, only to get out again a moment later, saying he would go to the garden before he left. It seemed the old man had the same idea as May, wanting to see the blooming flowers one more time.

"Father, it's very hot right now in the garden. When you come back, you could go during the cooler evening time," advised Bichu, but the old man seemed not to hear her, as he kept walking. The rest of the group gathered there exchanged knowing glances of exasperation, before following him.

It was scorching hot in the garden, as Bichu had warned, and all the flowers were wilted and listless, the grass crisp and singed by the fierce heat of the day. The old man stopped under the shade of a willow, allowing the cool shade to envelop him, and narrowed his eyes toward the glaring light of the garden.

A small smile played upon his lips; the university campus was a nice place for an old man. For half his life, he had been busy with revolution, and being on the front line for so many years had made him understand the importance of smart, talented people. Every action in life was made by people, and if they had a good head on their shoulders and their minds were sharp and intelligent, that could only be for the best.

Past the garden, between the leafy tendrils that trailed like curtains before his vision, he could see the rows of classrooms, and two other university buildings, in the near-distance. It was a spot he had stood in many times, watching the students coming and going with books under their arms, engaged in inaudible discussions. Regardless, the sight of them would always arouse faint hopes within him, that not everyone and everything was doomed. Where there was learning, there was potential for a brighter future, less likelihood of making the same mistakes as past generations. Now, it was the middle of the summer vacation and the campus was quiet. It was still beautiful, but it didn't please the old man nearly as much, to see the grounds empty of bright minds.

Not knowing what the old man was thinking, everyone's eyes were drawn to the iridescent cosmos, though no one was in the mood to fully enjoy their beauty.

"These flowers are in full bloom," Tantai Mian sighed.

"Grandfather, take one more look," said Kiddo, suddenly looking up at the old man, remembering his sister's words.

Compelled by the sweet voice of Kiddo, everyone took another look, the old man included. He was beginning to feel uncomfortable in the heat, the shade from the willow blocking the direct ferocity of the sun from above, but unable to block the hot steam that rose up from the ground. As they were talking, sweat began to well up on the old man's brow, trickling down the side of his face in warm rivulets.

Bichu looked at him, concern furrowing her brow. "Father, please get into the car. Brother Mian has business to attend to in town, and it wouldn't be fair to keep him."

Tantai Mian shook his head, not wanting to cause a fuss. "It's okay, I have time. I was invited to talk about the power supply in north China this afternoon, but it could well have been canceled... I don't know. They sometimes do that," he yelled, close to the old man's ear so he might hear better.

The old man said nothing, he just waved his hand a little at Bichu and Tantai Mian, before heading back across the garden to the spot where the car was waiting. Without another word, he got in.

As the car pulled away, Bichu went inside to make some

last-minute arrangements. There was still so much to do, but she knew it would have to wait, as she moved towards her room, to begin the ritual of getting dressed up. With their mother otherwise engaged, Amah Zhao helped the kids to change their clothes and put on their wedding outfits. Kiddo wore a light blue navy suit that made him look very smart, and once he was fully dressed, he began to march back and forth in the room like a soldier, saluting every time he turned. May, meanwhile, was dressed in a white georgette dress with a flounced collar and cuffs, that made her look sweet and graceful. Her beautiful face emerged from the ruffled collar like a bud standing upright, the centre of a pretty white flower. She was wearing a pair of shoes woven with thin red and white leather strips, the red standing out vividly against the crisp white, giving a pop of colour to the outfit. Amah Zhao scooped her up with a delighted smile on her face and set the girl down in front of the mirror, exclaiming: "Look at our young miss! How beautiful she is!"

May thought she did indeed look very pretty, and took the opportunity to squeeze onto the stool alongside her mother. Bichu was focusing on elegantly painting her face with a variety of pots and brushes scattered around the vanity table, and May looked on in awe, transfixed by the artistry.

"Mother, can I have some make-up?" she asked, leaning against her mother, smiling. A large, oval-shaped mirror, embedded in the hardwood frame of the vanity unit, and carved with elaborate clouds and airy patterns, reflected the image of the mother and daughter clinging to one another, with their eyebrows arched, and their eyes full of laughter. There was no mistaking they were related, and it pleased Bichu to see her sweet daughter, looking so like her. Picking up a bright red hair band from a tray she kept on the table, she placed it on May's head and answered: "To be natural is the best way for children to look beautiful. You don't need make-up – it makes you look too made up, and would spoil this pretty face of yours." May didn't say anything although she was slightly disheartened as she continued to watch her mother combing her hair. Bichu had very long, thick black hair, the most enviable kind, and May watched as she gathered it all together with the ease of familiarity, before binding it up into a perfect bun on the back of her head. It was the style handed down from her mother, Madam Lü, and one Bichu would hand down to her daughters. Madam Lü's bun was well known in Fuyang county[14] and was named 'the Lü Bun', in her honour. Her three daughters, Bichu and her two sisters, had all worn their hair long in their youth, and put it up in a bun once they were married. Now, Bichu's bun had never received the same attention as her mother's did, in such an enormous city like Beiping, but she remained proud of it, every time she drew it up into that familiar style. As an added flourish, Bichu decorated her bun with a pin. A red 喜 (xi), meaning happiness, forged out of red flannel, hung at the tip of the pin and trailed down across her silky black hair.

Satisfied with her hair, she picked a pair of oval, emerald earrings from her jewellery box, sliding them into her ears, and selected a matching brooch to fit onto her collar. The jewels glinted in the sunlight glancing in through the window, adding a touch of sparkle to Bichu's appearance. Looking in the mirror, she assessed her face; her fair skin didn't need much in the way of make-up, so she was done quite soon, selecting products from only a few pots, though May remained entranced by the action of applying it. Finishing up,

---

[14] Fuyang county: (阜阳县 *fuyang xian*) is a prefecture-level city in northwestern Anhui province. It borders Bozhou to the northeast, Huainan to the southeast, Lu'an to the south, and the province of Henan on all other sides.

mother and daughter were smiling at each other in the mirror, when they saw Earl come into the room.

"Mother, it's not fair – all of you are going to town, leaving me behind," Earl said, sulking.

Bichu frowned slightly. "Aren't you going to your concert? Has it been canceled? If it has, you should come with us," she suggested patiently, knowing her eldest was prone to capricious behaviour.

Earl sighed. "Of course it's not canceled, I have to be there to collect the entrance fees."

"Is Zhang Xinlei going, too?" May asked, out of curiosity.

"It's none of your business," the big sister snapped, glaring at her younger sister..

"It would be better if you didn't go tonight. Seriously," recommended Bichu, after giving it some thought,. She was concerned about Earl, who was as stubborn as a donkey and equally hard to harness. "Are your classmates going with you?"

"Of course they are," retorted Earl, casting one more glance at her younger sister and brother before whirling from the room, a black cloud hanging over her head. Earl was ever the whirlwind, and Bichu wasn't quite sure what she was going to do with her unruly eldest daughter, if the stormy winds of her demeanour didn't settle soon.

With everyone dressed and ready, they all went outside, where the two children climbed into the car, taking the backward-facing seats as they usually did. Bichu and Fuzhi got in after them, exchanging a glance as they both looked toward their beautiful children, sitting opposite. The couple could say a lot without saying anything at all, and a whole conversation was silently underway. With so much uncertainty looming over Beiping, both of them shared the same concern – for now, their children were happy, but there was no telling what challenges they might face in their journey through life. War brought complications, and the Meng couple simply hoped it would hold off for long enough that their youngest might enjoy the remainder of their childhood.

"Don't forget to remind Cousin Wei to take his bug catcher with him," Kiddo whispered to May. They also exchanged a knowing look with each other. Once, during Wei's stay, they had caught a dozen fireflies and set them free in their room. It had been a glorious moment, the three of them holding a firefly convention, before Bichu cut it short, giving them a long, serious lecture on why it wasn't acceptable. They had promised never to do it again but, despite the telling-off, it seemed they hadn't learnt their lesson after all.

"Professor Meng, what's your opinion on the situation now?" Old Song was a very disciplined driver, who never presumed to speak with his passengers, nor did he spread a word of their conversations, his lips perpetually sealed. But today was a most peculiar day, and he felt compelled to ask.

"We don't have many options. We have to fight back," Meng Fuzhi answered, with his usual calmness.

"But we have so many good things in Beiping. If the war hits the city, what are we going to do with those things?" Old Song asked.

Meng Fuzhi knew the National Palace Museum had been busy sorting out its most valuable collections to deliver to Nanjing, to keep them safe should war break out. He guessed that might be a solution, though he knew it couldn't be done with every valuable thing in the city. Sighing softly, he muttered: "If we are going to face the destruction of the entire nation, who are we saving Beiping for?"

Old Song nodded sadly. "You are definitely right, professor."

The car drove off the campus, exiting the beautiful realm of cooler air and lush fauna, the avenue shaded by two lines of Chinese Scholar trees quickly disappearing behind them. May, sitting on the backward-facing seat, could see the disappearing avenue better than anyone, and she watched it intently until it had completely disappeared from view. Closing her eyes, she could almost smell the sweetness from the trees. Instinctively, she waved to the retreating university gate and said a cheery, "Goodbye!"

Bichu laughed at May: "We are coming back this evening. You are treating this like a farewell." Her heart missed another beat at the word 'farewell', her mind ever-conscious of what the future held. Would there be a day when it would be 'farewell', for good? She shuddered, pushing the thought from her head.

She wasn't the only one. Everyone's heart missed a beat at the thought of such a goodbye, as they watched the towering gate getting smaller and smaller. The car took a turn, and the gate disappeared.

It was an easy drive to town and, as they reached it, many of the stores were still open. Things looked peaceful, nothing bad seeming to linger in the air, though Old Song seemed on edge. "Not so many people. There are not so many people on the street," muttered the driver.

May and Kiddo looked out of the windows with curiosity, their faces pressed up against the glass. Old Song's words seemed strange to them; compared with the campus during summer vacation, the children thought there were lots of people on the street, more than they'd seen in a while. The car took Xizhimen street and drove on, as the signposts on both sides of the street receded behind them. Kiddo looked ahead as far as he could, a giant copper kettle catching his attention. He pointed at it with his chubby fingers and laughed heartily: "What a giant tea kettle!"

"It's for the shop selling millet noodles," Bichu answered, looking to where her son was pointing.

"There's one near Aunt Jiangchu's house," added May, eagerly.

Meng Fuzhi laughed: "You kids growing up on campus don't know much about the city. You are quasi-Beiping natives; we are a class separated from the masses."

The two kids paid no attention to the quasi-Beiping natives label, all their attention focused on what was going on outside the car windows. It was true, they were a little sheltered at the campus, but they loved the sights and sounds of the city.

Driving by Xidan district, the family noticed that some shops under the archway were putting up their blinds, ready to close up early. It seemed not everyone was oblivious to the dangers lurking overhead.

"Do you think Wei Feng will show up on time?" Bichu asked, a little worried after their encounter earlier.

Fuzhi shrugged. "He always manages to. Even if he doesn't make it today, it's not that important in the grand scheme of things – compared with wars, weddings are a trivial thing."

After traveling down several more streets, the car arrived in good time at the Euro-US Alumni Association, located on the south bank. They passed the gate and entered the parking area. With only a few cars there, the lot looked rather deserted, compared with the bright lights and gaudy banners that hung in front of the lobby. It was crowded in there, a flurry of voices rippling out towards the car. As they got out, they could feel the mixture of happiness and excitement in the air that always seemed to come before a wedding.

Wei Feng's father-in-law, Ling Jingyao, came out to greet them. He was of noble stock – a professor of French literature at Yiren University and one of the pioneers of the drama movement, while his father had served as a minister in the late Qing dynasty. Though he was not a tall man by any means, the extra meat on his bones added a jovial flavour to his personality that made him seem larger than life.

As they entered the building, it was evident that the whole hall of guests was not fixated on the wedding, as they ought to have been, but on the war instead. It was likely what Wei Feng would have wanted, given his inclination that conveying gratitude and respect to the army was far more attractive than the prospect of officially becoming a bridegroom. To him, the war mattered more, and it seemed several of the guests shared his opinion.

"Has Wei Feng arrived?" Meng Fuzhi asked, looking around.

"He just got here. He's getting changed as we speak," Ling Jingyao answered, before turning to greet Bichu: "My wife and our daughter Xueyan are in the east hall," he said, but before he could finish speaking, his wife Yue Hengfen hurried up to them. She exchanged greetings with the Meng couple, her eyes sliding enviously from Bichu's smiling face to her dark green, elegant silk *qipao* with yellow and red polka dots, and lingering for a couple of seconds on her matching jewellery. Once her scrutiny was finished, she turned to her husband, her voice anxious: "The car that was sent for the maid of honour has just come back. She said she couldn't make it. Her parents won't allow her to leave the house. What should we do? She should have told us earlier!" she whispered, her manner flustered. The maid of honour was Ling Xueyan's classmate, who lived in the southern part of the city. Not waiting for her husband to reply, Yue Hengfen continued: "I mean, I understand why her parents wouldn't allow her to go out. We are at war, after all!... but, well, my family has just run into the war! Do we have any other options? Do we?"

"If we could beat the brazen provocation of the Japanese, that would be something to celebrate," said Meng Fuzhi, casually. "Can you manage without the maid of honour?"

Yue Hengfen frowned thoughtfully. "Xueyan might be upset. The dress and everything was arranged for the maid of honour! Goodness, this doesn't bode well for a wedding!"

Bichu finished evaluating Hengfen's outfit, as she had done hers – she was wearing a thin dark scarlet silk *qipao* woven with a goldish-grey pattern that suited her very well. Bichu noticed that her petticoat was dark scarlet, too, giving her quite an imposing silhouette. Lying flat against her chest was a red agate pendant, trimmed with gold, leading up to a chain of the same rich metal, and the pure lustre from the agate indicated its supreme quality. Satisfied with what she saw, Bichu stopped studying Yue Hengfen, and turned to help the host and hostess: "Is a substitute acceptable?" she asked.

"Aunt Bichu! Uncle Fuzhi!" The crisp voice cut through the crowd, catching everyone's attention. The whole room turned to look and found Tantai Xuan and Tantai Mian hurrying towards Bichu. Tantai Xuan was going to be a sophomore after the summer vacation, and was a student in the foreign language department of Yiren University. She was one of those girls that everyone remarked upon, agreeing how beautiful she was, with her delicate facial features, very fair complexion and smooth skin attracting attention wherever she went.

Her younger brother, Tantai Wei, muttered his greetings

rather shyly, but when he looked at his Aunt Bichu, his eyes shone with sincerity. He was a good-looking teenager, sharing a similar, genetically blessed appearance to that of his sister, with bright eyes and long, neat eyebrows that shaped the structure of his handsome face. Having greeted the elder members of the big family, he turned to talk to May and Kiddo, preferring their company to that of the adults.

"You two are here," Bichu's eyes brightened up with an idea. She patted Tantai Xuan on the shoulder and cast an enquiring glance at Hengfen, who smiled her confirmation to Bichu, as Bichu brought the girl forward for closer inspection.

Hengfen nodded approvingly. "I have met Miss Tantai before. I know her," she said, putting her hands around both their waists, as she walked between Bichu and Xuan, guiding them to the east hall. After a few steps, she realised another role for the wedding was missing, and asked Bichu to fetch May, as May, Wei and Kiddo had already joined the kids from the Zhuang and other families at the east end of the hall.

Mrs Zhuang was the second wife of Zhuang Youchen and Zhuang Wuyin's stepmother, and although she was English in origin, her tall and slender figure made her feel she was quite qualified to wear the *qipao*. Indeed, it suited her well. She was in the middle of talking and joking with May, when she looked up to see Bichu coming towards her. Brushing herself down, she took several steps toward Bichu and extended her hands in greeting: "Mrs Meng, what do you feed your children? They are beautiful! You must give me some tips." She beamed, glancing delightedly towards May and Kiddo.

Bichu smiled. "We have a bit of a problem," she explained. "You see, we have already borrowed Wuyin for the wedding, but now it looks like we also need May. There's a role that needs filling."

Mrs Zhuang clapped her hands together. "Let them do it! What a special wedding - May and Wucai, two flower girls holding the bride's train together! They'll remember this for the rest of their lives!"

"The most special thing today is the gunfire at Marco Polo bridge," her husband Youchen commented, putting a dampener on Mrs Zhuang's enthusiasm. "We Chinese are very proud of this moment." His wife, who was much taller than he was, looked down at him, her eyes full of admiration. It was an expression she held only for her husband and, inspired by her admiration, Youchen continued: "If we fight, we have a good chance of winning. What would horrify me is if we didn't fight at all."

"This is not the whole case," interjected Qian Jingming, a lecturer from the Chinese department who was close by. "The government has its reasons for fighting or not. Look at the country! Do you think the country can withstand another war? In the last century, they did exactly that – they fought several wars, and every single one ended up being a bigger disaster for everyone."

"What are you saying then?" said Youchen, a little lost.

"We must resort to negotiation," Qian Mingjing sighed, as if it were obvious. "How's your experiment going? It would be a real pity if it were interrupted," he asked, changing the topic. It was clearly a subject that interested him, as he began to speak in-depth about it, going on and on about Youchen's experiment, the war partially forgotten for the moment. It was interesting to Qian that Youchen should be such an attentive listener, and he was only too happy to have a captive audience. Bichu nodded and smiled where appropriate, and asked Kiddo to stay with Wei, as she excused herself from the discussion and took May through the crowd, heading for the east hall.

The dressing room in the east hall was even livelier than the grand hall, though there were only a few people within. As Bichu and May entered, they were engulfed by a wave of sweet-smelling fragrances and the ring of laughter in their ears, as they looked around, taking in the sight before them. The dressing room was in a fair amount of disarray, with dresses hung everywhere, making the room look rather crowded, as if there were more people in there than there were. Sitting in the hairdresser's chair was Zhuang Wuyin, a striking mixture of her English mother and her Chinese father. She was wriggling this way and that while the hairdresser struggled to blow-dry her locks into something resembling elegant hair, while, behind a silk screen, the bride, Ling Xueyan, was sitting upright, all dressed up and ready for the ceremony. Her white wedding gown was billowing up around her, making her look like a princess, torn straight from the pages of a storybook. She had finished her preparation at home and arrived early for her special moment. There was a tremor of anxiety in the air of excitement that hung across the room.

"Sis Ling looks like a fairy!" May exclaimed merrily, her eyes wide with awe. "A fairy in the clouds!"

Xuan was ushered over to the beautifying station, where she stood patiently as Mrs Ling and Old Amah Sun set about dressing her up.

"Is this one qualified?" asked Bichu, gently pushing May in front of her.

"She just needs to blow-dry her hair a bit. Wucai is almost done," Mrs Ling said, holding the maid of honour's dress up to Xuan, to see whether it was a good fit or not. When she was satisfied that it would fit, she handed it to Old Amah Sun. After so much seriousness, Xuan made a monkey face in May's direction, making her giggle joyfully. The happiness was wiped from her face a moment later, when she saw what the hairdresser was doing to Wucai's hair.

"Oh, no! I don't want that, I don't like blow-drying," protested May, remembering when Xueyan had taken her to a hairdresser once. It was a horrifying experience to have that hair dryer blowing hot air around her head, and it wasn't one she particularly wanted to repeat, though it didn't seem she had much choice in the matter.

Bichu knew better than to upset Mrs Ling, who was a known perfectionist with a great eye for detail. Although the guests were distracted by the war, this was her only daughter's wedding, after all, and Bichu was determined to try and make things right, to make up for other peoples' wandering minds. So, Bichu wiped the smile off her face and gave May a serious look that silenced the young girl's cries of dismay.

When Wucai was done, she hopped down off the chair. Her dark, red-tinted hair was fluffy from the hairdryer, and matched her blue eyes beautifully. She smiled at May, as May took a deep breath and climbed into the chair, without having to be called.

"This is a very brave young lady," said the hairdresser, praising May.

Behind the screen, Xuan could be heard complaining. "This dress is too tight! I'm going to be strangled to death!" she cried, before collapsing into a fit of giggles at Ling Xueyan: "Sis Ling, I'm doing this for you!"

"There, there!" Old Amah Sun murmured, trying to calm Xuan down. "It's just a little bit tight… just a little bit. You'll be okay."

"Why would you pick such a hot day to get married?" Xuan added, trying to relax in the tight dress. The heat made it ten times worse.

Her latest complaint went unanswered, as someone was sent to ask whether the bride was ready. All the guests were gathered in the grand hall, awaiting her arrival, and Ling Jingyao was waiting outside the east hall, ready to deliver his daughter to his new son-in-law. With firm instructions from the two directors, Mrs Ling and Mrs Meng, everyone was in position. Xueyan stood up, with Xuan by her side, May and Wucai holding the bride's train behind Xueyan. Once everyone was in place, and knew what they were doing, the screen was then removed.

Holding the piece of fine gauze in her hands, May suddenly wanted to sneeze. Her sensitive nose couldn't stand all the strong, sweet smells that swamped the room, hanging in a tangible mist all over the place, inescapably pungent. She had been holding the violent sneeze back for a while, but she simply couldn't hold it anymore. The sneeze erupted from her nose with a loud 'achoo', provoking an angry glare from Mrs Ling.

May blushed, feeling embarrassed but relieved to have the itch in her nose gone. "I will never, ever sneeze at my wedding when I am the bride," said May to herself. For her, to be a bride was a wonderful thing, and something she hoped to be one day. It was the closest thing to a fairytale princess she knew she was ever likely to get.

The door opened, and in walked Wei Feng and the best man, Li Yuming, a former classmate of Wei Feng. Both wore black suits, which showed off their charm and looks. They both looked incredibly handsome and smart, dressed up to the nines, to the point where May felt she couldn't look at them as she used to; they didn't even seem like the same boys she knew.

Taking her eyes off them, May and the bride held their heads half down, while Xuan and Wucai held their heads high with their eyes wide-open. Wei Feng approached and took up one of Xueyan's gloved hands, the fine material covering up to her elbows, but he wasn't looking at his bride – instead, he was smiling at Xuan. It was clear he hadn't expected Xuan to be the maid of honour, and the sight of her, standing so close to his bride-to-be, was a pleasing one. In his eyes, both Xueyan and Xuan were stunningly beautiful, though he could not have chosen between the two, who was the more beautiful. He was familiar with Xueyan's beauty, his eyes accustomed to seeing it, and though she looked dewy and positively glowing on this particular day, he couldn't help but be drawn in by Xuan's beauty. Sensing her groom's wandering eye, Xueyan gave the hand holding her arm a little pinch, forcing Wei Feng to hurriedly take back his gaze and smile embarrassedly at his bride. At least he had the decency to show his mortification at being caught out.

"You go first. We'll be right behind," instructed Hengfen. Wei Feng and the best man obeyed the order and obediently left, while Ling Jingyao came over to Xueyan and offered her his arm. With their arms linked, the bridal party walked slowly to the grand hall, as the band began the Wedding March. May and Wucai walked behind Xueyan very solemnly, trying to figure out the optimum distance between themselves and the bride, so the gown wouldn't be pulled too tight or too loose as they held up the train. It would be a shame to ruin the silhouette of the dress now, given how beautiful Xueyan looked in it. May felt the pressure of her duty upon her, as she continued to walk, holding the flimsy white gauze.

The wedding itself was a testament to the great efforts both families had put into bringing it together on the day. Ling Xueyan had wanted a church wedding. It was something she had dreamed about since she was a little girl, envisioning the way she would be asked the all-important question by the priest, in that solemn, reverent atmosphere: "do you take this man to be your lawful wedded husband? Will you love him and keep him company as long as you both shall live?" And she knew she would answer with all her heart: "I will."

It might have happened, had Wei Feng not claimed he was an atheist, flat-out refusing to agree on a church wedding. Mrs Ling proposed they might invite her uncle, the vice mayor of Beiping, Miao Donghui, to host the wedding instead. However, Wei Feng had been even more strongly opposed to this idea, given that he didn't like officials either. After what seemed like endless discussion on the matter, they had finally agreed to invite Professor Zhuang Youchen to witness the wedding, seeing as Mr Zhuang had taught Wei Feng, and enjoyed the prestigious academic standing of his position at the university. Besides, he didn't take any stand in politics, which suited Wei Feng well. In addition to a variety of speeches, they had decided that the wedding ceremony would include traditional rituals like exchanging of rings and bowing to the parents. When Wei Feng would later recall the wedding, and the little moments within it, he would always have this gentle mood of dissociation, since it mirrored his own life – neither eastern nor western, neither fish nor fowl.

The band stopped the music, allowing the new couple and the best man, the maid of honour and the flower girls to walk past the rows of seats. They came to a halt beside sweet-smelling swathes of fresh flowers, that had been put up just in front of Zhuang Youchen. Many seats were still empty, but there was joy in the air. It was a happy moment, and the onlookers watched the new couple with wide, cheerful smiles. Bichu and Hengfen stood by their husbands on either side of Zhuang Youchen, glancing nervously around the grand hall, hoping everything would be fine.

Professor Zhuang began:

"It is a remarkable day today. Why? Because today I have found the answers to two questions which have been bothering me for quite a long time. The first question is why have the Chinese people always allowed themselves to be beaten down by the force of other nations? It is said that Confucius and Mencius are the causes of so many deep-rooted bad national habits, so that anything that can be done by one Chinese is doomed to fail if done by three. One Chinese is a Chinese, two Chinese half a Chinese, and three Chinese, no Chinese. But today, I saw the Chinese people united together to achieve something great – they have forced the invaders to leave! It is true that, for almost a whole century, our country has never managed to fight against invasion, but past failures cannot serve as new dooms. We cannot wait for failures to happen again. To resist, we still have hope! To surrender, we can only perish!" Youchen's voice was not loud, but it caught everyone's full attention. This question weighed more on their minds than the wedding. At the word 'surrender', a wave of sighs drifted across the hall.

"As for the second question, the answer is a lot easier. Mr Wei Feng and Miss Ling Xueyan are a match made in heaven. Everyone agrees with this fact. I had been wondering why the two were still not married, but today, I found the answer. They have been waiting for this great moment! At this great moment, they are…" As if to echo his words, and witness this great moment, a deafening gunshot interrupted his sentence.

More rumbling sounds came from the distance, panicking the congregation. The whole afternoon, prior to this momentous occasion, people had only heard the distant sound of sporadic gunfire. With it kept at bay, not close enough to worry them, they had been able to stay calm. But now, the sounds, though still relatively far away, were loud enough to alarm the ladies present. Some of them stood up, but after looking at others seated around them, they sat down again, steeling their nerves.

"We are witnessing a great moment," Youchen announced, giving free rein to his passion. "They have been waiting for the Chinese nation to stand up; they have been waiting for a peaceful and happy life; they have been waiting to put their hearts into their chests, their brains into their heads without sparing a thought about how to avoid those disasters. We shall never forget this moment. We have been waiting for this moment for a hundred years – when children grow up to get married, their weddings will be surrounded only by their loving families and friends, sweet flowers and melodious music. But today, we cannot do without guns. We need guns!"

The hall fell silent. Even the master of ceremonies (MC) forgot to proceed, distracted by the noise and the stirring rhetoric of Youchen. Hengfen and Bichu exchanged a look and motioned May and Wucai to put down the train and take the two trays to the new couple. May gave her tray to Wei Feng, and Wucai gave hers to Xueyan. Cushioned on the red velvet lay two knotted rings made of gold, forged with fine craftsmanship. Wei Feng took the ring from the tray and put it on Xueyan's finger. Her trembling palms were covered by the lace trimmings of her fingerless gloves, and her fair thin fingers revealed some blue veins as the ring slid onto her finger. Looking at these fingers, he was moved. He realised that she was now his wife! Uncertainty crept into his mind –

how was he supposed to love her, take care of her, and protect her? How much time was he allotted to play the role of a good husband in such a situation? It wasn't a position he'd ever been in before, understanding that this delicate creature was now his responsibility.

Fuzhi delivered his best wishes, before Jingyao stepped in to talk about how lofty love was. He then recited a few lines in French from *La Nuit de Mai* by Alfred de Musset, before jumping to the lines by Juliet from *Romeo and Juliet: "My bounty is as boundless as the sea, / My love as deep. The more I give to thee, / the more I have, for both are infinite."* It would not count as an auspicious quotation on any account, and his wife shot him a series of warning looks, but he didn't see them, his mind too focused on the words at hand.

The ceremony continued, though there were disturbances among the audience. Miao Donghui came in late, dressed in a long silk gown with a short thin sleeveless silk jacket knitted in patterns of clustered flowers. Everybody turned to look, wondering what news he brought, but he kept waving people to sit down as he took a seat in the last row. Several guests nearby cosied up to him for some information, but he would not give them the news they desired, as he pointed at the new couple and kept smiling without saying anything. It wasn't the time or the place, not yet.

Finally, the MC announced the conclusion of the wedding. A cheer went up, as the newlyweds walked out of the grand hall to music, their arms linked, just as their lives now were. The ushers steered the guests towards the banquet hall, so the festivities could continue, but Hengfen hurried to Miao Donghui: "I'm sorry, uncle. I thought you were not coming, so we didn't wait for you."

"Nonsense, stick to your schedule. You didn't need to

wait for me," Miao Donghui said, smiling, though he looked rather exhausted.

"Are we negotiating?" Meng Fuzhi came to ask.

Donghui nodded. "Yes. There was a skirmish in the afternoon. Now, the two sides are sitting around the table. The best option would be that both agree to withdraw from Marco Polo bridge at the same time." When he was a young man, Miao went to study in Japan, majoring in railroad engineering. He served one deputy minister in the traffic department but, being born with a silver spoon in his mouth, he had been out of work for a long time. Saying that, he was an enthusiastic philanthropist and had dedicated lots of his time and effort to fundraising for the municipal government's construction of Beiping. It was the main reason he had later been assigned the position as one of the vice mayors of the city and, with his political attitude being ambiguous at best, it made him popular among the different sides who continually tried to gain his favour. "Is Mr Lü not coming? He didn't show up last time when Master Merciful came to share his interpretation of the Diamond Sutra."

"If those who repent for their sins are forgiven, no one will take the iniative to repent," said Meng Fuzhi with a bitter smile.

"Negotiating! They are negotiating," Miao Donghui nodded comfortingly at Meng Fuzhi, and greeted other acquaintances from varied backgrounds, as they came up to greet him, hungry for information. "It looks like it will take more than one negotiation to reach any agreement. They had a battle just now, and the first talks after such an event rarely breed success but the Japanese prime minister declared it's still too early to think about sacrificing peoples' lives, or to snatch a tenuous peace."

"This way, uncle," Hengfen called, wanting to steer Donghui in the direction of the banquet hall. "Yesterday, I took Xueyan over to pay her respects, but you were off listening to sutra interpretations."

"I am no capitulator." Miao Donghui didn't answer Hengfen. Instead, he continued to talk to Meng Fuzhi: "But this is a decision which will affect the lives of 400 million people! Individuals like you and me can give our blood to serve our country, we can make any sacrifice, but for the government, they have much more to weigh up before they can come to a decision."

"When they weigh up the balance, they should consider the wishes of the people first," Zhuang Youchen said firmly.

"That's for sure," said Donghui, still deep in discussion as they reached the banquet hall. There were about 20 round tables in the hall, all covered with bright pink, painstakingly embroidered table cloths, and decorated with fresh flowers that gave a sweet, summery scent to the hall. The space was bright and airy, lit by two rows of gilded chandeliers that hung ostentatiously from the ceiling. Waiters in their smart, crisp uniforms were standing respectfully by the tables with their hands at their sides, awaiting their first task of the proceedings. The guests seemed to be waiting too, and when Miao Donghui reached the table set up in the centre, he nodded to the guests and took his seat. Taking their cue from him, others then began to sit down at their tables too.

Discussion continued, the babble of it rippling across the room until, a short while later, the Wei couple came out after changing their clothes. May and Xuan and other youngsters had all gathered at the two tables on the outside edge, where they would be out of the way of the adults. Li Yuming came to join Kiddo and the other kids, and immediately an excited conversation started. May thought Ling Xueyan was stunningly beautiful, and proclaimed that when Xueyan was in her wedding gown, she looked like a fairy. Now, she had put on a red silk *qipao* with a hollowed-out finish, adding a youthful freshness to her elegance. May watched the newlyweds as they wandered towards Miao Donghui to propose a toast, when the hall fell into sudden darkness.

"The lights are out," Xuan said, not greatly concerned.

May and the other kids weren't bothered either, because it wasn't completely dark outside, and the stray rays of the fading sunlight were still shining in through the windows. But there was some disturbance in the centre of the hall that did give cause for anxiety, as the waiters brought up candle holders to the tables as quickly as they could. Each holder had five candles in it, bringing a different ambiance to the hall, showering it in a hazy glow of romantic light.

Despite the soft glow, everyone felt somewhat uneasy, and although the food was delicious, it was hard to enjoy with the weight of the world on their shoulders. The children, sitting at their table, were the only ones showing an ounce of bawdy, celebratory excitement, as they busied themselves filling the glasses in front of them, so they could toast and cheer like the adults did.

Wei filled up the glasses for May and Wucai, the other boys following suit, thinking it looked like a very proper thing to do.

Xuan complained woefully: "Why will no one fill up my glass? Am I too old to be taken care of?"

It looked like Li Yuming had overheard Xuan, as he came over to the table to speak with the beautiful Xuan: "I have long heard of Miss Tantai. What a straightforward lady she is!" he said, teasing her slightly.

"You are the tennis guy?" Xuan laughed, her pink cheeks so radiant that they challenged the blush of the wine in her glass.

"Yuming is the champion of the Beijing College and University Open Championship and you just called him 'the tennis guy'?" Wei Feng exclaimed, chuckling. He and Xueyan were going table to table, to thank and toast the guests that were present and the two that had arrived at the kids' table. Gleefully, Xuan flashed a look at Li Yuming, before drinking up the wine in her glass merrily. A sweet chuckle rising from her throat, she even showed the newlyweds the empty bottom of her glass.

"What a carefree lady! I like Xuan's way of doing things," Wei Feng added, and although Xueyan might have felt a pang of jealousy, she refused to allow those thoughts into her mind. Instead, Xueyan looked at Yuming and Xuan with a gentle smile on her face, wondering if it might be the start of something.

Bichu walked toward them as if she had something important to say, but before she could say anything, a wave of turmoil hit them, with the arrival of a message that "the city gate is closed!".

The city gate was closed! The message was delivered by Miao Donghui's secretary, and the news brought panic with it. Gates and doors hold a special significance for Chinese people, stemming from their understanding of the universe and the flow of things – if a door is closed, that's a bad omen, if not a catastrophe, and the fact that the city gate, an entry point of such valuable importance, was closed left everyone jittery.

The message affected the newlywed Wei couple most of all, since they couldn't go out of town to enjoy the well furnished bridal room that Bichu had painstakingly decorated, in a grand display of effort from both the bride and the bridegroom's families. However, all was not lost, as the Ling household had already prepared a room in expectation of the bride returning to her mother's home, as was tradition, three days after the wedding ceremony. It was not hard to imagine what a luxurious room it would be, with all those exquisite decorations laid out under the keen supervision of Hengfen. Wei Feng had been specific about not leaving their wedding to reside with the in-laws, preferring their own space, but then the onset of war meant they'd run out of all other options.

It wasn't quite as simple for many of the guests from Minglun University, who had to excuse themselves to begin the hunt for a proper place to stay overnight in town. It wasn't what they'd expected, knowing they would need to call on all their friends and relatives living in town, to see if anyone could put them up for the night. They had promised to visit many of them while they were in town, but now that they couldn't get out of town and were forced to stay, it suddenly made them feel homeless. They would have to call in any favours they could, to put a roof over their heads for the night.

Bichu was searching anxiously for Fuzhi, amongst the crowd. A smile was still hanging at the corners of her mouth, despite everything. They spotted each other in the crowd and walked up to one another, their eyes communicating with that silent, secret language, as they always did: "Is it on?"

"Yes, it's on, although we will have to go through many hardships," said Fuzhi, sadly.

Bichu nodded, keeping a brave face. "I know. Shall we stay at father's?"

"We should," Fuzhi confirmed.

May and Kiddo had overheard the conversation, and exchanged a look, before turning sorrowfully to Tantai Wei. It seemed the fireflies and the campus would have to wait, although May hoped they had not said farewell to it for good.

Tantai Wei, however, was surprisingly quite delighted: "Let's just put off our firefly meeting. We can all hang out in town instead – there are lots of fun things to do here." He was the only one who was genuinely happy about the prolonged stay in town, because he wanted May and Kiddo to stay with him as long as possible. It was hard with the other two being so far from the city, but now he could show them his world, and let them see how much fun it could be.

A while later, the various wedding parties began to leave, the festivities somewhat soured by the news. Tantai Wei didn't let May and Kiddo out of his sight, as they parted ways, certain that they would somehow get away from him. Even as he and his sister Xuan got in the car and headed home, he pressed his face against the back window, to double check whether the car May was in was following behind.

PART 3

Next to Shicha lake, the house at No. 3 Chestnut Street would be called a mansion. With No. 2 and No. 4 on either side, the three places stood out distinctly from the neighbouring buildings, with their imposing, sombre gates and tall roofs carved with lions, tigers and mystical beasts like kirin (or *qilin* - Asian mythical creatures with hooved feet). They looked majestic, their mouths open mid-roar, fangs sharp and ready to bite, stone limbs stretched out and ready to pounce. Each building had a gothic air to it, that enthralled passersby, making them wonder what lay beyond the curved iron gates and savage stone guardians.

The three mansions were once part of one big property, belonging to Zhang Zhidong, one of the four most important ministers in the late Qing dynasty. No. 3 was the central part of the property, and standing in front of its gates loomed a gigantic screen-wall, made up of dark grey tiles that bore an elegant pattern of elaborate bats and ornate turtles, symbolising happiness and longevity for the house it belonged to. The screen used to have a huge painting of a blooming lotus on it, a mirror image of Shicha lake, but Grandpa Lü asked for it to be painted white when he bought the building more than 20 years ago. Now, it was just a plain, blank screen-wall with the original tile frame.

Where there had once been two medium-sized stone lions flanking the entrance, they stood no longer, having been removed to the back garden, their sentry duty at an end. Instead, a pair of scrolls bearing a couplet written by Weng Tonghe[15] had been put up on each side of the gate. The scroll on the left read: 'Listen to different opinions while maintaining your own, pay attention to the details while looking out for the overall pattern'; the one on the right read: 'Remain down-to-earth while nurturing ambition, leave your comfort zone and be ready to face challenges'. In fact, it was Fuzhi who had gone to the Commercial Press, which sold these ready printed couplets, and chose that one, thinking that it might suit Lü's taste. Grandpa Lü had indeed liked it very much and even now, every time he passed by, he would pause to read the couplet aloud.

Two things had led Grandpa Lü to buy such a big place. The first was that he wanted to live with his daughters, but he didn't want to live at his in-laws' place. He figured a house this size would come in handy, with enough space for all three daughters and their families, without them stumbling over each other all the time. Besides, he had a sound business mind, and knew that transforming land into real estate was far safer than turning it into cash.

His oldest daughter, Suchu, moved to Yunnan province, about 2,000 miles away, when she got married, but he assigned space for her and her family regardless, should they ever choose to return. His second daughter Jiangchu and her husband Tantai Mian had busy social lives, so he gave

---

[15] Weng Tonghe (翁同龢) 1830–1904; courtesy name Shuping (叔平) was a Chinese Confucian scholar in the Qing dynasty. In 1856, he obtained the position of *zhuangyuan* (状元), the highest level of achievement a scholar could attain in the imperial examination, and was subsequently admitted to the prestigious Imperial Academy.

them the reception hall and the third section of the building, feeling it was the best part of the property for their needs. His youngest daughter, Bichu, and her family lived out of town, so he gave them the smaller compound, with a small garden, to stay overnight when they came into town to visit. For himself, he took the fourth, innermost compound, which was designed for the master of the mansion. As for the rest of the house, the south wing in the front compound was given over to guestrooms, that were constantly occupied by a colourful, vibrant array of guests. For the last two decades, however unstable things were beyond the walls, when the gate was closed, inside the mansion it was a peaceful paradise. A true place of calm and tranquility – a rare find in a city so busy and bustling.

When the car reached the gate, Fuzhi had an odd feeling, as if they were seeking shelter from an unseen danger. Although, saying that, he knew precisely what the danger was. It was strange, pulling up to the door of the mansion; he hadn't planned to come over, given that Grandpa Lü had chosen to forgo the wedding, but now Fuzhi was forced to knock and ask for a place to stay. No, this was not his plan at all. Despite his concerns, he knew there was a nice part of the property assigned to him and his family, inside the Lü residence, where they would be safe and comfortable, and for that he knew he should be grateful.

On the way, Bichu suggested they make a detour and go to Xizhimen gate to see if they could find a way to get out of town; she had a growing concern for Earl, who would be alone at home if they couldn't find a way to get back, but Fuzhi assured her it wouldn't work. All the gates were closed; there was no way out. Old Song also added his two-cents-worth, noting that it might not be a good idea to drive about now, given the potential upset raging through the city. There was no telling who might be out and about. No, the Lü residence was the only viable option they had, for the time being, as their car and Tantai's arrived at the grand mansion at exactly the same time, much to Tantai Wei's delight.

The street was quiet, and although it wasn't late, all the doors were closed. No one was out, enjoying the relief of the cool evening, as they used to. The giant white screen-wall shone in the fading light, grimly solitary on the road, like an ancient ghost, seeking solace. The evening lacked the laughter and chatter of passing citizens, their absence sorrowfully noticeable.

Once the two cars had come to a standstill, Wei jumped out of his car and hurried to open the door for the Meng couple, his excitement palpable. As the black, wrought-iron gate started to open, he shot into the building to report to his parents that Aunt Bichu and her family had arrived. His father, Tantai Mian, and his mother, Jiangchu, had a business dinner at Tongheju restaurant, which was why they were absent from Wei Feng's wedding, but, during the meal, duty had called Tantai Mian back to his company, and so Jiangchu had gone back home alone after the meal was over. She was standing in the reception room, talking with Amah Liu, the servant in charge of the main compound; they were discussing the latest news about the city gate being closed, Jiangchu mentioning that her sister's family might be coming over, seeing as they lived outside the city and would be unable to return, due to the new restriction. Wei rushed into the room and reported to his mother that the Meng couple had arrived. Taking her leave of Amah Liu, she hurried out to greet them, Tantai Wei running on ahead. Before she had even passed the garden and reached the hallway, Bichu and Fuzhi had entered the ornamental inner gate, which served as a means of separating the mansion into the quarters reserved for guests, and the section reserved for the hosts. When they saw each other, they found themselves at a loss for words.

Jiangchu was two years older than Bichu, but the two sisters shared a remarkable physical resemblance. Once, when Jiangchu had paid a visit to Minglun University, several professors greeted her outside the Mengs' garden, believing her to be her sister. She had felt quite strange, having so many people behave so familiarly with her – it was only afterwards that she realised who they had mistaken her for. You see, as similar as the two sisters were in appearance, they had very different personalities – Jiangchu was sharp and smart, where Bichu was gentle and quiet; Jiangchu looked wealthy and elegant, while Bichu looked natural and dignified. Their different life experiences had carved out their different personalities, making them the ladies they were.

The reception hall, a grand, sumptuously furnished room, also served as the living room for the Tantai, but Bichu and the rest of the group didn't stop to rest there. Instead, they walked towards the back of the mansion, where Wei's German shepherd Henry came out to greet them, wagging his head and tail good-naturedly, his tongue lolling in the fading heat. Henry was good at distinguishing relatives and friends from strangers, seldom making mistakes.

All of them walked to the outside living room in the master compound and sat down, although Bichu excused herself, looking for a phone so she could call home to check on Earl. To her dismay, the line worked but no one picked up the phone.

Fuzhi smiled, not wanting to worry his wife. "Maybe Earl is still at her concert," he suggested.

Bichu put down the phone reluctantly and decided to

wait for a while before calling again, later. "Is father already asleep?" she asked.

"Amah Liu has gone to check. I guess he probably is," answered Jiangchu with a shrug.

As they talked, they heard the rustle of a curtain being raised. A moment later, a small, middle-aged woman in a thick, grey silk *qipao* entered, her small round eyes gleaming like tiny black buttons. She was the second wife of Grandpa Lü. When his wife died in his 50s, his life fell into chaos without her familiar company, with all sorts of unexpected inconveniences popping up, things he had never even anticipated before losing her. Although he was reluctant at first, many friends suggested he find someone else to take care of him in his old age. It was a popular thing to do then, among those in similar situations, although people refrained from terms like 'taking a concubine'. Anyway, she was as far from his concubine as it was possible to be – she was his wife, in law and in his eyes, although she would never replace the one he lost. It was the thing that made Grandpa Lü stand out from his contemporaries; he had insisted on giving his second wife a legal marriage, although it was not entirely the done thing. Although legally and formally married to Grandpa Lü, Zhao Lianxiu didn't gain much due respect in the family; she never enjoyed the same prestige as the deceased Madam Lü had enjoyed.

In fact, rather than 'step-mother' or any other form of endearment, Jiangchu and her sisters addressed Zhao as 'aunt'. They did this for two reasons; the first one was due to her less than noble origins. Zhao Lianxiu was born to a poor family in a small county in Yunnan province, where her father was a carpenter. She came from humble origins, and would not have been the expected choice for someone as eminent as Grandpa

Lü. When Suchu, Grandpa Lü's eldest daughter, and wife of the commander of the Yunnan division, Yan Liangzu, had a trip to the Stone Forest, a notable set of limestone formations about 80km away from the provincial capital Kunming, she came across this woman, Zhao Lianxiu. Given the place and situation in which Suchu had found this woman, the sisters found it difficult to see her as a match for their father. Their second reason was that she was two years younger even than Bichu, the youngest daughter of Grandpa Lü. Suchu's plan had been to find a qualified maid, rather than a wife for her father, and definitely not someone her father would formally marry. When Grandpa Lü told his daughters that he wanted them to treat Lianxiu as an equal, Suchu and Bichu agreed, showing no hard feelings. They were sweet-natured, and wanted their father to be happy, but Jiangchu was vehemently against the idea. Her opposition to the marriage never worked, however hard she tried, which led to the flagrant attitude of derision and neglect towards Lianxiu that still prevailed. It didn't matter that Lianxiu turned out to be a virtuous woman, dedicated to serving her husband, Grandpa Lü. Jiangchu would never accept her.

Lianxiu smiled and greeted everyone, her manner respectful but tinged with caution, as she said, or more accurately, reported: "Master is already asleep. He wanted to wait up for you and to ask you about what happened, but it got dark and he went to bed," she explained, as she went over to take May's hand. Lianxiu adored May, and each time May saw her, she felt the same pull of closeness. It would never be prudent for her to call Lianxiu 'grandmother', but it was an endearment she felt, regardless of the title. Saying that, despite their affection for one another, when Lianxiu was out of sight, she hardly came to May's mind at all. May wondered if it was, perhaps, that the other members of the Meng family so rarely referred to her on any occasion, that it seemed she didn't exist. She thought that might be why it was so hard to keep her in the forefront of her mind, because every time May saw her, May felt as if she was a familiar stranger, and longed to know more about the woman.

"I have looked forward to your arrival a few times, but you never showed up. It's nice that you are finally here, and can stay in town for more days than normal," Lianxiu said, taking May's hand. She then tried to take Kiddo's, saying: "Your grandfather is not concerned at all. To quote from him: 'if a bomb doesn't drop on our head, we should just get on with our lives.'"

"Wei, take your cousins to your room. When the west garden is ready, you kids should go to bed," Jiangchu said, not liking Lianxiu's proximity to them. It was the order the three children had been waiting for, and they were already heading out before she had even finished her sentence. Lianxiu took her hand back with an awkward twist, and let May go. With the children gone, she sat down in the chair near the door, still smiling, despite Jiangchu's cold glare. It wasn't like her to stay so long – she usually came in to greet them, staying for a couple of minutes before excusing herself again, but this time she lingered.

Wei's room was a small apartment in the west section of the master compound. Behind the rows of rooms of the compound was a garden running all the way to the back. It gained its name 'wisteria garden' from the prolific amount of wisteria that thrived in it. A vine was hanging across the window of the room facing the garden. May loved that scene.

"Lights off, lights off," May called out when Wei entered the room and turned on the lights.

"May wants to see the wisteria," Kiddo explained. When the lights were off, they saw the leaves and the dancing shadows. A thick vine as big as a child's arm lay diagonally across the window. "Why don't you have fireflies in town?" Kiddo asked. "Fireflies dart to and fro everywhere in the countryside. Can we go back home tomorrow?"

"If the city gate is open, then we can," May assured him.

"I don't think so. Come! I'd like to show you my map – are you done with the wisteria?"

May nodded to let Wei know he could turn on the lights. The room was lit up. A beautiful model plane painted light blue hung from the ceiling in the middle of the room. That was a model Wei had finished during the summer vacation. A big hand-drawn map, another summer vacation assignment, was lying on the desk. Wei had a big work desk, bigger than his father Tantai Mian's office desk. The big desk was divided into different sections according to subjects: maths, history, geography, aeronautics, etc... May went over to study the map while Kiddo nagged Wei to take the model plane down from the ceiling. When they got it down, the two squatted on the floor and began to study it.

"I guess you two are going to fly planes when you grow up," said May, leaving the map behind to join the two boys.

"I am going to MAKE planes," corrected Wei. "People should fly up into the sky like birds, or we will be too pathetic. Birds probably look down upon us humans from the sky the way we'd look at lower creatures like snakes."

"I am going to make planes," parroted Kiddo. "And to fly like fireflies." He looked at May: "May won't make planes. We'll give May rides in our planes."

"I can clean up your planes," said May. She had no interest in making planes, but she thought planes might be very much like houses, which needed cleaning all the time.

"If we ask Xuan to take a ride, she'll definitely say: 'Never. I don't want to fall from the sky and die!'," said Wei, amused by his own words.

"Cousin Xuan is so beautiful today. As beautiful as Cousin Xueyan." For May, all brides were supposed to be the most beautiful women.

The three studied the plane for a while before they returned to the map. Wei marked out all the places where the Japanese armies were stationed. "So many?" May was surprised. "Where is Marco Polo bridge?"

"My map is not so detailed. Do you think I should add it on the map?" Wei picked up a pen.

Then came Amah Liu who had been asked to put May and Kiddo to bed. Wei wanted to follow, but Amah Liu said: "Madam Jiangchu just asked you to go to bed, too. She'll be with you shortly."

"Tomorrow we are going to Shicha lake."

"Do you think you will be allowed to go out of the gate? Come on, my young master."

"Then we'll go to the back courtyard and build canals," said Wei. That rarely visited back courtyard with tall wild grass was a mysterious place for the children. Standing amid the tall wild grass was a small ancient two-storey building. Servants said it was occupied by fox spirits, and deep into the night, tiny red lanterns would be lit up and hung in the building. Of course, no one had ever seen those red lanterns.

The three whispered among themselves a while longer before they broke up for the night. May and Kiddo took the passage in the east wing to reach the main courtyard. Surrounding the main courtyard were 14 tall, spacious main rooms, with the bordering eaves hooked together. Standing in the yard were two giant crab-apple trees and two elms, deeply rooted with rich branches and thick leaves. In the centre was a giant fish tank with lotus growing in it. Two were blooming haphazardly. It was quiet and dark. Only the lights in the passage were on. The sweet smell of tuberoses filled the air. The kids slowed down considerably not to wake up their grandfather with their footsteps. "Just run along! You kids won't wake up your grandfather in such a big garden," said Amah Liu.

They went west and entered the full-moon shaped entrance into a smaller courtyard, which was designed to be a study or a music room. It was small in size but splendidly designed. Lilac grew along the surrounding wall; in front of the south section of the wall was a delicate mini rock garden; beside the rock garden was a flowerbed planted only with herbaceous peonies. The lights in the room filtered through the window frames and spilled peacefully over onto the well-spaced trees and flowers. They lifted up the door curtain to see Fuzhi sitting at the table and Bichu busy sorting things out. Amah Liu helped the two kids wash and get into bed before she excused herself.

A while later, someone was calling outside the door: "Aunt Bichu, are you still up?" Bichu knew the person calling was Lü Guitang, a grandnephew from the same clan as her father. Grandpa Lü didn't have a son, so all the men in the county claimed to be Grandpa Lü's clan members. Guitang was literate and taught for some years in a private school in the countryside. Last year, his wife died of illness and left him with a pile of debts. He couldn't make a living and repay the debts in the countryside, so he took his daughter Lü Xiangge with him and sought refuge from Grandpa Lü. His plan was to find something to do with Grandpa Lü's help and to pay off the debts step by step. Among the steady streams of guests coming and going in the south wing, Guitang was the most sober, loyal and honest one. Grandpa Lü always invited him over to the main courtyard for a chat and to ask for his help with some of the house chores. His position in the big family was half relative and half servant. From the top to the bottom, it had become a kind of routine to address him by his name instead of by any title. Grandpa Lü wanted to send Xiangge to school, but Guitang said Beiping was not a place for them to stay long. Their priority was to pay off their debts. The father and daughter had found some transcription work and had gradually paid off some debts over the past few months. Life had become easier for them.

"Come on in and say hello to Aunt Bichu and Uncle Fuzhi," Lü Guitang said, lifting up the curtain, and entered the room, followed by her 16-year old daughter Xiangge. Each time Bichu met Xiangge, she found the girl more grown-up and more attractive. Yet her gut feeling also told her this girl was smart but not so sincere. She wore a starched light-blue cotton shirt and loose trousers. When she walked, the loose legs of the trousers flapped rhythmically back and forth. Although it was a peasant's style, she had her own brand of charm.

"Is little aunt still up?" She was referring to May.

"No, no! Not now! Do come in!" May and Kiddo were tossing and turning in their bedroom, having difficulty getting to sleep. Xiangge looked at Bichu to see whether there was any trace of disapproval. She decided there was none, and she took out of her pocket two pyramid-shaped sachets stuffed with spices and wrapped with bright-coloured silk yarn with long shiny strings at the end. She smiled, and said: "I made these for little aunt back during the dragon boat festival," and into the bedroom she went. May and Kiddo's cheers were heard without delay. They cheered literally at everything.

Earlier, Bichu phoned home again but still no one picked

up, so she decided to go to the master compound and try again. In the living room, Fuzhi had finished a brief talk with Lü Guitang about the current situation. Guitang was worried about delaying Fuzhi from getting to bed and was ready to leave, but Fuzhi wanted to know how things were in the countryside, so Guitang continued: "Someone from the clan wrote to me, saying life in the country is even worse. One whole village was afflicted by some plague. People first got burns in their eyes, then they had fever, then their right legs were incapacitated. There is never enough to eat or to wear, these people are barely surviving, not really living at all. How could they not be ill? If the Japanese invade, they don't stand a chance of surviving. What are the Japanese after this time?"

"They want to take over north China first, so they can invade the whole country," Fuzhi answered. "It comes down to just one thing – whether we Chinese have a strong will to resist. If we give up north China now, the war will be fierce later."

"Uncle Fuzhi! I don't want to hide this from you," said Guitang, no longer holding back: "I always feel I am a useless loser. Although I know how to read and write, I am far from being educated; I grew up in the countryside, but I don't know much about how to farm. People like me spend their whole lives just eating, living and killing time. If one day I turn out to be of some use fighting the Japanese, I won't have anything to lose." He heard the laughter from the bedroom in the back and cast a glance in there: "I know for sure Aunt Bichu and Aunt Jiangchu will take care of Xiangge for me."

Fuzhi was touched. When the chips were down and the time came to decide between prospering or perishing, most

Chinese were determined to make whatever sacrifices were required of them. He didn't know how to summon up such determination. He kept silent for a while before he began: "We are going back to the university tomorrow. We'll have to leave father and the place in your care. Thank you."

"It's my good fortune that I have the opportunity to serve Grandpa Lü and stay by his side." With these words, he stood up and told Xiangge it was time to leave. Walking out of the room, Xiangge was still promising she would come over tomorrow to teach May how to make dolls with cloth scraps. She and her father then said goodnight to Fuzhi.

Bichu came back a while later and told her husband she had finally got through to Earl, and went inside to check on the two kids.

"Your big sister is at home. She's all right. Her concert was held on time as scheduled," Bichu told the two children, fondling Kiddo's hair. "Daddy and I will go back tomorrow, and you two need to stay here. You have had lots of fun in town, haven't you?"

The town encompassed a world that was rich and full of all sorts of new wonders. The two kids used to complain they didn't stay long enough every time they stayed in town. But upon knowing their mum and dad were going back home and leaving the two of them behind in town, May immediately cast away the two beautiful sachets. She wanted to go home: "Why do we have to stay?"

"I want to go home!" added Kiddo.

"You just stay for a couple of days. When things are better, we'll come to take you back home."

Fuzhi went into the room. "Grandfather is excellent at

telling stories about things that happened in the past. Your cousin Wei will take you to play in…" He didn't have time to finish his sentence. The four of them all felt the same - that the loveliest place in the world was Square Teakettle, and no one wanted to leave it.

"Can we still go back?" May pulled the cover up to her nose, showing only two enormous watery eyes.

"I think you can," Fuzhi didn't have a better answer.

"Just a couple of days. Now, you go to sleep," Bichu assured her.

The two kids could never have imagined in their wildest dreams how long it would take them to get back home. When they did go back, they were grown up. Their beautiful childhood had passed them by and turned into a memory buried deep in their hearts. And those fireflies had gone and become vague images in their dreams.

The Heart of the Wild Bottle Gourd

My dear children, this was the first time I saw you in such loose pajamas, your clothes not quite fitting, and it was my first time, too, to tell you a story, though you two were already asleep.

How I wish I could have kept sitting with your mum by your bedside like this, safeguarding your sweet dreams, praying silently for you.

This tale hails from the big, ancient mountains, passed down from generation to generation. It is a primitive tale, untainted by the rush and tumble of our times.

My tale began, as ordinary tales do, with once upon a time. Once upon a very old time, far far away, there was a village. Outside the village, there was a field full of bottle gourds growing wild. No one ever planted them. It seemed that they were already growing there when the world came into being, and that they would continue to grow long after we were gone. In spring, the vines and branches twisted together with the lush, vibrant leaves, leaving a cool green shade on the ground, keeping it moist and nourishing even in the height of summer. When autumn arrived, golden gourds appeared among the vines, growing high and low, making the vines sag, as they popped up between the leaves like lanterns waiting to be lit. All the villagers loved these golden gourds, marking the passage of time by their shape and size. When a baby was born, its parents would go to the gourd field and claim one gourd for the baby. Taking a piece of paper, they would intricately cut out the name of their child, and tape the word to the gourd, letting it be known who the gourd belonged to. When the gourd was ripe, they would take it home and cut the small tail part off, making an opening so the plant could be dried out, turning it into a perfect container, to be kept within the household until it could serve no further purpose.

To claim a gourd for the babies had become a village tradition, revered alongside other traditions, like giving babies their first bath three days after their birth, the baby's 100-day celebration to wish it 100 years of longevity, and a grabbing test to check a child's vocal ability on the baby's first birthday. Hence, every child in the village had a gourd hung by their bedside, and in some of the girls' bedrooms, the gourds were carefully placed into delicately hand-knitted nests, with all their treasured belongings surrounding them.

Then, one autumn, a fierce enemy invaded the village. What enemies? No one ever knew for certain. All they knew was that these soldiers wore leather jackets, and carried sharp weapons with them, wherever they went. They burned and robbed, looted and massacred, stopping for nothing and nobody. Any survivors were forced into slave labour, made to do back-breaking work until they felt that they, themselves, might break. The enemies tore through the towns and villages, plundering valuables, taking anything they fancied. Then, they happened upon the field of gourds, and the names pinned to the plants. They asked what these names meant, but when they learned the story, they burst into cruel laughter. As a final act of vicious torment, they gathered all the children of the village together and killed them all, beheading them one by one.

After the deed was done, they picked all the gourds and tried to cut the tail parts, so they could use them as containers too, as they had been told to do by the surviving villagers. They chopped at the thick vines with their swords, as sparks flew around the blades. No matter how hard they hacked, the gourds weren't even dented. They slashed, smashed, and crushed the plants, but to no avail – they couldn't even make a crack in the gourds' thick skins. Infuriated by the defiant gourds, the villains lit a huge fire, bigger than any the villagers had ever seen, and dumped all the gourds into the tall flames. Golden beams of light spiraled and sparked within the fire, brighter than the flames themselves. It kept burning all day and all night, but the gourds were still perfectly intact. The enemies panicked, believing the gourds to be possessed, and threw them into a stream, watching with relief as they floated away.

In the rapids, the gourds floated and sank, sank and floated, over and over again, bobbing up and down in the water. The stream was flooded with gourds, ducking and diving in the rapids. According to some witnesses, a piercing cry of fury was heard, erupting from the water, shaking the whole valley. Some said that the objects floating in the stream were not gourds after all, but the heads of those poor children.

With a piercing cry, the gourds floated away, disappearing into the distance.

The next spring, the vines and branches twisted together with the same lustrous leaves, as they always did, casting the same cool shade across the ground. It was the same when autumn arrived, the golden gourds appearing among the vines, just as they had always done, growing high and low, popping up among the leaves like lanterns waiting to be lit.

My dear May's eyebrows furrowed tightly together, as if she was about to cry. I didn't know if she was trying to figure out what dreams were put into the gourds, to make them grow the same, breathing fresh life into the lost children whose names had belonged to them?

Kiddo kicked his feet against the side of the bed, his face puzzled. You two were just like puppets, the taut strings of your fate grasped firmly in the iron grip of war. I found myself worrying about you and the future you deserved, which had become so unpredictable, snatched away without your say-so. I was worried about the millions of youngsters that made up this nation, with their youth set to be consumed by the vicious flames of war. I was worried about all the things yet to come for our country, and what that meant for us all.

Amid all the chaos and confusion, the word 'motherland', so noble and sacred, was engraved on the heart of many Chinese. It was hard to explain to you what that word meant, and in all honesty I didn't understand it myself, yet I felt drawn by it – a magnetic attraction. It was not the government, nor the system. Both were replaceable. It was smaller than that, it was about your family, your hometown, your 'Square Teakettle' you loved so much, and my university, for which I had dedicated half of my life. It was at the epicentre of the history that bore witness to our nation's struggles, and the splendour that rose from hardship like a phoenix spreading its wings, the rich and fertile earth still bearing fruit in a ravaged land. The word belonged to our time-honoured, glorious past and the terrible, uncertain present. Our motherland was irreplaceable. The thought of her brought a lump to the throat of any honest Chinese citizen, and warmed the blood that ran through one's heart, spurring the nation on to protect mother China.

I was a coward, at the time, who never dared to indulge himself in the thought of fighting for that honour, or fighting for her, our motherland. I always wished I could do something truly good for my family, for others, and for society as a whole, but my attempts always fell short. I knew I might never be able to achieve this, and so I didn't dare to try. My failings led me to admire all the kinds of loyalty and persistence that I could not find within myself, just like those wild gourds, growing amid adversity and suffering, year-in, year-out, yet never letting hardship break them.

I remember that the night was painfully quiet, with dull bursts of gunfire rumbling in the distance. Your mum came to me, her face ashen, and said in a soft, scared voice: "What will tomorrow bring?"

My dear children, I didn't know then and I don't know now – what tomorrow will bring...

CHAPTER II

Part 1

Let us turn over one page in the book of time. Today was the 9th of July.

Earl woke up with a start from her dream. It was quiet all around. She jumped out of bed and drew apart the pink and dark grey curtains to find the pale line of the sky. The grass was the same dark green as it was the day before. The small stream running through the garden shimmered in the dim daybreak as it always did. Outside the window was the same scene she had been seeing for more than a decade, which was gradually waking up from the darkness of the previous night. The happy tweets and chirping of sparrows added life to the early morning. Nothing had changed.

But Earl felt something inside her had changed. Did she have more? Or did she have less? She was not sure. She drew the curtains and went back to bed. Looking around her room with its simple but comfortable furnishings, she didn't find anything missing, or anything redundant.

On one of the walls was a glass cabinet. Inside were rows upon rows of plant specimens.

On the side of the cabinet was a crucifix. From the positioning of the crucifix, one could tell that the owner was not a follower of Jesus. The owner's glance paused at the crucifix and she raised her wrist, as was her habit. The wrist watch was no longer there. In its place was a slightly pale mark around the smooth wrist.

The concert last night! How extraordinary!

Earl was considered to be a music fan since she went to so many concerts. Someone like Earl came from families that would learn to play a musical instrument or to participate in choirs to sing Christmas carols around Christmas time, just like other upper-class young ladies did. But because Earl had huge stage fright, she'd rather check tickets at the entrance to concerts. Many informal performances needed extra hands to help. These extra hands were usually passionate volunteers. Earl was never passionate, though she was a free extra hand, but she was very serious about her ticket checking. Her white shirt and black skirt had become her working uniform. She guarded the entrance dutifully, blocking anyone who was late and tried to enter once the performance had already begun.

The concert last night was held in a private university near Minglun University. Earl, her classmate Wu Jiaxin, and Jiaxin's cousin Zhang Xinlei, whose name sounded exactly like Thunderhand (literally, thunder in the palm of the hand), rode to the concert together. Jiaxin's brother, Jiagu, was also a student from Minglun University, so Jiaxin got permission to stay in the girls' dormitory to prepare for her college entrance examination.

The concert was held by a community group, which was a popular form of association in such a private university. They held lots of activities to attract new student members. Not many people had arrived when they got there. The person in charge was very pleased to see the three of them. Upon arrival, Earl immediately stood by the entrance.

She made several exceptions to let in those who showed up late that night, given the fact that it was a peculiar night.

When Earl finally sat down, several performances had already finished. She was always half-hearted during concerts, not because she enjoyed daydreaming to the accompaniment of music. She was not a dreamer herself, and loathed daydreamers like her younger sister May. Music gave her a break in life during which she could just sit there, not thinking about anything, not doing anything, not worrying about being asked why.

Today she was totally absent-minded, and couldn't remember a single performance. She didn't even realize she was at a concert until Mrs Liu, a famous soprano, was on stage.

Mrs Liu's maiden name was Zheng Huiyuan. When she married, she took her husband's family name and called herself Liuzheng Huiyuan. She was a professor at Beijing's National School of Arts, and was one of the few singers who could hold her own solo concerts. Her first song was '*Parting Tune with A Thrice Repeated Refrain*'. Her voice was capable of reaching very high notes, but it didn't sound sharp or forced like mediocre singers' voices would. Her voice was generous and smooth. When she finished the last two lines 'out of the Yangguan pass in the west, you'll find no old friends', she lowered her head, letting the applause from the audience roar and echo. She did not bow.

She kept the same position for a long while. Her pianist looked up at her, anxiously waiting for her signal to start the next song. She did not give any signal. Suddenly, she raised her head and began:

"I am sure everyone here today has heard the news that war has broken out at Marco Polo bridge. It is a great war.

All the songs I have performed in my life would be no match for one single bullet fired by our soldiers at the front. Just now, I decided to say something. I have to say something. We should go to the front to demonstrate our gratitude to the soldiers, to encourage them to fight more, and fight harder! We have their backs, they can count on our solid and strong backing. Without them, how can I find a place to sing and you a place to listen to my songs?"

The audience burst into applause. She kept silent for a short while before starting her second song. On the photocopied concert program, her second song was '*Ave Maria*', but she sang '*Along the Songhua river*'[1] instead. "Oh mother! Oh father! When could we gather together?"

When her song stopped, the audience stood up one by one.

Someone shouted: "Defend North China!"

Another shouted "Beijing can't be a second Shenyang!"

Some people went to the stage and began to toss cash and coins onto it. A sturdy young man came to the stage, raised his arms to quieten everyone down, and made a loud, short speech, saying they planned to take gifts as tokens of gratitude to the army, but they didn't plan a fund-raiser here and now. Since Mrs Liu had made such a significant start, everyone could make his or her donation now for tomorrow's presentation.

One took out two large cartons; the pianist ran to the back of the stage and fetched several wooden boxes. The audience started to move forward and put things into the containers.

---

[1] 'Along the Songhua (Sungari) river' (松花江上 *songhua jiang shang*) was a patriotic song popular in the War of Resistance Against Japanese Aggression. The song describes the lives of the people who lost their homeland along the Songhua river, after the Mukden Incident of 1931 in Northeast China. It was written and composed by Zhang Hanhui.

Some didn't, they just put things onto the stage. Earl was quite embarrassed for she didn't have any cash nor did she wear any jewellery. Jiaxin stood up and took off her watch. Earl appreciated Jiaxin's quick-wittedness and hurriedly took off her watch. Thunderhand hesitated for a while before he joined the crowd pushing towards the stage.

The boxes were already filled; piles of loose cash and coins were scattered on the stage. There was not much jewellery. The audience were almost all students, so there were lots of watches. Earl felt sick at the sight of a denture with two shining hooks.

Earl, who was sleeping with her arms behind her head, raised one arm and looked at her wrist. Her thin wrist looked rosy with the imprint of the watch no longer there. That had been a gift from her parents for her 15th birthday. She thought, if mum wanted to give her a new one, she would have to decline the offer so that the donation would be a genuine act of sincerity on her part. She moved the calendar aside and pulled a delicate alarm clock into a square space in front. She was going to count on it from now on.

"My young lady, are you awake?" Since Earl was the only one staying in the main rooms, Amah Zhao had put up a temporary bed under the bay window.

As all the members of the Meng family were in the habit of getting up early, Amah Zhao assumed Earl had woken up and entered her room without asking. She took the liberty of drawing open the curtains.

"Madam Meng called several times last night. She is worried about you. Next time, you'd better go with your father and mother instead of going alone. We are at war. Things are different now," she said, repeating what she had already said a couple of times the night before.

Earl didn't respond. She pulled the light-yellow silk comforter up around her and turned around, pretending she was still asleep.

Amah Zhao continued: "Alright, it's still early. Just stay in bed for a while longer. When would you like to have your breakfast? I'll let Chef Chai know."

"I don't want anything. I will have nothing. Don't prepare breakfast for me." She pulled the comforter all the way up and covered her head.

Amah Zhao was well aware of her young lady's temper and knew better than to antagonise her, so she didn't say anything more and carried on cleaning the room.

Earl's mind drifted back to the previous night. When the concert was over, the person in charge of the event specifically told everyone to go back home together and to be more careful.

She rode her bike back with Jiaxin, Thunderhand and several other students from Minglun University. They had taken the same route many times before. The road had a village on one side, and a babbling brook on the other. They used to talk and laugh happily all the way, remarking among themselves how beautiful this ordinary country view was. The previous night, they had taken the same route. The road, the village, and the brook were bathed in bright moonlight, peaceful and clear.

But things felt different somehow with the realization that their lives were about to undergo tremendous changes, so tremendous as to be beyond their imagination. They felt excited. Troubled but excited.

"I have been thinking about this all day," Thunderhand said. "We may not be able to continue our studies."

"I want to go to the front. We should," Jiaxin said.

"I want to go, too!" Several more responded enthusiastically.

"Meng Liji, how about you?" It was Thunderhand.

Earl didn't talk much in front of other people and always waited to be asked. The atmosphere of the concert was still lingering in her mind. She thought it was the young people's mission to go to the front and kick the invaders out.

She kept thinking for a while before she said something else instead: "What should we do about our studies?"

A dog's bark from the village quieted them down. One after another, more dogs followed suit. The barking sounded more like whining than their regular night-time alarm as if they were terribly upset. The barking spread far away in the darkness and echoed faintly in the distance.

"Looks like these dogs have smelled war in the air," someone commented about the dogs barking.

When the group reached the university, the gate was already closed. The campus guards asked them several questions to confirm their identity.

When they finally decided to open the gate for them, they warned: "Looks like you certainly don't know what is happening. You still have the guts to go out."

Yes! What was happening? Earl said to herself. What was happening was a national crisis. The nation was in peril. She gazed at the curtains that draped silently, hardly able to block the rising morning sun. What was happening outside the window?

Amah Zhao came in again: "Someone sent a letter and asked when Mr Wei would go back to the university. I left the letter on the redwood desk in the home office."

By the door of Fuzhi's home office, stood a small redwood desk. When mail and newspapers arrived, the servants would leave them on the desk for Fuzhi. In fact, Amah Zhao didn't need to remind Earl about the letter. But now Mrs Meng was not at home, Amah Zhao assumed she should be extra careful.

"Mum told me when she called last night they would come home when the city gate was open. How could I possibly have known when Cousin Wei would come back to the university? What should I do now? It looks like I should stick to my studies. Whatever happens, I should take the college entrance examination."

Thinking about her preparation for the exam, she jumped out of her bed, quickly made herself presentable, and got her biology book out. She was going to apply for the biology department at Minglun University. She read her book for a while and suddenly became angry at her parents for leaving her behind, alone at home.

"Mum and dad just don't care about me." She was more sad than angry. The lines on the book became blurred. She pointed at one line with her index finger and read aloud: "seeds — embryo — pollen…"

She forced herself to read a few more lines before she cast the book aside and looked out of the window. She saw Wuyin riding his bike beyond the lawn, reading, holding the book with both hands. He kept reading and riding his bike forward slowly.

Earl never liked children, teenagers included. But Wuyin was an exception, not because he could ride a bike and read a book at the same time and have no trouble steering with his hands off the handlebars, but because of his different personality. He was courteous. He was cold. Under that coldness lay something mysterious. Earl vaguely felt they had something in common.

"Hey! How can you be so focused on your book with the noise of gunfire?" Earl asked. It was indeed quiet around them. "Do you know we are at war?"

Wuyin's handsome facial expression was as cold as usual. The war hadn't reached him, yet. He got off his bike and bent down to pick up a yellow flower.

"How about you? If you were me, would you be preparing for the entrance exam?"

"I sure would," said Wuyin, eyeing the yellow flower.

"What are you reading?" Earl asked.

Wuyin held his book toward her and answered: "Analytical geometry." He held up the flower: "May got one once, saying she was getting it for you to make it into a specimen."

"I guess you picked it for her?" said Earl, with a wry smile.

"No, I didn't. She did," Wuyin answered seriously.

Earl tried to say something, but she finally decided not to and just nodded coolly. Wuyin nodded back and got back on his bike with his book.

Earl watched him disappearing into the distance and went over to the front gate.

In front of Square Teakettle was a low circular flowerbed. A Buddhist pine was planted in the centre surrounded by flowers. Its smooth branches stretched through the willows, and twisted all around the rockery, reaching for the university gate. Earl stood there, pricking up her ears to catch any sound of an approaching car. She cast a casual glance at the rockery and spotted someone coming up behind it. At the sight of the person, Earl felt the whole world had brightened up and that the flowers were extremely beautiful. She was delighted upon seeing who was coming.

It was Xiao Cheng, the youngest professor in the biology department. He was in his mid-30s, with fair skin and a slender figure. His distinctive facial features only added to his charm. He came toward Square Teakettle, with his usual unique unworldly and unrestrained air. He was idolised by the students in the department. They reckoned his knowledge, his capacity, and even his appearance were all top-notch. He set a 'perfect' example.

"Professor Xiao, my father hasn't come back yet. Is the city gate open?" Earl took several quick steps forward to greet him. "Please come in."

"I was told that the gate was open early this morning, so I thought your father had come back," smiled Xiao Cheng. "I've got something for your father." He hesitated whether to go in or wait until Meng Fuzhi came back. "Why didn't you go into town for the wedding?"

"I had a concert last night. Mrs Liu gave a performance."

"Zheng Huiyuan?" Xiao Cheng asked, with much interest.

"You know her?" Earl countered, instinctively.

He didn't reply. Then they heard a car pulling up. "I'm coming!" Earl shouted in the direction of the approaching car. She was so happy to see her parents again. It seemed such a long time ago that they had left.

The car stopped at the front gate. The Meng couple stepped out of the car one by one. Earl went over and grabbed her mother by the hand. Bichu looked at her daughter. She couldn't imagine how much this daughter of hers had suffered during the night. The thought brought a big lump to her throat and her tears welled up. She took Earl's arm and mother and daughter went into the bedroom. After Meng Fuzhi and Xiao Cheng sat down in the living room, Xiao Cheng took out a flyer and showed it to Fuzhi.

"A student delivered this to me a moment ago. This is how things should work."

The photocopies were blurred, but it was not hard for Fuzhi to figure out the content. It was a communique issued by the Communist Party of China (CPC) after the Marco Polo bridge incident: "Beijing and Tianjin are in peril! North China is in peril! The Chinese nation is in peril! To launch a war of resistance by the whole nation is the only way out." At the end of the communique, there was an appeal: "Let's arm ourselves to defend Beijing, Tianjin and North China! Let's defend our country and our land until the last drop of blood!

All Chinese compatriots, the government and the army, let's unite and build a solid great wall against the Japanese invaders! The Kuomintang (KMT) and the CPC should work together to fight against fresh attacks by the Japanese invaders! Expel the Japanese invaders from China!"

"This is in line with the wishes of the Chinese people," Fuzhi said, putting the flyer down quietly.

"I think so. Cooperation between the KMT and the CPC is the only way out." Xiao Cheng's crystal-clear eyes widened: "I thought you would go crazy when you saw the flyer, you sincere leftist!" He said 'sincere leftist' in English.

Fuzhi smiled: "Since I am sincere, I need to be objective. The government is like the eldest son in a family, shouldering all the responsibilities. Before the government decides to do anything, it must consider every possibility. When it begins to do something, it faces all kinds of constraints. This country has been poor and weak for so long, it is not an easy decision for the government to make. The CPC is like the youngest son in the family, with fewer burdens and more insights. The CPC has done the right thing."

"You are quite right. I guess, no one who teaches in the university is for negotiation," said Xiao Cheng.

"When I was in town, it was said that the fighting had stopped. My guess is that: either both sides will retreat to where they were before, or the Chinese army will retreat and leave the Marco Polo bridge in the hands of the East Hebei Army[2]. But do you think the Japanese will stick to their word? No, they won't. The Japanese are just trying to appease the Chinese to buy themselves a couple more days to stage something bigger and worse."

Fuzhi stood up while he talked and began to pace up and down. He checked the mail and papers lying on the small redwood desk and picked up a photocopy. It was the same flyer Xiao Cheng had brought with him. "I actually have one." They smiled at each other. Both knew, tacitly, who had asked it to be delivered to Square Teakettle.

"Youchen must have got one, too," said Fuzhi.

"I'm going to Nanjing, to Lushan (Lu mountain). It's time to launch total resistance against Japanese aggression by the whole nation. I will also protest against the fallacy of turning Beijing into a cultural city," Xiao Cheng said. "Miao Donghui's proposal is written in rhythmical prose characterized by parallelism and ornateness. It sounds quite impressive."

---

[2] The East Hebei Army was established from the former soldiers of the Peace Preservation Corps that had been created by the Tanggu Truce on 31 May 1933. The Army participated in the Marco Polo bridge incident and the battle of Beijing-Tianjin. They launched the Tongzhou mutiny on the morning of 29 July 1937. After the mutiny was put down by the Japanese, the East Hebei Army was disbanded.

"It used to be forgivable to indulge in such fantasy. But it is not if he persists in that vein. I don't think the government would agree. What the last mayor did can be categorized as 'fantasy', but what they are trying to do now is fallacy. They are just surrendering the city to the Japanese!" Speaking of the last mayor of Beijing, both remembered the farewell party. Mr Yuan, the last mayor, was very interested in turning Beijing into a cultural city. He vigorously renovated the two ornate archways, the no. 4 East Archway, and the no. 4 West Archway, replacing the wooden frames with cement ones. He also built a road to the Summer Palace, and published *An Overview of the Imperial Palace* with a beautiful cover design and ornately bound. But he was asked to resign for his readiness to comply with the demands of the Japanese, and was given an ultimatum to leave Beijing. Before his departure, he hosted a farewell dinner party at the Beijing Hotel and invited many celebrities. Fuzhi and Xiao Cheng were invited, too. During the meeting, Mayor Yuan raised an empty glass to propose a toast. He raised the empty glass, bottom-up, without saying a word. He repeated his silent, empty toast several times at the tables where the most prestigious guests were gathered. Before all the courses were served, the secretary from the new administration informed him it was time for him to leave. He was silent for a moment and then said: "I've been given such a short amount of time!" He stood up and respectfully bade farewell to all the guests present with his hands joined in front of his chest. The dinner party broke up quickly after his departure. A hush came over the assembled guests and not a single person raised their chopsticks.

Despite the passage of several years, his recollection of the occasion was no less gloomy. Xiao Cheng said: "Who could imagine this is happening right now on Chinese soil? I don't know what will happen when I am in Nanjing. My colleagues in my department will cover for me. You don't need to worry about that."

Fuzhi nodded: "If things go well, I will go to Lushan around the 25th."

Earl appeared at the door to the living room: "Father, you have a call from the president's office." Fuzhi stood up to take the call. She came over to a wicker chair with a high raised back and leaned against it. She smiled at Xiao Cheng:

"Are you going to relocate the university?"

"I am not sure. But I guess it's about time."

"Should I still prepare for my college entrance examination?" Earl asked, half addressing the question to Xiao Cheng, and half to herself.

"Of course, you should! Especially in wartime, we need to keep training qualified people to meet the country's needs. Who else can do that?" Xiao Cheng always felt that Earl was somewhat odd and affected, unlike May, who was innocent and natural. But of course, May was still a kid.

Earl asked again: "Should I apply for the biology department? Should I study biology?" She looked rather lost.

"Before I took up biology, I was very much into philosophy. Life is so strange, so strange. There are several advantages if you study biology, I think. First, unlike maths or physics, without specific talent, it won't be easy to keep going; unlike the humanities, either, if you don't excel among the top few, you will fall into the ranks of mediocrity. But, if you study biology, you can always end up as a specialist."

Did that mean I was mediocre, so I should apply for the

biology department?, thought Earl, blushing: "I also think life is so strange."

Fuzhi came in and waved to Earl to leave them alone. He said to Xiao Cheng: "President Qin called from Nanjing, asking me to host an administrative council meeting for him. The purpose is to inform everyone to stand by and await instructions. He had left for Lushan for the first session of talks. But he was late."

"OK. I will leave this afternoon then. Not sure when we will meet again," he said and stood up, reaching for the flyer.

"Just leave it here. I'll take care of it and mine," Fuzhi told Xiao Cheng, hurriedly. He said to himself: "This guy is lucky to be a bachelor." But he didn't say it out loud. It would have sounded like a taunt.

He saw Xiao Cheng off on his bike. Earl came to tell him he was wanted by Zhuang Youchen on the phone.

When she found Xiao Cheng had left, she couldn't hide her disappointment: "Mother just said she wanted to invite him to stay for dinner."

"Dad wants to discuss this with you. Since the city gate will stay open for the next two days, why don't you and your mother go to town together? You need to focus on your studies."

"How about you, father?"

"I'll stay on campus," answered Fuzhi, scooping up the things on the little redwood desk, and went to his home office before going to answer the phone.

"I'm at the lab," Youchen said at the other end.

"I just arrived at Square Teakettle a moment ago. You were fast."

"Wei Feng is not with me."

"Is he wanted?"

"Mrs Ling called, saying he disappeared early this morning."

"Shall we call the newspaper to print a notice for a missing person?"

"How would we write the notice? 'We have a lovely son-in-law missing?'" Youchen said humorously. "If you see him, tell him the lab needs him, too. Luckily, we can still work like we used to. One more minute of work is one more minute gained."

Both put down the phone to grab that extra minute.

Part 2

It happened exactly as Fuzhi had predicted. On the third day after the truce, the Japanese army broke its word and launched an all-out attack on Wanping fortress. Right at noon, July 13th, a fierce battle erupted outside the Yongding city gate. People in the southern part of Beijing could hear everything clearly. People trembled with cold shivers of fear at the waves of gunfire, despite the customary July heat in Beijing. People in the northern part of the city couldn't hear the gunshots, but the boom of artillery rang in their ears as well. People were panicked. People were excited. Word on the street was always "where has our army reached?". It sounded like we had an invincible army. Newspapers had never sold out so quickly. Radios, which were still rare at that time, became the new luxury. Those who had one always kept it on for the latest updates of the battle.

The atmosphere inside no. 3 Chestnut Street was unusual, too, like that outside the gate. Grandpa Lü had finished his sutra readings and was waiting impatiently for the morning's newspaper. He had asked many times why the paper hadn't arrived yet. It was as if the low, dull blasts might have passed for summer thunder for him. Just before noon, he asked whether it was going to rain. Zhao Lianxiu raised her voice and explained to him that it was the approaching gunfire. Years of companionship had taught her never to withhold any information from Lord Lü.

"So, the battle is approaching the city," he said to himself, and began to pace the spacious living room with its floor paved with square bricks. An old rug was laid between two rows of chairs in the main part of the room. He always paced along one single row of bricks and never took a wrong step. Lianxiu was sitting in an antique, high-backed chair by the window. The wicker work on the back of the chair was worn through and the hole had been mended carefully with a small piece of fabric of the same colour. Although the patch had been skilfully applied to the chair, it still stood out. In her eyes, such a chair in such a position was a proper match for her position in the family. She was always doing some needlework, knitting or stitching. This work of hers was of no practical use, so what she did when she had finished an item was to break it back into yarn and start again. Now, she was too upset to do her usual needlework. The bamboo hoop she used for her embroidery had been left by the tea table beside her for quite some time.

"So, the battle is approaching the city?" asked Lord Lü, interrupting his pacing up and down as he turned toward her.

"Lady Jiangchu said we need to think about where to hide." The pitch of her voice was habitually high, but not confident. In the past, when the country became very unstable, some of their friends and relatives went south; others went to the foreign settlement in Tianjin. But Lord Lü was against either option.

"To hide from what?" The old man stopped abruptly in the middle of the room.

"Father, you are already up." Jiangchu raised the door curtain and entered the room, followed by a roar of gunfire. "The situation doesn't look good. No one knows where those artillery shells will land. We have rooms in the German hospital. Many of our friends have gone there. My husband and I hope father could move there and stay for a couple days."

The old man didn't move as if he wasn't able to figure out what his daughter had said because of his poor hearing. Jiangchu then continued: "The kids will be excited to spend some time with their grandfather."

"The kids need a safe place to stay," said Lord Lü, pondering. "Go to the German hospital..."

"The Miaos, the Lings and several relatives are going there, too," Jiangchu hastened to explain. "The wives and children of those deputy managers in Mian's company want to go as well, but there are already no rooms available. We have booked the big family rooms," she added.

"The kids should go," said the old man. "Carry on with your arrangements, but don't include me. I'm not going anywhere. When will your sister Bichu come to town?"

"The telephone line stopped working again this morning. Now that the battle has begun, I don't think Bichu and Fuzhi can enter the city. May and Kiddo are both staying with Wei in his room, practicing calligraphy with their writing brushes." Jiangchu paused. But she didn't wait long before beginning again: "I am going to ask the kitchen to serve lunch. Then father can leave for the hospital."

"I'm not going anywhere!" The old man resumed his pacing, a signal for Jiangchu to leave him alone.

"How could we stay at ease in the hospital without father? Besides, it's completely inappropriate to leave father behind."

"You all go along," the old man said amiably while keeping up his pacing. "I am already at the ripe age of 76 and I would die content if I can witness the Chinese army fighting off the foreign invaders. I will be alright with Lianxiu for company."

"Father, it's quite convenient there. And it's just a short drive…"

The old man started walking and waved dismissively at Jiangchu. She knew that nothing would change her father's mind, so she said: "Have it your way then, father." She turned around and prepared to leave.

Lianxiu hurried to her and whispered: "How about moving his lordship to the underground chamber in the back garden?"

"I have considered that option. You try your best to talk him into moving to the German hospital. I still have things to deal with." With these words, she left.

It was almost noon. The only relief from the heat of the day was provided by the round-ridged roof overhanging the reception hall and the water sprinkled on the ground twice before noon in the garden. Jiangchu went to her room. She asked Amah Liu to prepare the clothes they would need to take with them and pressed the bell to summon their attendant Liu Fengcai. She wanted Liu to clean up the building in the back garden.

"The building would provide protection against stray bullets. Some neighbours came to ask whether they could hide in that building for a couple of days," Liu Fengcai reported to Jiangchu rather timidly.

"It's all in their heads," Jiangchu snapped impatiently. "Clean it up first."

The telephone rang. Yue Hengfen called to say she and Xueyan had arrived at the hospital. One room per family. It was indeed quite a decent arrangement in wartime. She also asked when the Tantais would arrive and mentioned to Jiangchu that President Qin's wife and children were there, too. Only after she had asked whether Bichu was in town did she also enquire whether they had heard anything about Wei Feng.

"Is he not at home with you?" queried Jiangchu, surprised by the question.

"He went out of town the day after the wedding, saying he had to deal with something urgent," complained Mrs Ling. "Now, he has been away for almost one week. He called home a couple of days ago, saying he would come back to town today. I don't think he will make it."

Jiangchu talked a while longer to show her sympathy before hanging up. Having calmed herself down, she went to her daughter Xuan's quarters in a small side garden in front of the west side of the main compound.

It was an apartment with three south-facing rooms. The two in the front had more sunshine than the one behind. The side garden, without a formal entrance, shared the door in the gallery leading to the reception hall, known as the Gallery garden. The rooms were finely furnished like the main apartment occupied by Jiangchu and Mian. The brown hard-wood floor and green screen windows were a fusion of Eastern and Western styles. The most eye-catching thing about the room was that it was full of dolls and figurines representing all kinds of races and nationalities from around the world. Some had blonde hair with blue eyes in hats with lace and short dresses; some had their hair in buns on top of their heads with long evening gowns, some were Scottish soldiers in kilts and tall black bearskin hats.

Xuan once boasted that she was like a child delivery goddess. When Amah Liu heard this, she told Lady Jiangchu:

"Young Lady Xuan's words are way out of line."

Jiangchu answered that she was quite out of line when she was young, but Xuan went even further than she did. Her husband then commented "like mother, like daughter". This was one of Tantai Mian's favourite phrases.

Xuan was in her bedroom, busy picking among the dresses of all colours, styles and materials, which were piled up on her bed. She was wearing a cerise silk dress with two white silk ribbons attached to the upper part like two suspenders. She was looking left and right in front of a full-length dress mirror. Her dress fluttered as she glided a few steps on tiptoes, dancing.

"Haven't you heard the gunfire? How can you be so carefree? Aren't you afraid that the Japanese might make their way into the city?" Jiangchu tried to be cross with her daughter. But seeing that innocent, delicate face, her heavy heart felt a tad lighter.

"Aren't we going to the German hospital? We are not afraid of the Japanese." She put special emphasis on 'we' as if by doing so, people like her wouldn't be afraid of the Japanese or anyone else.

"There's a party at the Grand Hôtel des Wagons-Lits at six this evening. Paul will come to pick me up." She glanced at the miniature clock on her bedside table. Inside the clock, there was a tiny figure holding a baton, which would strike a tiny gong at the top of each hour.

"He'll come by half past three. When the party is over, I'll go directly to the hospital and meet you there. Don't leave her behind." Her eyes rested on a giant doll lying on her bed.

The doll was a little girl in a white silk dress. She had a big forehead, big blue eyes, and was named 'Shirley' after the popular Hollywood child star, Shirley Temple.

Paul's invitation was delivered 10 days ago, before the war began. Jiangchu looked at Xuan and said: "The party might have been cancelled."

"They wouldn't have." Xuan raised her chin as she always did and tilted her head: "The Americans wouldn't be afraid of those weeny Japanese."

Jiangchu shared her daughter's confidence about the Americans. She pondered for a while and decided it would be safe at the hotel. When she got ready to leave, she heard a cough from Liu Fengcai outside the door:

"Mr McAllen from the American consulate has arrived. Should I invite him to wait in the reception hall?"

"Just show him in here," Xuan said, before Jiangchu could say anything.

Paul once mentioned he would like to see her huge collection of dolls. Besides, she was properly dressed. Why should she waste the time she had spent on getting dressed up? She probably wouldn't pick the same dress to go to the party.

Deprecatingly, Jiangchu walked out of the bedroom and stayed in the living room. "He is coming to tell you the party has been cancelled," said Jiangchu.

Xuan answered: "No. He's coming to confirm whether I will go. To remind me. I'm positive about that."

In the garden, they heard the sound of footsteps from

leather-soled shoes. Liu Fengcai raised the door-blinds to let in a young American man with a tall, neat build. He spoke fluent mandarin:

"Mrs Tantai? I can see the resemblance between your daughter and you. I mean, Miss Tantai looks very much like you."

"Welcome, Mr McAllen. Please take a seat." Jiangchu stood up.

Xuan came out of her bedroom. She looked more dazzling than a fresh flower with her snow-white skin in that brightly-coloured dress.

Paul's eyes lit up. He went over and bent slightly to shake her hand, and turned to Jiangchu politely: "Were you troubled by the gunfire at Marco Polo bridge?"

"It hasn't been peaceful for the last several years. And this is not the first time we have heard gunfire. But I don't know how long it will last this time."

After exchanging pleasantries, Paul looked as if he was still not going to mention the party this evening. Xuan ran out of patience: "What's happening about the party this evening? Has anything changed?"

Paul smiled: "I was just about to ask. Do you think you can still make it?"

"Why not?" Xuan was surprised he would ask her such a question.

"Nothing can change our plans." Her tone made it seem as if there was something special about the party.

Paul didn't answer immediately. He just looked at Xuan. With the admiration in his blue eyes waning, they just stared at Xuan dully. Jiangchu was a bit annoyed by Paul's lack of response and she raised her voice:

"So Mr McAllen is going? We were just wondering whether the party might have been cancelled."

Paul took his gaze off Xuan and looked at Jiangchu: "No, the party is still on. We are not at war with the Japanese. I came to look for an answer to a question which has been puzzling me for a while. Allow me to be frank."

He made a little bow towards Xuan: "I hope Miss Tantai won't hold this against me. The Marco Polo bridge incident is a great event for the Chinese nation. China is awakening. So, I was wondering how Miss Tantai and other Chinese from similar upper-class families would react. Are you excited? Are you concerned about your own country? My assumption was that you wouldn't be going to the party this evening."

"I see." Jiangchu stood up: "Mr McAllen must be otherwise engaged?"

"I think if you have no interest in the party, then the feeling in your heart is consistent with your appearance. But if you are still interested in going, I'll come to pick you up at half past three." Paul poured out what he had been thinking, regardless of the consequences. When he finished, he stood up.

At these words, Xuan's first reaction was how ludicrous this foreigner was! Then her face turned red, redder than the colour of the dress she was wearing. She looked around to find a big thick carved-glass bowl on the table next to her, and felt the impulse to grab it and smash it on Paul's head. But she quickly calmed herself down. A slight, scornful smile appeared at the corners of her mouth.

She slowly stood up and said: "To save that nice image of yours, I think it won't be necessary then."

"Are you mad at me?" Paul began to feel uneasy. He

continued with sincerity: "We are friends, and I think friends should be honest with each other."

"Every Chinese is a patriot who knows how to love his or her country without being told to do so," answered Xuan. "Except for turncoats." It suddenly occurred to her what the definition of 'turncoats' was.

Paul didn't say anything. About half a minute later, he bade farewell. Both mother and daughter kept silent for a long while. Then Xuan went back to her bedroom and took off the new dress, keeping only her white silk petticoat on. Then she swept all the piles of clothes off the bed onto the floor.

"Mum, are you there?" Hardly had the words come out of his mouth than Wei charged in. He bearhugged Jiangchu who was still in a trance.

Every time Jiangchu saw Xuan, she felt delighted; every time she saw Wei, she was over the moon. Now she was looking at Wei, smiling while trying to rub his head like when he was young, but instead resting her hand on his shoulder. That boy had grown to be so tall that she couldn't reach his head anymore.

"What's up?"

"May wants me to ask you if we can stay here with grandfather if he is not going to the German hospital. We can keep him company."

"You only have thoughts for May!"

Jiangchu was a little bit jealous but her smile didn't fade even a whit: "Everyone is going to the hospital. Grandfather may change his mind and go there a day later."

"I'm definitely not going!" declared Xuan in her bedroom, resolutely.

"My little ancestors! What do you want? Don't I have

enough troubles on my plate?" She changed her tone and looked at the sister and brother with a more sombre expression.

Amah Liu raised the door-blinds and entered: "Secretary Huang from the company has come to say master won't be able to come home, so he sent Secretary Huang to help with the move to the hospital."

"Invite Secretary Huang to have a rest in the main rooms. Get ready to serve lunch. I'm on my way." She gave one more look at her two children but didn't say anything. Amah Liu called outside the door-blinds, saying Jiangchu was wanted by Mrs Ling on the phone.

On the phone, Hengfen asked Jiangchu to move to the hospital as soon as possible. "People have noticed your rooms are still not occupied and they have been trying to grab them. Luckily, Jingyao reacted quickly and told them to take a hike."

"Is Mr Ling at the hospital with you?" Jiangchu didn't expect him to be there.

"We have to have at least one man here! How can we womenfolk handle everything?" answered Hengfen.

Jiangchu mulled over Hengfen's words for a while before answering: "Would you please try your best to keep our rooms? We'll go as soon as possible. In case we can't make it, I'll call you and let you know."

"In what case? You do know how hard it is to get even one room, don't you? You just take the kids and get into the car, then you are here. It's not only stray artillery shells we are worried about. Those soldiers going astray are more terrifying! Who knows what will happen…"

"My situation is much more complicated than yours. I just

envy you: once you issue an order, your daughter and your husband just obey it," said Jiangchu.

"Ah-yah! Speaking of my situation, our Xueyan hasn't had her orange juice yet! I need to see to it right now." For people like Hengfen, they were probably unaware of the fact that fruit and vegetables had their seasons.

After hanging up the phone, Jiangchu had time to talk to Secretary Huang. He was a tiny man. When he spoke, his eyes and nose were pinched together obsequiously. Jiangchu decided it was no use talking to him at all, so she called her husband. Tantai Mian said briefly that if the kids wanted to stay with their grandfather, it would be hard to change their minds. The real reason for a sudden change of plan was their daughter's sudden refusal to leave. But Jiangchu didn't mention that to Mian.

"Or they can go and stay in the building in the back garden. The building has a cellar," Mian reminded her.

"It has already been tidied up. When are you coming back?", asked Jiangchu.

"I can't leave until late in the evening." Jiangchu could hear someone was asking him questions.

"I'll come back as soon as possible."

Jiangchu hung up without waiting for him to finish.

A series of loud gun shots rang out as Jiangchu hastened toward the back garden. Amah Liu asked whether Jiangchu would have lunch first before going to the back garden. Jiangchu told her to serve Secretary Huang and the kids first. Wei, May and Kiddo wanted to tag along; Xuan locked herself in her bedroom.

Secretary Huang, as an old acquaintance of the family, saw what was going on, assuming he wouldn't be of much help, and then asked to be excused. Jiangchu took the kids, passed along the gallery, then through the main garden, and took the small eastern alleyway to the main compound connecting the back garden and the main compound. The door, which used to be locked at the end of the alleyway, was now open. Liu Fengcai and his helpers had cleaned it up, but they didn't have time to replace the broken light bulb, so it was very dark in there. Kiddo clutched May's hand while Wei grabbed May by the other arm.

When they got out through the small door, they immediately felt the difference. Although the sun was still high in the sky, they felt cooler in the garden. The wormwood shrubs were almost as tall as Wei; several willows grew nestled among the shrubs. Green slimy worms were twisting at the end of their silk hanging from two elm trees. Among these plants and creatures towered a small three-frame house built on a brick-and-stone platform, a classic construction method. The paint had long since peeled off, but one could still discern that it was once resplendent with carved and painted beams and rafters.

An elm worm dropped and dangled in front of Jiangchu. Wei stepped bravely in front of her and led the way. "Mind your step, mum," he would remind her from time to time as if danger lurked ahead on the gravelled pathway. After walking around several big rocks randomly scattered on the pathway, they reached the building. The door was wide open. Liu Fengcai and another attendant, together with two guests from the south compound, were cleaning the doors, windows, tables and chairs.

The three kids, chattering excitedly, tried to run upstairs. But Jiangchu stopped them just in time.

Liu Fengcai went over to Jiangchu and asked: "Madam,

would you like to have a look at the cellar? It is the safest place in the building. But it's really very small."

Upon these words, he led Jiangchu to the cellar. The entrance to the cellar was set on a loggia at the back. The wooden board covering the entrance had been removed. They had cleaned up the inside. The cellar was designed to be the boiler-room to provide heat for the building when people came to enjoy the snowy view in winter. It was the only building equipped with a boiler-room in the house. It wouldn't have been much fun in the freezing cold to try and appreciate the snow, would it?

Jiangchu took a few steps downward. Having figured out there was barely enough space for two beds, she instructed the men to set up a bed for Lord Lü and another one for Wei and Kiddo to share to keep their grandfather company; the womenfolk could stay on the ground floor.

She walked back to the ground floor. The three kids had run to the grass under the loggia where there used to be a ditch filled with water from Shicha lake. It had long since dried out, revealing a layer of glistening gravel at the bottom. Kiddo went over and grabbed a handful, but he dropped the stones at once, exclaiming: "It's burning hot!"

Wei and May were so amused that they couldn't help clapping their hands at Kiddo's reaction, laughing.

"The sun is burning hot, too. Aren't you afraid of getting sunstroke? Come on now back to the loggia," snapped Jiangchu.

May hastened to take Kiddo by the hand and walked back to the loggia, but Wei had disappeared into the grass.

"Watch out! There might be snakes!" Jiangchu shouted out, agitated.

Amah Liu grabbed a bamboo stick and dived into the grass after Wei.

"About the neighbours asking for shelter, what do you say, madam?" Liu Fengcai reminded Jiangchu.

Jiangchu glanced at the room. The windows in the back and front had loose frames. It seemed more like a cave than a room to her. She was already thinking of putting up two screens to divide the room into inner and outer sections. She knew she couldn't refuse shelter to the neighbours, particularly at a time like this, but she was also very much aware of how reluctant she was.

"It's already a big mess here. Why should they try to come over and make it messier?", she said to herself, while instructing her men: "Put up a partition screen here. Make sure both doors are open. Let them take the back door."

Then she heard the kids yelling merrily: "Grandpa! Grandpa is coming!"

She turned around to see her father coming over in the scorching sun with his walking stick, with Lianxiu by his side, holding his arm.

"Father! What brings you here? We are not ready yet." Jiangchu advanced to greet her father.

"Ah anyway, it's better that you come earlier rather than later."

The old man slowly ascended the steps and sat down in the room. Lianxiu handed him a wet towel taken from the flat-bottomed bamboo basket she was carrying, but the old man didn't take it.

He looked around the room: "I haven't been here for two years. It can take at least 10 people."

Jiangchu felt resentful that her father cared so much about

the neighbours instead of his own daughter, and that she hadn't had her lunch yet but he hadn't even bothered to ask. Mindful of this, Jiangchu decided to keep silent.

Liu Fengcai smiled ingratiatingly and said: "Madam Jiangchu has already asked us to carry the screens down. We are going to fetch them. The backdoor is also quite convenient for the neighbours."

The old man looked at the backdoor, which was sealed tight with nails. Outside it was Shicha lake. Knowing it must have been Jiangchu's idea to let the neighbours take the backdoor, he sighed softly: "They can take whichever door suits them best. Who knows how long they can use these doors!"

He rose up and walked to the steps leading to the second floor. But Jiangchu stopped him:

"Wei and the kids tried to go upstairs just now. I didn't let them because the staircases have long been neglected. Father, please wait until they are properly repaired."

The old man looked at his daughter gently and said: "You have exhausted yourself taking care of so many things. Now I am here, and I am already in a safe place."

He then turned to the kids gathering around him: "Granny Lianxiu said you still haven't had your lunch. Go with your mother and take your lunch now."

Jiangchu didn't leave with the kids until she had made one more thorough check of the rooms.

The old man asked Lianxiu to help him upstairs. Slowly, slowly, they climbed up the stairs. Liu Fengcai wanted to go and clean up first, but the old man wouldn't listen. So, Liu Fengcai followed them up, opened the windows, then began to clean the chairs.

A draught came in when the windows were opened. It felt cooler than downstairs. The old man stood by the window, looking at Shicha lake, half of which was covered by lotuses in full bloom.

He smiled and said to Lianxiu: "Who would imagine it is the artillery shells that have sent us up here to appreciate the lotuses!"

Lianxiu answered: "You are standing in a draught. I don't want you to catch cold. How about we stay for a while and then go downstairs?"

There was no wind on the lake. The flowers and leaves still floated in the water. On the left lay a long dike with a shelter under which snack stands used to be clustered. But today, few stands were to be seen. On the right stood houses upon houses clustered together along the lake shore and Gulou, the Drum Tower, towered under the blue sky. Even though one could hear the crackling of gunfire and roar of artillery in the distance, it was still so quiet here. It was too quiet for an enormous city like Beijing.

Lord Lü tapped rhythmically on the windowsill, chanting the lines from Xin Qiji's[3] 'A Song of Dragon and Water: On Climbing up the Healthy and Hearty Tower':

"I look at my trusty long sword,
and pound the railings with my hands,
but nobody knows why
I climb the high tower."

Lianxiu didn't dare to respond.

He turned around to look at her: "This is the time when

---

[3] Xin Qiji (1140 – 1207) was a Chinese poet and military leader during the Southern Song dynasty (960–1279).

all men should fight for their country. I am ashamed to have outlived my usefulness. How many times do you think we still have to climb up high like this?"

Lianxiu beamed a comforting smile and answered: "Anytime you want to come up, then we will come up. But it's not safe up here now. Let's go downstairs."

Lord Lü didn't answer. Instead, he sat in an old chair. Gazing at the lotuses, he sank into a trance.

The flowers were somewhat listless in the scorching sun, but even the subdued colours were loud enough for the blurred vision of an old man. Gradually, he figured out the silhouette of the Bell Tower behind the Drum Tower. The two towers stood in harmonious contrast with each other.

"How can we face our ancestors if these buildings are going to be destroyed in the war? Why can't we fight the invaders and expel them from our territory? What unworthy descendants we are!" He was yelling at himself silently.

The proposal to establish Beijing as a city of culture emerged in his mind. What did they mean? When the pirates came, the owner told them:

"Halt! You cannot have these things. I cannot have these things. Let's share! Let's just share!"

Did they mean that? Were they so naïve? Or were they so stupid and so cowardly to bring up such a treacherous proposal? I, Lü Qingfei, would rather die for my country than live in shame! How could I be so useless during a national crisis?

"Why did you let my father go upstairs? He should stay in the cellar!", came Jiangchu's raised voice from downstairs.

Liu Fengcai clambered all the way upstairs and smiled ingratiatingly: "Please, your lordship! Madam Jiangchu is asking you to come downstairs."

As if to testify how important it was to go downstairs, a barrage of heavy artillery fire boomed, shaking the window frames, causing them to creak. The old man got up and went downstairs.

Jiangchu met her father with a very unhappy expression on her face, glaring at him with disapproval: "My hands are already full! How can you add more trouble?"

With a very straight face, she said: "Mrs Zhuang called to let us know they are staying at Dong Jiaomin Xiang[4], with one of their foreign friends. She asked where Bichu and her family are and she wants to invite May and Kiddo to stay over for several days. What's your opinion, father?"

"I guess Fuzhi may not be willing to do so. Although the Mengs and the Zhuangs are very close friends, now the Zhuangs are also guests in someone else's place."

Jiangchu thought for a while and said: "Then let's wait and see how things go."

The room on the ground floor had been divided into two sections with screens. Lots of whispers and controlled footsteps could be heard. The neighbours were coming in, careful not to disturb their hosts.

"Prepare some tea and snacks for them. They can't take everything with them," said the old man.

---

[4] Dong Jiaomin Xiang: also known as the Beijing Legation Quarter, the area in Beijing where the foreign legations were located between 1861 and 1959. In Chinese, the area is known as Dong Jiaomin Xiang (东交民巷), which is the name of the *hutong*, a lane or a small street, that runs through the area. It is in the Dongcheng district, immediately to the east of Tiananmen square.

"Father, would you please go down to the cellar and lie down for a while? Don't worry, it's already long past your nap time. I'm afraid you might tire yourself out," suggested Jiangchu.

The old man nodded: "Right. In theory or in practice, I am quite experienced at fleeing from war." He then went to the cellar to lie down. Lianxiu tucked him in, put down the gauze net, and withdrew.

It was shady and cool in the cellar. The four brick walls tinted with moss reminded the old man of prison.

"How's my youngest daughter at the university? I cannot cause more trouble for the elder one," thought the old man.

Gradually he fell asleep. In his dimming consciousness, he was a young lad again, fleeing from bandits. The bandits who were active in the border area between the provinces of Henan and Anhui were called 'cudgels' by the locals because most of these bandits used to be peasants, who were forced to 'take up cudgels' and rise up in rebellion when life became too hard for them to survive, and then they joined gangs and became one of them. Rebellions had been in existence for hundreds of years.

Grandpa Lü was his father's only son. Every time, when the bandits came to loot, his parents would hide him in the bay-wall in the minor quarters of the residence.

Once when many more bandits came, his whole family had to evacuate into the hills outside the village, leaving behind only the family guards and servants. Another time, they had to take to the hills again.

The hills were like a quiet retreat with lush trees and surrounded by tranquillity. It should have been an enjoyable place. Qingfei, the young Grandpa Lü, was intrigued. While the others were busy setting up chairs and tables, he clambered up onto a big rock and looked downhill. Dark smoke billowed above the Lü residence.

People shouted: "Fire! Fire! The minister's residence is on fire!"

Four members of the Lü family had been ministers during the reigns of the Jiaqing Emperor[5] and the Tongzhi Emperor[6], and long after the family's fortunes had declined and it was not as prominent as it once had been, locals still referred to it as 'the minister's residence'. The scene was chaotic with people running around shouting and screaming. In the distance, they could clearly make out red flames more than ten feet tall ripping through the dark smoke.

Qingfei was stunned at the sight. People were running about, calling his name, searching for him. Someone found him on the rock, brought him down, and took him to his mother. Later the family guards came to report that bandits had broken through the village wall and burnt the ancestral temple.

An ancestral temple didn't matter much. What mattered to Qingfei was that one of the daughters of the well-off landlords kidnapped by the bandits for ransom was his fiancée, Zhang Mengjia, from a neighbouring county.

---

[5] The Jiaqing Emperor: (嘉庆帝 *jiaqing di*, 13 November 1760 – 2 September 1820), personal name Aisin Gioro Yongyan, was the seventh emperor of the Manchu-led Qing dynasty, and the fifth Qing emperor to rule China from 1796 to 1820.

[6] The Tongzhi Emperor: (同治帝 *tongzhi di*, 27 April 1856 – 12 January 1875), personal name Zaichun Aisin Gioro, was the 10th emperor of the Manchu-led Qing dynasty, and the eighth Qing emperor to rule China. His reign, from 1861 to 1875, which effectively lasted through his adolescence, was largely overshadowed by the rule of his mother, Empress Dowager Cixi.

The two families had just exchanged betrothal presents. Mengjia's grandfather was a retired provincial governor. The Zhangs had immediately used their connections and managed to ensure Miss Zhang's return within two days. But rumours were already rife among the Lü family. It was only because the Zhangs had more influence, politically and economically, than the Lü family, that the latter didn't dare to propose cancelling the wedding. But rumours could never be suppressed by any outside authority, hence their popularity in the Lü clan.

The young Qingfei thought otherwise. He felt the incident just added mystery to his fiancée that he had never met. Sometimes he even imagined her as a heroine. Of course, it never occurred to him that later during his decades of efforts to revolt against the Qing dynasty, Mengjia would be the first one to teach him about revolution.

How beautiful young Mengjia was back then!

> *What a slender figure in gauze*
> *as fine as a cicada's wings;*
> *What beautiful cascading hair*
> *cloaked in floral scents.*

He wrote these lines of poetry for her after their wedding. She was as light as a soap bubble, transparent, iridescent, and always intangible. Soap was rare back then. Her voice was light, too, with a distinct but distant tone.

"There are good people among the bandits with very good manners," Mengjia told him in her light voice when asked about that incident.

"They had no choice. No one with any alternative would have chosen such a desperate path!"

It was the first time Qingfei had ever put himself into someone else's shoes and looked at social problems from a new point of view. He had already passed the imperial examination at the provincial level and was expected to pass with the highest grade, be appointed to be a high-ranking official, and serve the imperial Qing dynasty. Influenced by advanced ideas and thoughts, many people had realized how corrupt the Qing dynasty was, how much suffering the people were subjected to, and were searching for a solution for the nation.

"Master, are you up?" Lianxiu asked in her even voice, followed by Jiangchu's with an emphatic tone: "Mr Miao sent a letter to you. It's private."

The old man woke up from his historical reverie and realized that the Chinese nation was now at the critical moment of survival or annihilation. To fight the Japanese! That was the way out for the Chinese nation! Getting old was a strange thing. One's mind couldn't help slipping back decades in time. He took the letter from Jiangchu and the magnifying glass from Lianxiu and began to read carefully. He hadn't been reading long before he suddenly sat bolt upright, ripped the letter into pieces and dashed the pieces onto the floor.

"Father, what's bothering you?" Jiangchu said.

"What did he say? We should figure out an appropriate response."

Lianxiu picked up the scraps of paper, pieced them together, and showed them to Jiangchu. The letter was mainly about a proposal for a truce because if Beijing became a battleground, many precious relics would be destroyed overnight. No amount of lives could compensate for such a loss. What the French and British troops, and the Eight-Nation

Alliance had done to Beijing during the Second Opium War[7] was a conspicuous and alarming example. Miao proposed to stop fighting and sign a truce, and invited Lord Lü to sign his name in support of Miao's proposal.

"Amid the deafening gunfire, with burning concern, I present what I see and sigh. All I am trying to propose is what would be worthy of our ancestors and our descendants. I sincerely hope you will join me in this action."

Jiangchu was confused about the last lines, so she just said: "Mr Miao's attendant is still waiting for your reply."

"Give him the blue stationery," the old man answered quietly.

The blue stationery was his unique notice of no response. The paper was printed with bright blue patterns and five words 'Best Regards from Lü Qingfei'. The recipient then knew Lord Lü wouldn't respond to any further contact in this regard. When he withdrew from the political stage, this habit of replying with his blue stationery had saved him loads of trouble.

"It might not be appropriate to reply with just the blue stationery," advised Jiangchu, always trying to be courteous. "How about a few words?"

"Yes, I am going to write a few lines. But not to Miao. To someone who understands!" the old man laughed.

Lianxiu had already set up on a small table, the writing paper, the inkwell, and the writing brush Lord Lü used when

---

[7] The Eight-Nation Alliance was an international military coalition set up in response to the Boxer Rebellion during the imperial Qing dynasty. The eight nations were Japan, Russia, Britain, France, the United States, Germany, Italy and the Austro-Hungarian empire. The Boxer Rebellion, or Yihetuan Movement, was a violent anti-foreign, anti-colonial and anti-Christian uprising that took place in China between 1899 and 1901.

he wanted to write. She also put *Guo Xiang's Annotation to Zhuangzi*[8] beside the writing materials. The blue stationery was in a small box. Jiangchu took out one sheet of blue paper and excused herself, turning over in her mind what she would commit to paper by way of explanation. She went to the reception hall and wrote several lines of polite greetings, and then sent Miao's attendant on his way.

Xuan unlocked her door and went out. She wanted to have lunch. Wei, May and Kiddo trailed in her wake.

"Have you had yours, mum?" Xuan asked, smiling as if nothing had happened. "I'm hungry," she went up to the food cabinet in the living room to look for something to eat.

Amah Liu said to Jiangchu smilingly: "I asked my young lady to have lunch earlier and she said she didn't want anything, so I cleaned up the table."

"Would you like some noodles?" Jiangchu asked Xuan. When she nodded to Amah Liu, her tone had switched to one of command: "Hurry up. Let them go to the house in the back garden when they have finished."

Shortly afterwards, Amah Liu fetched a bowl of noodles with pink shelled shrimps topped with boiled tender leafy vegetables. Xuan tried it and said it was delicious. Upon hearing her words, Wei and the other two kids, who hadn't had a proper lunch either, asked if they could share. And another bowl of noodles was produced from the kitchen for the three kids to share. They really enjoyed it.

Did they assume the war was just like sharing a bowl of shrimp noodles, boisterous and joyous?

---

[8] Guo Xiang (郭象) is the author of the most important commentary on the classic Taoist text Zhuangzi (庄子), named after 'Master Zhuang' which, along with Laozi, was one of the earliest texts to contribute to the philosophy that has come to be known as Taoism (道家 *daojia*).

PART 3

The city gate was closed most of the time. When it was open at random hours, it didn't stay open long. Just like the ongoing battle, which was fierce at times, and suddenly died away at other times. The papers were full of passionately patriotic editorials and requests from college students volunteering to join the army, mixed with reports about truce talks. Fuzhi asked Bichu to go to town with Earl, but Bichu wanted to come back and stay with him after sending Earl to stay with her aunt Jiangchu. The university used to run shuttle buses between the city and the university, but they had been cancelled these days.

That day, Bichu asked Old Song to drive her and Earl to town. When they arrived outside Xizhimen, the city gate there was closed. They waited for a while to see whether it would be open. It was the first time that Bichu had realised how useful the city gates were in Beijing.

"It would be better if they could keep the enemies outside the city!" she thought.

Having stepped out of the car, she looked up at the imposing gate tower on top of the gate. Slivers of thatch pierced the sky like lances. Earl remained silently seated in the car. Old Song had gone to ask for information. He came back soon, running, saying it was not safe to hang around and that they'd better leave. Then they went back to the university. The only lucky thing was that the telephone line was still in operation. The line was completely dead only on the 13th. It worked properly for a couple of hours each day, so Bichu could keep in touch with Jiangchu. May and Kiddo had never left her side since they were born. Now both had been away from her for several days. And there was a war going on! Bichu's heart was torn in two.

Wei Feng came to Square Teakettle that day, telling them the battle was going their way and that the Chinese army's morale was sky-high. Some universities were jointly preparing to express their gratitude to the army at the front. Wei Feng hadn't been back to town since he had left the day after his wedding. Yue Hengfen, his mother-in-law, had called Bichu many times to complain about Wei Feng. Sometimes Professor Zhuang would also be on her complaint list. While Wei Feng was very busy with his experiment with Professor Zhuang, who was deeply worried that all their efforts would be in vain if the war aborted their experiment and wanted to finish it as soon as possible, he was also involved in all kinds of off-campus activities. Preparing an expression of gratitude for the fighters at the front was just one of those many activities.

"At the concert held several days ago, Mrs Liu launched a fund-raising effort for an expression of gratitude," Earl said.

"That one actually happened. But we forgot to get a permit, so we were not allowed into the camp. We just delivered a letter and gifts of gratitude," Wei Feng said.

"This time, we have already made contact with the army and we are going tomorrow."

"I want to go, too!" Earl blurted out.

Her parents were stunned for a moment and then exchanged a glance. They knew this daughter of theirs was never one to be fun-loving or to get involved in any activities. Earl didn't pay any attention to her parents' reaction, but looked at Wei Feng, waiting for his answer. "Will it be a problem for you?" asked Earl.

Wei Feng didn't know what to say, and looked at her parents instead.

"Of course, you can go," Fuzhi said. "Earl can represent us and go on behalf of our family."

"Yes, you should go," said Bichu. "Just be careful and always listen to your cousin Feng."

"It's not complicated. You just stick with the others and walk together. We are going to sing some songs. You know them all," said Wei Feng with a smile.

"You look exhausted," said Bichu. "When you can go into town, remember to squeeze in some time to see Xueyan," she told Wei Feng.

"Things are not so bleak. Many of us share the same goal: we don't want to be conquered. If we don't want to be conquered, we need to fight hard to drive the enemy out of our country. Everybody feels the same about this," said Wei Feng.

"Xueyan wants to move to the university and stay with me, but her mother won't let her," he added.

Before he got married, he already addressed Yue Hengfen as Yue Mu, literally meaning 'Mother Yue', which sounds exactly like mother-in-law in Chinese. For him, it was more a joke because he was emphasizing Hengfen's family name, rather than the relationship that later developed between Hengfen and him.

"We didn't have the opportunity to enjoy the bridal room so carefully arranged by Aunt Bichu. What a loss for the two of us!" He had been feeling guilty about not being able to use the room which her aunt had gone to so much trouble to prepare.

Fuzhi smiled: "You don't owe your aunt an apology. The Japanese do. Some professors are writing an open letter to the Nanjing administration. I will sign that letter, too."

Wei Feng said excitedly: "I just knew you would!"

Bichu asked: "What should we present to the soldiers? There's still time for some characters on embroidery. I'll contact some of the ladies to make a rush job of it."

So saying, she rose to her feet to look for some suitable material.

Wei Feng knew that when the news of the Bailingmiao victory came, this aunt of his had led more than a dozen wives from rich families to pull an all-nighter to sew cotton-padded winter coats for the soldiers on the front line to show their gratitude.

"Would you please ask Earl to bring it with her tomorrow?" he said. After these words, he got ready to leave, declining their invitation to stay for lunch.

Early next morning, Earl rode her bike to the school gate and found three trucks parked there. Many students had already gathered around. She was parking her bike when she heard someone calling her by her official name 'Meng Liji'. She raised her head to see Wu Jiagu and his sister Jiaxin. All three were happy to see each other.

Jiaxin said: "We thought you wouldn't come. You know, because of your preparation for the entrance examination."

"Aren't you doing the same thing?" Earl answered.

"Jiaxin wasn't allowed to tag along at first, because we already have too many people. Well, she wouldn't listen," answered Jiagu.

"She's trying to make her contribution," someone standing next to them said.

People stood around the trucks, talking. Wei Feng was discussing something with a couple of guys in front of the truck. When he noticed Earl, he waved at her to come over, and asked: "Who wants to take the passenger seats in the cabs, you and the other girls?"

All the young girls, like Earl, refused to sit in the cabs. Earl passed him a package wrapped in a cloth cover.

Inside was the banner Bichu and the other wives had made overnight. Once everyone had arrived, they climbed into the back of the trucks. The *qipaos* of Earl and Jiaxin were ripped down the side, but both were too excited to pay any attention to this minor embarrassment. They were so excited that one couldn't help thinking whether their visit to the fighters on the front line was an insurance for further victory, or a guarantee that they would be saved from the plight of being conquered and enslaved.

Earl and the Wus took the last truck. The trucks in the front stirred up enormous clouds of dust. Before long they were covered in dust like terracotta figures. The coolness of the morning dissipated as the sun rose. Many students were wearing straw hats; some female students even put up their parasols. But neither hats nor parasols helped much in the sultry air.

Sweat trickled down their faces, leaving distinct trails. When they arrived, their faces were filthy. Luckily there was a creek beside the road, so they were able to wash their faces a bit before they went into the barracks in three rows.

A small team of soldiers stood neatly in the open area of the barracks. Earl and Jiaxin were surprised to see so few of them. They had been expecting to see a powerful army with thousands upon thousands of soldiers and horses, the mountains and plains covered with heroes, all well equipped with a fine arsenal of weapons. This tiny batch of solders looked so solitary. They didn't look grandiose, either.

"What's this place?" Earl and Jiaxin asked each other at the same time. They later figured out it was the Nanyuan barracks located in Fengtai district, south of Beijing. Two officers went up, shook hands with the representatives, and welcomed them.

More and more trucks arrived carrying students from the city. There were far more students than soldiers. People in colourful clothing were clustered around a small group of khaki uniforms. The soldiers didn't look solitary any more. They were surrounded by passionate admirers.

Earl didn't know the person who spoke on behalf of the students. His speech was impassioned, but somewhat too formal and bookish. Wei Feng presented the gifts – towels, cans, and other items were laid on a row of tables. He opened the package Earl had brought him and asked three students to hold up the banner. On a strip of printed cotton cloth were four big Chinese characters cut out of red cloth '*guo zhi gan cheng*' (国之干城), meaning heroic defenders of the nation.

Wei Feng stood in front of the banner and made a short speech:

"The officers and their men have a mission to fight the enemy, so few can be present today. Not many students have come to present their gratitude, either, but those few who have come represent not only the college students in Beijing. They also represent their families. I am confident to say that we represent many more. We represent the broad masses of the people. We are here to show our support for you. We are, and always will be, strongly behind you! You are using your flesh and blood to build a new great wall for the Chinese nation. Because of you and your sacrifice, the Chinese nation has survived the fate of destruction!"

People's emotions were stirred. With a lot of hustle and bustle, the banner was hung up under the eave. An officer advanced two steps toward his men. Before he could speak, successive waves of heavy gunfire rang out. After a short silence, he shouted: "one – two!" The soldiers then began to sing aloud. Although their voices were husky and somewhat out of tune, their singing was magnificent and yet sad at the same time. Many years later, Earl could still recall their singing, loud and clear.

The last line of the song was 'we'd rather die than surrender'. It was first sung in a regular register, and then repeated in a higher register. The two officers joined the chorus, then the students. With the accompanying music of rumbling gunfire, the sound carried over the fields and up into the clear, cloudless sky, echoing far and wide.

The students' performance was cancelled because they had to leave the site as soon as possible. Earl and Jiaxin ran over to the soldiers and gave them their straw hats. Earl's had delicate patterns on it and was given to a young one with a round innocent face like a child. Jiaxin's was plain and was given to a middle-aged one with a stern poker face. They climbed back into the truck and left for the university. No one talked on the way back.

From time to time, someone would start singing "We'd rather die than surrender! We'd rather die than surrender!"

Were these students just taking a serious oath on their lives with the soldiers? 'We'd rather die than surrender!' It was an oath taken by the Chinese nation!

When she got home, Earl began to feel unwell and skipped dinner. In the evening, she had a fever. Dr Zhu, the family doctor from the school infirmary, had been detained in the city, so they had to ask the doctor on duty to come over and have a look. The doctor said Earl had sunstroke and prescribed some medicine. Earl took the medicine, but her condition deteriorated during the night. She threw up and had diarrhoea. Bichu got up in the night several times to check on Earl. The next day, the vomiting and diarrhoea stopped, but she still had a very high temperature.

On the third day, Earl didn't feel any better. People said that the Xizhimen gate was open twice a day at that time, once in the morning and once in the afternoon. They decided to take Earl to town to get proper treatment.

Fuzhi thought it was alright for him to go into town with Bichu this time since he was still on summer vacation and there wouldn't be much at the university for him to do. He sent someone to Wei Feng, asking him whether he would need a ride. But Wei Feng was not in his dormitory. His whereabouts were unknown since he had come back from the trip to the military barracks. The guy then went to the laboratory to find Professor Zhuang alone, who said that Wei Feng had been sleeping in the lab for the last two days, and now it was his turn to sleep in the lab. Fuzhi and Bichu then had to take Earl to town without Wei Feng, accompanied by Amah Zhao.

They arrived at Chestnut Street without any delay. May and Kiddo flew into their arms with loud cries of joy, with Wei at their heels. It was not convenient to take care of the sick Earl in the building in the back garden, so the Meng couple decided to stay in the west garden as usual. Dr Zhu was sent for and arrived in no time. He said Earl had caught acute tonsillitis. He prescribed some medicine and asked her to take a good rest. The building in the back garden had lost its charm for the three kids, so they just crowded into Earl's room, trying to help and hand her anything she might need. Xuan came over when she heard that Earl had become ill after her visit to the barracks.

"How did you come up with the idea of going to the barracks!" Xuan said, wide-eyed, looking so much like her doll Shirley. "Did you think that your visit would bring us victory?"

"What makes you think that we won't be victorious?" Earl retorted feebly.

"Who said that? I didn't say that," said Xuan, laughing: "What I meant is it was not worthwhile. Look at you. One visit, and now you are lying in bed."

"It was enormously worthwhile!" Wei blurted out. He and his sister had very different personalities, but they were very close.

Usually, Wei would put up with all kinds of nonsense from his big sister and laugh it off with his gentlemanly generosity. To shout at his sister like that was rare.

Earl and May didn't have similar personalities, nor was their relationship very close, and they always locked horns like bulls. But now, May admired her big sister. She was even envious that Earl had made a visit to the barracks. She was envious that Earl was ill, and she didn't agree with what her cousin Xuan had said. Her bright eyes were fixed on Xuan, though.

"Really, you all disagree with me?" Xuan was still smiling. "What a tough break I have been having recently. Why do I keep running into souls that are so passionate about war? Anyway, I'll do whatever I like. I'm not going to let war stand in my way or affect my life."

"Then why do you go to the building in the back garden to hide from the shelling?" asked Wei.

He was thinking of mentioning Paul, but he was also afraid of hurting his sister's feelings, so he dropped it.

Xuan decided she wouldn't stay any longer as Earl was lying comfortably in bed while she had to bicker with the smaller kids. "Alright! Alright! I have no more to say," she told Wei, which also served as a goodbye to Earl, and went into Bichu's room to say hello.

Bichu and Amah Zhao were busy tidying up May and Kiddo's clothes, and Fuzhi was not in the room. She stayed for a while and then left.

Fuzhi was in Lord Lü's room. They were talking about the newly arrived newspaper with Chiang Kai-shek's speech at the Lushan talks. In his rather toughly worded speech, Chiang had clarified that the bottom-line position of the central government was to hope for peace and prepare for war, and to seek co-existence internally and survival externally. The old man had asked Lianxiu to read the paper to him first, and then read it again by himself carefully with his magnifying glass.

He said to Fuzhi: "The first half of my life was dedicated to fighting against the Qing dynasty, and the last half was against Chiang. When I retired to live by Shicha lake, I shut myself off from the outside world. If, this time, Chiang is willing to unite the country and fight for it, I'll support him."

Fuzhi said: "The most important thing now is the cooperation between the KMT and the CPC. United, we can fight the Japanese. We have read the resistance declaration from the CPC." He then summarised the declaration.

The old man was very pleased: "The hope lies in the fact that this war against the Japanese might also serve to be a turning point for the nation."

He then said: "Your nephew, Mr Wei, is unusual. My impression is that scientists do not care much about politics. Not only does he care, but he feels deeply about it and is prepared to take action."

Fuzhi reckoned that the declaration reminded the old man of Wei Feng, so he explained:

"We actually don't know where he stands politically. When he was a student, he studied hard. His professor Zhuang Youchen was very proud of him. In the past year, he has been involved in many off-campus activities and has been a little bit neglectful of his research. He is very capable and is a passionate patriot. What I am worried about is that his research might suffer in the future with all the activities he has been doing."

The old man nodded thoughtfully:

"There has to be someone who's willing to direct their energy toward politics. Otherwise, who will see to the fate of the country? To be frank, when I was young, I was ashamed to become a scholar focusing on my research. I shouldn't really be saying this in front of you, so please don't take this personally. I know you and most of your colleagues are all scholars with a down-to-earth attitude. However critical the situation is, if we have this valuable power made up of you scholars, then we have hope. As for me, I have long outlived my usefulness to serve my country. Miao Donghui asked me for my signature on his proposal to turn Beijing into a cultural city. That really set me off. I had planned to write a passionate article against such a proposal, but in the end, I only came up with two limericks. Still, I want to share my feelings with someone who understands."

He asked Lianxiu to fetch the specially designed stationery with his two poems on it. He handed them to Fuzhi: "Before I took up the brush, I felt the words gushing out of my heart. But when I put them on paper, they became so dull and plain. Just take them home and read them by yourself."

Fuzhi took the stationery and kept it in a safe place. He talked with the old man about the university for some time then bade him farewell and went back to the west garden. He invited Bichu to read the poems with him. On the paper were two poems entitled: '*On Recalling My Thoughts*'.

On Recalling My Thoughts

One

In front of Buddha, worries sent me to pray, gnawing.
Those depressing poems brought me to tears, streaming.
Moths obsessed with darting into the fire intent on destruction were dormant by day;
Fish transformed into birds hurried south.
Charlatans were omnipresent but never punished.
How did a passionate patriot turn into a hermit
Who frequented such an eminent monk?

Two

The motherland is subjected to so much pain,

Bullied at bayonet point by a neighbouring country.
People carrying all colours are on stage one by one.
All sides should fight shoulder-to-shoulder
like brothers on the battlefield
To save the country from invasion.
During the crisis, senile like an old horse in the stable,
I volunteer to shoulder my responsibility
though I'm not so able.
My love of my country never dwindles with age.
I too heard the gunfire on Marco Polo bridge.
To save the country, let's talk less and work more.

The old man had poor eyesight and trembling hands, but his handwriting was legible even though several strokes overlapped. The couple didn't say a word after reading the two poems.

Fuzhi sighed: "Will our descendants, worthy or unworthy, understand us and the significance of having a strong motherland free from any bullies?"

"As such a passionate patriot, father is a rare case. Few at his age would be as passionate as he is. How could he claim to be 'a passionate patriot' who turned 'into a hermit'? No one has ever seen him calm and cold like a hermit!" said Bichu.

"In the long run, we have to move the university to the south. Father should leave Beijing as well. Although he has been far removed from politics, he is still a major political target."

"Leave Beijing?" Bichu was surprised at these words. "Aren't we still fighting?" she asked.

"We'll certainly fight the Japanese. But if things are no longer stable in Beijing, it won't be possible to run any

Wei answered: "It's true that I am still not old enough. But you are wrong about me. Why can't youngsters fight in the war? Youngsters are Chinese, too, and have a duty to fight for their country."

Liu Fengcai smiled: "My young master, you are ambitious and courageous. But I really can't believe that you can go to fight in the war. Your mother wouldn't let you."

Lü Guitang said: "Not likely. His old lordship might."

As they were talking, Amah Zhao came for May and Kiddo. May tugged on Wei's sleeve to ask him to go with them, but Wei ignored her. He wanted to stay and talk more about the war. So Amah Zhao took May and Kiddo away. When they passed the Wisteria garden, Amah Zhao began to talk:

"Young ladies shouldn't mingle with the male servants. Besides, they don't have anything of interest to talk about," she said to May.

Kiddo interjected: "Lü Guitang is going to fight in the war, so is Cousin Wei."

May hurried to explain: "He meant when he grows up."

"I don't see how the war has anything to do with you two. You have nothing to worry about." Amah Zhao then sighed, "but for the country folk, it's really tough. We must deal with more donations, taxes, and extra recruitment of soldiers. Lots and lots to worry about."

As the battle intensified, more neighbours came for shelter. Jiangchu had asked for the screens to be moved inside twice, leaving less and less room for the family. Fuzhi declined to go to the building in the back garden, and Bichu decided to stay with him; Earl didn't want to move either; only May and

Kiddo stayed in the building in the back garden because it was more fun with so many people there.

That night, Amah Zhao took the two kids from the building in the back garden to the west garden to wash before going to bed, then Kiddo said he didn't want to sleep in the building in the back garden that night. He wanted to stay close to his mum. May was unwilling to leave, too. The five of them then sat together in the living room. They didn't talk much, but the peaceful atmosphere made all five of them feel as if they were back at Square Teakettle. The war was, for a very brief moment, far away from them.

"Madam Meng, are you still up?" Amah Liu asked outside the door-curtain before she lifted it up to enter. She had been sent by Jiangchu to deliver a message from Mr Miao, saying that the East Hebei army had staged a mutiny[9] and dealt the Japanese troops a heavy blow when they took Tongzhou and Fengtai. The message, in Amah Liu's words, was to the effect that:

"His Lordship Miao informs Her Ladyship Jiangchu that the East Hebei army has defeated the Japanese and seized Tongzhou and Fengtai. They are going to take back Langfang in the coming days!"

At the confirmation of the victory, everyone was exhilarated.

"They are going to take back Langfang in the coming days!" said Kiddo, imitating Amah Zhao. They all laughed. Fuzhi was also excited, but his excitement was mixed with concern.

---

[9] The Tongzhou mutiny (通州事件 *tongzhou shijian*), sometimes referred to as the Tongzhou incident, was an assault on Japanese civilians and troops by the East Hebei army in Tongzhou, China on 29 July 1937 shortly after the Marco Polo bridge incident that marked the official beginning of the Second Sino-Japanese War.

He imagined that maybe, just maybe, our righteousness could defeat the enemy and protect our people.

Seeing everyone around him so happy, he was touched, and chanted to himself:

> 'All the citizens burnt incense
> To thank heaven that we have won.
> We have already taken back Tongzhou
> And it won't be long
> Before we take back Fengtai.'

When the kids went to bed, the Meng couple went out to the garden for a while. The moonlight was like the mist from an enormous waterfall. The flowers shimmered with a silver lustre. The two weeping willows were like delicate statues, standing still in the yard. It was quiet. Too quiet.

"Why is it so quiet?" whispered Fuzhi.

Compared with the intense gunfire over the last few days, it was strangely quiet tonight.

"Maybe they are preparing for a big battle tomorrow?" said Bichu.

"It was also quiet last night and the night before. But we always heard some gunfire."

"There's no gunfire. Not even sporadic shots."

They went to sleep in dead silence. Late into the night, a cacophany of noise intruded into Fuzhi's dream. He felt as if he had been shoved hard several times toward the edge of his dream, on the verge of waking. Suddenly, he woke up. He collected his thoughts and figured out that the noise was being made by footsteps, horses and carriages from the south. He got out of bed, went to the west wall and listened intently. Heavy footsteps sounded like they were coming from just outside the wall. But he knew they were coming from Di'anmen toward the back gate of Beihai lake. The footsteps sounded measured and rhythmic. Each step thumped like a blow on the Beijing earth. He listened for a while and went back to the covered passageway.

Bichu came out, and whispered: "Is that troops passing by?"

"Yes. They are going from east to west," answered Fuzhi hesitantly.

Why were such measured footsteps heading from east to west? He suddenly remembered his lines of verse:

'We have already taken back Tongzhou
And it won't be long
Before we take back Fengtai.'

How ironic! The moonlight shone gently. Something plopped down in the bushes. Amid the heavy footsteps, they suddenly heard the shrill cries of a child, the kind of startling cry that pierced through the darkness of the night.

The couple looked at each other, deeply upset. The child's crying became fainter as time passed. The footsteps and the sound of cart wheels became more and more frenzied, like sweeping waves, or roaring thunder, shattering the all-enveloping dark silence, shaking the Beijing earth, which encompassed the time-honoured history and culture of China, and shaking the sinking hearts of this middle-aged couple.

Part 4

Fuzhi would never forget the bleakness in Beijing on the morning of 29 July 1937. It looked like a giant beast, with its hairs standing up on its neck and muscles tensed, with every nerve cell jangling and ready for a fight, which suddenly collapsed onto the ground. Every cell in its body dead, cold and stiff, waiting to be slaughtered by a merciless enemy. Fuzhi felt he was one of those dead cells.

Fuzhi got up later than usual since he had stayed up until midnight. Bichu had gone to the kids' room to check on them while he was getting dressed.

"Uncle Meng!" Lü Guitang called out in the living room.

Before Fuzhi could finish dressing, Lü Guitang had already dived in and threw himself in front of Fuzhi, with his knees on the floor. He held Fuzhi's legs.

"What? What happened?" Fuzhi tried to help Guitang up with one arm, while the other arm caught hold of his sleeve.

"Doomed! We are all doomed!" Guitang raised his head, tears streaming down his face. "Our army has evacuated. We have lost Beijing!"

The noise last night was the army evacuating! Fuzhi heaved a long sigh, and helped Guitang to stand up. Guitang asked: "Should I inform his lordship?"

Bichu had come out on hearing Guitang. Her hand was resting on the bedframe, her eyes fixed on Fuzhi. Tears rolled silently down her face.

"Later. Let his daughters tell him the news later," said Fuzhi, after taking in the news.

"The fortifications in the southern part have been torn down. It was neat and solid yesterday, but it lies there dead now. Uncle Meng, what should we do?" Guitang asked, sobbing. He didn't wait for Fuzhi's answer and shot out with his face covered in his hands.

"I'm going out to have a look," said Fuzhi, holding Bichu by the shoulder and helping her to sit down. He hurried out without waiting for her response.

Although there had been a war going on, most of the shops in the northern part of the city had been open for business as usual. Now they were all closed. The streets were empty. No one came out to clean their shopfronts. The glorious morning sun shone on an overwhelming, strange peace. Di'anmen stood in its usual place, so good-natured, and so incompetent. The three doors in the gate were like three big mouths with their jaws gaping open. They were mouths that couldn't speak. They were incapable of describing the indignation stirred up by the evacuation of the previous night; they were incapable of conveying the trauma inflicted on Beijing. They were dumber than dumb. No yelling. Nothing but silence.

South of Di'anmen was a police station, which was empty now. Further south, there was a small bicycle repair shop. It was open. Fuzhi approached it to see a man fiddling with a bike, squatting on the ground. Fuzhi had been standing there for a while when the man began to talk:

"I saw it through a crack in the door. Is it really the case that our troops can't fight?" He stopped for a moment before starting again: "The sand bags have been removed. If you walk a bit further, you can see for yourself."

They were total strangers, but they felt so closely connected in the empty street with a shared destiny and identity — they were conquered slaves destined to live a miserable life trodden under the boot of the triumphant Japanese invaders!

Fuzhi waved his hand dismissively and turned back, heading home. The sun had risen high in the sky. Some people opened their doors to fetch water. They all had gloomy expressions on their faces. Fuzhi felt his legs were heavier than lead. He could hardly drag them along. When he reached the entrance of Chestnut Street, he found Liu Fengcai waiting on the street, looking up and down. When he saw Fuzhi, he ran to him and grabbed him by the arm, saying Mrs Meng was worried and had sent him to look for him.

When Fuzhi arrived home, Bichu just stammered one sentence before being engulfed in tears: "How can we live on?"

Fuzhi didn't reply.

It was almost noon. Jiangchu and Bichu decided to go and see their father in the main compound. Lianxiu greeted them in the living room. "His lordship is lying in bed. He said he doesn't want to see anyone."

Jiangchu's face immediately darkened. She snapped at Lianxiu: "Who told him?"

"Father would have got to know sooner or later," replied Bichu, hurriedly.

Lianxiu dropped her head and remained silent for several minutes before talking again: "When Lü Guitang came in, his lordship had noticed something was wrong, so he kept asking. Then Lü Guitang gave up and told him the truth."

Jiangchu sighed. Bichu's eyes were wet again. The two sisters took a few steps down the garden. The lotus leaves in the fish tank were withered and dried. Each of the two seedpods was already half rotten. Things have turned out to be so desperate and bleak.

Jiangchu called Miao Donghui to ask for more details about the evacuation. Having known Fuzhi was staying with them, Miao asked Fuzhi to talk over the phone. Both ends of the line remained silent for a long while after they had exchanged greetings with one another. It was Miao Donghui who broke the silence:

"It was an intense battle at Nanyuan. Deputy Commander Tong Lingge and Division Commander Zhao Dengyu were both killed."

Fuzhi uttered only one word "ah", and said no more.

Miao continued on the other end: "Fortunately, all the relics in Beijing are intact. It's a reassuring piece of news."

Fuzhi just said "en" followed by silence.

Miao went on: "Zhang Zizhong is now the interim mayor of Beijing, and the chairman of the Hebei and Chaha'er standing committee. To be frank with you, a friend who works for the newspaper told me that. No one informed me about anything."

"Beijing will soon no longer be a place for Chinese people anymore. Will you remain in your position?" asked Fuzhi.

"You asked the wrong question, Fuzhi, ha-ha," said Miao, forcing a laugh. "It is not about whether I am willing to stay or not. It's all about whether they are willing to let me stay or not. Even when Beijing becomes someone else's Beijing, we will still have to live on like slaves dependent on their masters. What I cannot let go is this city, our Beijing city, the city handed down to us by our ancestors!"

He paused and then asked: "The city gate is going to open this afternoon. What should we do with the colleges and universities? People are all concerned about this."

"I need to get out of town as soon as possible. China is broken, but we Chinese are not!" Fuzhi didn't want to go on, so he said goodbye and hung up.

Mrs Zhuang called a moment later, to say that she and the kids were alright and asked Fuzhi to send a message to her husband. She wanted him to know that she was ready to leave town to stay with him.

"The kids are safe," she added rather hesitantly. "I'm ashamed of myself. We are too safe."

Fuzhi was unable to say a word, as if his power of speech was lost when Beijing was lost. When he hung up, he went to prepare to leave town. Bichu wanted to go with him, but he said no, saying he had Amah Li and their chef Old Chai to take care of him and that the kids needed her here. Bichu understood that it would be too much to ask her sister Jiangchu to take care of their father and all the kids. She reluctantly agreed that Fuzhi should go back to Square Teakettle alone.

Time passed very slowly. Finally, it was afternoon. Fuzhi asked Old Song to give him a ride out of town. The streets were quiet. Only a couple of shops were open for business. They had to open because, for these families living hand-to-mouth, to be closed meant to starve with no income. They didn't encounter any checkpoints along the way. When the car arrived at the university gate, the campus guard saluted as usual. Fuzhi told Old Song to stop the car and asked the guard whether they had encountered any disturbance. The guard answered that several days ago, Japanese fighter planes had bombed Qinghe, which luckily didn't cause many casualties. Things were alright on campus. He then asked Fuzhi: "It is said that Song Zheyuan[10] and his army have evacuated. Is it true?" Fuzhi nodded. The guard burst into a loud, tearful cry. Old Song was so stunned on seeing this that he forgot to restart the car.

Fuzhi went to Zhuang Youchen's house first. Mrs Zhuang loved Chinese-style houses, and that was why they had chosen this house to live in. He went through a gate with double doors painted in a traditional Chinese red colour and found no one in the garden. The grass was overgrown, reaching the steps leading to the rooms. He stood in the garden for several minutes until a servant came to inform him that Youchen hadn't come home for several days. He had been staying in the laboratory and had his meals delivered there. Fuzhi nodded and got back into the car heading for Square Teakettle.

The lemon-yellow gauze screens were the same. The rooms were decorated with the same furniture. But Fuzhi felt things had changed a lot. He went from one room to another, opening the door to look into each room. They were all strangely empty. He didn't dare open the door to his home office. How would he feel if his work and manuscripts were tainted with the sadness of being conquered?

"Sir, you are back! Did you have a smooth trip?" Chef Chai Fali and Amah Li trotted in to greet him from the passage connecting the servants' quarters with the main rooms.

They gathered excitedly around Fuzhi and bombarded him with questions:

"Where is Madam?"

"How about the two young ladies and the young master?"

After firing all their questions at him, they calmed down

---

[10] Song Zheyuan (宋哲元; 30 October 1885 – 5 April 1940) was a Chinese general during the Chinese Civil War and the War of Resistance Against Japanese Aggression (1937–1945).

and returned to their usual reserved manner, standing with their hands draped obediently by their sides.

"Thank you for having worked so hard. I am sorry for what you have had to go through during our absence," said Fuzhi gently.

The roar of aircraft engines could be heard in the distance, coming toward them. The planes hovered overhead for a while and then headed west. A series of thunderous bangs reached their ears.

"The enemy is dropping bombs," said Old Chai. "Sir, you should go to the basement in the university library."

Fuzhi didn't reply immediately, and then said: "You two should go."

Old Chai said: "Others in the family are staying in the library basement. I asked Amah Li to go too, intending to stay myself to take care of the house, but she didn't want to go. So, both of us stayed here."

Fuzhi nodded with a smile: "All right. Everything proceeds as usual."

Old Chai and Amah Li said yes. Old Chai went back to the servants' quarters while Amah Li remained in the room and began cleaning it.

Having dropped about a dozen bombs, the fighter planes continued hovering in the sky. Fuzhi guessed that the planes were bombing Xiyuan. When in town, they hid from the bombardments in the building in the back garden; when on campus, they went to the library basement. Hiding like this became a regular part of their lives and their destiny now. He slowly went to his home office. Having summoned up his courage, he opened the door to see messy piles of books and even messier piles of manuscripts. The sight calmed him.

He stood by his desk for a moment, caressing the crystal paperweight on the piles of papers. He couldn't sit down to work now, although he very much wanted to. He had to contact President Qin first.

He couldn't get through on the phone. The fighter planes were still hovering overhead. He decided he couldn't stay at home, waiting. He had to go to the Qins and together they might work something out. Zhuang Youchen arrived before he left the house. Their mutual impression of each other was that both looked so much older than when they had last seen each other, but neither mentioned it.

"I'm finishing my experiment. Three more days and it'll be done." Youchen started, before Fuzhi could say anything.

He then smiled apologetically: "Sorry! I'm only thinking about my experiment!"

"Della said she wants to come and stay with you," said Fuzhi, delivering the message, even though he knew full well that Youchen wouldn't let her come.

He continued: "The university has to move south. We can't go on like this for very long."

"It's OK for you 'arts' guys," said Youchen. "You just need to wrap up your papers and pack your books into boxes, and then you are all set to go. But for us 'science' guys, what can we do with our labs? New ones can't be built in one or even two years. The two key elements that define a quality university are its faculty and facilities. Well, the second one is going to be crossed off the list."

"If there is still anyone alive, the first one is always available."

"Not exactly!"

The fighter planes finally disappeared. Youchen said he was starving. Very likely he forgot to have lunch.

Fuzhi said: "Maybe your butler forgot to send you your lunch?" He pressed the bell to summon their chef, Old Chai, to prepare some snacks, which were put on the table in a moment.

Youchen said: "I need to eat as much as possible. Who knows what will happen later."

He immersed himself in the food. Soon he had emptied a blue-and-white porcelain bowl and a tall dish.

He asked, all of a sudden: "What did I have?"

Fuzhi hadn't noticed either, so he pressed the bell and summoned Old Chai again. Old Chai said:

"It was wonton and a pie made of ham and shredded turnip. I just learned how to make the dish. Did it not taste alright? I probably didn't cook it correctly."

Youchen replied immediately: "No, no! It was terrific."

Old Chai then said to Fuzhi: "I have prepared the same dishes for dinner. Will that be OK, master?" Chai couldn't find any more ingredients, but he tried hard to make the best of what was available.

Fuzhi told him anything would be fine. Someone was ringing the doorbell. Old Chai went to open the gate and found Qin Xunheng standing outside: "President Qin!"

Qin Xunheng was thin, but not weak, and looked like someone you could rely on. Everything from his appearance to his knowledge marked him out as a model university president. Minglun University had several presidents in the late 1920s. No one had stayed in the position longer than half a year until Qin Xunheng came along. He had his special ways of dealing with the authorities politically, motivating the professors, and educating the students. After the Marco Polo bridge incident, he had cut short his visit to Nanjing for the Lushan talks and hurried back to Beijing. He was now standing in the living room with his usual calmness as if he were not in a war zone and hadn't noticed any fighter planes dropping bombs.

"I was just about to go to your place. Youchen is here, too," Fuzhi said.

"The planes have gone, so I came out to have a look," he said in a hushed voice.

He spoke very slowly and deliberately. There was a saying among the students that it would take President Qin a thousand days to make a decision on something but that, once he had decided, he expected to finish it in one day. "I knew you would come back to the campus once the city gate was open."

They then exchanged information about the evacuation. President Qin sighed:

"Both Deputy Commander Tong Lingge and Division Commander Zhao Dengyu died a heroic death. Last month when Tong Lingge visited our school, he encouraged students to work for him. Dozens of students signed up. What has happened to those students?"

There was a moment of silence.

Fuzhi then said: "We have to let our students go. I think many of them will join the army to fight against the Japanese."

"What about our school?" Youchen asked.

"We must move it to the south. Fuzhi had come back just in time. We are going to have a meeting tonight to discuss the details about moving to the south."

"Moving to the south?" repeated Youchen, though it was not news to him.

The school had held several meetings to talk about it.

But when the words came out of President Qin's mouth after Beijing was abandoned, they felt different, more real, somehow.

"That's the only way out. Do you have any other suggestions?"

"Luckily, we have a big country," Fuzhi opined, forcing a bitter smile. "In times of crisis, we can always move to the south and wait out the crisis in the eastern reaches of the Changjiang (Yangtze) river, hopefully."

"We always hoped we wouldn't have to do this. But it is an unavoidable fate determined by the last 100 years of history — we are left with no alternative. We have to take refuge."

After seeing things through the historical lens of the last century, Xunheng was calm. Youchen gently rubbed his hands together and talked about how to move the lab equipment. He then told the other two he had to go back to his lab. Xunheng wanted to go to the students' dormitory.

After Youchen and Xunheng left, Square Teakettle fell into deathly silence which tried to engulf Fuzhi and crush him. He walked fast toward his home office and shut the door behind him as if this would shut the deathly silence outside.

In the days following the meeting that night, Fuzhi spent his mornings in the office attending to the dismissal of students. Each one got 20 yuan as expenses. For those who wanted to team up, they were to travel with two or three team members to Changsha. Although not many students stayed on campus during the summer vacation, Fuzhi still had a lot of matters to deal with.

In the afternoons, he would go to the library to take care of the books. Many books had been shipped, but there were still many left behind. The storeroom was stuffed with piles of books in no particular order. Boxes of books were piled high. The books on the shelves were in a mess. Some rare editions were just lying on the dirty floor, which was made of a thick layer of glass and used to be kept spotlessly clean. The roof was made of the same material. Looking up, one could see the milky sky through the glass of fog and cloud; looking down, one could see the opaque water from the lake. From between this glass roof and the glass floor had emerged so many great people who had played a role in accelerating the country's historical development.

Fuzhi loved this store room, the valuable thoughts from the best human minds stored in the books, the knowledge, and the glass floor. He kept picking up books from the floor. Not knowing where to put them, he would wipe the dust off the covers with his sleeves before handing them to the librarian following him. He would mop the floor too, with his sleeves.

"Professor Meng! What's the point of tidying the books up now? We can't move them. We are doing this for the Japanese," whined a librarian, holding a big pile of books in his arms.

Fuzhi froze. As the dean of teaching, he had discussed many times with the president, the secretary general, and the director of the library what measures they should take to move these books. They hadn't yet decided. Maybe they couldn't move the books at all. But he felt he had to say something. It had been growing inside him, stretching his body. He felt his body had grown bigger.

"We will come back!" He almost shouted.

Those who had immersed themselves into sorting out the books looked up at him; some were wiping their eyes with their hands, dirty with dust.

Someone muttered: "We will come back!"

Fuzhi went back home from the library in the scarlet setting sun. He wanted to shout at the top of his lungs on the campus: "We will come back!"

It felt like his chest was going to explode with the indignity, the pain and the shame. He was so overwhelmed with these emotions that he barely had the strength to drag his feet back to Square Teakettle.

In the flowerbed near the gate, one side of the Buddha Pine tree was bathed in the glorious red hue of the setting sun, while the other side was engulfed by darkness. It looked so lonely. Fuzhi picked up his pace, heading for the bedroom. But he found Bichu sitting in her old rocking chair. She got up from her chair on seeing Fuzhi, and tried to smile as usual, but her tears streamed out first rather than her smile. Fuzhi sat down and asked:

"What's wrong? Are the children alright? How about father?"

She nodded and tried several times to dry her tears. She finally managed to speak in between sobs: "They are all safe. Don't worry."

She slowly told him what had happened on her way back to Square Teakettle, her tale punctuated occasionally by wrenching sobs.

Bichu came with Della in a car which belonged to the British consulate. When they arrived at Two Elms district, they were stopped by a group of armed Japanese soldiers and asked where they were heading. When they found out the car was from the British consulate, they left Della alone, but demanded Bichu open the parcel she was carrying. It had some spare sets of clothes. A soldier picked the clothes out one by one with his bayonet and tossed them all on the ground. Bichu and Della kept silent. When their eyes moved from the clothes on the ground to the roadside, they grasped each other's hands.

The Two Elms police station was down the road. In front of the station lay two bodies, one face down and the other face up. There was a third body in the door, with half of the body on the street. All were in police uniforms. One civilian was tied to the door frame, his head drooping. His bald scalp was so shiny in the sunlight. No one knew whether he was dead or still alive.

Bichu didn't dare to look at first. But when the bound man raised his head slowly, the big scarlet birthmark caused Bichu to scrutinize him more closely. "Peddler Guangdong!" Bichu was shocked.

She then looked around and found the toppled containers which Peddler Guangdong always carried with him. Those delicate boxes and glasses were scattered all over the ground. Bichu was scared and furious. She wanted to cry out loud, and protest, and confront the soldiers. Her face must have betrayed her boiling thoughts because a Japanese soldier raised his gun and pointed it at her.

"What do you want?" Della asked in English. They couldn't understand Chinese, anyway.

"Do you belong to any regular army? How can you point your guns at a woman?" She then explained they were spouses of two professors at Minglun University and they were going back home. Another soldier looked at Della with a poker face, and then pointed his gun at her.

Bichu and Della's hearts almost stopped in the face of the two dark muzzles. They loosened their grip on each other, and sat up straighter. They didn't say another word.

A soldier who looked like the head of the gang came and looked in through the car window. He waved impatiently at the two soldiers to step back. The driver didn't dare to do anything. His upper body was resting on the steering wheel. He was trying his best to squeeze himself into a tiny bundle to attract as little attention as possible. The soldier in charge waited for a while and knocked on the windshield to ask the driver to leave. The latter hurried to start the car. Either the driver was too nervous or there was a problem with the car because the engine roared for a long while but the car wouldn't move. These couple of minutes lasted an eternity for Bichu and Della.

The car finally moved. But the driver didn't dare to speed up. They hadn't driven far before they heard a gunshot. The two ladies turned their heads back to see Peddler Guangdong slumped forward on the ground with a bloody mess over his shoulders. Della covered her eyes with her tender, white trembling fingers.

Bichu clasped her hands together and whispered to herself: "Don't be scared! Don't' be scared!"

Her tongue was stuck in her cheek, completely numb. She couldn't utter a word.

Fuzhi didn't know what to do except stand by her side, and mumbled: "There, there." He felt he had failed her to let her suffer such terror. The heavy emotions dragged on, adding to the shame of a husband who had failed to protect his wife. They were too weighty for him to say anything.

"The stores in Hutai county had all hung up Japanese national flags," Bichu sobbed.

"What the university can do is to move south," said Fuzhi.

"What we can do is to move with the school, leave Beijing

and migrate to the south. Let's talk this over when the school is settled, shall we?" He gently stroked Bichu on the shoulder. For Fuzhi, that was already the most tenderness he was capable of expressing.

Bichu gradually calmed down. She raised her head and looked at Fuzhi: "We don't need to talk this over. Let's just move with the school. I don't mind hardship, just — well, in the afternoon, you…"

She could only speak in broken sentences while she grabbed Fuzhi by the hand.

"President Qin is going to leave the day after tomorrow. It will be announced in a meeting tomorrow," said Fuzhi.

Bichu slowly let go of his hand and said: "You should eat and have a break now. I'm OK." She stood up, heading to the bathroom to wash herself. The couple went to the dining room together.

The next day, the last meeting of Minglun University in Beijing was held at President Qin's residence 'Round Rice Steamer'. All the professors sat in the living room with a big French window facing a colourful garden in full bloom. No one said anything. The atmosphere was suffocating. The attendant came into the room several times, bringing tea and other beverages. Few touched them.

President Qin, sitting in his armchair with ebony armrests, started in his deep voice:

"Beijing is lost, but the country remains. The 400 million Chinese still have hope. We are now shouldering more responsibilities than ever because we need to train qualified graduates for the country. During my stay at Lushan, when Generalissimo Chiang Kai-shek and I talked about the future of the colleges and universities in Beijing, Mr Chiang said:

'It's hard to predict the future of North China. We can give up one town, or even one city, but we cannot give up a single student. Nor a single teacher.' Our school has made necessary preparations in Changsha. Tomorrow, I am going to go to the Ministry of Education first and then head for Changsha. I'll be waiting for you all in Changsha."

He then talked about the status of moving books and lab equipment. It was agreed in the meeting that Professor Zhou Senran from the chemistry department would stay on campus with the director of the administration office until everyone else had left. Li Lian from the Japanese department would join the effort because of his fluency in Japanese. Zhou Senran had decided to stay in Beijing to take care of his aging parents and his wife who suffered from health problems.

"Word on the street is that the Japanese troops will be stationed in the city. Our campus might be taken over," said Zhou Senran.

"So be it," Qin Xunheng said. "With our colleagues moving to the south, we'd better set up a transit point in Tianjin."

All present at the meeting agreed that the foreign settlements in Tianjin might make the necessary arrangements much easier.

Something occurred to Youchen. He spoke up: "I will be the liaison between our university and the British settlement."

Having never thought about this, some were rather taken aback by Youchen. Others found the proposal very appropriate.

Looking at those who agreed, Xunheng was a little hesitant: "We have specific officials taking care of the liaison. I guess it won't be a very complicated business."

Looking at Youchen's shiny eyes, a tide of emotion rose in

Fuzhi's heart. He said loudly: "If we can borrow Youchen from his experiment, he can manage anything that is complicated."

With nobody disagreeing, Xunheng nodded his consent. They continued to talk over some details about the Tianjin transit point and agreed it would be Youchen's responsibility, and that he would also take care of the supporting funds for the staff who were on their way south and for the transportation of books and lab equipment.

Probably inspired by Youchen's proposal to seek assistance from the British settlement, Zhou Senran asked: "Is it possible to ask the American consulate to protect the campus?"

His voice was so low that it seemed he was posing the question to himself.

"With the skin gone, to what can the hair attach itself?" Fuzhi said.

"It won't work." Others agreed with him.

Zhou Senran kept quiet for a moment before crying out loudly: "I will follow President Qin's command. I know what I should do is to take care of the campus before I hand it to the Japanese."

His cry triggered tears from several professors who sobbed out loud, tears trickling down their cheeks.

"I think, we WILL come back," Qin Xunheng stood up and said, his voice trembling and tears streaming down his cheeks. He first shook hands and said goodbye to Zhou and Li, and then to Youchen, and then everyone else.

Holding Fuzhi's hand, Qin said: "I'll see you later."

The setting sun lingered on the two faces filled with pain and solemnity, and burning tears flooding down their cheeks.

The wet spots on their clothes glistened.

CHAPTER III

Part 1

After the Chinese army's evacuation of Beiping, there was no more gunfire or artillery fire. No. 3 Chestnut Street seemed to have regained its previous order before the incident. But it was all superficial. People felt lost once they no longer had to worry about dodging bullets or shells. For the first few days, Grandpa Lü was quite serious about reading the newspaper. He just couldn't believe that the fierce defence was suddenly history. He would hold his magnifying glass, sit by his desk, and search for any news about a counterattack by the Chinese army. The newspaper arrived rather late on August 9th and he couldn't stop hoping and said to Lianxiu that maybe the evacuation was a clever ruse by Song Yuanzhe. When the newspaper finally arrived, he opened it to see two prominent lines of captions:

'Yesterday the Japanese Army Entered and Occupied Beiping from Three Directions via the Yongding, Chaoyang and Guang'an City Gates'.

There was also a message from the Japanese commander to the people of Beiping:

'Dear citizens, I, your commander, am now in Beiping to maintain law and order.'

At the end of the message, he told all the people of Beijing "not to worry". Imagine! The invaders were telling the invaded not to worry about the forthcoming slaughter! From that day on, the old man stopped asking for the newspaper. When it was his newspaper time, he just remained seated in his chair in a daze. Jiangchu told Lianxiu she should keep reading the paper for Grandpa Lü since it was always better to know one's enemy, and knowledge about what was going on in the outside world was not a bad thing, either. But Jiangchu herself didn't read the newspapers at all.

In mid-August, Tantai Mian received instructions to leave for Wuhan to develop the electric power industry in the south of China. When he left, Jiangchu put her whole heart into making arrangements for life in the residence. She didn't know how long she could maintain such a life, but she knew she would try her best to do so. Tantai Wei, May and Kiddo were listless for several days after Tantai Mian's departure since they had lost their usual interest in things. As time went by, life became more and more normal. Jiangchu also began to supervise their homework, and arranged time for them to play, so the kids began to think about how to amuse themselves.

The neighbours who had asked for shelter in the building in the back garden had long since moved back to their homes. The back garden, which had been desolate for years, had returned to its usual tranquillity after several days of liveliness. Wei found that the lock on the door to the passage could be opened with a piece of a wire and they could go into the back garden without asking Liu Fengcai to do them a favour and open the locked door for them.

That day, after his regular nap, Wei went tearing into the west garden as he always did to find May and Kiddo had just awoken from their naps. Kiddo was throwing a temper tantrum at Amah Zhao, shouting "No! I won't! I won't!", his two small stout legs peddling hard in the air. Amah Zhao, knowing how Kiddo would always listen, and how hard it had been for the kids recently, was not annoyed at all. She kept smiling and finally managed to talk sense into Kiddo, who agreed in the end to finish the thick mung-bean soup stewed with rock sugar and sweet osmanthus flower. May was languishing under the window, holding a book, her beautiful head inclined slightly to one side, concentrating on the book. Wei would always feel that image of May was permanently imprinted on his heart in retrospect.

"Let's go into the back garden," Wei said mysteriously, which successfully diverted Kiddo's attention.

"Can you open the door?"

"I know how!"

Amah Zhao smiled at May and said: "The back garden has only been closed for several days, now it has become so attractive to you kids."

Before she could finish, Earl walked over from her room and asked what Kiddo was shouting about. Everyone fell silent.

Wei spoke up in the end: "He's missing Aunt Bichu."

"The city gate will be open in a few days, and then mum and dad will be joining us soon." Earl took hold of Kiddo's hand and comforted him. That was peculiar.

After some maintenance, the back garden was quite different. One could see distinctly the gravelled pathway zigzagging its way to the building in the wild grass. Beside the path was a freshly dug pit filled with a lot of ash from burnt paper. The path led the kids all the way to the back of the building.

They stopped at the dried-up creek and played 'war' there. Lü Guitang had cut down the tall wild grass along the curved 'banks' long ago. Wei had shovelled up the earth and piled it into various shapes: the square one was a building, the rectangular one was a plane factory, and the round one was a bunker. May and Kiddo were busy helping to add pebbles around the side of the mounds with their two small pairs of hands. Wei asked May and Kiddo to play being the Japanese army, and he played the Chinese army. He 'used' a machine gun to shoot 2,000 Japanese soldiers. May and Kiddo each represented 1,000.

"Lie down! Lie down! Both of you are dead!" Wei yelled at his two cousins proudly. May and Kiddo didn't want to lie down on the ground, so they just stood where they were.

"I need to send a battle report!" Wei shouted. "Grandfather will be very happy to see it. We killed 2,000 of the enemy!"

"Let's go and write the report," suggested May. Taking advantage of the opportunity, she took Kiddo's hand, jumped over the ditch and ran over to the room. That would save them from lying down on the ground in the sun.

"We have pens and paper here," she said, swiftly taking out a pen and some paper from the drawer, and sat down to 'draft' the report.

She took more pieces of paper out and handed them to Kiddo: "These are for you."

Wei stopped insisting that "you are dead" and joined in the drafting. After heated discussion, they came up with the following:

"Tantai Wei, General Commander of the Chestnut Army, with his two captains, Meng Lingji and Meng Heji, killed 2,000 Japanese invaders."

May said: "Cousin Wei can represent 1,000 of the enemy." She added one more stroke onto the Chinese character for 'two' (二), to make it 'three' (三).

Kiddo looked at his sister with admiration: how could she be so powerful? He yelled: "We won! We won!"

The three of them were having a lot of fun when they heard people coming up the steps. It was Jiangchu and Xuan, with Liu Fengcai following behind carrying big piles of newspapers and magazines in two baskets.

"Here you are!" Xuan then asked her mum: "Should we tell them?"

Jiangchu didn't answer and just looked at Wei, who was drenched in sweat, testy and impatient. Wei could tell from the stern expression on her face that she was really annoyed.

Xuan continued talking to her brother: "How old are you now? I can't believe you are still playing such childish games. It's definitely only suitable for Kiddo!"

"We were fighting the Japanese! Or I wouldn't do it," explained Wei.

Jiangchu spoke up: "Wei, you are twelve! How could you take your younger cousins to play in the scorching sun? Beiping is now under Japanese rule. The police have ordered all newspapers and magazines which might offend the Japanese to be burnt. There might be house searches in a few days. You are old enough to know how important this is. You mustn't tell anyone what we have burnt. You can't tell grandfather, either. He'll be very annoyed."

Liu Fengcai had started a fire in the pit by the gravelled path, and began to open the newspapers and magazines and toss them into the fire. Wei suddenly understood what the pit was for. He stared at the rising flames engulfing those fragile pieces of paper, many of which were historical. Anything mentioning 'Japan' or 'Japanese' ended up in the firepit. *The Three Principles of the People* and the lectures of Sun Yat-sen didn't survive, either. Liu Fengcai kept tossing paper into the fire. He now took up a big piece and tossed it into the fire.

It looked so familiar! Wei leaped over and snatched it out of the fire. It was his hand-drawn map, the one with all the locations where the Japanese army was stationed.

"Why did you want to burn my map?" He held the map tight against his chest, furious.

"I took it. I was going to talk to you about it," said Jiangchu, lowering her voice.

"Anything that might cause trouble has to be burnt, not to mention your map, which is clearly marked with 'invaders'. My dear boy, you will draw a new one when we beat the Japanese and drive them out of our country."

She tried to reach for the map, but Wei drew back and refused: "How could the Japanese meddle with our family affairs?"

Xuan sniffed: "That's because we are a conquered people!"

"A conquered people? How could we be a conquered people?"

May, who was standing by his side, gave him a tug and whispered: "Because Beiping has been taken by the Japanese."

In the middle of all the upset, Fuzhi and Bichu came past the shade of the willows. Kiddo ran to Bichu, grabbed her hand, and hid his face against her back. Immediately, a big wet spot appeared on the back of her plain dark-green silk dress. May approached her mother, her eyes wet with tears.

Fuzhi went over to Wei and took the map from him: "During your father's absence, it is you who should take care of your mother and your sister. You should be helping, not causing them trouble. We have failed to protect Beiping. How do you think we could still protect your map? We need to burn it, and later we are going to recover our lost land."

As he was saying these words, he picked out a KMT flag: "This needs to be burnt, too."

He put the flag onto the map, and put them both solemnly into the fire. He stood there silently and respectfully. Others couldn't help but stand respectfully, too. Everyone was silently staring at the fire nibbling away at the flag and the map. The edges of the map curled up. The blackened paper didn't disintegrate into ashes until the fire had been burning for a long time. Then the part with the white sun caught fire. The flames, which were almost invisible, were steadily consuming the glaring white sun. Liu Fengcai gave it a poke with a stick, then the white sun burnt to ashes. Then the flames crawled up onto the part with the blue sky.

"Unworthy! What unworthy descendants we are!" Fuzhi struggled to hold back his tears.

Tears streamed from Wei's beautiful eyes and rolled down his cheeks. Making no attempt to dry them, he let them flow freely. His strict and formal education had taught him to love his family and his motherland. 'Motherland' occupied a sacred place in his heart, but now he had to watch the sacred symbol of the motherland, the national flag, burn in front of him. He had to take part in mourning the loss of his beloved Beijing with its time-honoured history. He had to witness and endure the invaders' boots tread on his and his motherland's dignity!

Jiangchu went over to Wei, stroking his hand, looking at the flag and the map until they had both been burnt, and then turned to Fuzhi and Bichu: "I have told Earl to sort out the books in your west garden. It's a good thing that you don't have many books in town — how's the university?" They were so eager to start a new conversation that they didn't try to take a seat in the room.

"Sister, Fuzhi is leaving," Bichu said gently. "But we need to talk to father first."

"What is there to talk about?" Jiangchu said: "All those who teach in colleges should leave. If they stay, they will really become the conquered! It's lucky for you two that you are together now and can talk things over. Not like Mian. He said he had to leave, and then he left. I have no one to talk to!"

"They have decided to relocate the university to Changsha. I will leave first for Tianjin the day after tomorrow," Fuzhi said gently. "In wartime, it is understandable that Mian left in a hurry. He didn't have much choice, I think. When the company is settled, they are sure to make arrangements for the employees' wives and children."

"We will stay. It's easier for Fuzhi to leave alone this time," said Bichu softly.

Jiangchu didn't respond immediately but spoke up after a while: "Have you moved all your belongings to town?"

"Not all of them, just some. Chef Chai will stay with us and take care of things. We'll see."

"How about Little Lion?" Kiddo suddenly interrupted.

Bichu lowered herself to look into Kiddo's eyes and said slowly: "Before we loaded the package into the car, he broke loose from the bag and ran back to the house. I searched for him for a long time but couldn't find him anywhere."

"Is he lost?" Kiddo's tears welled up again.

Bichu comforted him: "Don't you worry about it. Amah Li is staying in Square Teakettle. She'll feed him."

Kiddo and May exchanged an encouraging glance, trying their best to hold back their tears. They knew a cat didn't count for much in such times.

"It's the right thing to do for Mian and Fuzhi to leave Beiping," Bichu told Jiangchu. "It's only a matter of time before the rest of us to leave, too. The one we need to talk about now is father."

"Father? Father is in his 70s, what can we do with him?" Jiangchu said.

"Our opinion is that father should leave Beiping. Although he is an old man now and has been off the political stage for years, his participation in the revolution and his non-cooperation with Chiang Kai-shek are known to many. It is very likely that the Japanese might want to make use of his reputation for their rule," said Fuzhi.

He added: "Mian once reminded us, too. 'If Beiping is lost someday, father would be the one we should worry about most.'"

"Be that as it may," Jiangchu, of course, knew how true Fuzhi's words were, but she also had something else on her mind: "If father moves, it is hard to predict what inconveniences will occur along the way."

Jiangchu's words were true as well. When the books, newspapers, and magazines had all been dealt with, the three ordered the servants to lock the door securely, and that the kids not be allowed to enter.

They thought father might have been awoken from his nap, so they headed for the main compound. When Grandpa Lü was told that Fuzhi was leaving, he said approvingly: "Good! It's right that you should leave. One by one. The sooner, the better."

"It's lucky that the Tianjin-Pukou railway[1] is still operating nowadays. No one knows what will happen later. Youchen and I will go to Tianjin together. He'll stay in Tianjin, while I will find someone to accompany me to Jinan for transfer to Changsha."

"That's good. Jiangchu and Bichu can take care of each other here," nodded the old man. He had a sudden coughing fit. Lianxiu went over and gently stroked his back, handed him the spittoon, and then a cup of water to rinse his mouth. She handled the series of movements with deftly and smoothly.

Fuzhi looked at Bichu, who said: "The one Mian worries about most is father. Fuzhi and I also think father should leave Beijing. It is too dangerous for you to stay."

"Safety is no longer the priority for a rice bag like me. I just eat and sleep. It's no longer significant to keep me safe," smiled the old man.

"Father should think about leaving Beiping. It would be intolerable to live at someone else's mercy, I am afraid," Fuzhi made one more attempt.

Upon Fuzhi's words, something occurred to the old man and he said: "Liangzu is always trying to invite me to spend some time in Kunming[2] and enjoy the winter-sweet flowers. I have always thought 'there's plenty of time for that', and the trip to Kunming has been put off year after year. If I go now, I will be going to seek shelter — but it is a good idea to start a college in Yunnan province."

---

[1] The Jinpu railway (津浦铁路 *jin* short for Tianjin and *pu* short for Pukou) runs from Tianjin to Pukou outside Nanjing, Jiangsu province. It was financed by the Qing dynasty, and is currently the main section of the Beijing-Shanghai railway.

[2] Kunming (昆明), known as 'the City of Eternal Spring' for its pleasant climate and flowers that bloom all year round, is the capital of Yunnan province, southwest China.

"Yes, it is! And father can stay with our elder sister Suchu there," Jiangchu chimed in with the old man.

"The long road lies far ahead, but which way is closer?" The old man smiled again.

He looked at his two daughters and said: "As long as you two are staying here with me, we can always make it. I know what Fuzhi has been trying to say to me."

"What did father mean when he asked which way was closer?" Bichu asked Fuzhi. She was packing Fuzhi's things in their bedroom. She had designed interior pockets on several articles of Fuzhi's clothing and asked Amah Zhao to sew them according to her instructions. The old man's words popped into her mind.

Fuzhi thought he had understood the old man's words, but he didn't intend to share with Bichu what was on his mind. Instead, he said: "I'm worried you are going to shoulder too much responsibility. The old have their own philosophy of life. As their children, we just try our best to understand them and do our part."

Bichu's tears were welling up. Fuzhi knew she was not only worried about the old man, so he said: "My trip to Changsha all depends on how the war goes. Once I'm settled, I'll see when is the best time to pick you all up. But I guess it won't take long."

Liu Fengcai spoke from outside the door curtain: "Master Wei and Master Ling have arrived."

Both Fuzhi and Bichu were quite surprised. These two were precisely the people Fuzhi most wanted to meet before his departure.

They went to the door to greet them both – the two of them had already come through the full-moon-shaped door to the garden. Ling Jingyao grabbed Fuzhi's hands, and Wei Feng called out "Uncle Fuzhi". Everyone looked sad.

They went into the living room and greeted Bichu. Having sat down, they exchanged news about what had happened recently. Jingyao and his family had been staying in the German hospital until two days ago.

"When we came to the street, we found Japanese flags all over the street. I was so lost that I felt I was in another country!" Jingyao sighed. "Hengfen and Xueyan are both doing alright. They only worry about Wei Feng. He came home two days ago. During such a tough time, when one should be home with one's family, he has been absent for several days, causing his family a lot of anxiety."

When Jingyao had finished speaking, he gave Wei Feng an accusing look but he pretended not to see it, and turned to Fuzhi and said: "Professor Zhuang has finished his experiment and has acquired rare data. This is something comforting."

Speaking about the departure of Fuzhi and Youchen, Fuzhi asked Jingyao what was his plan.

Jingyao said, pensively: "The country is now suffering. Even someone useless like me wants to do something. My family has lived in Beiping for generations, so I really fancy taking a look in the south. But Hengfen is worried about how much suffering we will have to endure once we are out of the comfort zone of our little dog-house of a home, and how long we can survive."

Bichu said: "There is nothing unbearable in life. It's more about getting used to things. Once you get used to something, it's OK."

"I'm afraid some people don't get used to it," said Wei Feng bitterly.

Jingyao looked disapprovingly at Wei Feng and said to Fuzhi:

"According to Miao Donghui, Beiping is the safest place because no one would be so bold as to destroy such a city with a time-honoured history and culture like Beiping. Anyone living in the city can share the same protection. It's just like sparing a rat to save the dishes. We are not rats after all. And we won't stand in their way. I will just teach as I used to. To be frank, it's also painful for me to change my way of life."

"Do you really believe the Japanese would let you enjoy your way of life as usual?" said Fuzhi, well aware of what his 'way' of life was after knowing Jingyao for years. It was not a complicated way. It was just an easy, casual and enjoyable way. Such an easy way was a perfect match for the city of Beiping. The long winding *hutongs*, the echoing cooing of doves, the birdcages hung high in the winds inducing many varieties of flowers to bloom in different seasons. Such an ambiance was visible at every nook and cranny in Beiping, nurturing all those who had been living there long enough.

"Do you really think you can wait all this out?" asked Fuzhi.

"I will wait until our army fights its way back," Jingyao said with ardent sincerity.

Fuzhi stood up and walked over to Jingyao: "You come with us, or with Wei Feng. Minglun University will hire you and you can start whatever course you like. You are 46 now. Are you going to spend the rest of your life waiting?"

Wei Feng said: "I have been asking father to leave Beijing. Mother and Xueyan can stay for a while since Aunt Bichu is staying, too."

Bichu said: "I'll take care of Hengfen and Xueyan and leave with them when the time comes."

"She won't leave," said Jingyao softly, and then he smiled: "I'm tied up, too." With Fuzhi standing in front of him, he tried to sit deeper into the sofa, as if to squeeze himself into a smaller shape to attract less attention.

"Sometimes I feel I know you so well that I understand whatever you do and whatever you say. At other times I feel you are such a stranger to me that I can't guess what's on your mind." Fuzhi walked away from Jingyao to the window, looking outside.

"There's nothing on my mind that you need to guess," Jingyao smiled again. "It's all listed there: cowardly, corrupt, hedonistic…. Leaving is indeed very necessary for an individual like me."

Speaking of leaving, his eyes sparkled. He was smart and knew himself, to some degree. He was well aware that he needed to leave and to change, which might pull him out of the situation he had been trapped in for years. But wouldn't that require a bit of a struggle? With this on his mind, he leaned back and tried to sit more comfortably.

"If you try to make a complete change, like change the soil of a plant, your life might be very different. Please leave with Uncle Fuzhi and Professor Zhuang! If you agree, the sooner, the better," pleaded Wei Feng sincerely. He almost said that if his father-in-law thought such a departure was too hasty, he would leave with him! But he managed to hold back his tongue.

"When I go back, I'll talk it over with the womenfolk," his narrow bright eyes dimmed on mention of the word 'womenfolk'. "We'll talk it over," he added, heaving a long heavy sigh.

They then went on to talk about the children. Bichu, after accompanying Wei Feng and Jingyao to greet Grandpa Lü, led them to the front compound to see Jiangchu.

Wei Feng asked Jingyao to go first while he went to the west garden. He found Fuzhi standing in the passage, with his hands folded behind his back. "Uncle Fuzhi," said Wei Feng, picking up speed at the sight of Fuzhi. "Uncle Fuzhi!"

"I once mentioned to you that I would leave Beijing soon. But I am not leaving for Changsha. I assume you have guessed," said Wei Feng. "I will probably go back to the university to teach. I love campus life."

"What's your plan for Xueyan?"

"I don't know yet. But she can't go with me this time. It's too tough for her. I think we will be separated for a while. It's still better than to be separated forever," said Wei Feng, forcing a smile.

Fuzhi didn't know what to say. Wei Feng didn't need any advice or back-up plans. He had more powerful backing than anything or anyone.

Wei and the other two kids ran into the room, all yelling happily "Cousin Feng is here!". Wei Feng lifted Kiddo high above his head and then set him down on his shoulders, while May tugged at his shirt and Wei stood by his side, smiling.

"I'm traveling to a faraway place on a business trip, so today I came to say goodbye to you all." Having lifted Kiddo one more time and put him down on the floor, he solemnly told the three kids about his departure.

"Are you going to fight the Japanese?" Wei asked.

Wei's question took Wei Feng by surprise. The latter

paused for a second before saying, with a smile on his face: "To fight the Japanese doesn't necessarily mean to kill them with guns. Those who properly carry out their responsibilities are fighting the Japanese properly as well. For example, you kids should study hard."

Wei listened attentively to Wei Feng without blinking his eyes.

"Where is Earl?" asked Wei Feng. Fuzhi asked May to go to the west apartment to tell Earl that Wei Feng was leaving. As a matter of fact, Earl couldn't have failed to hear them talking in the garden in her west apartment behind a Rhododendron bush. The door-curtain made of mottled bamboo was hanging still. It was quiet inside.

May reappeared after a while, saying: "Big sis said she doesn't want to see anyone now." There was not even one word of goodbye from Earl, and May was too young to say goodbye on her sister's behalf. Knowing how peculiar Earl had always been, Wei Feng decided to give up on seeing her before he left.

"Are you going to the same place where daddy is going?" asked May, looking up at Wei Feng.

"Not this time. Maybe we'll end up in the same place." What Wei Feng was thinking was that he might as well go to Changsha later, or Fuzhi might go where he was going now, a lot later, of course.

"You'd better stay together," said Kiddo, looking up at Wei Feng. "When I miss daddy, I will miss you as well. That will save me from missing you separately."

These funny childish remarks added more solemnity to the proceedings. Everyone stopped talking.

Tantai Wei wanted to accompany Wei Feng to the front

compound. Fuzhi and the two kids walked with them until the two reached the full-moon-shaped gate. Wei Feng turned around, bowed deeply towards Fuzhi, then turned back, dashed across the garden and sped into the alleyway.

Tantai Wei tagged along, and asked with great reluctance as Wei Feng was leaving: "When will you come back, Cousin Feng?"

"What is your big sister doing?" asked Fuzhi.

"Nothing. She's lying against the head of the bed, thinking to herself," replied May.

The two kids followed Fuzhi into the room. "Can we leave with daddy, can we?" Kiddo asked Fuzhi, tugging the lower edge of his gown.

"Last night, I had a dream. I dreamed about Cousin Wei's map. It was standing in the fire. It refused to fall down."

Everyone around was silent. Kiddo continued: "It's scary when daddy is not home."

"What are you scared of, my dear boy?" Fuzhi asked affably, lowering himself to Kiddo's level and stroking him on the head.

Kiddo's big dark eyes widened as he answered: "I'm scared when daddy is not at home."

Having realized how redundant his question was, Fuzhi pulled the two kids close to him, one on each side, and explained slowly and carefully why he had to leave alone first. He also assured them that once he had settled down, he would ask their mother to bring them to meet him without delay.

The next day, time at No.3 Chestnut Street literally flew by, especially in the west garden.

Time didn't have any intention of pausing even for a split second. Words couldn't slow it down. Needle and thread couldn't slow it down. Locks on the cupboards and luggage couldn't slow it down. Time stubbornly stuck to its course, ticking away relentlessly. When it reached dusk, everything was finally ready.

Bichu rubbed each cash note to soften them and put them into different secret pockets sewn inside Fuzhi's clothes. Fuzhi's luggage only included one case and one basket with netting on top. Not even a single book was packed. After dinner, the case and the basket were taken outside the door to the living room.

Fuzhi told Earl: "You are the oldest child and you need to help your mother to take care of the rest of the family. And you need to take care of yourself, too. May and Kiddo will stay at home, skipping school, but you need to go to school. It's great to have the determination to fight against the Japanese, but you are not allowed to participate in any activities. You are still young and you need to focus on your study. When you grow up, your country will need you in many ways."

"I'll see you off, Dad," Earl said abruptly. "Mum and I will see you off."

"How can you strut out and see me off at the station? We are like dejected dogs!" Fuzhi smiled bitterly.

He looked at Bichu and said: "Your mum shouldn't go, either."

Bichu, who had been looking down at the floor, raised her head and said: "I'll stay in the distance and see you go into the station. Will that be okay?"

"You don't need to do that," replied Fuzhi. "No matter

how many miles you go to see me off, the parting will come in the end."

How hard it is to part when one doesn't know when the one you care about so much will come back!

The next morning rolled in. Fuzhi was accompanied only by Lü Guitang to the station, who carried Fuzhi's luggage for him. Bichu followed the two jinrikishas to the entrance of Chestnut Street. Fuzhi waved at her repeatedly to go back, and she finally stopped, rooted to the spot, watching the two drivers running. The gaping mouth of Di'anmen city gate swallowed Fuzhi up. The jinrikishas became smaller and smaller in the distance while Jingshan mountain grew taller and taller under the clear sky.

When the three children got up, they found Bichu sitting quietly in the room. They came up to her, but she waved her hand and stood up to clean the room like she always did, which was messier than usual.

She told the kids calmly: "Daddy has left."

Part 2

When Fuzhi set off on his journey in the bright morning sun, Ling Jingyao and his wife Yue Hengfen were lying in their soft bed under a brocade canopy, bickering. They were not arguing over anything substantial, but reproving and rebuffing each other, far from where they had started. They had many fights on the topic of Jingyao's departure.

Each time Hengfen would fly into a rage before Jingyao finished listing the reasons why he should leave: "Why can't you just stay and let us carry on leading a simple life? Why do you have to leave? How could you even think about leaving your home in the care of only two women? Yes, it's true that we have lots of relatives in Beijing. But can they do the husbandly duties which are your sole responsibility?"

"I know my responsibilities as a husband and a father. But I also have my responsibilities as a citizen. Besides, why don't you mention your responsibilities as a wife and a mother?" When Jingyao told Fuzhi he couldn't leave, he was counting on Fuzhi to help him to evaluate his reasons for staying; but when faced with Hengfen, he had to clarify the reasons why he should leave.

"What are my responsibilities as a wife and a mother? Enlighten me! I am very ready to be enlightened by you." She sprang up and leaned on the headboard, tossing the pea-green silk comforter onto the floor. Her body, wrapped in her silk-embroidered night gown, revealed its determination not to see reason as her words had done.

Jingyao sat up and leaned against the other end of the bed. Both of them were ready to talk, but Hengfen got a head start:

"Since I married you, how have I benefited? Any expenses, your food, your clothing, your entertainment, are all covered by my family. What have you done? You just recite a few lines of French poetry that you have memorised and that no one understands, or you enjoy going to operas with your eyes on the stage. All you have done is to be a master of the house. Now you clap your hands and claim it's time for you to show your loyalty and dedication to your country. And you think you can just get up and leave? Did you think it would be so easy?"

Jingyao just replied: "You picked me in the first place. I didn't pick you!"

Hengfen was convulsed with fury, her eyes staring at Jingyao, her finger pointing, unable to utter a word, but her anger just rattled around in her throat like a cat purring.

That "You picked me!" was like a sword through Hengfen's heart. The Yue family was once one of the richest families in Beiping and Hengfen was once a celebrity socialite. It might have been because of the traditional values in Chinese culture that businesses tended not to last long unless the family formed marriage alliances with families serving the kings and emperors and later the government, that Hengfen's father set his sights on the youngest son of a former minister, Ling Jingyao. The Ling family had long since lost its former renown, and Jingyao was just a poor student back from his overseas study, so Hengfen's mother was against her husband's proposal to marry Hengfen to Jingyao. But Hengfen was somehow deeply attracted by Jingyao. She was so taken with his charm and unaffected demeanour. She had been on tenterhooks after seeing him, and she told her mum of her secret love for Jingyao. Supported by her father, she realised her dream and married Jingyao.

Only after the marriage did she find out Jingyao was not only obsessed with literature, but that he was a keen theatregoer who spent 30 days a month at the theatre! It seemed that, for Jingyao, what was on the stage looked more real than reality. He laughed and cried sincerely at what was going on on the stage, but he was indifferent about what was happening around him.

He was rather indolent and neglectful, without any set time for his meals or sleep, and was never serious about his teaching. When he was happy, he could prattle on and on for hours, but more often than not, he failed to show up to conduct classes for several weeks in a row.

He played his research by ear and never stretched himself. Rumour had it that his French might have been learnt in the type of cafés in France where the air was thick with liberty. He didn't care much about such words. The material wealth of the Yue family secured him a comfortable life style, and blurred the lack of understanding between him and Hengfen. Thus, 20 years had passed like the blink of an eye for Jingyao.

Hengfen, as a proud and arrogant daughter of a rich family, had quite a temper. She had assumed that her husband would be one of the most wonderful gentlemen on the planet. It was far beyond her expectations to have married a man like Jingyao. But she had picked him, which was somewhat strange for a family like the Yues at that time. When her parents were still alive, she would complain to them. But when they were gone, she could only complain about her fate. Wasn't it true that she had picked him?

Hengfen gasped, tears streaming down her cheeks. Usually, Jingyao would feel sorry for her and surrender before they reached such a stage. But today, he just stared blankly. That agitated Hengfen. To distance herself from him, she got off the bed, kicked the silk comforter off onto the floor with her bare feet, walked to the chaise longue under the window, sat down, and began to weep loudly.

The chaise longue, custom made from the south, was intricately woven with strips of rattan. The hardwood parquet floor in front of the chaise longue was covered with a milky white Persian rug, on which lay a fine woven mat leading to the bed. Her delicate feet were now kicking the chaise longue. The room was filled with her weeping, enveloping Jingyao tightly.

He wanted to tell her: "You are like a shrew!" But he managed to hold his tongue. Would a ferocious fight lead him to break off the shackles of family? He felt very sorry for himself because he hardly felt any lofty sentiments anymore. He needed understanding and compassion to help him get over his shortcomings. He wanted to be an upright man! But he couldn't. Each time when he summoned all his courage to have a try, he felt a heavy burden pulling him down, down, down. He assumed that the burden was his family.

But how much family responsibility had he shouldered? He had never supported his family. Although he had the title of professor, he was not one of the best and was not teaching in one of the top universities. What he earned was barely enough for his own spending and for some impractical small gifts for his wife and daughter. If he left, it wouldn't matter much to his family, but it mattered a lot to him. His personality needed it. But Hengfen didn't get it. She just wanted to grab his body, caring nothing about how pathetically his soul had fallen.

Both felt they were the most pathetic in the world. Hengfen needed an excuse to stop crying, but Jingyao wouldn't offer any. Their bedroom, located at one end of the upstairs level, had a glass door to the corridor, which blocked any noise from the room. They were free of embarrassment since however fierce their fights were, they wouldn't be heard.

The standoff between the two lasted for a while until Jingyao gradually calmed down and regained his indifferent attitude. He said coolly: "It's seven. I'll press the bell for breakfast."

He actually didn't have a set time for breakfast, the way he didn't have any set time for any activity in his daily life, so he had to press the bell every day to let the servants know when he needed it. This was a habit he had brought back from Paris. He had indeed been a poor student in Paris, but he had enjoyed his leisurely ways there. Maybe such laziness was in his blood as was sometimes the case with people from big decent families that had fallen into decline.

At the mention of breakfast, Hengfen remembered her daughter and her promise to have breakfast with the young couple. How could her daughter suffer from the same ill luck as her to have married Wei Feng who didn't stay at home at all? There was no denying that the Japanese invasion was the priority, but one couldn't simply disappear into thin air the second day after one's wedding and not come back for several days afterward! Was Jingyao's attempt to leave inspired by Wei Feng?

Mindful of this possibility, Hengfen found she hated this father-in-law and son-in-law more than the Japanese. But for her daughter's sake, she had to save the face of her son-in-law. With these thoughts, she gradually stopped crying. Jingyao checked his watch and pressed the bell.

Ah Sheng, the maid in her usual white apron, came into the room with a tray in her hands. She put the tea-set on the table with a marble top and a hardwood frame at the end of the chaise longue. It was delicate Wedgewood chinaware made in England. Ah Sheng, sensing the seriousness in the air, said smilingly: "Madam, there are freshly picked white champaca flowers. Would you like some when you comb your hair?"

Hengfen didn't answer. Ah Sheng looked at Jingyao leaning against the bed rails, with one leg crossed over the other. She didn't dare to say more and then swiftly excused herself.

Jingyao automatically switched his legs and kept staring at the ceiling. Hengfen, having remembered so many things she had to deal with, heaved a long sigh, and went to the bathroom. Their discussion about Jingyao's departure died as so many previous ones had, without the slightest rapprochement.

"Mum and dad, are you up?" Xueyan's clear, crisp voice came up from outside the door.

She opened the door. Her slender figure drifted in. She was wearing a new green silk *qipao*. The colour was a combination of three shades of green - light, emerald and dark. Her face was shining with the lustre of a fresh morning.

She glided to the bedside and complained sweetly to her father: "How can you still stay in bed? The tea is all set." She turned to the small table and took the teapot to pour two cups of tea.

"Where is mum?" She didn't wait for an answer before walking to the bathroom. She opened the door to find Hengfen standing in front of the dark-green sink, lost in thought. There were traces of undried tears on Hengfen's face.

"Mum, have you been crying?" asked Xueyan. "Mum, don't cry!" She held her mother by the shoulder. She had known this sentence since she was very little.

Seeing Xueyan's young face in the mirror, Hengfen directed all her attention to her daughter's happiness. "Is Wei Feng up?"

"He got up a long time ago," replied Xueyan, dropping her head a little and smiling. She looked up at her mother and asked with concern: "Why were you crying? Did dad tell you again that he wants to leave?"

Hengfen nodded, covering her face in a towel.

"I hope you won't be upset if I tell you that Wei Feng said he will leave, too," Xueyan told her mother hesitantly, though she agreed with Wei Feng that he should leave and she wanted to leave with him. It didn't matter where they went as long as they were together. But if she left, too, her mother would be left alone. Looking at the towel, she didn't venture to tell her mother what she had on her mind just now.

The fact that Wei Feng was leaving was not unexpected by Hengfen. It would have surprised her if he wasn't. For the last 20-odd years, it had always been the three of them. If she could have kept the three of them together, it would have made her happy. A son-in-law was never a real son. But her daughter had to suffer the absence of her husband. Maybe the Chinese army could fight its way back? With all those thoughts swirling around in her mind, she hastily tidied herself up, and took Xueyan downstairs heading for the dining room, ignoring Jingyao who was taking his tea in silence.

"Dad, please come and join us," Xueyan asked apologetically. Because Wei Feng had risen early, the whole family's breakfast schedule had to be brought forward.

The dining room was located downstairs and connected with the reception room. The arched windows in the rooms all had colourful tinted glass, which used to be Hengfen's father's favourite. May had been here a couple of times and felt like she was in a chapel. Normally, Hengfen and the other two didn't have formal meals, so they usually used the smaller cosy waiting room instead. When Wei Feng was here, they had meals in the dining room. All the servants knew how it worked. The table had been laid with shining tableware. The fish-shaped chopstick rests and napkin rings were all cloisonné. On one corner of the table stood an engraved glass vase with a wide opening. It had fresh flowers Xueyan had picked from the garden. Wei Feng, standing by the table, was staring at the vase, lost in thought.

"Hello," Xueyan reminded Wei Feng of her mother's presence. Wei Feng went up to greet Hengfen. He looked exhausted, not like a happy newly wedded bridegroom.

"You've been back for several days, why haven't you recovered yet?" Hengfen asked. "Are the dishes not to your taste? I remember you mentioned that you liked the steamed silk-thread rolls from Tongheju Restaurant. I ordered some from them yesterday. Try them."

The three sat at the table. The servants waiting at the table immediately served them with glutinous rice porridge.

Wei Feng couldn't help asking: "Where is father?"

"He eats when he wants. For the last couple of days, he has been trying to keep up with your schedule. Did you visit the Meng family the day before yesterday?" Hengfen wanted to talk before the meal.

"Did Professor Meng suggest that you and Jingyao leave Beiping?" On seeing Wei Feng, she suddenly realized there was one more person whom she hated even more than her husband and her son-in-law.

Wei Feng found it hard to answer such a question, so he smiled: "I stayed and played with May and Kiddo while Uncle Fuzhi and father talked. I didn't know what they were talking about. Uncle Fuzhi left this morning. I think life in Beiping is going to be quite tough. I have been employed by Minglun University as a lecturer. Now the University has been moved to Changsha, I have to move with it, too. If I stay, I won't have a way to make a living and I can't live off you like this."

He involuntarily looked around as if he could see the footsteps of war hanging outside the door. How long could they linger on?

What was bothering Hengfen now was a completely different kind of concern. She had assumed that her son-in-law, a top graduate from Minglun University, and a young lecturer, would become a prestigious professor after studying abroad. What else would he be? The near future with the Yue family's wealth and Wei Feng's social status would be beyond being splendid and glorious! Besides, Wei Feng was so different from Jingyao. Jingyao was easygoing and lazy, while Wei Feng was rigorous and industrious; Jingyao was negligent, while Wei Feng was perceptive. He was precisely the one to restore the former glory of the Yue family. But then the war came! Things just changed overnight! Everything became so weird and strange. Her home, her world, was doomed to encounter enormous difficulties. But these two men - father and son – weren't trying to figure out how to take care of the family but only thinking about leaving! How could they shove all the responsibilities on her alone?

She grew silent, and then answered indignantly: "We are a family. How could you say you live off me? The whole family will depend on you!"

Wei Feng, having seen that the topic of leaving had already been raised, decided to take it further:

"This war has been the consequence of years of plotting. The Japanese won't be satisfied just to have seized North China, so China will surely launch a total resistance against Japanese aggression. Our nation is fed up with all these foreign bullies, so every Chinese is willing to fight back. It's just like the old saying 'an army burning with righteous indignation is bound to win'. But it would be naïve of us to think that we can await victory by just sitting comfortably at home. In my opinion, father should leave Beiping. Not to mention the responsibility of an adult man to his country, for father's own safety, he must leave!"

Wei Feng looked at Hengfen with deep sincerity. "Father has his reputation in cultural circles. It's very likely that the Japanese might force him to work for them."

He carefully avoided words like 'turncoat'.

Xueyan grabbed his hand in appreciation under the table, and looked at Hengfen with the same sincerity as her husband's: "Let's leave together, mum! All four of us!"

Hengfen's body recoiled at those words. She said: "What did you say? You are leaving, too?"

Xueyan answered hastily: "Not this time! Let dad and Wei

Feng leave first and see how things go. I'll wait with mum and we will go later."

"What shall we do with our home?"

"Mum, do you mean the house, the furniture, the garden? All these things belong to people, but people are not attached to them. Wherever we stay, as long as the four of us stick together, that's where our home will be!"

Looking at Xueyan, Hengfen shook her head slowly. How could her daughter have changed so much? She had been married for several days and now she and her son-in-law were speaking with one voice!

She didn't want to lose her temper in the presence of Wei Feng, so she said rather coldly: "It doesn't matter much to me wherever we go. But you'll be the first one who can't stand the hardships."

"I can! I can!" Xueyan answered like a spoiled child.

Hengfen's face was still buried in her porridge as she continued eating.

Alerted by Hengfen's reaction, Wei Feng said: "This isn't a decision that can be made just like that. We'd better talk it over with Granduncle Miao first."

He eyed Xueyan as if to warn her not to say any more. They finished their breakfast rather absent-mindedly each preoccupied with their own worries.

The big issue had been finally raised. For Wei Feng, this already counted as an achievement. Hengfen ignored them and went on her regular patrol around the house. The young couple went back to their bedroom hand in hand. Their bedroom was located at the other end of the second floor, with a very similar structure to Hengfen and Jingyao's bedroom. A small living room was attached to this bedroom with chic new rattan furniture, including two lounge chairs with adjustable chair backs, two short round-backed armchairs, one beside each lounge chair, and a small round table with calla lilies and carnations ordered by Xueyan from the flower shop. Two stylish blackwood chests of drawers, a wedding gift from Miao Donghui, were positioned against the wall. In the Ling residence, Wei Feng could only breathe freely in this small world of their bedroom. But the sight of the chests of drawers depressed him. Miao Donghui possessed some mysterious power which could pull his home in a different direction from where Wei Feng wanted it to go.

"Feng!" Once Xueyan was in the bedroom, she became brisk and light-footed. She went into the bedroom to have a look and then walked out, calling Wei Feng just by his given name 'Feng'. This one character, was an endless source of happiness for her. She wouldn't trade anything in the world for it.

"Xue!" Wei Feng couldn't help uttering the lovely name louder. Xueyan looked at him, pouting prettily. He held her silky arm and led her to one of the lounge chairs, while he himself sat in one of the short round-backed armchairs. The two of them just looked at each other in silence. Smiles lit up their two fresh faces radiant with youth. Wei Feng took up her hand and kissed it from the finger tips all the way up, not missing one inch. Xueyan, with eyes half closed, wanted so much to purr like a cat.

"I hate to tell you this, but I know I must," Wei Feng muttered, holding both of her hands to his lips. His wife's eyes, full of limitless trust, brought out his tender love and sense of guilt. His wife was like a clear crystal, with each nerve cell quivering with love for him. But he couldn't share all of his secrets with her. He had a cause greater than his love, his family, or his research, so sacred for him because it was vital to the happiness and progress of the whole Chinese nation.

"Are you leaving tomorrow?" Xueyan's bright eyes were filled with trust, understanding and gentle sadness.

What Wei Feng felt so sorry about was that he could only tell her when he would leave. "Not so quickly. I can stay for at least one week. But with things happening so fast, it's possible that I won't stay that long."

He pondered for a while and then continued: "I will come back to get you."

"When?" Xueyan smiled hopefully. When? He couldn't answer. He put those tender finger tips against his lips.

"Can I leave with you?" begged Xueyan. "I won't be a burden to you, and instead, I can take care of you. Don't you believe me?"

"I don't," teased Wei Feng. "You'll burn the rice. It won't taste good."

"I can't burn a whole pot of rice!" Xueyan said thoughtfully. "I'll eat the burnt part and leave you the good one." Her expression was so serious that it stirred a multitude of tender feelings in Wei Feng's heart, buoying them both up in a river of love.

There was a knock at the door. "Miss, Madam has asked you to come downstairs," Ah Sheng said from outside the door. Hearing no response, she continued: "Mrs Miao and several other ladies have arrived."

Xueyan didn't answer, her eyes gazing at Wei Feng until he let go of her hands, and then she answered slowly: "I'm on my way."

"What has this granduncle of yours been busy doing?" asked Wei Feng, tidying up Xueyan's earlocks.

"Their family has spent some time in the German hospital, too. He has been kind to us. I think he might be studying Buddhist scriptures every day." She suddenly kissed his cheek, more like a peck, and smiled: "Please excuse me for a while." With these words, she slipped away from him and out of the room.

This was the first time Wei Feng had been alone in the room. He had never really set eyes on the furniture either. Now he took his time pacing up and down the small living room and the bedroom, immersed in such unbridled bliss and abysmal distress, which both excited and unsettled him. He felt he didn't deserve Xueyan's sincerity and love because he couldn't reciprocate with his whole heart and soul. He couldn't even offer her an explanation. He felt he was betraying her when he had to keep his mouth shut about what had been keeping him busy, all those meetings late at night, secret recordings of broadcasts from Yan'an and delivery of those recordings to influential professors. He couldn't tell her that he was going to take a road of hardship and danger, and that he was not leaving for Changsha, but for the soviet area. How could he promise her happiness? He was not even sure how he could realise his promise that he would come back to get her.

Why did he marry Xueyan? Wei Feng looked back on the marriage which appeared to be so perfect. His eyes stopped on a small stand inlaid with mother-of-pearl carvings. A notebook with a washed-leather cover and a clasp was lying on it. Last night, Xueyan had mentioned this notebook to him.

Tilting her head a little with this notebook clasped to her chest, she smiled at him and said: "This is my soul." With these words, she thrust it into his arms.

"It now belongs to you."

"Your diaries?"

"My diaries."

The image of her holding this notebook, which was almost sacred, warmed his heart. He understood that she wanted him to read her diaries because she wanted to give each and every cell of herself to him, but sometimes the spoken word is not as convenient as the written word.

Wei Feng stood in front of the stand for a while before solemnly opening the notebook. On the first page was the title: 'My Rebirth'. It looked as though her diary entries began from the very first time she met Wei Feng a year ago. He hesitated for a while and turned the page. This page had a delicate embossed pattern. A note written on a slip of paper had been inserted onto the page:

'To my darling husband. Let this go with you and stay with you forever wherever you go.'

Xueyan knew she couldn't follow her husband and stay with him, so she was asking her diary to do these things for her. Wei Feng's hands trembled as he turned the next page.

July 12, 1936, Monday

It was a peculiar day today!

School was out for summer vacation two days ago. Dad had been saying we would stay in Fragrant Hills[3] for a couple of days, and today we finally made the trip a reality and went

---

[3] Fragrant Hills (香山 *xiang shan*) is a public garden at the foot of the western mountains in Haidian district in the northwestern part of Beijing. It consists of a natural pine-cypress forest, hills with maple trees, smoke trees and persimmon trees, as well as landscaped areas with traditional architecture and cultural relics. The *xiang* in the name refers to incense, not fragrance per se. This name derives from the name of the highest peak Xianglu Feng (香炉峰), a hill with two large rocks resembling bronze-cast incense burners at the top.

to the small house in the hills. I had planned to go to a movie with my classmate and pay a visit to Tantai Xuan today, and wanted to come here tomorrow. But mum and dad wanted to do it today. So, here we are.

Wei Feng was rather surprised to see Tantai Xuan's name popping up first this diary entry entitled 'Rebirth'.

It was much cooler here out of town. And it was so green! I like this type of green colour. But the loud noise of the cicadas was annoying. The nap time was rather long. Mum said it was confusingly long and she was talking about dad, of course. I ordered shaved ice. It was delivered from the Fragrant Hills Hotel.

Was she delaying? Was she afraid of writing down the most important moment? Why did she mention Tantai Xuan first, and then the shaved ice?

A giant cherry lay on the shaved ice. When I tried to enjoy the cherry, Professor Meng and his family arrived. It was not correct to say 'his family' because Earl was not present. Instead, Professor Meng was accompanied by one of his relatives. He was a handsome young graduate from the physics department of Minglun University.

His name was Wei Feng. I didn't know what his name Feng actually meant, but I felt as if he were enveloped in a halo, which lit up the whole room.

Wei Feng smiled: alright, I have come on stage identified as 'one of Professor Meng's relatives', and a handsome graduate.

As I stood up to greet them, I knocked over the shaved ice. The table was definitely out of my way! I hurried upstairs to change. May followed me. She was a smart girl. And sweet, too. She tried to share some interesting things with me about what happened in her school. I really wanted to listen to her, but I didn't hear her at all. The few dresses I packed didn't offer me many options. It was May who finally made the decision for me to take the slightly shiny pale-yellow dress, which looked very nice contrasted against the green of the surrounding trees.

He smiled at me. "I heard that Miss Ling is a student in the psychology department. Why did you choose psychology?"

Can I tell him that I have no idea why I chose psychology? For me, I didn't care much what I studied - it was all the same to me. I didn't want to waste my energy on any major, but a college graduate is a title which matters a lot for a young lady like me. "I like psychology," I answered.

He appeared to like the answer.

Wei Feng tried very hard to recall the same occasion. Yes, he remembered that pale-yellow dress, but he felt sorry that the person who wore the dress that day didn't make any impression on him.

They didn't stay long before saying that they would go back to Minglun University. Wei Feng mentioned that he would come back to Fragrant Hills two days later because he wanted somewhere quiet to write his dissertation. When he was asked where he would stay, he said he would rent somewhere at the foot of the hills. Mrs Meng said the place didn't provide meals for lodgers. I suddenly spoke to mum:

"Can we invite Mr Wei to stay with us? It's quite convenient here." Everyone looked quite surprised by my suggestion.

Mrs Meng spoke up first with her regular smile: "You have so many spare rooms you should provide some convenience for others."

I didn't hear what mum and dad said, but mum gave me a studied glance.

He hesitated to accept the offer at first and then looked at Professor Meng. Finally, he said he would like to come.

How lucky I am that I have come here today!

She should have gone a day later, so that she might have found someone other than me to make her happy.

July 15, 1936, Thursday

He came with lots of books and his halo. When he entered, the whole room lit up. The lush trees had dimmed the rooms.

Mum let him stay in the smaller room downstairs. He kept the door shut until meal time. He was polite and good-mannered, and had dad's absent-mindedness, too.

I had been reading an English novel entitled Little Women. I like the family's quiet and loving third daughter, Beth.

I invited him to swim in the enormous swimming pool at the Fragrant Hills Hotel, but he said he couldn't make it because he had to read. I went with my friends instead. It was a rather disappointing experience, though. It would have been too cold in the water, and too hot if one sat poolside. Then we decided to order cold drinks to enjoy in the passage. But the drinks tasted horrible.

What was he doing?

July 20, 1936, Monday

After dinner, several friends came round to invite me to go for a walk. He went with us. They were talking about the newly released movie Mariners of the Sky. Those who had watched it all said how amazing it was. I didn't want to talk. He didn't talk, either. Then someone mentioned the students' demonstration with a coffin several months ago. He gave a long speech, saying the deceased, Guo Jing, was a student patriot, and that young people should keep themselves up-to-date with national affairs. Someone whispered in my ear, asking whether he was from the politics department. That was so funny.

What he said was all correct.

I have known him for eight days now. It is safe to say that he is brilliant and well developed in terms of his overall character. I know nothing about the formulas he has been dabbling with. He possesses a passion which radiates around him. He loves his country. Dad loves his country, too, but it seems dad has never worked out what he should do for his country. He is so beautiful! He is the most beautiful person in the world.

He is my ideal. He is my dream.

A smile crawled up at the corners of Wei Feng's mouth, a bitter smile. He remembered that scene because since then, his mind had fallen into a constant chaos of confusion and struggle. He thought Xueyan was adorable, but adorable in the sense that a flower or a bird was adorable. It never occurred to him that she might be his soul mate, who should be a comrade cherishing the same ideals as him, rather than a naïve young lady from a wealthy family.

He hinted to her that he was not suitable for her. He even exaggerated his shortcomings to put her off, but all his efforts were in vain. When the summer vacation came to an end, the two were already as close as two peas in a pod. The

Ling family, from the servants to Mr and Mrs Ling, had all treated him as a future member of the family, but he was still struggling within himself.

He turned to another page at random, which happened to have recorded his struggles.

August 30, 1936, Sunday

The new term is about to begin. We are going back to town tomorrow. Mum told him he could stay as long as he wants, but he declined and said he should have left a long time ago. I didn't get what he meant.

It is much cooler these days. This morning, before we headed for Shuangqing Villa, he reminded me to put on a coat. For the last two months, he has seldom looked me in the eye. I have been wondering whether he actually recognises me. It looks like he does.

He has been looking gloomy recently. I guess he is not as happy being with me as I am with him. I am not happy, indeed. I am delighted to be with him without knowing precisely why.

Numerous flowers with names I don't know lined the road along our route. He picked some flowers for me from time to time. Once, when he handed me a flower, he even looked me in the eye. Before he spoke, he heaved a long sigh:

"Have you heard this expression: that 'in the whole of North China, there's no room to put a writing desk?'"

Am I an utter fool who knows nothing about current affairs? He smiled. I wanted to ask him whether taking a walk with me had wasted time he could have spent better loving his country. But I didn't say anything because that would have been rude.

The steps leading to the front gate of the villa were most peculiar. At first, all you could see were steps. But as you kept climbing them, all of a sudden, the trees inside the gate, the pond under the trees, and the path around the pond all came into view.

He said slowly: "Life is like climbing steps. Many things just pop up like that unexpectedly. This is a very interesting gate."

I said: "The gate is quite beyond my expectation. But whether you want to enter or not is up to you."

But there was no other road to take. One could retrace one's steps.

"But time cannot go back," he said. Did he feel the same way about the fact that what had been imprinted on one's mind couldn't be wiped away?

Wei Feng covered up the diary, lost in the memory of his struggle last year. He had joined the Anti-Japanese Publicity Group in January, and later the Vanguard for the Liberation of the Chinese Nation; in February, he had joined the Communist Youth League, and was formally approved to be a CPC member in June.

He used to have the firm belief that no matter how many lives he had, there wouldn't be enough to dedicate to the great cause. But then Xueyan walked into his life. Her tender love for him was like a tight net trapping him from every side. He wanted to wriggle free. When the new term started, he decided not to go into town. He didn't go into town as he had decided, but couldn't stop calling her every single day. They once talked on the phone for 100 minutes! So, he had to go against his own better judgement. But he was not completely willing to give up his struggle and continued to torture Xueyan and himself.

When he opened the diary again, time had moved on to the snowy winter.

December 23, 1936, Wednesday

Today, he told me he didn't want to get married because people like him were not suitable for marriage. I didn't know how to respond. I think he was warming me that we should put an end to our relationship. I feel he has been hiding something from me, and he hasn't told me the whole truth. I wanted to ask him whether he meant he was not suitable for marriage, or I was not suitable to marry him. The words almost rolled off the tip of my tongue, but I swallowed them. How could I dare ask him about marriage?

We went to have dinner at the Kissling Restaurant. He looked serious, so serious that I became anxious. My tears dropped into my soup. I kept my head lower and lower, so he wouldn't notice. He did notice, but he didn't look at me. He kept fiddling with his knife and fork. A long while later, he asked what classes I was attending these days. He sounded like my dean! I wasn't going to many classes these days.

When we walked out of the Dong'an Mall, I asked him to come home with me and stay awhile, but he refused, saying he had other things to do, and left in the direction of Lantern-Fair Street. I suddenly noticed it was snowing. Snowflakes danced in the sky and drifted toward him. He picked up his pace. I was sitting in the car, looking at him. How much I wanted to go and ask him where he was going and if I could give him a ride, but I remained seated in the car. His figure slowly disappeared into the dancing snowflakes. There was nothing for it but for me to return home.

I felt lost. I felt so lonely! What should I tell mum? Will she look down on me?

The next paragraph was a blur. It was not hard to tell they were tear stains. If their relationship had ended there and then like that, Xueyan would have been in luck, thought Wei Feng. He had intended to end the relationship. Fuzhi and Aunt Bichu had also reminded him that if he continued like this, he would be toying with Xueyan's feelings, and his feelings as well.

He had made up his mind to do it thousands of times until that day he finally gave her a hint. But the consequence was only a few days without calls. He didn't expect he would miss Xueyan so desperately. How many smart ideas did that delicate, foolish head contain! How could she come to the conclusion that irises looked like funny masks? Why had he never thought of that? She had such strength in her slender body to back him up. Whenever he was troubled by physics or politics, her presence calmed him to such an extent that he could always work things out. Cutting off the connection with her was like cutting his water supply. He felt he had become demented.

Even Professor Zhuang, who was always slow in such things, was stunned by the change in him. Professor Zhuang had been telling him he should follow his heart. Now it seemed he had finally figured out where his heart wanted to go. Then Lao Shen, who was his immediate contact and leader in the organization, asked him to meet to talk over his personal relationship issues. Lao Shen pointed out that such a marriage would be helpful to build up connections with the upper class.

That made up his mind. But then he became unsettled again, afraid that Xueyan's parents might disapprove since he had never given any serious consideration about where the Ling couple stood about him marrying their only daughter. Now when he thought about it, he reckoned they might long have felt what an ill match he was for their daughter. But first he needed to get permission from Xueyan's parents. He remembered it was the second day of the New Year on the traditional Chinese lunar calendar when he visited the Lings. The reception hall was crowded with guests. He located Jingyao among the crowd and the two went to Jingyao's home office.

At first, Jingyao thought Wei Feng was going to share a story about the stage with him. It took Jingyao a while before he suddenly realised what was happening, and then he jumped out of his chair, patted Wei Feng on the shoulder, and kept saying "Good lad! Good lad!" Wei Feng said he should also ask for Hengfen's permission — he forgot how he had addressed Hengfen at the time. Jingyao promised him rather authoritatively that there would be no problem at all.

In a few days it would be spring. What a spring!

He turned the page over and froze.

December 25, 1936, Friday

It was Christmas Eve yesterday. Mum invited many guests, some of whom are my classmates. I stayed with them for a while and went back upstairs to my room as I knew they would enjoy themselves without my company. I couldn't bring myself to have a good time with them no matter how hard I tried because of Wei Feng's absence. A world without him is no world for me at all!

I stood on the balcony for a long time. The strong north wind was blowing relentlessly, spreading its extreme coldness over the cold half-moon and over the chilled land. I had been thinking a lot about things. Late that night, mum came to my room to check on me. She knew what was happening. She told me there is no shortage of nice men in this world, that I am young and still have lots more opportunities, better ones, and that I shouldn't be moaning over someone like you. I know I shouldn't worry my parents, so I decided to tell them my plan.

I am going to a nunnery. Mum was taken aback at my decision. She threw her arms tightly around me. Tears streamed down her cheeks. I hadn't expected that my decision would be such a blow to her. I am willing to go to a nunnery, just like the nuns in my college, dedicating their lives to God, and living a peaceful life. It's a simple life, and a happy one, too.

Wei Feng never knew she had ever had such a plan. His heart quivered. He kept reading.

Mum then said she was going to ask him to propose to me. I was not happy with that. I'd rather be a nun than ask him to propose. He had told me he didn't want to get married because what mattered most was his cause. I get it. But will I stand between him and his cause? Every cell in my body will burn to ashes for you even it is just for your smile!

Is there anyone who can help me? Lord? Where is my Lord?

Another blurred paragraph appeared. Wei Feng clasped the diary tight to his chest when a gentle hand was laid on his shoulder. He took the hand, put down the diary, and held the author in his arms.

"How am I worthy of such love?" Wei Feng muttered.

"I ran back to you. So, you have read it?" Xueyan again pouted lovingly.

Wei Feng gazed at his wife's tender, loving eyes, and sighed softly.

"I am not asking you to tell me anything in return," Xueyan's eyes became wet. That tender and beautiful pink flush spread all over her cheeks. She craved to know everything about her husband, but she also knew how important it was to respect him and his privacy.

"You are the dearest little wife!" Wei Feng wiped a tear from her pink cheek. "What are those wives downstairs up to?" He asked casually.

"They want to play mahjong. I told mum it was not a good idea, but she wouldn't listen. She's afraid of hurting people's feelings."

"Aren't you afraid of hurting people's feelings?"

"I'm only afraid of hurting your feelings."

He held his ingenuous little girl even tighter! How he wished that time would freeze at that moment!

Part 3

A couple of days later, Ling Jingyao was having tea alone in the small living room attached to their bedroom, one cup after another. He drank black tea with milk and honey. The black tea was just common Keemun black tea, but the honey was from a senior tenant and bee farmer working for the Ling family in Shanxi province, a connection of the former minister, which had nothing to do with the Yue family. The honey had a smooth but transparent consistency like pork fat. Jingyao didn't have a sweet tooth, but he liked to add some honey in his tea which, to some degree, almost represented his independence from the Yue family.

Several years ago, when he was closely associated with opera circles, he followed some opium addicts and became addicted himself. He was lucky to have quit in time. Holding his cup, he let his thoughts float in a world of fantasy. A stinging bitterness arose in his heart. How he wished he could take one puff of opium, now! Ah Sheng came to clean up the room. He was ashamed of himself for thinking such a thought and withdrew to sit on the balcony. Creeping euphorbia and morning glory crawled across the exquisite latticework trellis frames forming a lush green screen which sheltered him from the scorching August sun, but not from the tempests of time or from the billowing waves in his heart.

A servant came upstairs to inform Jingyao that Mr Miao was here, and madam was asking Miss Xueyan to come down to greet him, too. Jingyao remained seated, with no intention of moving from his chair. Later, the servant came into the room and told Jingyao madam was asking whether he was still in bed. Jingyao stared at the servant with narrowed eyebrows until the servant grew anxious that something abnormal might have grown on his face. A moment later, Jingyao started to make his way downstairs.

The reception hall was enormous. In the centre stood a complete set of exquisitely carved and ornamental blackwood furniture. At the west end was a set of Victorian-style sofas and a shiny grand piano, which was seldom played. All the guests were received at the east end, where the furniture was changed according to the season. Now the east end was replete with a complete set of rattan chairs and couches. Each item was a work of art.

On one of the works of art sat Miao Donghui, who was in a pale-white fine silk gown. With his fair skin and fine demeanour, he looked like a work of art, too. Hengfen, focusing keenly on Miao Donghui, and Xueyan, half-hearted, were sitting in their usual rattan chairs with oval backrests.

"It is said that our army had planned to burn the imperial palace during their retreat, but the counsellor at the American embassy intervened. I can still feel fear creep into my mind when I recall this." Miao Donghui acknowledged Jingyao's presence smilingly, and continued:

"It didn't take much time to restore order in Beijing. People are hardly aware anything has changed. So it looks like the

Japanese do know how to do things." When he noticed that Jingyao had walked slowly to the chair opposite him and sat down, he got up and took a seat by Jingyao. He talked to Jingyao confidentially:

"However life changes, we are the conquered in this city, who have to bow their heads to live their lives. It's justified if one wants to leave Beijing. But, personally, I think people like us would suffer two disadvantages if we leave, and enjoy three benefits if we stay."

Jingyao turned to look at that old but still handsome face, and said to himself: enlighten me!

"People like us all share one thing in common, that is, we have been used to being pampered. Let's not talk about how to lead a comfortable life, but survival is the most basic thing, isn't it? Let's focus on your case. You want to leave for Nanjing because of your patriotic enthusiasm for your country. But do you think those hundreds of thousands of citizens who stay in Beijing don't love their country?

Meng Fuzhi is leaving because his Minglun University has been moved. Your Yiren University hasn't, and it will remain functional in Beijing and will begin a new term in September. It's not easy to keep things functioning in Beijing at all. You should stay and make your contribution to it instead of running away on others' heels.

The above is the first disadvantage. I was told that Meng Fuzhi wanted to employ you. Do you know his political orientation? Do you know why he has not been promoted to be president of Minglun University? Because he is a leftist!"

After seeing how shocked his three listeners were by this revelation, Miao Donghui paused with a smile to give them time to get over the shock.

"Everyone knows this fact, although it is not that obvious. It's dangerous if you want to rely on him, who cannot guarantee you either a comfortable life or your personal safety. This is the other disadvantage. The most important among the three advantages has been repeated on many occasions, namely, that Beijing is the safest place. Such an ancient city of time-honoured culture should belong to all mankind."

"But they are trying to eliminate us all from mankind," said Jingyao indignantly.

"That's just propaganda," Miao Donghui smiled condescendingly, and said: "They have to unite people like us to sustain their rule."

What typical turncoat talk! Jingyao said to himself. But he also found that some of Miao's words did make sense. He didn't have time to dwell on it because Miao continued:

"The new mayor called me yesterday, saying he wanted me to be the honorary deputy mayor. That requires me to work for the Japanese and I won't do that! He said the title was just a title and he wanted me to do something substantial. Now that Beijing needs peace and stability, he wants me to help them stage an opera."

"Isn't it too early to stage an opera?" Jingyao sneered. "It takes time for people to get used to the new environment."

"It won't be long before things cool down. How about we make some preparations first? It is still not certain that it will be on," Hengfen suggested carefully, looking at her uncle, and then her husband.

"Forgetting the nation's warfare,
you spend your days in comfort and diversion.
Can you bear to order me about,

considering the hardships that I bear,
and ask me to accompany you
in drinking and merrymaking?"

After chanting some lyrics from the famous opera *The Peach Blossom Fan*, Miao Donghui sighed softly, paused, and said: "Such an enlivened atmosphere might do the Beiping city folk some good."

"I saw them build the courtesan's quarters,
saw them feast and make merry.
But I saw, too, how the building collapsed.
Broken dreams are the most real,
and sights once seen are hard to forget.
Though it may seem hard to believe,
the old dynasty has already fallen."

Though Jingyao didn't think much about the proposal to stage an opera, Miao's chanting reminded him of more opera lyrics.

His heart sank with bitter sadness. Clapping his hands to beat the rhythm, he slowly repeated the line *"sights once seen are hard to forget"*. A strange hunger crept into his heart. Like those who longed for delicious dishes, he craved opera, Beijing Opera, Kun Opera, or drama, anything. One look at the stage, and the grand curtains slowly being drawn apart, would induce in him a pure childlike joy. He hadn't been to the theatre for almost 50 days! How had he survived that?

"Since *'the old dynasty has already fallen'*, why should they ask us to stage an opera and *'spend the days in comfort and diversion'*"? Xueyan asked in a low voice.

Miao Donghui ignored Xueyan.

*"How could I shed my endless tears of blood and lament?
How could I shed my endless tears of blood and lament?"*

He was still chanting with his hand beating softly on the armrest of the chair.

"If we manage to stage an opera, we might be able to save several lives." He then lowered his voice: "Since the Japanese army took over the city, they have arrested many people, saying they are CPC members. It is said they will launch another round of large-scale arrests."

The three members of the Ling family didn't feel any connection with the CPC, but they all felt offended to varying degrees upon hearing about the forthcoming arrests.

"Who gives them the right to arrest people like that?" Xueyan said to herself.

Hengfen suddenly remembered something with a jolt: "The notices on the street informed us to burn books. If anything against the Japanese is discovered, the whole family will be incriminated. Uncle, do we need to do that, too?"

Miao Donghui answered immediately: "Yes, of course. My house is being check out, too. They may not come to search us, but we need to be prepared."

He suddenly became uneasy: "You should start checking. Jingyao, think about the opera. With your expertise, you'll be sure to make a success of it."

Before he left, he invited the Lings to dinner at his place next week, and said that if Wei Feng was home, he was invited as well.

Hengfen hurriedly said: "Wei Feng has gone out to run some errands, or he would come to greet you. He'll surely go with us next week."

Satisfied by her answer, Miao Donghui left. The Ling family went to see him off. When his car disappeared from sight, even Hengfen breathed a sigh of relief.

Jingyao was sent to his home office by Hengfen. His spacious home office had nice bookcases, set against the four walls, filled with books, and were equipped with beautiful glass doors, although the books were not arranged in any order. He was very keen to buy books but lazy about reading them. He loved novels by the famous French romantic writer Prosper Mérimée, and had finished reading his complete handsomely-bound collection. He was once determined to translate the collection into Chinese, but still hadn't wrapped up his translation of the novella *La Vénus D'Ille*[4] after two years.

Now he was required to sort these books out, deciding which ones should be saved, and which ones had to be burnt. This was a tougher job for him than asking Hercules to clean out that stable! What he wanted to do was to retreat into a corner and chant and enjoy *The Peach Blossom Fan*. Where was this book indeed? He opened a bookcase at random, took out *Thaïs*[5], sat on the sofa, and began to read. Why couldn't he understand those lines from a book he had read so many times?

Some low whispers reached his ears. He looked up from his book to find Xueyan and Wei Feng standing in front of him.

---

[4] "La Vénus d'Ille" is a short story by Prosper Mérimée written in 1835 and published in 1837. The story is about a statue of Venus that comes to life and kills the son of its owner, whom the statue believes to be its husband.

[5] *Thaïs*, published in 1890, is a novel by French writer Anatole France. It is about a monk who attempts to convert Thaïs, an Alexandrian libertine beauty, to Christianity, but discovers too late that he is obsessed with her beauty once the purity of her heart is revealed to him. The novel inspired Jules Massenet's famous opera of the same name.

"I think we should go and help father," Wei Feng said affectionately. "How about we deal with the foreign-language books later? The newspapers and magazines published before and after the Marco Polo bridge incident are a priority."

Xueyan was already digging into the messy piles of newspapers and magazines. She had become a yes-woman attached to her husband and willingly followed whatever he said with a sense of perfect happiness. It seemed she and her husband had grown to be one.

Jingyao just cracked a smile. Having put *Thaïs* back, he took up *Weimiao Sheng*, or *Subtle Voice*, the Beijing Buddhist Association monthly.

"This one should be no problem." He waved the magazine at Wei Feng, put it down, took up a book by Molière, and began to read it with a feeling of dreary deprivation.

He had translated Molière's comic verse the *Daredevil*, from the very first page to the end, but it had never been put on the stage. Realizing it was also a book in a foreign language, he hastily put it down, took up a magazine entitled *Dongfang (The Eastern Miscellany)*, and checked the pages casually to show he agreed with Wei Feng.

Wei Feng's mind was weighed down. Xueyan's brilliant face made his heart ache, and Jingyao's casual indifference worried him. Both struck notes of discord in such times. Both forebode bigger disasters.

"For humanity, justice, freedom and peace, we are willing to sacrifice, regardless of the cost!" Xueyan read aloud.

"This is the open letter by the professors at Beijing University with an appeal to fight against the Japanese. And this is the students' open telegram to the Nanjing government: 'stop negotiating, mobilize all walks of life, expel all the

Japanese armies stationed in China, protect our territory and take back our land. All the youth in North China are awaiting assignments!' There's more," she continued excitedly:

"An open telegram to Generalissimo Chiang Kai-shek from prestigious professors: 'Our nation is in crisis. We cannot sit still and await our doom!' It has Uncle Fuzhi's signature." She smiled at Wei Feng. "This one is an editorial: 'A critical moment has been reached. It is high time for the Chinese to prepare to die!'"

"I remember all of them! They were all published in the newspapers on the 28th ," said Wei Feng. "The army retreated on the 29th."

"Have those professors left already?" asked Jingyao, raising his head.

"I think they have all left. Will they be in danger if they are still here?"

"Mr Miao just mentioned that the Japanese will launch a large-scale search for CPC members. But they are aiming at supressing the anti-Japanese forces. I don't think only the CPC is resisting Japanese aggression," answered Jingyao.

"That's for sure," Wei Feng agreed calmly. "Did he mention any detailed arrangements?"

"I don't think he knows any. Even if he knows, he wouldn't mention anything to me." Jingyao turned back to his book.

"He said they might be heading for the Xishan (West Mountain) area in a couple of days," Xueyan added gently.

Wei Feng seemed not to have heard Xueyan and kept moving books. Hengfen came to check on their progress. She was sulking because the ones in charge of the kitchen had reported to her that no shrimps or fish could be found in the market today because they had all been given to the Japanese army as 'gifts'.

"See? You are being bullied and now you have to send gifts to the people who are bullying you. This is defeatist, slavish talk!" Jingyao cried out, tossing away *the Eastern Miscellany* he had been reading.

"Mother is here! That's wonderful," said Wei Feng. "Would you please ask the servants to burn all of these newspapers and magazines? Look, Xueyan has become a muddy girl."

A fine sweat oozing up on Xueyan's tender face added a rosy touch to it, far from being a 'muddy girl'. "I need to go upstairs for a while," he looked at Xueyan. The latter immediately left with him.

As they were going up the stairs, Wei Feng whispered to Xueyan: "I need to pay a visit to Mrs Zhuang."

"You said you would be staying at home these days."

"I will be back in no time." He took off his silver grey silk gown and hung it over his arm. After kissing Xueyan on her cheek, he went out of the room. Before he reached the stairs, he couldn't help going back to their room to find Xueyan rooted to the same spot. Upon seeing him, Xueyan threw herself into his arms and wept.

"I'll be back in no time," assured Wei Feng. "There! There! Don't cry..."

He went out of the house. As he walked across the garden, he looked up to discover Xueyan was looking at him with a smile squeezed in between tears. "Feng! Feng!" she cried out loud. That was quite unusual for her since she never raised her voice when she talked.

Her Feng waved at her, gesturing her to go into their room. Then he strode off.

Having walked past Zongbu Hutong (Lane), Wei Feng saw some jinrikishas on the street. The drivers were waiting for business in a very narrow shaded area, listlessly wiping their sweaty faces with towels. The sight reminded him it was almost noon. The small grocery store on the corner was still closed. As the only pedestrian on the street, the heat from the sun and the hot gazes of the drivers were all focused on him.

"Where are you heading, sir?"

"We are not going to the west part of the city, sir." One of the drivers had guessed Wei Feng might be from one of the universities in the western suburbs.

Wei Feng wanted to go to East Siqianliang Hutong. Normally it would have been much faster to take the tram, but the tram was still not working properly, so he decided he would take a jinrikisha to East No. 4 Hutong first. The jinrikisha passed along South Minor Street where they ran into a couple of policemen. The nine districts in Beijing with the 12 city gates and 3,600 *hutongs* were all exposed to the boisterous heat. Wei Feng was quite uneasy in the seat under the small bit of shade cast by the small sunshade made of light blue cotton cloth upon seeing the sweat streaming down the naked tanned back of the driver pulling the vehicle.

"Are you from Minglun University, sir?" The driver slowed down and tried to start a conversation. "I knew who you were as soon as I saw you. I used to shuttle to and fro between the city and the western suburbs."

How Wei Feng wished that he could have arrived at Old Sheng's place in a gallop! He also felt sorry for the driver. Although he was all for the elimination of such jobs, he took them so frequently for lack of better means of transportation.

"You don't have many passengers these days, do you?" he asked. "Do you earn enough to feed your family?"

"We work hand to mouth and day to day." The driver levelled the handle bars. "Our stomachs are smart and flexible, but I just hate to see my kids suffer from hunger. And this is just the beginning."

When the jinrikisha had almost reached East No. 4 Archway, Wei Feng saw a tram wobbling past, its iron wheels clunking and clanking on the iron rails, making a huge racket that could be heard miles away. "It would have been much faster if I had taken the tram from Dongdan," thought Wei Feng, and he asked the driver to pull over by the roadside. He took out several banknotes of one, two or five jiao denominations, jammed them all into the hands of the driver without counting them, and turned to leave.

"Thank you, sir!" The driver cried out loud behind him.

Wei Feng waved his hand at the driver and walked off. He felt the impulse to run, but he checked it. Instead, he walked even more slowly than usual. Most of the stores were open, but the street was deserted with few people around.

"Is Old Shen still at his place?" thought Wei Feng, secretly hoping Old Shen had already left. They had expected the arrests, but they hadn't expected them to happen so quickly. A sudden burst of marching footsteps came from behind him. He turned around to see a squad of armed Japanese soldiers going through the East No. 4 Archway heading northward on their regular noon patrol. These archways, which had undergone maintenance a few years back, basked gloriously under the sun. Now creeping out of that glory was a deadly viper.

A sudden dizziness seized Wei Feng. He dived into a *hutong*, turning back from time to time. The Japanese soldiers went past the exit of the *hutong* with the blades of their bayonets glinting in the sun. He had a good look around and figured out he was near the original site of Fulong temple.

"That explains why the jinrikishas are reluctant to take the main streets!" thought Wei Feng. He was aware he didn't know his way around the *hutongs*, so he exited the hutong onto the main street. When he arrived at Qianliang Hutong, the back of his gown was soaked through with sweat.

Old Shen's place was an ordinary traditional Beijing-style courtyard house. The front door was closed tight like others in those days. He pulled the cord on the old doorbell.

The door opened slightly after a long while. Half a wrinkled face appeared in the crack in the door. That was the old owner of the house. Though he recognized Wei Feng, his one eye still looked Wei Feng up and down through the crack before he handed Wei Feng a book and whispered: "Page 29." Then the door was closed again.

Clutching the book tight in his hand, he left. It was an old romance entitled *Hua Yue Hen* by Wei Zi'an6. Old Shen might have been on a watch list. He tried his best to walk as normally as possible. Looking around, he found the street was empty, and it didn't seem like he was being followed. With that realization, he gradually settled down.

There was a tiny public toilet beside the street. He walked in. Having made sure it was empty, he took out the book and turned to page 29. In the space at the top of the page were two words 'leave soon' in Old Shen's handwriting. Under the words was a circle with three arrows pointing in three

---

[6] *Hua Yue Hen*: (花月痕), literally meaning 'traces of the flowers and moon' was a romance written by Wei Xiuren (魏秀仁), 1818-1873, who styled himself Wei Zi'an (魏子安), in the late Qing dynasty. The novel focused on the love stories of two gifted young scholars and their wives who used to be prostitutes. It was the first novel in China to take prostitutes as its protagonists.

directions - A, B, and C. The words and drawing, though done lightly, pounded heavily on his heart. He tore out the page, carefully shredded the part with the writing and the drawing on, and tossed the pieces into the pit.

He didn't dare to linger there, so he followed Di'anmen Street to the north. Although he had no specific destination in mind, he knew for sure he couldn't head back home. When he reached Houmen bridge, he took a random turn westward and found he was by Shicha lake. Through the shroud of vapour on the surface, one could see several lotus leaves drooping languidly in the lake. The branches of the weeping willows along the bank were listless, too. Several pedestrians were visible, who were also enervated by the sun. He tried his best to slow down to allow himself more time to collect the thoughts churning around in his mind and sort things out.

He had been given a mission: to inform the three contacts, A, B, and C, that a recent meeting had been cancelled, and he had to leave Beijing now. The three contacts were in three different locations, one in the southern part of the city, and two in the western suburbs. If he went to inform the one in the southern part, he could then follow his plan and leave by train. What if he went to the western suburbs? How could he go there? Was Old Shen safe? How about his other comrades?

In the student movements he had participated in, he was recognised as a man of courage and prudence. But now, he was beside himself with fear. When he had made a stand against the government and the authorities, it was still an issue of different forces in China, and it was still an internal affair. However ruthless the struggles were, he had never been cut off from his party. Now he had to face the powerful and brutal Japanese aggressors all alone! Would Xueyan and her parents be spared? Maybe that old Mr Miao would help them get through it.

When he finally decided to take the train, he was already on the west dyke of Shicha lake. The summer bazaar along the dyke had ended more than a month ago, now there were only sporadic stands selling snacks and toys. The monkey man was automatically walking the monkey wearing a funny mask without his usual loud gong beating to enliven the show. He just led the monkey to a trunk, where the monkey took a new mask and put it on, then he let the monkey walk around in circles, then back to the trunk for another mask, and then walk around in circles again.

A boy of about seven or eight with dirt all over his face was holding a ragged hat to collect money.

"You are so generous!" Wei Feng heard someone say in English.

On hearing these words, he looked up to see a very slim young lady dropping a banknote into the hat. When he looked more carefully, he could see that it was Tantai Xuan with her American friend Paul standing beside her.

"Hello!" Xuan saw him out of the corner of her eye and immediately walked toward him in high spirits.

"How did you end up here? Where is Mrs Wei?" The way she addressed Xueyan as Mrs Wei sounded sarcastic. Wei Feng, failing to understand why she was being sarcastic, greeted Paul politely.

"We just came out for a walk. It's no fun back at home," Xuan complained, and then looked at Wei Feng, full of curiosity. "Really, what brings you here? Why aren't you going to visit us?"

"I just wanted to go for a walk," Wei Feng answered flatly. "Aren't you bothered by the heat?"

"I took a bet with Xuan," Paul said. "I told her there were some stands along the dyke, but she wouldn't believe me and wanted to check it out for herself. So, here we are."

"It seems there's not much to bet on." Xuan's eyes glanced over the handful of stands. The farmers' produce was no longer fresh in late August, but was still displayed on some stands. Without sparing a glance at the shelled lotus seeds and water chestnuts on shredded ice, Xuan just walked on, closely followed by Wei Feng. Ahead of them lay the famed restaurant on Shicha lake — Huixian Tang. All of a sudden, a Japanese flag with a burning red colour assaulted their eyes. Wei Feng staggered. Xuan and Paul stopped walking.

"So, these all belong to the Japanese now," sneered Xuan. Paul looked at the two Chinese with sympathy. Wei Feng had a strong urge to leap up, snatch the flag off, tear it to pieces, and trample all over it! How he wished to leave Beiping! Now!

Xuan looked away from the flag and turned to Wei Feng. She could feel waves churning around her.

"So, Mr Wei, how about coming over to our place?" Her tone was cheeky and jocular, but there was sincerity in her eyes. She had already figured out that Wei Feng needed some R&R (rest and recuperation).

"I can't go," thought Wei Feng, and he started to walk away determinedly from the restaurant. How conspicuous and dangerous for the three of them to stand there, staring at the flag?

Xuan and Paul joined him, and the three walked slowly toward the shade under the trees along the dyke. When he was sure there were no strangers around, Wei Feng stopped and asked: "Is Paul driving today?"

"Yes, he is," Xuan answered on Paul's behalf. "His car is parked in front of our house."

"Can I ask for a ride?"

"No problem," answered Paul, happily. "Where to?"

"Out of the city by Xizhimen city gate," answered Wei Feng frankly, weighing in his mind whether his decision was right or wrong.

Paul looked at him and asked: "Are you going to Minglun University?"

Wei Feng looked at Paul in return, but didn't answer.

"Let's go to the Summer Palace!" suggested Xuan cheerfully. She knew Wei Feng was interested in politics and actively involved in student movements, and she guessed he might be in trouble right now.

"I want to go to the Summer Palace," repeated Xuan.

Wei Feng's eyes widened in disbelief — one of the three contacts worked at the Summer Palace Estate Management Office, and Xuan wanted to go there! But he maintained a rather solemn silence, and refrained from revealing his intentions.

Paul cast an enquiring glance at him, and then said: "If both of you are interested in going, there is no reason why I should say no." As if by prior agreement, the three walked toward Chestnut Street on hearing Paul's words.

"Aren't you going in to say hello to Aunt Bichu?" Xuan asked as they approached the gate of No. 3 Chestnut Street.

Wei Feng shook his head. Xuan didn't go in either. Instead, she lept into the passenger seat of Paul's car parked in front of the gate.

"It's burning hot!" She bounced up when she sat down, but

had to sit down again because of the space, fanning herself frantically with her delicate small sandalwood folding fan.

When Paul and Wei Feng had taken their seats, Paul started his car. Wei Feng turned back and looked nostalgically at the gate of No. 3 inhabited by an old man, his uncle and aunt who he respected and loved, and the cousins he cared about so much. It was not his home, but his life had been intertwined with theirs in that place since his childhood. How could he leave all this behind so easily? His heart pounded in his chest. The image of Xueyan seeing him off at the balcony melted away in his eyes, blocking everything. Was it so easy for him to leave behind Xueyan, his beloved wife?

"This is too hard for me! This is too hard for me!" His heart moaned.

"What's that book?" Xuan asked Wei Feng, turning in her front seat as the car passed the back gate of Beihai lake.

'*Hua Yue Hen*," he replied, holding up the book to show it to her. "I've been trying to read the poems and verses in it." He couldn't find a better excuse.

"If you're not reading it now, you can put it in the compartment under the seat," said Paul as he was driving.

Wei Feng lifted up the seat next to him and put the book into the storage compartment.

"Well," continued Paul. "I think I'll never understand any of those poems and verses."

At the Xizhimen city gate, the car was not stopped to be inspected, so they went out of the city without any trouble. When the car passed Gaoliang bridge and headed for Hutai town, all three in the car heaved a sigh of relief.

"You were right to have decided to take Xizhimen city

gate," Paul said. "There are checkpoints in the train station. I think it started today."

"So, you two have figured out that I am leaving?" Wei Feng asked in a relaxed manner, smiling. "I am so lucky to have run into you."

"WE are the lucky ones," Xuan smiled. "Or we wouldn't have thought about paying a visit to the Summer Palace."

"We might be the first visitors after the Marco Polo bridge incident," Paul said in a measured voice.

There weren't many people or cars on the road. Besides, Paul was a very good driver. So it didn't take them long to arrive at the remains of the Old Summer Palace. From there, taking the road to the right, one could reach Minglun University; taking the one to the left, one could reach the Summer Palace. Paul slowed down, turned back and gave Wei Feng an enquiring look.

"I can't go back to the university," Wei Feng inclined his head slightly to the left, and said: "How pathetic it is that one has a home that one can't go back to!"

"I can only go as far as the Summer Palace. I can't go further west," Paul told Wei Feng frankly.

"That will do." Wei Feng had already conceived a plan. Once he had found the member of the National Liberation Vanguard for China, Wei Feng would inform him as he had been instructed. Then Wei Feng would climb over the West Mountain and head for the North Hebei anti-Japanese base area.

They bade farewell to one another in the curved courtyard known as the Fan house in the Summer Palace. Xuan took all the cash she had from her white leather handbag and pressed it into Wei Feng's hands. Wei Feng didn't try to decline the favour.

"See you," he said. "Please do me a favour and give Xueyan a phone call."

"What should I tell her?" Xuan asked seriously and sincerely.

"Tell her what you have seen today." Wei Feng felt something was trying to burst out of his body. When could he tell Xueyan what he was thinking without asking others to deliver the message? He didn't want to ask anyone else to deliver his message.

"I will," Xuan's voice turned hoarse. "I will go and pay her a visit."

"And please tell Uncle Fuzhi and Aunt Bichu I have left." Looking at Xuan, Wei Feng felt she was representing all of his relatives and friends, all of Beijing, which he was leaving behind. He found it hard to let go!

Paul offered Wei Feng his hand, and said solemnly: "Have a safe trip."

"Thank you. I will always remember your kind deed."

Paul gestured to Xuan that they should leave now, and they started heading toward the exit of the Fan house. They passed under the huge wisteria frame, and disappeared.

The green courtyard remained a picture of serenity without any moving creatures. Even the cicadas kept silent. Wei Feng's knees failed. He dropped onto the lawn involuntarily, and kissed the velvety earth with its fine needles of new grass. My love, my home, my laboratory, my Beiping, I will come back!

A Letter Which Was Never Delivered

Xue, My Darling Beloved Wife,
How I wish I could have delivered all the following words

to you all by myself! I have masses of such words, but I would prefer to meet you, sit beside you, hold you in my arms, and say these words to you. Even if I could do so, I still wouldn't be capable of expressing them all to you. I have been so focused on thinking how to write a letter that is worthy of you, my beloved wife, that it has grown to be such a terrible weight on my mind. But I am also aware that this is a letter which will never be able to be delivered to you.

We are a couple and are supposed to be a team. There is no doubt that we are the right halves for each other. But I can't give you all of me, and I am not entitled to do so. That's why I have to leave you behind, husbandless, and to cry alone! It is not my choice. Our time has chosen this path for me.

In the entry that recorded our first meeting in your diary, I appeared to be a graduate in the physics department devoting myself to my study and research. I was not so devoted to physics at all as I looked at the enemy's artillery that was aimed at us! When there was already no room for a desk, how could students focus on their study? I hadn't cared much about my desk for quite a long time, indeed. I had been working on how to fight against the enemy's guns and artillery instead. Now you know who I was then and who I am now, would you regret having ever met me, my beloved Xue?

I have managed to pass through the blockade and have arrived safely at a farmhouse, waiting to start the next leg of my journey. Please don't worry about me. I am safe. What happy news it is to know one is safe! How I wish you were here beside me! But all I can do is to write a letter to you, not on a piece of paper, but in my heart. A letter without written words.

It is a typical summer night in the northern countryside. When I sat down on the kang (a heatable adobe bed), my heart went back to where I had come from. Recollecting how far I have come, I felt my heart was filled with stirring heroic and tragic feelings. Have I taken myself too seriously? I have heard people say young college students are too romantic and not pragmatic enough.

The fall and winter of 1935 was a turning point for me, and for many of my generation, too. It was a tradition at Minglun that the first and second year students had military training included in their curriculum. One of the activities was horsemanship which was open to all students at Minglun. A couple of graduates, including me, signed up, and were trained together with the freshmen and sophomores to learn how to ride horses.

How wonderful it felt to ride a galloping horse! One cannot understand such an experience until one has learnt how to ride a horse. It's like you won't feel as free as a fish in water until you have learnt how to swim. We also learned how to jump on and off the horse when it is cantering. We were almost as good as the cavalry. Our coach was a captain surnamed 'Wang' from the 29th Army. He always mumbled to us: "You guys need to learn well. One day, it might come in handy. Who knows when!" It was supposed to be a three-month training session, but one week before the end of the session, Captain Wang declared rather suddenly that he wouldn't be coming again the next day.

All the trainees were taken by surprise and asked why, but Captain Wang only explained: "It was the university's decision to cancel the training. They have to cancel it." Later we figured out that such training was a violation of the He-Umezu Agreement, specifically to the non-hostility rule. Just imagine: we Chinese are deprived of the freedom to be Chinese on Chinese soil! We are not allowed to carry on our military training! We are not allowed to ride our horses!

Captain Wang and his horses left the campus via the west gate. The sound of hooves disappeared into the distance along the uneven road lined with poplar trees with endlessly falling leaves. The hooves sounded slow and reluctant. They couldn't come back on campus anymore. All of us trainees gathered around the gate to see them off. Several students had tears welling up in their eyes. The reason why I joined the military training in the first place was to learn how to ride a horse, but then when I looked at the horses in the distance, I realised my heart was not lingering on riding horses. I realised we Chinese were just like those horses, which were ridden and driven by human hands.

This realisation came rather late for those of us who grew up in rich families which maintained their normal life and study even in times of war. When the December 9th Movement[7] happened, I realised it more. I realised that tolerance of the Japanese encroachment would only bring extinction to China and the Chinese nation! I realised that patriotism was not a crime! We realised that the government should be reminded about these facts. We demanded to fight against the Japanese invasion!

You heard about the above-mentioned things a long time ago. Now I always see the image of you listening attentively to me, so gentle, so focused, with your unique sincere sentimentality. I am always moved by this image of you. What are you doing now? Are you sitting alone in the light? Are you leaning against the rail on the balcony looking at the moon? Whatever you are doing, my darling Xue, please, please, don't cry!

---

[7] December 9th Movement: commemorates what happened on 9 December 1935, when students from colleges, universities and middle schools in Beiping, with the support of the CPC, staged a revolt against the Japanese invasion. It was the first wide-scale nationalist student movement led by the CPC.

The parades on December 9ᵗʰ and 16ᵗʰ have awakened many Chinese. It's a rather peculiar phenomenon that the development of history has been marked by the student movement since China moved into the 20ᵗʰ century. For example, the May Fourth Movement[8] ushered in a new era of cultural movements. A year and a half later, after the December 9th Movement, began the total resistance against Japanese aggression. Who knows how many more student movements will promote the development of China's history?

In one's lifetime, loneliness is an inseparable part of one's life because people always have things in their spiritual world that they cannot share with others. Even when one is included in a collective, one may still feel unable to blend in wholeheartedly. Is it a problem for intellects like mine? In my 25 years, I have experienced two sacred moments of enlightenment. One happened during the parades.

So many people, with both youth and a bright future in prospect, gathered together and formed such an unparalleled strength. Dozens of us lined up, arm in arm, supported by lines behind us and supporting the lines in front of us. The armed military police were nothing in front of us! The bayonets were nothing in front of us! Loneliness failed to slip in between us. An enormous spiritual power filled the space between the earth and the sky. In the fields on a bleak winter's morning, we walked with measured footsteps, cracking the unmelted snow underfoot. We felt that each step was like consolation and redemption for our grieving, pathetic country!

---

[8] The May Fourth Movement was an intellectual revolution and socio-political reform that occurred in China between 1917 and 1921. It reached its peak on May 4ᵗʰ, 1919, hence its name, when thousands of students rallied in Beijing to protest against China's unfair treatment in the Treaty of Versailles. The movement aimed at national independence, individual emancipation, and social and cultural reconstruction.

On December 16th, we took so many detours until we reached Xibianmen city gate, one of the seven outlying city gates. I and a dozen other students took a railway sleeper, and used it to ram the iron gate. We chanted slogans to synchronise our movements. When the iron door gave in and was cracked open, that sacred sensation I felt reached its peak! Still holding the heavy weight of the sleeper, we burst into cheers! It felt like we had cracked open the iron gate of the Japanese rulers, and the iron gate locking up our nation's mind!

Why did these scenes occupy such a prominent place in my memory? It is because such pure emotions at these moments of enlightenment have become much fewer in specific struggles and confrontations, that my awareness has greatly improved. I first joined the Vanguard of the Liberation of the Chinese Nation, and was soon accepted as a formal member of the CPC. When I met you, I already no longer belonged to myself. That's why I can't give you all of myself.

The second moment when I felt that sacred sensation was when Professor Zhuang and I finished our experiment. It was rather fleeting because I was in such a hurry to organise activities to fight against the Japanese that I didn't have time to relish that moment of success. Physics now is so remote for me since, without independence, scientific development is impossible. What we need most now is our right of subsistence!

The CPC is capable of leading our nation to fight for our subsistence and prosperity. This is what I believe. I think I can explain it in detail to you later when we meet again. I had hoped my wife would also be a party member, like me, a comrade, which was rational enough. I have met many excellent female comrades, but it never occurred to me that my fate would be linked with any of them. But you, my darling

Xue, however hard I tried, I couldn't find a way out of your net of love. We are are a perfect fit for each other in life, but the reality is that we have to be torn apart and cut off communication with each other. My darling Xue, you won't blame me, like your mother would blame your father, will you? I still insist that father should leave Beiping. If I hadn't left in such a hurry, I would have tried my best to persuade him to leave.

I am so sorry, my beloved wife! I will write a few lines and try to get them posted, but I don't know when they will reach you.

The owner of the house has returned, bringing in our team leader. We work in teams. Now it's time for our meeting. I imagine you sitting beside me, taking part in my first meeting on my arrival in the base area.

CHAPTER IV

Part 1

Summer had come to an end without anyone noticing. The weather felt like a tank of cold and hot water that hadn't been well mixed together — the steaming heat was gradually penetrated by a separate coolness. The breeze from Shicha lake in the evening was cool, too; but the Japanese national flag hung so high in front of Huixiantang Restaurant that it was suffocating. It was hard to miss the big red circle from any direction around Shicha lake. That red spot tinged everything red with its redness, from the dark green mountains, the moon obscured behind the clouds and the crystal-clear lake water, to the short and tall houses nearby.

Most of the shops and stores had reopened. First-class theatres like Zhenguang and Cathay were open for business, too. Giant advertisements with words like 'tragic and romantic' characteristic of Hollywood movies were hung up. But nothing could escape the shadow of the big red circle. People trudged by it oppressed by the heavy load of its weight. From the outside, it looked like the habits of the city folk of Beiping were carrying on as usual; but from the inside, the inhabitants of Beiping felt crushed by a heavy weight, not their usual leisurely way of life.

On August 8th, Generalissimo Chiang Kai-shek declared in a message to the army:

"Our patience has reached its limit! There is no room left for further retreat! The whole nation will unite together and fight against the Japanese invaders to our last drop of blood!"

On August 13th the Second Battle of Shanghai broke out.

On August 14th, the Republic of China led by the KMT issued a declaration of war against Japan, sharply denouncing its invasion of China and claiming it was determined to realize its human right of self-defence. Many people in Beijing listened secretly to the broadcast from the Nanjing government and relayed the declaration to others.

Bichu relayed the message, too, copied it with a large writing brush and delivered the copy to her father, Grandpa Lü, who held the paper in his trembling hands and kept reading it again and again.

Tears rolled down along his whiskers, shining as he choked with sobs: "This is the turning point for the nation!"

He took out the seal with the four characters '*huan wo he shan*' (还我河山), meaning 'give us back our territory' (literally 'rivers and mountains'), which had been through several revisions already, and asked for more soap bars for Tantai Wei and Kiddo to practice on repeatedly with him until he was satisfied. He then carved the four characters onto two exquisite golden seal stones, a material which no one could recognize.

Later he was told that some senior citizens wanted to establish an army which they called the 'senior scouts' to go to the front and fight the Japanese army, so Grandpa Lü demanded that all the residents of No. 3 learn martial arts. He promoted himself to be the coach, and gathered everyone to practice every couple of days. Jiangchu and Bichu were privileged to be exempted from practice; Tantai Xuan was always absent, turning a completely deaf ear to her grandfather's orders; Earl never showed up; Lianxiu, Lü Guitang and Lü Xiangge dared not say no; only the three little kids sincerely enjoyed such an activity. Books, games and martial arts made their days more enjoyable. The threatening heat of summer was thus consumed having fun.

One early morning in mid-September was supposed to be the day when the new school term began, an achievement of the puppet Education Department's backbreaking efforts. Tantai Wei took his bicycle and went out of the black-painted gate of No. 3 Chestnut Street. Once he was on the street, he jumped onto his bike and sped along, leaving behind Liu Fengcai's urge "to be more careful". With his feet peddling swiftly, the bicycle rushed toward Di'anmen city gate. He had been stuck at home since Wei Feng's wedding in July. His heart was pounding with joy on seeing the approaching lush green scenery of Jingshan mountain, the shining pavilion standing on the mountain, and a few pedestrians on the familiar streets.

Like any other 13-year-old boy, Tantai Wei loved his school, his teachers, his classmates, his classroom and his playground. Everything sounded so much fun to him from the knowledge he learned in the classroom, to the games on the playground, from the myriad pet phrases of the teachers, to the bitter bickering among his classmates.

Usually he would pay several visits to his school during his summer vacation. But this one was special because he had stayed at home the whole time. Although he had Kiddo and May for company, they were different from the people he used to meet at school. Now his father had left, so had Uncle

Fuzhi. It felt different at home during his father's absence, but he was lucky that he still had his school. It was true that Beiping has been taken by the Japanese, but what were the Japanese going to do with me, Tantai Wei? He said to himself. He examined the pedestrians he met and found no Japanese. Having passed those racing rickshaws and rattling trams, he and his bicycle reached the Lantern Market Crossroad in no time. When he saw the school gate, he flew into it like a darting swallow.

Many students had arrived earlier. Everyone was happy and excited. "Hi! Tantai Wei!" Lots of students greeted him and he said "hi" and greeted many in return. But there was something peculiar mixed with the happiness and excitement which was particularly in evidence among the teachers. Their smiles seemed rather more forced and bitter. He ran into Zhuang Wuyin on the edge of the playground. Both were happy to see each other, but they just said "hi" and stood and talked, not like the girls who would laugh and jump on seeing each other.

Zhuang Wuyin was in ninth grade and Tantai Wei was in eighth grade. Both were in the school brass band. Besides, their parents were on good terms. That was why the two became very good friends.

"Is Meng Lingji staying at your home?" Zhuang Wuyin asked immediately after saying "hi".

Tantai Wei felt the question was inaccurate because his family and May's family were staying together; it wasn't the case that one family was staying at the other's home. Besides, my home was May's home and hers mine, thought Wei. But he didn't see the need to correct Wuyin, so he just answered: "They have been staying in town since they came from the

Euro-US Alumni Association."

He then added: "We have been having a very good time. But we were not allowed to leave home."

"It was no more fun in town than in Minglun," Wuyin pondered. "My father has left. He is now in Tianjin and isn't coming home. So the distance doesn't matter at all."

"My father has left, too. He left earlier than Uncle Fuzhi did," Tantai Wei said.

The two boys looked at each other with a kind of pride mixed with sympathy. Several more students gathered around them and said their fathers had left as well. All these fathers were going to fight in the war, of course. They walked alongside the playground, chatting happily, waiting for the opening ceremony. They waited for a long while but didn't see any sign of the ceremony starting.

"Classrooms! Go back to your classrooms!," the teachers of each class informed their students. "There is no opening ceremony. Each class will have a brief meeting in their classroom."

Disappointed, the students hurried toward their classrooms.

Tantai Wei's class teacher was Mrs Fang, a genial lady in her 40s. She kept silent for a long while even after everyone was seated, her eyes behind the thick lenses fixed on the teacher's table instead of glancing gently from one student's face to another as she used to. The air was so heavy that even the naughtiest and most daring students behaved themselves.

"The headmaster has informed us that we are not going to have an opening ceremony. He said what he wanted to say is what he has always said at every opening ceremony. He hopes you will all study hard since knowledge is always a valuable commodity. What I want to tell you is that although the school term has begun, you can't have new textbooks today as you used to because all the textbooks need to be revised."

This caused consternation among the students. "Why do our textbooks need to be revised?" They whispered the question to each other, but soon quietened down and focused their attention on their teacher.

"There will be changes in your curriculum, too, but I have still not been informed of the details. One thing is for sure. There will be a Japanese class included." Mrs Fang tried so hard to force these words out of her lungs that her face turned purple. She didn't dare raise her eyes to look at her students, and her arms were braced so tensely on the table instead of resting naturally by her side as they usually did. She didn't know what to say next. The class plunged into a deathly silence.

"Madam!" A student raised his hand. It was Tantai Wei. He stood up without waiting for his teacher's approval. The ivory colour on his face had turned red, and the delicate corners of his mouth were quivering.

"I won't learn Japanese. I'll learn English as I always do."

Mrs Fang was still figuring out how to respond to his request when another student stood up and said: "I won't learn Japanese, either."

Then several more stood up. Then the classroom echoed with the cry: "I won't learn Japanese!"

Mrs Fang hurriedly raised her hands and gestured to them to quieten down: "Please lower your voices! Please!"

She lowered her voice and said: "We have Japanese supervisors now! Oh heavens! Oh heavens!"

She took out her handkerchief and wiped the streams

of sweat off her brow. She tried to wipe her tears, but big teardrops smashed onto the table before she could reach for them. She hurried to wipe the table with her handkerchief instead.

"Order, please!" she said through her sobs. "We will get into trouble." Her students had no idea what trouble they would be in, but a weeping teacher was enough to arouse their sympathy and a strong sense of masculine responsibility. The class quietened down. A smaller boy sitting in the front began to cry.

"Oh! Please don't cry!" Mrs Fang kept muttering the student's name to sooth him. She tried several times to say more. When she failed, she turned back and faced the blackboard, stiffening her back and trying her best not to lose control of herself. The door opened. The headmaster entered together with the director of teaching affairs and a man in a light-coloured suit.

He must be the Japanese, the Japanese who had taken Beiping, who had compelled our fathers and brothers to leave the city, the Japanese who were hijacking our education system. Looking at that gentle face, Tantai Wei felt a surge of blood rush straight to his head. When the headmaster entered the classroom, he stood in front of Mrs Fang with her partly obscured behind him and began to talk in no time.

"This is Mr Miura Kenro. He is going to teach you Japanese. He is going to make friends with you, too."

He cleared his throat and continued: "There are not enough Japanese teachers now in Beiping and we are one of the first schools to have been chosen to start Japanese classes. Mr Miura suggested he would like to meet you as early as possible."

Upon these words, he felt he was at his wit's end to figure out what to say next, so he extended his hand to invite the Japanese man to say something. The Japanese man happily took one step forward and gave a speech in his thickly-accented Chinese to the effect that although Japan was a tiny country, it was powerful and determined to establish friendship and goodwill between the two countries. He was aware this school was one of the best middle schools in Beiping and that the students were all smart. He wanted all his young friends to learn Japanese well for the sake of better cooperation with his country and his fellow countrymen in the future. His attitude was not at all cocky, but sufficiently conveyed his deep conviction that his country was powerful. His proud eyes glanced directly at the students, like he already belonged here.

Dead silence strangled the air in the classroom. All the students bowed their heads. He stared at them for a while, turned around, and left the classroom, followed by the headmaster and the dean. The students kept their heads bowed for a long while because of their fathomless humiliation until the faint voice of Mrs Fang delivered the message: "You are dismissed!"

Most of the classes were dismissed earlier than usual. The happy boisterous atmosphere around the school gate early in the morning was replaced by a frustrated silence among the dismissed students. Some were still in high spirits because they hadn't had any visits by Japanese people to their classrooms and were still free of the immediate pressure from the presence of an actual Japanese person.

Tantai Wei ran into Zhuang Wuyin again. Both lowered their heads for fear of looking each other in the eye. Before Wuyin got onto his bike, he turned to Wei and said: "I had planned to go back with you to find May and Kiddo, but now I don't think I am in the mood anymore."

Wei nodded understandingly. They went their separate ways on their bikes.

When Wei arrived home, Liu Fengcai came out to take Wei's bike, and joked: "Did my young master pick a fight with his classmates?"

Wei ignored him and went directly back to his room. Tossing his school bag onto the bed, he sank into a chair and became lost in thought. Upon hearing the noise, Jiangchu came into Wei's room, with sheets of folded new brown paper to make book jackets for Wei's new textbooks. Seeing how annoyed Wei was, she took his hand and asked what had happened.

"We are going to learn Japanese. The new Japanese teacher came to our class and gave a speech!"

He took the sheets of brown paper from his mother and said: "We haven't got any textbooks. They need to be revised."

Jiangchu was dumbfounded at the news, then she said: "Whatever you are required to learn, you learn it well. It will come in handy someday. You kids just focus on your study, and nothing else."

"What is May doing? And the others?"

"Grandfather is coaching May and Kiddo at kung fu (Chinese martial arts); your sister is going with Earl to see whether Earl has been accepted by the college she has applied for. There will be notices." Jiangchu stroked Wei's head gently and reassured herself that her son was just upset and offered more comforting words.

Wei told her: "Thank you. Don't worry about me, mum.

Just leave me alone." He took out an abridged English version of *Robinson Crusoe* and began to read.

Without his grand hand-drawn map, his gigantic desk looked rather empty. The model airplane hanging in the room only had its left wing because he had never been in the mood to finish it for the last two months. He turned a couple of pages until he found out that his mother had left unnoticed, then he got up from his chair and circled around the model, mulling over in his mind whether he should finish it or not. But finally, he sat down again, read a few more pages, and turned to stare at the model.

A while later, he heard a rustling sound outside the door. Lifting a tiny corner of the pleated white muslin curtain, he found Kiddo's chubby body leaning against the door, peeping hard into the crack between the door and the frame. He tiptoed to the door and jerked it open all of a sudden. Kiddo jumped and looked up at him with a smile.

"Why aren't you coming in, my little Sherlock Holmes?" Wei asked Kiddo.

The latter answered: "I'm not sure what you are doing. Maybe you are still doing your homework." Kiddo walked in, saying: "May is still doing her recitals with grandfather. I have finished, so I came first."

He went directly to the big pile of blocks and started building things, while continuing to talk: "I'd like to go to school, too. It's so much fun."

Wei's smile evaporated. As a sensitive child, Kiddo immediately perceived the change and stopped talking. He didn't talk for a long while until he asked, rather slowly: "What happened at school, Cousin Wei? Did your teacher punish you? Our teachers at the kindergarten never scold us or punish us."

Wei picked up a block and added it to Kiddo's work, answering: "No, my teacher didn't blame me or punish me. My teacher is, she is, pitiful — you wouldn't understand."

Kiddo kept his head bowed and remained silent for another long while. He spoke without raising his head: "I understand. Because the Japanese are now in town, so daddy left, we can't go back to Square Teakettle, where Little Lion has been left behind."

Tears welled up in his big, innocent eyes. When he looked up at Wei, they tumbled off his face. Wei went to the bathroom. Before getting a towel for Kiddo, he rinsed his face with cold water first. He went out of the bathroom and asked Kiddo to wipe his face with the towel.

He thought for a moment and then asked: "Neither your father nor my father are at home. We are the men of the family and we can't cry. Which book are you reciting?"

Kiddo nodded obediently and answered proudly: "Grandfather asked me to recite *The Three Character Primer*, too, but each time I do less lines than May does."

"I met Zhuang Wuyin at school." The happiness of the occasion came back to mind. "He said he and Wucai will come to visit us."

"When will Brother Zhuang come?" May's sweet voice reached them before she did. She wore a short cotton-padded winter coat with a red-and-blue checked pattern and a white flannel blouse on top. A shiny tangle of something or other was hanging around her neck, her hand fidgeting with it, her face beaming with a smile.

"I'm done with my recitation. Grandfather is asking you to join the kung fu training."

Her joy infected Wei and Kiddo, and both smiled. Pushing the Japanese and Robinson Crusoe to the back of his mind, Wei grabbed Kiddo by the hand, and the three together flew into the garden in the main compound, chattering all the way about which Sunday they should invite the Zhuang kids to come over.

In the main courtyard, the lines were being formed. At the end of the steps stood the three kids with Kiddo in the middle. Behind the kids was the second line consisting of Grandpa Lü in the centre with Zhao Lianxiu on his left and Lü Guitang on his right.

When everyone was in position, Grandpa Lü looked around and asked: "Where is Xiangge? Why hasn't she arrived?"

"There's no need to wait for her." Lü Guitang took one step forward to go and look for Xiangge, but he stopped when he saw someone coming from the wisteria garden.

Xiangge ran through the gallery to the yard, smiling apologetically, and said: "I was transcribing and forgot the time. Sorry to keep you waiting."

Her long hair was folded up into neat braids. Her half-new short coat made of green machine-made cloth hugged her figure amking her look neat and well presented.

Grandpa Lü nodded at her approvingly. He didn't pay much attention to his granddaughters due to his view that men were superior to women, but he seldom failed to appreciate how capable Xiangge was, saying young as she was, she was more sensible and capable than most young ladies from big families. She was the best at learning kung fu from him, too.

"Spread your feet, a little wider than your shoulder

width," the old man began giving orders, and shouting out his instructions punctuated with pithy phrases that he had invented himself:

> *"Front, one, two, three.*
> *Give me back the sea.*
> *Back, one, two, three.*
> *Give me back the sea.*
> *Left, one, two, three, four, five, six and seven.*
> *Give me back my land and my men.*
> *Right, one, two, three, four, five, six and seven.*
> *Give me back my land and my men.*
> *Fight until our last breath,*
> *Our efforts will never cease!"*

The old man's trembling voice was resonant, echoing around the garden. The others repeated after him with muffled voices, while Jiangchu urged them to keep the noise down in case they were heard.

The old man learned how to box in Shaolin style when he was young. The Shaolin-style martial art dates back to 1600 AD at the end of the Ming dynasty. Its first principle for anyone who was going to learn this school of martial art was that "anyone who learns the martial art should aim at restoring China to its former glory", which represented young Grandpa Lü's intention exactly.

In later life, however busy he was, running hither and thither, he never forgot to practice it. The horse-stance exercise when one took three steps forward and three steps backward, had a special meaning, namely, that wherever one went, one would not forget China, the centre of the world.

The number seven also had its significance, covering seven parts of the body from one's fist, elbow, shoulder, hip, knee and foot to one's head from left to right. He taught the kids the simplified version and felt very happy that he could integrate the training of mind and body.

The kids worked hard at every movement without looking for an easy way out. After several training sessions, they were quite skilled with the movements. Today, Wei put even more heart into the practice. Each of his movements was completed with vehement intensity as if he was hitting an enemy. The more he practiced, the lighter his heart felt. May was an excellent trainee, too. Each of her jumps, dodges, squats or attacks looked agile and beautiful. Grandpa Lü watched them practice very attentively and praised them for their progress.

"Okay! May and Xiangge try a combat," he ordered, wondering how far they could go.

May, who just reached Xiangge's shoulder, looked delicate against Xiangge. She tugged her white flannel vest, and stood in an alert fashion. Xiangge had leaped one step back upon hearing Grandpa Lü's order. The two began. One attacked, and the other dodged. It was quite an impressive scene. Wei and Kiddo cheered them on. May and Xiangge made several turns and approached the lotus tank under the pomegranate tree.

They hadn't learnt many moves, so before long they had finished what they had learned. May felt exhausted after the 'combat' and was ready to perform the last move which marked the end of the set when she felt a pain in her wrist. She cleared her mind and found Xiangge had grabbed her wrist with a smile.

Who on earth could have such a smile! May was stunned at what she saw. It looked like Xiangge's smile had two layers.

On the top layer was her regular ingratiating, obsequious smile, but the layer beneath it was imbued with a rare ferocity, a brutal impulse intent on tearing to pieces everything within its sight. Besides, the training didn't include any movement like grabbing people by the wrist!

"Ah!" May cried out in terror.

Xiangge didn't let go of May's wrist. Instead, she tightened her grip and stared May in the eye as if to challenge her; "just show me what you've got!". The others looked on in bewilderment at what they were "fighting" for. Lianxiu came to her senses and ran to them.

She took Xiangge's hand and said: "You both have tender skin and bones. Just wrap it up, would you?"

"I was just horsing around with little Aunt May," said Xiangge, releasing her grip. The bottom smile dissipated speedily and utterly, leaving only the top layer of sweet smiles.

Not wanting to get Xiangge into trouble, May refused to show her wrist, which was left with a crimson weal from Xiangge's grip. She was rooted to the spot, lost in her bewilderment about how one could pull off such a smile. Wei and Kiddo ran to her and pushed her in front of their grandfather, who stroked her head lovingly and said girls shouldn't make any fancy moves when doing martial arts. Having spoken highly of Xiangge's solidity in practice, he dismissed his 'team', and took the two boys with him into the master compound for seal carving practice.

When Lianxiu took May's hand and was ready to leave, Xiangge stopped her. "Little Aunt, please stay. I'll show you how I can jump with the skipping rope."

May paused, searching for the bottom layer in Xiangge's

smile but found only the sweet charming layer between her rosy lips and neat white teeth.

Xiangge took a tall narrow wooden bench and her rope. She lept deftly up onto the bench and started skipping with the rope gently and gracefully. She did alternating skips with the tip of only one toe touching the bench at each skip. That she was able to skip at such an amazing speed on such a narrow, tall bench made it seem like she was airborne. She swung the rope so fast that the swings made a whooshing circle around her. It was a dazzling circle even if it was not a glaring white halo.

Upon seeing the impressive performance, May had long pushed that savage grin and the weal on her wrist to the back of her mind, and laughed happily, crying: "Let me have a try! Let me have a try!"

Amid the laughter, Jiangchu, Tantai Xuan and Earl entered. Xiangge lept to the ground and disappeared in no time with the bench and her skipping rope.

May snuggled up to her Aunt Jiangchu and listened to Xuan, who was describing how nervous she had been when she was reading her notice of acceptance to Yiren University, and how excited she had been when she had found Earl's formal name 'Meng Liji' on the list.

"Aunt Bichu!" She called toward the west garden. Bichu went out upon hearing Xuan, who was in high spirits on seeing her aunt. Her voice rang out. Earl stood by her side with a sullen, straight face as if she hadn't been the one to have been accepted by the college, or as if there had been a mistake about her acceptance.

She told Bichu blankly and shortly: "I have been accepted. Third place." And she went back to her room.

"Xuan looks much happier than Earl does," Bichu said to her elder sister Jiangchu. For the Meng family, a Catholic university like Yiren didn't count as a formal university. But Fuzhi told Earl she had to get registered, so she could be transferred to 'formal' universities later when they moved to the rear area. The fact that Earl didn't disrupt her parents' arrangements was something to be thankful for.

"I ran into Professor Ling," Xuan continued. "There's still no news from Wei Feng. He sent his greetings to Aunt Bichu, mum and grandpa."

She then laughed to herself first before saying: "Can you guess what students say about Professor Ling? Those in his French class have made a popular rhyme about him:

> *'Ling's always late;*
> *Ling doesn't know how to punctuate;*
> *but he stays around like our clock'."*

"How does he stay like a clock?" Jiangchu didn't get it.

Bichu thought for a while and said: "Maybe it's because of his casual attitude. He doesn't take anything seriously, and others might take it easy on him and not point out his faults. So, he stays."

"True! So true!" said Xuan. "That is something you can only see in a university like ours."

But Jingyao did take something seriously, which was the stage. Wei Feng's departure left the Ling residence in a gloomy mood. Xueyan was so deeply buried in her sorrow that she wouldn't eat, drink or sleep, and she faded as time went by. Hengfen was buried under piles upon piles of frustrations and concerns — she was worried about her daughter; she blamed Wei Feng for his sudden departure without a proper goodbye;

she was not satisfied with her husband. For Jingyao, Beiping was suffocating like an enormous airtight tank and his home was a miniature one.

Since his favourite stage drama was still not allowed to be performed, all he could do to quench his thirst was to invite a few friends from his Beijing Opera circle to come over to his place to talk about some plays, sing a few lines, and walk a few steps. So, for the last month, most of his associates were from this circle. Melodious music and songs from different roles could be heard from the reception hall.

People found it hard to open their mouths to sing at first, but once they started, then it all flowed naturally. Soon songs from different roles were lingering in the air. Some first-class performers had shut themselves indoors, but Jingyao's sincere invitations brought them out of their confinement to enjoy themselves with the others. Jingyao had said no to Miao Donghui's proposal to let him stage a performance, but in effect Jingyao was helping with the preparation.

Being surrounded by decent guests was part of Hengfen's upbringing and later became customary for her. Presented in front of crowds of guests, she had no time or room for her sorrows and frustrations. She would complain about her husband in front of the guests, and he would reply humorously, and the guests would tut good-humouredly at both of them. Those moments seemed to be the most harmonious and happy ones for her and Jingyao. That was why Hengfen never shut out any guests. How could a family be defined as a thriving one if the luxuriantly furnished reception hall was silent, without the pleasant, animated sounds of lots of people talking and laughing floating up into the air, the shiny grand piano standing alone free of the flurry of fragrances and dresses, the works of art from the rattan chairs to the antiques without anyone to appreciate and admire them? That would be a genuine waste! Jingyao derived pleasure from his friends in art circles while Hengfen derived hers from entertaining the artists and other guests. They enjoyed that momentary mutual peace amid music and songs.

The voluntary performance had a dignified name — Winter Charity, although how many of those who were suffering from hunger and cold would benefit remained unknown, but it did offer solid comfort to the consciences of those who participated in the performance. Somehow Jingyao managed to stage the performance in the best of spirits. One more surprise was that he even saw eye to eye with Miao Donghui on many things during the preparation. Everything went as planned. When the day of the performance was just around the corner, an argument between Jingyao and Miao Donghui finally cropped up.

The performance was scheduled for mid-October. A couple of days before the due date, someone mentioned in a seemingly casual manner that they had heard that Jingyao had been appointed as vice director of the preparation committee for the performance, and wondered whether this was a formal position. Jingyao was taken aback at the issue and vehemently denied the appointment, saying that what motivated him all along to prepare for the performance was his enthusiasm for Beijing Opera and his admiration for the excellent artists. How could he accept such a position without solid involvement? He confronted Miao Donghui on the phone the very second after the guests left.

Miao gave his answer after a long silence:

"Yes, the news is true, but it is still not final. The reason for appointing you to the position is that you are supported and admired by many because of your passion and devotion for the performing arts, even though you are not from such circles. You deserve it."

"No matter how much I am supported, I can't take the position. You know very well why not."

"I know, I know. This is not my decision to make. I'm telling you, several people really have tried hard to be included on the committee list…"

"No! Absolutely not me!" Jingyao declared resolutely. "Should I pay you a visit? Or would you please inform me whom I should visit? I'd like to visit them and ask them to take me off the list!"

Mr Miao comforted him in a conciliatory tone: "Alright, alright! You need to be more cautious. I'll try my best to get you off the list."

Seeing that his wife and daughter were standing beside him, listening attentively, he added: "That would be very gracious of you. I absolutely won't take the appointment!" Then he hung up.

Hengfen remonstrated with him without a second's delay: "See? I told you not to invite those people to perform at home, and you wouldn't listen! You have made yourself such a prominent target!"

"Who told me to listen to that dear Uncle Miao of yours, then?" Jingyao retorted sarcastically.

"Dad!" A smile lit up Xueyan's face, her eyes full of concern and admiration for her father. Seldom did she see Jingyao say anything with such strong conviction. Her smile was so bright that it clearly signified: "That's my dad!"

Since Wei Feng's departure, Xueyan had never exuded such a bright smile. Jingyao was dazzled by his daughter. His sense of guilt deprived him of the courage to look his daughter in the eye. He had lived a life in the clouds, drifting here and there, day after day. He was quite fanciful. He did wish that his daughter would have a down-to-earth attitude, free from unrealistic dreams. But it turned out that his daughter was even more fanciful than himself. How could she have indulged in such a gigantic fantasy as to marry Wei Feng? It was a joke! He and Hengfen had many disputes over what kind of responsibilities the two of them, as Xueyan's parents, had in such a marriage, but of course, no dispute was ever brought to any conclusion.

"The performance is going to be stunning. You two should go and have a look." He tried his best to sound convincing and forceful as if he had done something that was sure to make his womenfolk feel proud of him.

On hearing these words, the gleam on Xueyan's face dimmed and she again descended into a cold misery. Hengfen cast an accusing glance at Jingyao and slid an arm around Xueyan's waist, saying: "We don't have time for that!" The two went upstairs.

On the day of the performance, Hengfen was present. How could she miss such an exciting occasion? Besides, she didn't want to offend her Uncle Miao, and she had to keep an eye on Jingyao to see what he was up to, as well. She sat with Miao Donghui's second wife, while Miao, the mayor and the department directors sat with the distinguished Japanese guests. Jingyao picked a seat on the right of the third row, facing the stage entrance.

On his way to the theatre, he had been gripped by an uneasy excitement, like a primary school student playing truant and going to see a Beijing Opera, although the cast was barely satisfactory with the absence of any famous actors. He previewed the moves and gestures of the actors in his mind. Thinking that these graceful things would be presented on the stage in a live performance, he felt a feather tickling his throat. It was like an alcoholic seeing a bottle within reach but having to refrain from taking it because he didn't want to trouble his conscience.

He took his seat and bowed his head to avoid any possible exchange of pleasantries. He didn't let his guard down until he heard the orchestra start with their drums and gongs. He raised his head slowly to enjoy a good look around the theatre. How long had it been since his last visit to the theatre? Two huge banners made of red Chinese silk hung in two lines from the ceiling of the stage assaulted his eyes. The first one read 'Winter Charity Performance from All Circles in Beiping', and the second one read 'Warmly Welcome the Japanese Imperial Army's Arrival in Beiping'. All the enormous characters were cut out of gold fluorescent paper. The second banner pierced Jingyao's eyes and heart, making him dizzy.

He gathered his senses and looked around the theatre. The same old illuminated stage curtains, the much-stained booths with paint peeling off them, and the narrow hard wooden chairs that had all given him so much pleasure! Here! Right here, he had been elevated into the wonderland of art time and time again! How wonderful! But the same place now was so gloomy without its former glamour. For Jingyao, the rhythm of the orchestra was out of harmony with the view of the theatre, stinging his eyes and his ears so pungently that he wanted to escape. Ultimately, there was no escape for him. He dropped his head, but he raised his upper body from his seat, determined to have a good look at the Japanese, to see whether they were superhuman.

Right at that moment, the deputy commander of the Japanese army in Beiping walked in, accompanied by the mayor. The orchestra switched to a happy tune called *Blessed Arrival*. Several Chinese people clustered around the Japanese raised their hands high, applauding, signalling the audience to do the same, but few responded. The theatre was submerged in an awkward atmosphere, so awkward even the loud beats of drums and gongs couldn't dispel it.

The person sitting next to Jingyao was a red-faced old man. Seeing Jingyao rising to look at the Japanese, he said rather disapprovingly and coldly: "We have lost Shijiazhuang. The Japanese military barrage balloons have been seen for two days."

Looking at the old man, Jingyao retorted sourly: "Then why are you here at a theatre?" The old man was choked into silence, wondering who Jingyao might be, and didn't say anything. The page from Miao Donghui came to inform Jingyao that Miao would like to meet him in the lounge during the break. Jingyao just stared at the page and gave no response.

The first half of the performance was a renowned comedic romance in Beijing Opera entitled *The Mistake in the Field of Flowers*, and the second half comprised two famous Beijing Operas entitled *The Emperor's Drunken Concubine* and *An Interrupted Dream While Strolling in the Garden*, a selection from the famous Kun Opera *Peony Pavilion*. The three were chosen after several rounds of discussion and careful calculation between Jingyao and Miao Donghui. They were totally devoid of the slightest offence to the Japanese. The leading roles were all females. The one in *The Mistake in the Field of Flowers* was young, beautiful, funny and smart; the one in *The Emperor's Drunken Concubine* was dignified and graceful, while *An Interrupted Dream While Strolling in the Garden* was full of song, dance, poetry and splendid imagery. These roles would surely provide fine entertainment to the distinguished male audience, and serve as a perfect opportunity to give the Japanese a glimpse into the glorious Chinese artistic form! Jingyao and Miao Donghui saw to it that the interval occurred as a perfect window in time for closer contact and communication between hosts and guests.

The drums and gongs beat faster, and the big curtains slowly drew apart. Jingyao held his breath, ready to enter his dreamland when an old man coughed hard in his ears. The actors scurried on stage with their typical small, quick steps and started singing. Jingyao's eyes were filled with blurred, multicoloured figures, and his ears were filled with a nasty mixture of sharp, squeaky voices from the actors performing the female roles and the deafening coughs from the old man sitting next to him. He was sick at the pretence of the maid who tried to make a pair of large-sized women's shoes for her would-be master to wear. How could *The Mistake in the Field of Flowers* be as nasty as this? He was angry at himself. How he wished he could just skip to *An Interrupted Dream While Strolling in the Garden*:

> '*All the flowers bloomed in such bleakness.*
> *All sweetness sank with sadness.*
> *Who's the lucky one left to enjoy the scene?*'

The music and dance in such lyrics were the best catalyst for his dream. He wanted to chase after it, like everyone else.

But today, where had his ever-intoxicating dream in the field of art gone?

For the very first time, he imagined a wall between him and the stage. The loud laughter and talking from the Japanese seated in the centre seats reached his ears. Why didn't the wall block those noises out? He counted the seconds until finally the half-time break came. The audience all stood up. In the chaos, Jingyao took the side exit and he was out in the street.

"Master Ling!" The Miaos' servant hurried to stop him: "Where are you going? The lounge is this way."

"Just tell your master I have a headache and I must excuse myself," said Jingyao. Seeing the servant standing rooted to the spot, he added: "Please tell Mrs Ling the car is waiting for her." Several jinrikishas quickly approached, hustling for business. He tugged the collar of his coat up around his ears tightly and boarded one at random, leaving behind the theatre in a blaze of light.

There were few people on the street, so the jinrikisha raced along. He reached home in no time. The garden was in complete darkness; the whole building was dark and still except for the glimmering light from the window in Xueyan's room. The gatekeeper turned on the road lamps in the garden upon his arrival. He lept up the stairs and scurried toward Xueyan's room.

Xueyan sat quietly in front of the window, a book in her hand, her eyes and mind transported beyond the book into oblivion.

"My poor, poor daughter!" His heart ached at the sight. He stood by the door.

"Dad!" she raised her head and called gently. Her tone was mixed with some gratification and disappointment.

"My poor, poor daughter!" Jingyao mumbled. "My poor, poor daughter!" he went over and held that delicate head on his shoulder.

Part 2

The gate of No. 3 Chestnut Street remained closed the whole time. Its superficial peace belied the tumult and bitterness which prevailed daily behind the dignified gate of the compounds. Mid-October already heralded an autumn chill in the wind, prompting people to replace their jackets with light coats. In previous years, the compounds in the residence would have fired up their heaters with the arrival of the cold dew, the 17th term according to the 24 solar terms of the Chinese lunar calendar. But since coal was in short supply this year, only Grandpa Lü's compound had the heater on; other parts of the residence were cold and gloomy without any fire. The awnings in the main garden had still not been stowed away, blocking the wan sunlight which lingered only on the top of the giant ash tree and refused to filter down into the garden.

One afternoon, the lingering, reluctant sun suddenly brightened up, bathing the residence in a warm glow. Lü Guitang and Liu Fengcai ran through the gate in excitement, each holding a letter in their hand.

Liu Fengcai handed Jiangchu a letter and said: "Mr Tantai's letter. Professor Meng has written, too."

Lü Guitang ran on until he reached the west yard and cried: "A letter! A letter!"

Bichu took the letter but she couldn't tear it open with her trembling hands, so she went into the room for a pair of scissors.

When Lü Guitang excused himself, he added: "Mr Tantai's letter has also arrived."

It took Bichu a lot of effort to open the letter. She quickly scanned it to ascertain that her husband was safe, then she scrutinized the letter character by character. Fuzhi said the university was going to be moved from Changsha to Kunming, and that things might be settled next spring.

May and Kiddo gathered around Bichu's knees by her seat and stared at the back of the paper with their unblinking eyes wide open.

"Daddy's alright. Daddy's alright." She kept muttering these words and drying her tears. She read the laconic letter over and over again.

When Jiangchu came, they exchanged letters. Both letters were quite short and succinct. In Tantai Mian's letter, he wrote "since my arrival in Nanchang, I have been busy. But things are starting to fall into place and I think it won't be much longer before we are reunited", implying that he would make arrangements to fetch them when he was ready.

Fuzhi didn't mention anything about being reunited. Jiangchu immediately realized her advantage over her younger sister, and was almost overcome with joy on such a realization, but a heroic thought took her: "I have to wait until she's told to go. How can she manage everything here all by herself?"

Grandpa Lü was informed, so were their close friends. Earl and Xuan were told when they came home from school.

Both were happy about the letters. Jiangchu was just waiting to let her son Wei know the good news. Wei had caught a cold and had been off school for several days. It was his first day back at school after his cold. Jiangchu felt he had been gone for such a long time. As the clock struck 12, she finally heard Liu Fengcai's voice in the garden: "Mr Wei's home".

Jiangchu gave instructions for lunch to be served before taking the letter to Wei's room, who was sitting quietly in front of his desk, with a pile of new textbooks.

Hiding the letter, Jiangchu approached Wei and asked jubilantly: "So, you've got your new textbooks?"

Wei remained silent. Jiangchu picked up one of the books and opened it. Having noticed a sullen anger clouding over his handsome face, she asked: "What have the Japanese done this time?"

"Take a look at this history book." He turned to a page and handed it to Jiangchu.

As Jiangchu read, her head went into a spin. In her dizziness, she could only remember roughly what the page was about. It said that it was at the sincere invitation from the Chinese people that the Japanese army had travelled across the ocean to help the Chinese people establish Manchukuo, a land of promise.

"Future history textbooks are also required to be written that way: we have invited the Japanese imperial army to occupy Beiping!" said Wei, turning to another page.

"Look! The *Twenty-One Demands*[1] is said to be an emblem

---

[1] The Twenty-One Demands (二十一条 or *ershiyi tiao*) were a set of demands made during the First World War by the Empire of Japan. The Prime Minister Ōkuma Shigenobu sent the demands to the government of the Republic of China on 8 January 1915. The demands, if ratified, would have greatly extended Japan's control over Manchuria and consequently over the Chinese economy, and were strongly opposed by Great Britain and the United States.

of the friendship between China and Japan!"

Humiliation, anger and frustration at being unable to do anything about it were raging inside Jiangchu. She said to herself indignantly: "Yes! This is definitely the way to cultivate an enslaved younger generation!" How could her son have anything to do with 'slavery'? She felt a pang in her heart. She tried her best to force an affectionate smile at him: "Who would ever believe such nonsense? Every family will tell their children the truth that…"

Wei didn't wait for her to finish: "I don't want to go to school anymore." He enunciated each word with determination.

"That's not going to happen. Look, your dad's letter!" Jiangchu felt so lucky that she had held back the letter until this moment.

Wei took the letter and read it avidly, once, twice… again and again. Tantai Mian mentioned in his letter that Wei and his sister Xuan should study hard because only knowledge could make one a valuable person. He also implied they should be prudent about what they said and did. Wei immediately felt his father's strong love across the hundreds of miles between them, protecting and supporting him. He won't let me be enslaved, fooled and subjugated! The grown-ups won't let the Japanese off the hook so easily!

Wei straightened his back and asked: "Can I do home schooling, like May and Kiddo?"

"Why aren't you having lunch?" Xuan dashed into the room like a whirlwind.

She grabbed the book from Wei, read a few lines, and burst into loud laughter: "This should be the 'pages full of fantastic talk', though it's not *A Dream of Red Mansions*! It doesn't deserve to be taken seriously by you two!"

"If they were your textbooks, what would you do?" Wei snapped back at his sister.

"I don't have such textbooks," Xuan answered triumphantly, confident in her better luck. "Even if I did, I'd still have a way out."

"What is your way out?" Wei asked, smashing the book onto the floor.

"Don't! It will cause trouble!"

Jiangchu hurriedly picked up the book and said: "My dear boy, let it go. There are still many more days to come, and we'll leave Beijing one day." Jiangchu tried to calm down her son.

"When? Mum, when will we leave Beijing?" Wei threw himself into his mother's arms.

Jiangchu gently stroked his back, turning over the thought in her mind that she would rather die than let her son be enslaved by the conquerors.

After again discussing with his aunt Bichu the issue of going to school, Wei finally agreed to continue his schooling. Two weeks later, something occurred which made Wei officially quit school.

At Di'anmen city gate, there used to be two traffic police stations on the left and right gateways, facing the central gateway. One policeman manned both stations and moved freely between the two as needed to direct traffic. Later, to better manage the traffic, the police moved to stand in the central gateway, which was part of Di'anmen Avenue.

Not long ago, the policeman was replaced by Japanese sentries, monitoring the streets in all four directions in the old police station like vultures. Both Liu Fengcai and Lü Guitang had repeatedly urged Wei to be careful when he rode his bike past the sentries because they might be looking for any excuse to apprehend offenders.

That day, Wei rode to school as he always did. When he reached Di'anmen city gate, he noticed that several primary students were bowing on the street. He looked again and found they were actually bowing to the Japanese sentries at the traffic station. He didn't understand. Before he went up to ask, he thought about his mother and aunt's numerous instructions about keeping his distance from those Japanese soldiers, so he sped up and tried to go past the station as soon as possible.

"Student! Hey, you, student!" A sudden violent yell stopped Wei in his tracks.

The yell was followed by more violent cursing. It took him a while to realise the curses were aimed at him. The Japanese sentry stepped off his circular stand and stood in front of him after a couple of strides.

"Didn't you see this?" He pointed at the notice painted around the side of the circular stand. The notice was in big Chinese characters, saying: 'All students from middle school and primary school should bow to the imperial Japanese sentry on duty".

There was only one thing in Wei's mind amid such chaos: to escape from such morbid humiliation at any cost. The Japanese soldier standing in front of him had an officious look. He didn't look so ferocious or monstrous.

"You see now?" The sentry asked, waiting for Wei to bow. A handful of loitering Korean vagrants approached, waiting for any orders from the Japanese.

Looking at the Japanese sentry in front of him, and some Korean vagrants behind him and to his right, he threw a scornful smile at the Japanese, jerked his bike toward his left, jumped on it and peddled off like crazy. On seeing this, the students near the stand took their chance and scattered in all directions in perfect unison.

The cry "Down with Japanese Imperialism!" burst out behind Wei, lingering long in the air. Many passers-by were shocked. They pricked up their ears wanting to hear more.

The Japanese sentry ignored Wei on hearing the cry and hurried to check in the direction from which it had come. But there were only a couple of old men leaning on their walking sticks, deaf, and with hoarse voices. How could they have made such a loud cry?

The soldier went back to the students but found none. Later, a legend became popular among the residents nearby, saying how dim it was with the blinding sand and rolling pebbles in the air, so the one who cried must have disappeared into the ground. People also believed that the event was quickly hushed up because the superstitious Japanese soldiers believed that the person must have been helped by some divine intervention.

Wei took every *hutong* he came across. Several turns later, he looked back and found no one was pursuing him. When he reached the east gate of Beihai lake, he dropped his bike at the gate and entered the park, trying his best to loiter in a relaxed way. But he didn't admire any of the scenery. Few people were in the park. A man in a suit around his 50s smiled at Wei and asked: "Playing truant?" That question made Wei realize it was conspicuous for a teenager to be in a park during school hours. He then stopped walking alongside the lake and headed for the lanes among the rocks and fountains. These familiar rocks of different sizes offered him protection like old friends, covering him from strangers. He stood on the stone bridge for several seconds, picked up his pace, and went out of the park via the back gate. Having made sure the way was clear, he rapidly crossed the street, took the west entrance to the Chestnut Street residence and arrived home.

That's how Wei finally dropped out of school. His mother and aunt forbade anyone to mention this matter, but the servants figured it out by themselves. Liu Fengcai and Chef Sun even suspected it was Wei who had shouted "Down with Japanese imperialism", but they didn't dare ask for confirmation.

On the Chinese lunar calendar, it had shifted to the 19th point on the 24 solar terms, which is where 'winter begins'. The temperature dropped day by day, then it snowed even before the 20th point, the 'snows a bit' point had arrived. The fall of Shanghai brought more chill to people's hearts, piercing through their puffy cotton-padded coats. It was gloomy and quiet inside No. 3 Chestnut Street with all the residents staying in their own rooms. The practice of martial arts had stopped long ago. But the one who had changed most was Grandpa Lü.

The old man used to be generous to friends, compassionate to servants, and respectful to Lianxiu, but he had become so short-fused at people these days except for his grandchildren. The reason behind his change was as clear as the lice on a bald head, and everyone could understand but was concerned about the consequences.

The Tantai family physician, Dr Zheng, was sent for. He said the cause of Grandpa Lü's ailment was that it was all too much for him and people of his generation to take. All he could do was to provide treatment for physical pains such as headache, but not heartache. The medication was mainly tranquillizers, which made Grandpa Lü depressed. In a fit of rage, he dumped all the pills onto the floor. Jiangchu and Bichu talked over whether they should ask for another doctor or send their father to a hospital.

"But father will never agree to go to a hospital," Bichu said. "I don't think doctors can do anything for him, either. But we do need one in case something unusual happens."

"Dr Zheng is available anytime, but it seems father doesn't trust him much."

"Dr Zhang from Minglun's infirmary is in town, we can send for him. He knows father and the two can always talk about Buddhism instead of father's condition."

Jiangchu grunted upon hearing Bichu's suggestion: "Father always listens to Miss Bichu. I'm pretty sure any doctor Miss Bichu recommends will surely be better, too."

Bichu, as a woman, was well aware of that particular feminine trait that meant however well-bred and cultivated a lady she was, she would from time to time nag her husband as if all her own troubles would be reduced after pecking at her husband. Even at times when Jiangchu had no worries at all, she would nit-pick at Mian. Now since the country was facing a crisis, and Mian was so far away, she had no one to peck and nag other than to whine at her own sister.

So Bichu ignored her biting remarks and answered rather seriously: "So if you think this will work, I will call Dr Zhang and ask for an appointment."

Jiangchu swallowed the harsh words on the tip of her tongue upon seeing Bichu's determination to endure whatever she was going to unleash on her, and changed the topic: "Aunt Lianxiu mentioned that Lü Guitang wants to join the army, but he's worried about father. Of all those staying in the south compound, Lü Guitang is the most grateful."

"Yes, you are right. Lü Guitang can't leave. We need a male hand here to help manage the house. With regard to the others, I think everyone has their own worries and burdens. Is there anyone else who mentioned anything about leaving?"

"A few more just talked about it, I think. They said they understand how hard it is to support such a big family, but they have no other option than to stay. Things will get tougher. What am I supposed to do then?"

"Well, that would be like the old saying 'we'll cross that bridge when we get to it'. We just can't worry so much in advance," comforted Bichu.

"Mummy! Mummy!" May sped up the steps, lifted up the door curtain, and rushed in, shouting. Though she was young, she had always been calm and hardly ever raised her voice like that.

"Grandfather is mad at Lü Guitang!" The two sisters sprang to their feet and asked for more details.

May answered: "When I had finished reciting my part of *The Three Character Primer*, grandfather was very pleased. Then Lü Guitang came in, so grandfather asked him whether he had found the book grandfather had asked him to find. I don't know which book he wanted. Lü Guitang answered that he didn't know grandfather wanted the book today, so he hadn't hurried to find it. Then grandfather flew into a rage."

May's small face was pale because this was the first time she had seen her grandfather so mad. Jiangchu and Bichu asked May to stay, and both of them hurried to the master compound.

It was deadly quiet in the master compound. The sweetness of the clove incense was still lingering faintly in the rooms. It was quite different from previous times when the old man had been mad — he would stamp on the floor, and his shouts would tremble the rafters of the house. The two sisters entered. The old man ignored them and kept pacing up and down along his 'brick trail' faster than usual. Lü Guitang was kneeling on the floor in the corner of the hall. On seeing Jiangchu and Bichu, he lowered his upper body toward the floor in a praying position — and he kowtowed to the two sisters. They were both rather surprised when they found Lianxiu kneeling on the floor in front of her seat.

Bichu didn't hesitate and went directly to Lianxiu to help her up. Jiangchu gave Lianxiu a piercing stare, shouting to herself: "Why are you making the situation worse? Anyone who didn't know better might well think you had broken some family rules!"

"I am sorry, I really have no idea why his grandpa is so angry," Lianxiu responded to Bichu's enquiring look in a lost, low voice.

"Father, is this all because of a book? If Lü Guitang can't find it, we will help. You don't need to be so upset," Jiangchu said in a raised voice so her father could hear her.

Bichu went up to the old man and silently joined him, pacing by his side. She could feel the tumultuous anger in the old man's chest raging against the outside world, and against himself, too. She didn't speak until she had finished several rounds with the old man: "Father, would you please take a break? You have been pushing yourself too hard."

After a few more steps, the old man stopped, his body wobbling a bit. The three hurried to his aid, and helped seat him in the reclining chair. He heaved a long sigh. Bichu could tell his old eyes still blazed with anger.

He said: "I want to read Yan Zhitui's article *Pondering*

on the Suffering of Life. It can be found in Li Baiyao's *Book of Northern Qi*, or Zeng Guofan's *Collection of Chinese Classics*. How can you tell me you can't find it?"

"Fuzhi's book collection is in the west garden. I'll get it for you now." Bichu remembered a few lines from the article: "Millions of people were in prison; thousands upon thousands of books had been burnt in the firepit. The whole nation was lost in its scholarly disgrace." Her heart sank with those words, but her face wore a gentle smile which served as a tranquilizer, calming everyone in the room. Bichu took the opportunity and asked Lü Guitang to get up.

Jiangchu said to Lianxiu: "Aunt Lianxiu, you should know better. Why did you ask Lü Guitang to come to the master compound to make father so angry? Whether father can live a comfortable life or not is up to us. You could have asked Wei and Kiddo to come for seal carving, or invited someone to study Buddhism before father got so upset. Either course of action would have worked out better. If father needs to read any book, you come to us. If we fail to make any aspect of father's life easier, you should come to our help and cover for us."

Lianxiu's thin figure appeared even thinner in her oversized cinnamon cotton-padded winter gown with a satin surface. She kept silent with her head low, her eyes downcast. Jiangchu was obviously well aware that Lü Guitang had been summoned by Grandpa Lü, not by Lianxiu, but she didn't dare to challenge Jiangchu and tell her it wasn't her fault. Her years in the Lü family had taught her one survival principle for any social relationship crisis — to clam up.

"It's me who should be blamed," said Guitang who had already safely reached the door to the hall when he heard Jiangchu accusing Lianxiu.

He added: "My incapacity should be blamed. I have wasted the efforts he has spent on teaching me."

Jiangchu turned to him and sneered: "So, if you had cherished father's efforts, you wouldn't have failed to find a book! Father is so worried about the country that he wants to read. You always say you want to fight the Japanese. Now Beijing has fallen, you…" Mindful of the fact that a month had already passed since Mian's last letter, she felt a lump in her throat, and couldn't continue anymore.

Lü Guitang waited for a while and then raised his head to check with Bichu who indicated with her eyes that he was free to go, and then he excused himself.

Grandpa Lü's anger had subsided and he immediately felt guilty. What would an article do for him? Could it help him fight the Japanese? How could he behave like a child throwing huge temper tantrums now and then, making trouble for everyone? What terrible things had he said to Lianxiu? He couldn't remember.

He searched for Lianxiu and found her standing behind her two daughters. He raised one hand, and bent his index and middle fingers a little bit to summon her over. When people saw this gesture, they knew the tempest was over. There would be peace in the residence at least in the following week.

Jiangchu still wanted to say something, but Bichu tugged her sleeve to make her drop it.

"Mummy!" Kiddo popped his head in the door. Wei and Kiddo always played the role of 'comforter' at the end of any tempest. But Wei was unwilling to come and play his role today because he was afraid that grandfather might ask him about how school was. Kiddo answered his call of duty as usual. The little guy felt sorry for his grandfather and even somewhat looked down on the old man who was no longer the kind old gentleman he had known so well two months ago back at Square Teakettle. Oh! How he missed Square Teakettle!

Kiddo sat on a stool by the reclining chair, stroking the old man's freckled skinny hand with his fair chubby one, while Lianxiu sat on the other side. Receptive to the tranquillity being channelled by the two of them, the old man closed his eyes, and his breathing gradually slowed down and became even.

"What are we going to have for lunch?" He opened his eyes unexpectedly and asked with interest. He had never shown any interest in food before. Kiddo felt a groan in his stomach, too.

"Yellow croaker (fish) broth," retorted Lianxiu. They hadn't had such a nice dish for a long time. The old man nodded, and waited quietly for lunch. Jiangchu and Bichu excused themselves, taking Kiddo with them.

Several days later, a notice from Minglun University was sent to Bichu, informing her to collect the family's belongings. Li Lian also called, saying several wives of other professors had made their visits. It was still safe in the suburbs and the office he oversaw to take care of things after the university moved was going to be dismantled soon. If they planned a visit, it would be better if they could make it sooner rather than later. He also sincerely regretted that he couldn't send a car to pick them up and apologised for the inconvenience. Bichu told him he had done much more than he should have when he decided to stay behind and take care of things. The fears and worries he had been through were unimaginable and he shouldn't blame himself for such small inconveniences.

She consulted Jiangchu when she had finished the call. Jiangchu asked: "Haven't you moved all the important stuff in here? There's nothing else that's worth such trouble."

Bichu wanted to go back because she longed to have one more look at Square Teakettle, but she realised this was not a justifiable excuse, so she dropped the idea.

There was a power cut around Di'anmen city gate that night. The chilly northern wind roared even more fiercely in the darkness. Bichu was knitting a sweater for Fuzhi in the flickering candlelight. She would knit a few lines, pause to check the lines inside and out, smooth the dark-grey woollen yarn, knit a few more lines, and so on. She would spend some time knitting like that every night, which made her feel a few lines closer to home.

There was a knock at the door. "Aunt Bichu, it's me," said Lü Guitang, announcing his presence outside the door.

"A classmate of Mr Wei Feng is paying you a visit. He is now at the south compound."

"What's his name?"

"Li Yuming. He said he used to visit Square Teakettle. 'Yu' is the character for 'universe', and… "

Bichu asked Guitang to lead Li Yuming to the west garden without letting Guitang finish his explanation.

A moment later, Guitang brought in a young man. In the dim light, Bichu saw a short figure with a wide face. She was rather surprised to find that it was not Li Yuming. The young man bowed deeply to her and explained:

"I was sent by Mr Li Yuming. He asked me to send his regards and to deliver a letter to you. He specifically instructed that the letter must be delivered to you only. He is expecting your personal response, too." He then handed Bichu the letter, and watched her carefully as she opened it.

The letter read: "Dear Mrs Meng, under one brick at the northwest corner of the flowerbed by the cherry tree in the garden at Square Teakettle lies a parcel. Would you please burn it for me? I have a hunch that you would be so kind as to offer your help." It was signed: "Li Yuming, who once enjoyed broad bean pilaf at Square Teakettle". He wanted to confirm his identity with Bichu in case she was suspicious of the author of the letter.

Bichu was shocked to realise they had hid things at Square Teakettle. What was it? She used to think Li Yuming was just a fun-loving dandy, but now it turned out he was more like Wei Feng. See? Everyone loved his or her country, though in different ways. If the thing had to be burnt, it must be something to do with fighting against the Japanese. Bichu was overwhelmed by the realisation that she could actually do something real to fight the Japanese. How could she say no to such an opportunity?

She told the young man: "Please tell Mr Li I will do exactly what he has asked me to do."

The young man smiled and bowed again: "Thank you so much, Mrs Meng. I am also a student from Minglun. My surname is Liu. I was introduced by Professor Zhuang to work where Li Yuming works."

"Where is that?"

"Everyone is alright. I have to excuse myself now." The young man didn't answer her question or stay any longer.

Bichu asked Guitang to see the young man out and book two jinrikishas for a trip out of town the next day. Upon hearing these words, the young man bowed again, and then walked into the withering north wind.

Early next morning, Bichu went out and sat on one of the jinrikishas. Amah Zhao covered Bichu's knees with a fine fleece blanket and tucked the sides in carefully. The driver put down the door curtain made of padded cotton. There were three small pieces of glass serving as windows in the two sides and the door curtain, providing light and a view for the occupant. Guitang's driver tried to cover his knees with a cotton-padded coat, but Guitang declined, feeling it improper for a person of his rank, so the driver just put the coat by Guitang's feet.

When they reached Xizhimen city gate, it was already broad daylight. The lines of people waiting to go out of town were shuffling forward. All those who took jinrikishas had to get off and line up.

The driver whispered to Bichu: "Don't worry. I have been in and out of town several times already." He had told her the same thing a couple of times already.

Getting out of the jinrikisha, Bichu walked slowly with the other people in line. Since she had time on her hands, she looked up and down the towering city gate. It had no idea that it had already been occupied by a new master!

The lines passed the gates and entered the urn-shaped cleanly-weeded barbican. The bare ground in the barbican looked emptier and bleaker. The lines moved forward mechanically in choking silence. Soon, Bichu saw a line of Japanese soldiers in khaki uniform. The sight of them unsettled her nerves. Was anyone aware she was on a mission? She could hear her heart thumping in her chest. She said to herself as she walked on: "Why should I feel scared? What am I scared of?" She gradually calmed herself down.

The closer she came to the Japanese soldiers, the calmer she became. Several of those in front of her looked like common folk, and they were allowed to go after being asked a few questions.

The two immediately in front of her looked like a couple, who were interrogated for several minutes. They had been required to explain why the two of them were going together, as if they were less likely to come back if they both went together. Then the Japanese soldier who was questioning them waved them on, and the policeman standing by ordered the two of them to step out of the line and wait for further instructions.

When it was Bichu's turn, she calmly stepped forward and said she was going back to Minglun University to fetch some belongings. "They are with me," she added, pointing at Guitang and the two jinrikishas. The two Japanese soldiers talked among themselves, then the policeman said: "Helping hands." They were then permitted to go. Bichu and Guitang got into the jinrikishas again. All of them kept silent along the way as if they were afraid of being heard.

When they reached Hutai county, Bichu asked the driver to pull up the door-curtain. Few people were visible on the street, though most of the stores were open for business. It looked quiet and peaceful. Bichu asked the two drivers whether they needed any drinks for fear that there might be no water at all at Minglun University. So the two jinrikishas stopped in front of a small teahouse on the South Avenue for a cup of tea. A man came out to greet them.

When he got close to the jinrikishas, he cried out: "Isn't that Mrs Meng? Are you going back to the university?"

It took Bichu one more look to figure out that the man was Old Wang, who used to deliver their orders of vegetables from Ruyi Restaurant. He looked so much darker and thinner that Bichu didn't immediately recognise him..

"Please come in and take a break. Don't worry. It's still safe around here," said Old Wang. Bichu then got out of the jinrikisha and entered the teahouse. It was a very small room. The front half was for business. Bichu guessed the back half must be for beds.

"I can't believe my good luck seeing you today!" Old Wang was genuinely delighted to see Bichu. "How are the professors? Have they all left? You see, I have opened a teahouse to make a living."

"Has Ruyi Restaurant closed down?"

"At first, our boss tried to carry on. But then the Japanese became more and more intolerable, so he closed the restaurant and let all the employees go. I'm telling you the truth, many people lost their means of making a living when Minglun University was moved to Changsha. Life is getting tougher each day. I try my best to make ends meet. Luckily, I'm still surviving," continued Old Wang as he made the tea.

The two drivers took the tea over, squatted down under the eaves at the door, and enjoyed their tea.

Old Wang's words reminded her of Peddler Guangdong. He was right when he said he was lucky he was still alive. She sat for a while and handed two yuan to Old Wang, who repeated: "You'd better go to the South, too! Take the young master with you, so there is a life for us to look forward to!" He tried to put a smile on his skinny and swarthy face, but it turned out that he was on the verge of tears.

A group of Japanese soldiers was stationed at the university gate, accompanied by a Chinese. Bichu showed the soldier the notice and she was allowed to pass. The drivers took up their vehicles and were getting ready to leave when they were stopped by the Japanese soldiers, asking them to move things. The drivers argued that they should be paid for round trips, but their requests were ignored by the soldiers.

Bichu was worried for the two drivers' safety, so she argued on their behalf with the soldiers. The Chinese looked at her, stunned, and then whispered to her: "They will let them go. Please! Don't argue anymore!" Given no other option, Bichu had to get out and walk through the gate.

The Chinese scholar trees along the avenue comprised bare twigs devoid of leaves; the road was very clean, even the weeds along the shoulders of the road had been eradicated. The water in the creek near the banks was frozen over. The road, the trees and the ice shared one thing in common — bareness.

She kept walking along the avenue for a while and then switched to a lane. Having passed the primary school attached to the university, she climbed up a hill where the withered wild grass had tangled together, blocking the lane.

She ascended carefully to the top and saw Square Teakettle and Round Rice-Steamer with their closed doors and windows. The driveways in front of the two houses were buried deep beneath fallen leaves, bearing no trace of human activity. Guitang went in front of Bichu to make a pathway for her. She picked up her pace despite the vines in her way and quickly descended the hill.

The half-withered crown-daisy chrysanthemums were almost as tall as the gate; layers upon layers of fallen leaves buried half of the steps leading to the gate. The rare warm sunshine in early winter couldn't dispel the bleakness and desolation that had accumulated over the past few months.

The creaking of the door when it opened sounded so creepy in the deathly surrounding silence. Bichu stepped in gently. It was dark inside the house with all the blinds closed tight. The stuffy air reeked. Bichu tried to turn on the lights and was surprised to see the power had not been cut off. In the dingy light, Bichu saw the rooms exactly the way they had been after they had packed up and left. The left-over furniture piled up in one corner was sealed with a thick layer of dust and covered in spiders' webs.

Bichu brushed off a big mass of spiders' webs and headed directly for the garden without checking whether some spiders were still clinging to her hair. She was startled when something white flashed by with a whoosh at the door to the corridor. "Little Lion!", she called gently, realizing immediately it must be the cat. Little Lion snarled and growled threateningly, retreated to the cat flap on the door, turned around, leaped out, and disappeared.

Bichu opened the door and entered the garden. She would take care of the cat later. The flowerbed was obscured by the cherry tree and a tall, sturdy wall of holly. She passed several bushes of lilac and winter jasmine until she reached the northwestern corner described in Li Yuming's letter. She felt the bricks and found the loose one. She removed it with some effort and took out a small package of papers wrapped in water-proof paper. She pulled it out and hid it immediately under her coat without worrying about the dirt. Looking around, she saw no one else in the deserted garden. Heading to the small garden where the kitchen was located, she noticed that the bleeding heart flowers transplanted from President Qin's garden had all withered.

Bichu had barely reached the kitchen when the doorbell suddenly rang like crazy. The whole house rattled with the hollow echoes. Bichu was greatly disturbed by the sound. She hurried to strike a match to set fire to the package of paper. But the paper was too damp. She kept trying more matches but the paper just wouldn't burn. The doorbell rang again after a short pause. Since the paper had finally caught fire, Bichu instructed Guitang sternly: "Remember to burn it all up." And she went to answer the door.

It was Li Lian, who looked short and stout, as always. But the look on his face was dignified, free from his usual grinning. Bichu put her hands over her chest and calmed down upon seeing Li Lian. This Li Lian and his wife were quite unique. Mrs Li was a devoted follower of some secret society. Li Lian was somewhat affected by his wife's belief. He once went into elaborate details of anecdotes about karma. Minglun wanted to fire him because of this incident, but Fuzhi stepped in because of Li Lian's excellent research on the history of the Ming dynasty, so he kept his job at Minglun. It was quite beyond people's expectation when he was appointed to stay on campus and help with the management.

Failing to find anywhere to sit down, Li Lian kept standing and sighed: "I am glad I have managed to stay for so long without running into big trouble. We are leaving in a few more days. How I wish we could leave now for the rear area. How's Grandpu Lü?"

"He is very grumpy," Bichu smiled bitterly. "Who wouldn't be anyway?"

"His case is different," Li Lian answered sincerely. "He has devoted his whole life for his country, but now look what has happened! He has to witness the fall of his beloved country. How could an elderly gentleman like him survive such a blow? The Japanese on campus told me that the government is planning to move the capital from Nanjing to Chongqing."

With the fall of Shanghai, it wouldn't surprise anyone with any common sense if the government were to move the capital. But Bichu was still shocked and remained speechless for a long while at the news.

"It didn't work for the government to reign over the area to the east of the Yangtze river. They have to evacuate, and they have to keep moving! It is lucky for them that China has such a vast territory that provides them enough space to evacuate and hide."

Li Lian continued: "The Japanese want to fight a quick war and finish it in no time. How easy it is for them to say that!"

"When can we leave? Fuzhi didn't mention that in his letter."

"I think it has to be when things in Kunming are settled." He pondered for a while and then said: "When it is time for us to leave, would it be OK if my wife goes with you, so you could take care of each other?"

"That would be great," smiled Bichu.

Li Lian said: "The passes to leave campus are issued by the Japanese office in the basement at the library. They won't let us do it. Wounded soldiers stay on other floors. Dead ones are often seen being carried out of the building. The gymnasium is being used as horse stables. You can see them walking their horses on the playground. Where are the people you brought with you to help with the moving? And the jinrikishas?"

Bichu explained what had happened at the gate. Li Lian then said he would send people to find new ones for them in Hutai county, and sent Lü Guitang to go with Bichu to apply for the passes.

"Sometimes I feel I am like one of those people working

in the puppet army, or the puppet head of the community," he laughed self-deprecatingly and bade farewell.

Little Lion reappeared from nowhere, lept up at Bichu's feet, looked up at her and meowed sadly. The cat looked skinny with its tangled, long, dirty hair; its sunken face with a pointed jaw wore a docile expression rather than the vicious hiss a while before.

"You have nothing to eat, do you?" Bichu bent down and petted it.

"How have you survived? Come to town with us. Don't you run away this time." It then lingered around Bichu wherever she went, rubbing her legs or tripping her with its body, looking up and meowing at her from time to time.

Bichu went to the kitchen to make sure the package had been completely burnt. There was only a small pile of black ash left. She went to Fuzhi's home office, picked up more papers, and asked Guitang to burn them at the same site. She went to the bedroom, the most comfortable room at Square Teakettle, where she had spent the most beautiful years while Fuzhi made remarkable progress both in his research and his teaching career, and where she had given birth to May and Kiddo.

More than 10 years ago, Earl was even younger than Kiddo was now when they first moved in. Every piece of furniture, most of which had been moved into town, had been carefully hand-picked by her. The bedroom dressing table had been left behind because of its irregular shape which defied packing last time. It looked so dead, lying against the wall under a white cover. The oval-shaped mirror had witnessed all kinds of lovely stages of the three childrens' lives as they were growing up, and the passage of her youth, too.

"Will I have any chance to live here again?", she asked herself in the sinking gloominess, weighing up the uncertain future. She then felt relieved that she had burnt the package and finished her mission. Besides, she had had the opportunity to visit Square Teakettle once again. Since she had claimed that she had come to move things, she felt she had better move something. She thought about the dressing table. Maybe she would select more pieces of furniture to move together with the dressing table. But who would be in the mood to dress up in front of a mirror?

Having packed what she had picked up, she went out of Square Teakettle, heading for the library. Through the grove behind the house, she saw the 'Leaning Against the Clouds' apartments were surrounded by barbed wire preventing her from taking the shortcut via the lanes, so she walked along the wire fencing. She didn't see the entrance guarded by two Japanese soldiers until she reached the auditorium. Bichu's heart almost leaped out of her chest at the sight of the two soldiers. She slowed down to calm herself before she entered the library.

Fuzhi used to have a room where she conducted research in the basement at the library. Bichu took May and Kiddo when she paid a visit once. Sometimes when she came to borrow some books about history and literature, she would drop by that room, too. Who was occupying that room now? She entered the basement by the side door. Looking up, she saw the spiral steps leading to the ground floor. A memory rushed back into her heart.

Not very long ago, May and Kiddo ran so merrily up and down the steps. They would run to the drinking fountain in front of the door, take a mouthful of water, hold it, fly up the steps and then spit the water down from the top of the steps.

And they would laugh so hard that they bent themselves double. They earned a solemn reproach for such wild behaviour in a place as quiet and serious as a library. Bichu raised her head and looked around. What she saw was only gloominess.

A Japanese soldier at the end of the passageway stared at the two of them. She suddenly realized she shouldn't look around and went directly to the officer. Having understood what she was up to, the officer with a grim face issued her the passes immediately and tossed them to her. She was relieved that she didn't need to pick them up from the floor.

As they passed the gymn, they saw in the distance a team of soldiers dragging a man with lots of shouting and screaming. They tied the man to a flagpole by the playground. There were almost twenty of them, but they formed a neat line in seconds and took their turns to jump on the man, hitting him hard with a loud yell. The man's heart-breaking howls of pain reached far and wide, adding terror to the surrounding bleakness.

"Oh!" Bichu turned white and looked back at Lü Guitang. She turned back and made an effort to steady herself.

"It is lucky we already got the passes before the beating," Guitang thought to himself, and whispered to Bichu: "Aunt Bichu, don't be afraid! Don't!"

Why did the path to the gymn seem endless? The howls from the beaten man ripped through the refreshingly chilly air, piercing Bichu's eardrums. The pain lingered on and on.

Li Lian didn't find any jinrikishas, so Bichu had to sit on a large handcart loaded with furniture. She grabbed the fastening ropes made of dried rice plants and tried to get up onto the cart. She failed several times before she was able to sit down. Lü Guitang found an old bicycle and rode along behind.

The sky was grey as snow and sleet fell. The man and his son pulled the cart with great effort. Guitang occasionally gave a push from behind. The son was 13 or 14 – the same age as Wei. The ragged shoes he wore were too big to fit him. He had to stop to pull them up from time to time as he walked. The driver pointed out several spots to them where he said many people had been killed. When they passed Two Elms district, the father pointed at the damaged police station and said: "Ten people were killed there. Some were soldiers from our army; others were just people killed at random."

His words reminded Bichu of Peddler Guangdong and his red-and-white head. Her ears were still ringing with the loud yells from the Japanese soldiers on the playground. She tightened her grip on one leg of the dresser in case she fell.

"Many have run away over the Xishan (West mountain). But I have responsibilities and I can't run away with them," he said, heaving a low sigh.

"What do they do then?" Lü Guitang asked excitedly.

"It is said that they go to Miaofeng mountain first. When their numbers reach 50 or more, then they fight."

The child whose back was bent double, pulling the cart hard, looked back. Bichu saw a flash darting in his eyes against the twilight.

Though Lü Guitang had no idea where Miaofeng mountain was located, the thought there was some connection with that world filled him with hope. Bichu thought maybe Wei Feng and Li Yuming were active there, too. She didn't want to know what she had burnt today, but she knew she had done something related with fighting the Japanese. That gave her great comfort! These people, with such differing family background, way of life, and world outlook, were now focusing on the same cause, which somehow brought them a shared intimacy and harmony as they travelled along this gloomy path.

When they reached Xizhimen city gate, a quick search by the Japanese soldiers at the gateway pushed the image of Miaofeng mountain so far away that they all fell silent.

The sleet became harder as it got darker. Bichu covered her head with her coat, and straightened her back from time to time. The houses beside the road looked more indistinct. The back gate at Beihai lake park had long been closed. The whole avenue extended into blankness. Shicha lake was veiled in a shimmering grey, obscuring the entrance to Chestnut Street.

Home! There was home ahead!

PART 3

It had been snowing for several days in succession. Some wives of the professors teaching at Minglun had arranged a gathering at the Zhuangs', and Jiangchu had been invited, too. Mrs Zhuang also agreed to let her son Wuyin and her daughter Wucai pay a visit to Chestnut Street that day. Wei had been looking forward to the day ever since he had been told the news.

It had been snowing extremely hard that day. The snow was falling in great flakes like cotton-wool. May loved snow, saying that snow was smarter than rain. She would sit in the gallery, watching the falling snow for hours. She liked to watch snowflakes swirling down from the sky, thick and dense, but never in a hurry and always maintaining their gracefulness. She also loved to watch the snow sculpt a jade tree out of the bare twigs and paint the yard silvery white.

She hated to see those messy black footprints on the pure white snow, and that was why she loved to sweep snow to save it from being trampled underfoot. Bichu appreciated May's reaction and the reasons behind it; Amah Zhao was proud of May, saying: "That is exactly Miss May!" Meanwhile Earl and Xuan, who seldom saw eye to eye with each other, both jeered at May's foolishness.

Early in the morning, Amah Zhao had cleaned the snow in the garden, but now the brick lane across the garden was white again. Seeing the white, May picked up a broom and was ready to take the steps down to the garden when Tantai Wei popped out of the full-moon shaped door. His well-shaped figure, with that radiant face, was framed in the round door. With those snow-white twigs by his sides, it conjured up a perfect image. From Wei's viewpoint, May looked as pretty as a picture too in her long scarlet cotton-padded coat, standing in the gallery with carvings and icicles of different sizes hanging under the eaves, silhouetted against the reflection from the snow on the ground.

"That broom completely ruins the scene!" Wei laughed.

"Stop! Stay where you are!" May laughed, tossing Wei a broom.

"You sweep from your end!" she ordered.

The two swept from the two ends of the brick path and met each other in the middle in a short while. When they straightened up and saw each other, they burst into loud laughter. They laughed so hard that they had to hold their sides. They ran on to the gallery and brushed snow off each other's coats. Wei came from the front garden. His hair was shiny with a thin layer of snow.

"What are you laughing at?" Kiddo, dressed like a ball of cotton, ran out of the room.

May asked him to go back and put on his knitted cap. Kiddo followed her instruction and went out again with his red cap on his head.

Wei flipped the furry ball on Kiddo's cap and declared: "Listen up, Meng Lingji and Meng Heji! I've got a great idea!" May and Kiddo automatically straightened their backs and stood still, looking up at him.

"When Wuyin arrives, we'll go and play in the back garden," said Wei, lowering his voice. "I'll ask Lü Guitang to do us a favour and unlock the door for us."

"We can see the snow on Shicha lake from the second floor!" May's delicate face shone.

Wei put his index finger to his lips to hush her: "Mum and Aunt Bichu will be out soon. We are not going to tell them so they won't make a fuss."

"Mum is now at the master compound. And Sister Earl isn't bothered to know what we're doing," said May. The three went into the room as they talked.

The heater, which was almost as tall as May, was burning with the vent covered to stop the coal from burning too fast. The light-yellow embroidered winter inside door-curtains were all customarily hooked up to let the warm draught enter.

"How about going to skate on Shicha lake?" Kiddo proposed. He had tried skating once last winter.

"But no one is out skating since the Japanese fought their way here," said May.

"What does skating have to do with the Japanese?" Kiddo was not convinced. With his head cocked to one side, he said: "Maybe it's all because the Japanese have nowhere to skate!"

"They probably don't!" Wei agreed. They suddenly felt how ridiculous the Japanese were, and burst out laughing.

There were footsteps from the garden. Amah Zhao announced outside the door: "Young Master and Miss Zhuang have arrived." She lifted the curtain, and Wuyin and Wucai entered.

"Hi!" They greeted and smiled at one another. 'Hi' was their usual greeting. Amah Zhao helped the recently arrived guests take off their coats and hang them up.

The sister and brother both wore Western-style clothes — knee-length overcoats with fur collars. They looked energetic and neat in their coats. Both Wuyin and Wei looked handsome and elegant, but Wuyin appeared to be always lost in thought, while Wei looked gay and merry.

"How much you have grown!" Amah Zhao muttered several times. "Mrs Meng said you all need to drink something warm." Later she came in with five bowls of sweet gruel made of beef-fat and fried flour served with fried sesame on a tray bought from the shop famous for its gruel at the back gate of Shicha lake. The fried sesame floating on top infused the room with a pleasant, warm sweetness.

None of them was in the mood for any snacks. They were busy exchanging information since they had last seen one another. Wei and Wuyin talked about school. Wucai, who was very close to Kiddo, didn't attend school either. She was very interested in May and Kiddo's homework. Bichu and Jiangchu came to say goodbye to them, then they got into the car and left. The five went to Wei's room and played for a while before they furtively headed for the back garden.

All five kids were very excited since the back garden itself was a very exciting place. Besides, their disobedience of the adults' instructions became even more daring when it was snowing! The door at the end of the gallery was half open with some light filtering through. Wei pulled the door completely open, and the passageway brightened up immediately. He sprang out with a single stride, followed by Wuyin and the other kids. They hollered with joy.

The master courtyard, though enormous, was shaded by the surrounding buildings while the back garden, which was already lit up by the snow, welcomed it without any reservation, with its ground white and relaxed, the rockeries white and more grotesque, and the ash trees, which used to be festooned with green worms hanging all over them during the summer time, white and respectable. The rickety building covered with snow looked decent, its cornices and roof ridges, carved like animal backs, marked the silhouette of the building with soft white lines silhouetted against the skyline, which looked so close.

Wuyin and Wei started a snowball fight without wasting even one second. Wucai made a snowball and handed it to Kiddo, shouting: "Attack! Throw it at Wuyin!"

Wuyin suddenly became a one-man army fighting both Wei and Kiddo. Wuyin tried to find May to help him, but he couldn't find her anywhere.

"I'm up here!" May leaned out of the window on the second floor. "There's a beautiful view up here!"

Seeing Wuyin distracted by May, Wei took the chance to stuff a handful of snow down Wuyin's collar. Wucai and Kiddo clapped and laughed at Wuyin's misfortune. Wuyin jumped up and chased after Wei. The four of them shouted, laughed and had a great time.

Lü Guitang popped his head out of the window by the staircase and hushed them: "Shush! Shush!" All the kids in the garden turned a deaf ear to him, and went on with their snowball fighting.

May stood by the window facing the south where she could see a panoramic view of Shicha lake. Such a snow scene was rather simple when it was just a vast land of white with the dyke painting a beautiful dark-grey curve in the distance, but the Drum Tower and the Bell Tower appeared as different shades of black in the snowflakes whose rate of falling had slowed, like those dark shadows cast by some papercuts. May gasped in admiration. It was beautiful! It was so beautiful!

The snowball-fighting warriors became snowmen in no time as they became covered in snow. Lü Guitang went down into the garden and dragged Kiddo into the building first; soon the other three followed. The snow had almost stopped. Wucai looked to her west and spotted some figures on the frozen lake surface.

"There are people skating!" she cried.

Kiddo asked Lü Guitang to lift him up so he could look out of the window. When he confirmed Wucai's words, he clapped his hands and cried: "I want to go skating!"

The wish to go skating immediately quenched their desire to continue snowball fighting.

Wei said: "Lü Guitang, you take us skating. None of you mention a word to anyone when we come back. Understand?" he looked seriously at the other kids.

"Yes!" They all agreed... even Wuyin.

May and Kiddo had been confined to the residence for almost half a year; Wei hadn't even been allowed to go outside for three months. Thinking about this, Lü Guitang sighed: "How come Chinese can't go out as they wish in Beiping!" He thought for a second and then said skating was out of the question, but he said he might manage to take them for a walk. He said he would go first and check who those people were before he took them out. The children jumped with joy. Kiddo ran to Lü Guitang and held his legs in appreciation.

It didn't take Lü Guitang long to come back and tell them that there were about a dozen students on the lake, and he couldn't find any nasty people, but he said they had to go quietly and come back soon before the womenfolk noticed, otherwise they would all be in big trouble. Then the six of them went to the front garden in separate groups. Before they went out heading to the west, they played for a while in the doorway at the gate.

Though Chestnut Street was empty, the kids still didn't dare to make any noise as they ran along the snow-covered street. They quickly reached Shicha lake. How much closer and more real the dyke and the frozen lake surface looked to them once they were right in front of them, compared to how they looked when they had been watching from the windows in the building in the back garden! There were many mounds covered tightly with snow. May said those snowy mounds were beautiful, but Lü Guitang told her they were garbage piles which had not been removed in time before the snow came.

Wei and Wuyin ran to the frozen lake surface while Wucai and May walked along the dyke. Lü Guitang held Kiddo's hand tight and walked with him on the ice, too.

A young woman, who looked like a college student and a novice skater, was pushing an ice skating trainer to help her avoid falling on the ice. The trainer looked like a wooden crate, commonly used by novice skaters in the northern part of China. That girl, who was in a red coat, blue trousers and a white knitted cap, was skating close to Lü Guitang and Kiddo when she saw Kiddo looking up to talk to Lü Guitang. She waved to Kiddo, inviting him to sit on her trainer. She looked at Lü Guitang and Kiddo with a kind, gentle and sweet smile. Kiddo smiled back at her, involuntarily. He wanted to ride on that trainer and he looked up at Lü Guitang for approval.

"Come! Come," the girl spoke. Her voice was as gentle as her smile, but her tone sounded so strange. Lü Guitang suddenly realised she was Japanese! He felt as if he had been stung by some hideous bug and hurriedly walked off with Kiddo.

The Japanese woman must have wanted company, thought Lü Guitang. He wanted to take all the kids back home immediately, but he couldn't shout out their names loudly enough. Standing on the dyke, he tried to locate the other four kids. He noticed Wei and Wuyin were heading in the direction of the Japanese girl. The four of them ran toward him happily after a while.

"They are Japanese," Guitang whispered to them. They sank into a heavy silence.

Lü Guitang hurriedly took his small group back home. On the way back, the gentle look from the young Japanese woman popped into his mind. None of the womenfolk in the residence had ever given him such a look. It might have been because the Japanese woman hadn't learned how to recognize a Chinese person when she saw one. He smiled bitterly and then was ashamed at himself for having picked on the womenfolk in the residence. "Don't be afraid! Don't be afraid!" He tried his best to comfort Kiddo.

Once they were home, the children went on playing with their toys, forgetting completely about the Japanese. Lunch was held in the Mengs' west garden. Xuan didn't come, and Earl stayed in her room, so the five children were extremely satisfied to have the table to themselves. Chef Chai made dumplings stuffed with minced pork and chopped Chinese cabbage, and four other different dishes. The kids were starving at the sight of the dumplings and other dishes, especially Wei and Wuyin who gobbled up the dumplings with a single bite.

Kiddo looked at the two with admiration and envy, and wanted to copy their dynamic efficiency but ended up choking himself. Wucai patted him on the back, and May told him he had already had too much and should stop, but he wouldn't listen.

Later he stopped eating and stood on his chair to sing loudly. "Knock! Knock! Knock! Who's there? It's Mr Merry. Hi Mr Merry! The door is open. Please come in! How are you? I'm very well, and you? I'm very well. Everybody is very well. All are very merry and well. Ha ha ha ha ha ha ha ha ha!"

The five of them laughed so hard.

A few days ago, Wei and May finished a popular work of fiction, Xue Dingshan's *Journey to the West*, written in the Qing dynasty, and Wuyin and Wucai finished *Robin Hood*. They mixed the plots from the two books together and retold the stories in their own way, thus the heroine, Fan Lihua, the Pear Blossom from Xue Dingshan's *Journey to the West*, married Robin Hood, while the hero of the Xue Dingshan book had a ferocious fight with Richard I - the Lionheart - of England. Of course, they had no interest in studying the difference between Chinese and Western culture. They just let their imagination run wild while the whim lasted.

Amah Zhao came back and forced Kiddo to take a nap. Kiddo asked Wucai to stay with him, and May and Wucai then kept patting and lulling him, treating him like a doll. The two boys despised such childish behaviour and went back to Wei's room to study some geometry problems.

Later in the afternoon, Jiangchu and Bichu came back, and Wuyin and Wucai went home. They all felt they had had a great day. May followed Bichu around like Little Lion did, trying to find an opportunity to tell her mother about their adventures on Shicha lake that morning, but she never did. At dusk, Kiddo suddenly felt a sharp pain in his stomach.

"You may have caught cold. Mum will rub your tummy," Bichu said, sitting with Kiddo on the sofa.

"Did you have something indigestible?"

"He may have had too many dumplings," retorted May.

Bichu nodded, and asked the kitchen to make some 'three herbs tea' made by frying three herbs - dried Chinese hawthorn, distiller's yeast and barley malt - and then boiling the fried mixture in a slow cooker to get the extract. It was a traditional remedy for indigestion.

The materials were readymade, so the herb tea was brought to Kiddo in a short while. Bichu made Kiddo drink it, but he didn't get any better. Supper was ready, but only Earl was sitting at the table. Seeing the fried dumplings, she grew gloomy, complaining she was getting the leftovers. She didn't like the millet gruel either. She got up and went to her parents' bedroom to find Kiddo writhing in great agony in his mother's arms. May was standing there and was so worried that her eyes were brimming with tears. She busied herself by handing a hot towel or some hot water in turn.

"If you love Kiddo so much, you shouldn't have taken him out this morning!" sneered Earl. "You all had so much fun!" With these words, she went back to her apartment.

May had wanted to tell her mother about the adventure they had had in the morning. Now she didn't know what to say after her elder sister's reproving message. She dropped her head and stood in silence.

Bichu waited for a while and then asked gently: "Did Kiddo have anything indigestible?"

"No, he didn't!" May explained, hurriedly. "We had a snowball fight in the back garden, and then we went to Shicha lake for a walk."

Bichu's face sank: "Who went with you?"

"The five of us."

Amah Zhao brought a heated salt bag and tried to put it on Kiddo's stomach. Bichu took it and put it aside: "If it is acute appendicitis, then this won't be suitable. A gentle rub might help to drive out the cold."

"Let me rub for a while," Amah Zhao took Kiddo in her arms and rubbed his tender belly with her coarse hand. Kiddo felt better.

Jiangchu, Xuan and Wei all came. Lianxiu came, too. She gathered all her courage and said maybe they should go to the back garden to burn some paper money because the children might have run into some spirit and offended it. Lianxiu worshipped a wide range of things from the sacred Avalokiteśvara (a compassionate Buddhist bodhisattva) to the mysterious fox fairies. Jiangchu grunted, and the others remained silent.

But Amah Zhao spoke up in a clear confident voice: "I have taken care of Miss May and Master Kiddo. I have been working for the family for almost 20 years, so please allow me to say this. I think it won't do any harm to show our sincere apology, though I'm not sure whether it will do any good. If you approve, Madam, I'll go and pray in the back garden."

Bichu didn't answer. She felt Kiddo's burning hot forehead, and talked to Jiangchu. Both agreed they should go to the hospital now before the curfew started. They sent for Old Song to get the car ready, and asked Amah Zhao and Liu Fengcai to go together. Then they got everything ready and dressed Kiddo.

"Mum, I'll go with you," said Earl, who had just appeared.

Bichu was touched: "You stay at home and help Aunt Jiangchu."

She looked at May and said again: "May is too young to

sleep alone in this room. Why don't you come and sleep here tonight?"

Earl didn't say anything. Before they left, Bichu said to Lianxiu: "About the back garden thing, I'd ask you, Auntie, to do me a favour. It's better to believe in such powers. Who do you think is the proper person to do it? Please see to it."

There was a power cut that night. The few bustling lanterns they had were too weak to dispel the darkness, tension and gloom that fell on the residence.

They arrived at the emergency room of Beiping Union medical hospital without running into any checkpoints. Bichu registered with a renowned specialist. When they sat down in the waiting room, Kiddo was already in a coma. After examination, Kiddo was diagnosed with intussusception (an intestinal constriction causing severe abdominal pains) requiring immediate surgery.

"Please arrange for your best surgeon," Bichu asked vehemently. Surgical operations were charged according to the surgeon's expertise and experience. An expert surgeon would charge hundreds of yuan for one operation.

The young nurse in white uniform looked Bichu over to quickly appraise this lady's identity and her likely financial standing. It was soon settled. A famous surgeon called Dr Guan agreed to carry out the operation. After depositing 400 yuan, Kiddo was taken to the operating room to be prepared for surgery. Bichu felt slightly less pressurised. .

Suddenly, hurried footsteps reached Bichu. She looked up to find a crowd of people flooding into the spacious passageway of the hospital, men and women, some in civilian clothes and others in military uniform, mumbling to one another. Bichu realized they were Japanese. A Japanese officer with a pugnacious look was carrying a child of Kiddo's age. Bichu stood up and hurried across to the other side of the room, keeping her distance from the crowd. A long time later, a doctor and a nurse came to Bichu, smiling apologetically.

"I'm very sorry," the doctor sounded guilty as if he had made a mistake. "That Japanese child has intussusception, too, and needs to be operated on immediately. They want Dr Guan to be their surgeon. But according to our hospital rules, since you already paid first, Dr Guan should operate on your child now. But the Japanese want you to find a new surgeon…"

"Why? Is the Japanese child's life more valuable than that of my child?" Bichu couldn't help but cut him short. "Since we have finished all the procedures, the hospital should have declined their unreasonable request. And remember, yours is a Christian hospital."

"We don't advocate such things, but we are running out of options. Dr Kuang is as good as Dr Guan, but less well-known. Would you like…" the doctor tried his best to explain.

"Then ask the Japanese to take Dr Kuang. Wouldn't that be fine?" Bichu offered her advice. Hurried footsteps were heard again, then the Japanese came to Bichu and rounded on her. The pugnacious-looking man was leading, followed by a woman in a *kimono*. They were apparently the child's parents. The man's ugly face looked anxious and the woman's face was stained with tears.

"I don't understand Japanese, and I don't speak English," Bichu began before the man started. "If you have any issues, please talk to the hospital." On seeing the Japanese approach, Amah Zhao stood in front of Bichu. Liu Fengcai was nowhere to be seen. The Japanese man spoke Chinese, though not fluent, but intelligible.

"The Japanese children have to shoulder lots of responsibilities in the future. They are going to help you found a happy country. Our Japanese children need the best doctor!" He involuntarily fingered the holster fastened to his belt.

When the Japanese came into the hospital, Bichu had felt scared, to some degree. But now, her fear had been replaced by surging rage. So, our Chinese children should give your children the opportunity to live, so you can come to rule them and massacre them! Bichu almost shouted: "You and your Japanese children can go back to Japan! Go skating back in Japan! Go and get an intussusception back in Japan! Get your treatment back in Japan!"

But she couldn't bring herself to do it. She had to swallow her rage. She shook her head to show she couldn't understand the Japanese officer, implying his Chinese was not intelligible, and then she said rather slowly: "This hospital has very strict rules, and we always respect rules. Don't mention hospital rules."

She was yelling at herself inside: "Darn the rules! The Japanese fought their way into China! What right do they have to talk about rules?"

"And an American hospital!" A very tall doctor in white approached them from the other end of the passageway. He was the American surgeon, Dr Dale.

He looked at the Japanese and said seriously: "Dr Guan called me. I will operate on your child."

The Japanese didn't know who he was and remained silent. The doctor who had first come to explain to Bichu then explained to the Japanese that this American surgeon rarely agreed to operate on a patient, and his fees were even higher than Dr Guan's, implying that Dr Dale was the best of the best.

The nurse nodded at Bichu to follow her and then led her away from the Japanese to the treatment room. Bichu saw Kiddo lying on a stretcher.

"Mummy, I'm scared!", Kiddo told her weakly, opening his eyes and grabbing Bichu by the hand.

"Don't be afraid, Kiddo! You have never been afraid of needles or bitter medicines, have you? This won't be any worse than that." Bichu's voice was trembling.

The nurse comforted her: "The operation is a safe one. You don't need to worry. Dr Guan is already in the operating room. Don't worry."

The nurse waiting in the operating room came out to get the stretcher. Bichu walked alongside the stretcher, stroking Kiddo's hand: "My Kiddo is very brave. Daddy will know how brave you are even though he is far away. You will listen to the doctor, won't you?"

"Tell May to wait for me. We are going back to see those fireflies," Kiddo told Bichu, opening his eyes again.

"You can't see fireflies until summer comes. You will be well long before that," Bichu assured him, holding back her tears. Kiddo didn't say anything.

When they were in the operating room, he suddenly said loudly: "Mummy! I'm not afraid at all!" He let go of his mother's hand. He turned to look for his mother's face, but the stretcher had already moved on.

The two embossed glass doors to the operating room were closed. Bichu was in an emotional turmoil: she was pained, anxious and angry. She wanted to cry out loud, but she couldn't. Tuning around, she saw Amah Zhao. Supported by Amah Zhao's arm, she sat down on the bench in the passageway.

My poor child! He told me he was not afraid because he didn't want me to worry about him! What if anything happens to him? How could I face Fuzhi? Kiddo is only six and the future should be his! But now he is lying on the operating table. He might not be able to walk out of that door again! He might not be able to go back home!

"Madam, don't just focus on the negative! He is being operated on and everything will be alright. We'll soon have the same young master, alive and kicking!" Amah Zhao handed Bichu a packet of biscuits. "You skipped dinner. Have some biscuits now." Bichu gently pushed the packet away.

Hurried footsteps approached again. The Japanese child was being moved to another operating room. The mother followed, tears running down her cheeks. Bichu almost felt sympathy for her. The woman left the operating room. When she saw Bichu, her eyes full of worry and anxiety transformed immediately into hatred and hostility. It was apparent she might be thinking how inconceivable it was that a hospital under Japanese rule could allow a Chinese to have access to a better doctor than them.

Fortunately, she didn't sit on the same bench as them, but moved on to wait somewhere else. Bichu sincerely hoped that the woman's child would survive the surgery. Maybe she hopes that my child won't, thought Bichu. Who cares? Dr Guan wouldn't work according to her will. What is Dr Guan doing now? Has he dealt with the intussusception? These thoughts made her anxious again.

There was a sudden rush of footsteps in the passageway. Someone who looked like common folk ran in Bichu's direction.

He was stopped by an agile nurse: "You have registered for a general surgeon. Please come downstairs with me."

"The doctor told me my child needs an operation. But I really don't have so much money."

"If you let an intern do the operation, it won't cost much." The nursed tried to calm him down.

The man's haggard face was twisted with anxiety, which looked somewhat terrifying in the dim light. He suddenly burst out: "I don't have even a coin!"

"This way! This way, please." The nurse calmly led him down the stairs.

The night was quiet, deathly quiet. Bichu's mind drifted back to the night when Kiddo was born. It was the same type of bitter winter's day. The master bedroom's windows had been covered tightly with thick dark-green woollen curtains. Everyone said the baby might be a girl because the old saying went that girls came in series of three.

When the baby was born, the happy surprise was like a gigantic ship lifting Bichu up from the tormented sea of pain during her labour.

"Professor Meng, it is a boy!"

"Professor Meng! Congratulations! It's a boy!"

Different voices offered their cheerful congratulations to Fuzhi. How pleased he looked! Though Fuzhi explained later it was all in her imagination, because a son or a daughter would have been equally good news for him.

And Kiddo — Meng Heji — what a perfect son he was! What a wonderful person he would grow up to be! Why were the doors to the operating room still closed? What a long night.

Five hours later when the first grey light of dawn filtered through the window into the passageway, a nurse came out of the operating room. Bichu jumped to her feet and ran a few steps toward the nurse: "The child, how is he?"

"The operation was successful. Please don't worry," answered the nurse with a smile. "Dr Guan said parents and relatives are allowed to stay with the child because of his young age. Please come and wait in the ward." She handed Bichu a small card with the number of the ward on it.

"See? I told you it would be alright!" Amah Zhao was beaming with happiness. "I'll stay. Madam, you go back and take a rest."

"No, I'll stay. He's still not completely out of danger." Bichu saw Liu Fengcai and then told him: "You go back with Amah Zhao and tell your mistress not to worry and not to send anyone else here. They won't be any help." When she was done with them both, she left for the first-class wards.

Bichu didn't have to wait long before Kiddo was brought to the ward on a stretcher. He was still under anaesthetic. The nurse gently moved Kiddo from the stretcher to the bed. Once that was done, Bichu walked close to Kiddo, tears rolling down her cheeks.

Kiddo's face was pale, his eyes closed, his breath weak but even. The layer upon layer of medical gauze on his belly formed a bulge.

"Kiddo! My poor boy!" Bichu sat by the bedside, caressing his cold little hands.

The nurse constantly monitored Kiddo's blood pressure. Then Dr Guan and Dr Dale came in and talked in whispers for a moment. Dr Guan told Bichu: "Mrs Meng, just be careful of infection. Everything is fine. Don't worry." Bichu was full of gratitude, but she couldn't say anything.

About two hours later, Kiddo slowly opened his eyes:

"Mummy! Where's Mummy?" His voice was coarse. He tried to pull out the gastric tube in his nose, but Bichu stopped him in time. She lowered herself to land a soft kiss on Kiddo's forehead. "Mummy's here. Mummy never left your side."

"I had a dream," Kiddo tried hard to speak. "I dreamt mummy and daddy left me with an old witch."

"The old witch's roof is made of chocolate," Bichu said tearfully.

Kiddo gave her a faint smile, paused for a while and continued: "But I didn't want to eat the chocolate. Somehow, May arrived. So, the two of us kept running. We ran and ran. We ran to look for daddy."

Bichu's tears dropped on Kiddo's face, and he closed his eyes to feel the warmth. His tears soon joined his mother's. Bichu dried Kiddo's tears with a handkerchief, and wet his lips with damp cotton to reduce his thirst.

"Mummy isn't going anywhere?"

"I won't. I promise. You relax and take a nap." Kiddo opened his eyes to find Bichu seated by the bedside. He sighed softly with satisfaction and succumbed to sleep.

In the afternoon, Jiangchu and Earl came. Earl said she would stay, so Bichu could go home and take a rest. Bichu shook her head.

"But how can you take so much? We have to take it in turns; Xuan, Amah Zhao, Amah Liu and I can all take our turns," said Jiangchu.

"Mum would rather die for Kiddo," said Earl with concern, but both her mother and her aunt gave her a shocked look.

"We'll talk about it tomorrow," said Bichu.

"Lü Guitang took the children out to play yesterday," Jiangchu said. "He has regretted it ever since. Now he's waiting at the gate. I don't think he should come in." Bichu nodded without saying a word.

Kiddo heard his aunt vaguely in his sleep and hurried to explain: "Aunt Jiangchu, mummy, please don't blame Lü Guitang. We begged him to take us out. He didn't allow me to run on the lake, either."

"It's all Wei's fault! He and Wuyin are big enough to know better. Wuyin is a guest, so it's all Wei's fault!" said Jiangchu.

Kiddo spoke with tearful firmness: "It was I who wanted to go most. But now I can't go anywhere." He felt uncomfortable from head to toe because the wound had begun to hurt. He didn't want to cry, but involuntary tears ran down his face.

Bichu said: "No one will blame Lü Guitang. Nor Cousin Wei. Anyone can get ill since birth, but what's more important is to recover as soon as possible. You haven't spoken to your elder sister yet."

"No one can see I'm here!" You wouldn't believe these were Earl's words when she visited her sick little brother in hospital. But she went to the bed, took Kiddo's hand and smiled at him gently. This was her most open way to show her utmost concern.

"Little Lion has been looking for you. I have asked Amah Zhao to give him an extra portion of pork liver to comfort him." Kiddo knew how rare such an action was from his elder sister. He nodded with great satisfaction and then fell asleep again.

Bichu stayed with Kiddo for nine days in a row until he was strong enough to leave his bed. The hospital wouldn't let Bichu stay with Kiddo in the ward, so she then hired a nurse to take care of him, and went back home to take a rest and take care of things at home as well.

Bichu came back to the hospital in the afternoon. As soon as she set foot in the passageway, she immediately sensed that something was wrong. Doctors and nurses were in and out of Kiddo's ward in succession.

"What's happened?" She picked up her pace and entered the ward.

The resident physician was standing by the bed. Kiddo was moaning although he was unconscious, his head wriggling in pain and his body twitching. His thin, long neck looked so fragile that it looked like it wouldn't be able to support his head which had become enormous.

"What has happened to my son?" Bichu darted forward but was intercepted by the nurses, who sat her on a sofa and explained that Kiddo had a fever and that the doctors were working on it.

"He was well yesterday. How could this have happened?" Bichu was lost in tearful anxiety.

The doctor explained rather vaguely: "Fever is not unusual after surgery. But someone as young as your son is more at risk of contracting a high fever. We are treating him for it now."

Dr Guan came in and told Bichu that Kiddo had been given medication to calm his nerves and to help fight inflammation. Psychological treatment might help a lot because a mother's company was better than any medicine. Later, Kiddo looked like he had lost all his strength to struggle, and he quietened down. Bichu stayed close, not daring to take her eyes off Kiddo.

Bichu was informed by the nurse that Kiddo's condition was worse because of a terrifying accident in the morning. Kiddo was leaning against the headboard of the bed, reading a picture book when the Japanese child charged into the ward unexpectedly with a toy gun in his hand. When he saw Kiddo, he fired at him. The toy gun made a very loud noise and the muzzle flashed. Kiddo was so terrified that he dropped his book. Then the Japanese child ran to Kiddo's bed and shouted at him in Chinese: "You are our slaves! You are our slaves!" A nurse caught the child and coaxed him out of Kiddo's ward. Kiddo broke down into violent sobs. He was in such a condition for quite a while.

"Slaves!" Bichu knew Kiddo was not only frightened, he was also enraged. She bent over and whispered in Kiddo's ear: "Have a speedy recovery, and we'll leave to join daddy."

"The old witch... is from Japan," Kiddo moaned feebly, forcing out the words.

"No, there's no witch where daddy is staying. There are no old witches there," said Bichu as she tried to soothe Kiddo, who seemed not to be listening to her at all, and he slipped back into his coma.

"Mummy will sing Kiddo a song." Bichu didn't care whether Kiddo could hear her or not, she hummed a lullaby without lyrics, stroking Kiddo's hands.

In the afternoon, Jiangchu and Della both came to visit, and to bring Bichu some special medicine for soothing children's nerves, but they were all rejected by the hospital. At dusk, Kiddo had febrile convulsions again, his eyes rolled, and saliva dribbled from the corners of his mouth while Bichu leaned forward, hunched over Kiddo. How she wished she could suffer for Kiddo! A nurse came and gave Kiddo an injection, then he gradually settled down.

"Mummy wants to tell Kiddo a story about fireflies," said Bichu, again ignoring the fact that Kiddo couldn't hear her, and began in her gentle voice to recite the stories May and Kiddo loved so much. Many fireflies were flying over the brook, and suddenly one dropped into the water. A water moccasin (a venomous water snake) hidden in the dark snapped at the firefly and took it back to its lair. The firefly's friends came to the kids living in Square Teakettle. It was Kiddo who worked out a brilliant plan and rescued the firefly from the water moccasin. All the fireflies formed two neat lines to thank their hero. The light extended along the brook into the far distance.

"What was the brilliant plan Kiddo had?" Bichu asked, caressing his sunken little face.

This was the best part of the story. Every time Kiddo came up with a new idea, but this time Kiddo gave no response. Only a faint smile could be seen at the corner of his mouth.

Bichu stayed awake all night long. Deep into the night, Kiddo had a third convulsion, but it was much less severe, although the high fever lingered on.

The following afternoon, a nurse came to inform Bichu that they had visitors. Seeing Kiddo asleep, Bichu left the ward and went to the reception room.

Miao Donghui and his wife were standing in the room, their eyes fixed on the door. Miao was handsomely dressed as usual, but he had a concerned look on his face.

When he saw Bichu, he gave her some medicine: "I've heard all about it. All about it. To save the child is the priority."

Seeing that delicate packet emblazoned with golden characters for the name of the medicine, and realizing it was a rare kind of traditional Chinese medicine made of bezoar for soothing the nerves, Bichu's gratitude surged up from her heart. She asked them to sit down and told them how Kiddo had been doing.

Miao Donghui said: "The worst thing that can happen in life may be to fall ill in such troubled times. I have always cared about Mr Lü, the Tantai family and the Meng family. Mrs Meng, please go back to the ward and take care of your child. We are leaving right now." With these words, he excused himself and prepared to leave. Mrs Miao didn't say anything, but kept a smile on her face. She put her fur coat back on, and brushed the sleeves. Her marten-fur coat gleamed in the dimly-lit room.

"Thank you! Thank you so much!" said Bichu with sincere gratitude.

"We'll all be very happy at your son's speedy recovery." The Miao couple went down the corridor and disappeared round the corner.

Bichu went back to the ward and found the resident physician standing by the bed. He lowered his body to check on Kiddo. "His temperature has dropped to normal," he told Bichu, who handed him the medicine from Miao Donghui.

He said: "Not now. You keep it." His voice sounded odd.

Kiddo opened his eyes, uttered a weak "mummy", and then fell back to sleep. Bichu then started to feel more at ease. She heard sobs. Turning around, she found two nurses sobbing at the corner of the room. The tears on the physician's face had not dried yet.

Nanjing had fallen.

PART 4

At the news that Nanjing had fallen, No. 3 Chestnut Street lost its soul.

May was grief-stricken. It was the capital city! But she worried more about Kiddo. When Amah Zhao came back from the hospital, she had been tagging along behind her, asking questions like: "Is Kiddo in pain?" and "Can he stand it?", as if Amah Zhao was some sort of specialist.

She also worried about her mother when she heard the adults talking about how Bichu hadn't managed to get any sleep for several days and nights in a row. She wanted to burn some joss sticks and pray in the back garden with Lianxiu that night, but was stopped by her aunt Jiangchu: "You little children shouldn't be bothered with that stuff. Whatever needs to be atoned for, Granny Zhao will see to it."

May didn't know how to regard it, and began to worry for Granny Zhao. She went to ask Earl about it but was reproved for being nosy.

In ten years, this was the first time she had not been able to see her mother for such a long time. Grandpa Lü had been informed that May and Kiddo had been invited to stay with Xueyan for a few days, so she couldn't go to the master compound. Wei was sent to a relative to keep her away from all the distress. Since Lü Xiangge hadn't got any transcription orders, she took on some sewing and mending work instead, and had no time to visit the west garden as frequently as she used to.

After finishing the day's homework, May would stay in the gallery for a while, then run around in the courtyard. She wondered why the enormous residence had become so empty and so crowded at the same time, and yet she found nowhere to put her heart.

When the biting northern winds blew hard, she would listen with her heart, enjoying the high and low-pitched howls. When it was clear, she would lean against the window, studying the ice marks imprinted on it by the cold weather on the glass, and the icicles clinging to the dried branches of the trees in the garden. She would also count again and again the icicles hanging under the eaves, gazing in wander at the many different shapes.

One day, she had a feeling that her mother was bringing Kiddo back home and she ran all the way to the gate, saying she was going to meet them at the entrance of the street. Lü Guitang stopped her and brought her back.

All those books which had seemed so interesting had become so boring. She spanked her doll Lilly twice, conscious of the fact that Lilly had done nothing wrong. It took her half a day to comfort Lilly and to right the wrongs. She even scolded her favourite doll Little Pitiful.

Little Lion seemed to understand how lonely she was, and always tugged her. When he tried to bite her or rub against her, she would push him away impatiently. She wrote a story, out of utter boredom, describing herself as a terrible cranky owner of a cat and a doll, which had agreed to escape from their owner together, but got lost and eventually had to return to their owner.

When Bichu came back that time, May felt like she was in heaven. But Bichu left again in a hurry, hardly paying her any attention at all, and didn't come back again for several days.

It was very cold that day. May didn't want to get out of her warm bed. She seemed to be stuck there by the frozen air. Amah Zhao wouldn't let her stay in bed, saying it was clear and she should get up and go and walk or run around for a while.

When May had got dressed, she heard a door open and went to Earl's apartment. But Earl kept her door shut and wouldn't let her in. She then loitered in the front yard, thinking about checking whether Xuan was back from school. When she reached Xuan's gallery garden, a smashing sound reached her ears, and then more smashing noises followed. Amid all the noise, she could hear Xuan angrily shouting: "I'll beat you! I'll beat you to death!"

May wanted to hold back but Jiangchu had already spotted her, and waved her to come in.

The graceful and pleasant gallery garden now looked like a place of execution. Three Japanese dolls were tied to the dead tree in front of the steps to the garden leading to the rooms. Their hair was messy and dirty with water. Xuan was hurling glasses at them. Her eyes were bloodshot, fired up with rage. Lying on the ground was her favourite tweed coat lined with grey squirrel fur. Amah Liu tried to pick it up.

"Throw it away! Now! Dump it in the trash can!" cried Xuan.

"Alright! Alright! No one's hurt. That's the luckiest thing. We'll trash that coat," soothed Jiangchu. "Look! May is here. Don't let your little cousin look down on you."

Obviously, Xuan was not afraid of being looked down on by a junior because she took another glass and smashed it against one of the dolls. This time a beautiful girl. When the glass hit her, the hair piled high on her head slipped sideways and her face was creased, making it look like she was in pain. A transparent hairpin dropped onto the ground. May vaguely felt that this doll too was a scapegoat for others' mistakes.

"Why don't I see any Japanese soldier dolls?" Xuan asked, pausing with a number of glasses in her hands. The other two dolls tied to the tree were an old man in a kimono and a boy monk in a red Buddhist robe. Both were drenched and their heads were drooping as if they were sorry for the shameful conduct of their compatriots.

"Mrs Ling and Miss Ling have arrived," Liu Fengcai announced, popping his head in the door to the garden.

Xuan smashed all of the glasses in her hands onto the ground, ran into her room, and locked herself in. Jiangchu went out to greet the mother and daughter with May, and invited them to sit in the reception hall.

Yue Hengfen looked the same, but Xueyan had lost a lot of weight, and also her lustre of a new bride in the summer. She was smiling, but her smile was soaked with bitterness. Her sapphire-blue silk gown with dark-gold sprigged lining looked rather dull, making her look even less vigorous.

They had come from the hospital and said Kiddo was getting much better. On these words, May leaned against Jiangchu and whispered in her aunt's ear.

Jiangchu then smiled at Hengfen: "May is really bored and wants to ask Xueyan to stay with her for a couple of days. Will that be OK?"

Hengfen answered thoughtfully: "It would be nice for Xueyan to stay with May. They both need some distractions."

Xueyan nodded with a smile. Something suddenly occurred to Jiangchu: "How forgetful I am! It is the winter solstice! You should stay with us for dinner. It has been such a mess that I almost forgot the important things. Too many things have happened. Xuan ran into a group of Japanese soldiers on her way home when she was off from school this afternoon. They forced her to walk in front of them. One soldier's bayonet even pricked her coat and left a cut there. She threw a huge temper tantrum when she got back. It is lucky nothing else happened. Isn't it horrible?"

Hengfen was shocked: "Those soldiers should be avoided as much as possible. It's too dangerous for girls to go outside. What a troubled time! How could you still allow Xuan to go to school?"

Xueyan asked: "Is Xuan at home now? I guess she won't want to see anyone."

Jiangchu answered: "You guessed right. She doesn't want to see people. Would you please stay so you can talk to her in the evening?"

"I have to get back. I have someone to serve. How can I have the pleasure of enjoying delicious dishes here with you all?" Hengfen sighed. "I should have been to send my regards to Grandpa Lü, but since Jingyao is not here with me, I'll excuse myself and not disturb him." Hengfen stood up and said she would go to the Meng's west garden to pay a brief visit.

When they entered the reception room, Jiangchu exclaimed: "Why is this room as cold as a cellar?"

The heater was huge and full of coal but it was smothered and only gave off a faint glow. With pity and affection, Xueyan took hold of May's hands in their fingerless gloves. Those fingers were icy cold.

"It's cold indeed. You don't have enough coal?" Hengfen asked.

Amah Zhao hurried to poke a hole in the centre of the coal in the stove with a poker that was three feet long.

Jiangchu reproached: "Why are you using the coal so sparingly? Don't you worry that May might catch a cold?"

"I'm not afraid of catching a cold," May hurried to explain.

"Miss May is so understanding. She won't let me burn the coal, saying she would rather save it for our madam and young master," Amah Zhao said with pride.

"It's lucky that May is healthy and strong. My Xueyan would do the same since she is also considerate and understanding. But if she did, she would have caught a cold a long time ago," said Hengfen, looking at Xueyan with tender affection as if Xueyan was still her little girl the same age as May.

"Has Earl come back?" asked Jiangchu.

"I heard the door open." May offered to check, but was stopped by Hengfen: "No need to disturb her. We'll just stay for a while." She had no interest in Earl, and thought she had already shown her politeness by presenting herself in the west garden. They sat and talked for several more minutes, and then Hengfen said goodbye and left for home.

May felt settled with Xueyan's company. The two of them had always adored each other. May liked Xueyan's tenderness and grace, while Xueyan loved May's naivety and considerateness. They shared something tacit in such a troubled world.

"It must have been terrifying to run into those Japanese soldiers!" May was thinking about Xuan.

"My mother advised me to find a job to keep myself

occupied. But of course, I'm not going to work for the Japanese. It looks like it's not a good idea to go out now," Xueyan said thoughtfully.

May said: "We will go to join my daddy, sooner or later. Will you come with us to find Cousin Feng?"

Xueyan forced a smile: "Your father writes to you from time to time, while your Cousin Feng's whereabouts are still unknown."

"Sis Ling," Earl opened the door and entered, greeting Xueyan flatly as if she saw her every day.

She took a seat and dropped her head in silence. Xueyan asked how school was going, She didn't answer but her pointed chin was quivering as if she was trying hard to calm herself.

She stood up abruptly: "Just now... just now, I, I was almost scared to death." Xueyan went to her side and held her shoulder, asking what had happened. May stared at her sister with her enormous eyes.

"I was riding back home when I saw a group of Japanese soldiers walking in the centre of the street, their bayonets shining on their shoulders. When they saw me, they walked toward me and they walked so close to me that I had to get off my bike. I was trying my best to get to the side of the road when they separated into two rows, forcing me to stand in between. They lifted their guns over my head with the shining bayonets." She paused.

May ran to her and leaned against her, muttering: "Sister, don't be afraid! Don't be afraid."

"I was not afraid then," Earl was thinking it over. "The Japanese solders kept walking. Dozens of shining blades hovered over my head. When they were through and gone,

I looked around. All the passers-by dropped their heads and eyes, pretending they hadn't seen anything. I thought it would not have been a big deal if one of the blades had dropped on my head and killed me right there. But I was grieved when I thought how dare those Japanese are on Beiping soil."

Earl sat down again, cupping her hands to cover up her face, her pointed jaw quivering.

"Cousin Xuan met some Japanese soldiers, too," May tugged at Earl's sleeve. "Aunt Jiangchu already knows."

"Don't tell mum," urged Earl gently. She lowered her hands, and then added: "I saw what happened to Xuan, too. When the soldiers left me alone, I didn't dare to ride again, so I pushed my bike and walked along the street. A moment later, a thunderous noise of footsteps arose behind me. The soldiers had returned in single file with a young girl walking in front of them. That girl was Xuan! She was walking calmly and fast in front of them. The solder behind her poked at her coat with his bayonet! They drove her for a while and suddenly all turned around and left. Xuan stood in the centre of the street, dumbfounded. She didn't hear me until I repeated her name several times. We came back home together."

Xueyan had never heard Earl talk so long and so much. She was at her wit's end to find anything comforting. Earl looked better after her long talk. Instead of going back to her apartment as she usually did, she stayed silently by the stove.

Dinner was due to be in Jiangchu's compound, but since Earl wouldn't go, the three of them decided to have dinner in the west garden. Jiangchu sent them two dishes. After dinner, Xueyan suggested they go to see Xuan. It was getting dark. The snow on the steps leading to the rooms looked whiter than usual; the crows nesting in the ancient ash tree outside the garden were calling incessantly. They found the master garden looked even more bleak with the boards and reed mats from the summer awnings in a dishevelled pile by the fish tank. A gust of wind sent the fallen leaves on the ground swirling around. They shuddered. Xueyan suggested that they come back after they had put their coats on. Before they turned to go back, they saw a figure heading toward them from behind the ash tree. It was Xuan.

It was almost half a year ago when Xuan went to tell Xueyan about her chance encounter with Wei Feng before his departure. She was wearing a coat with a lilac silk surface. Her fair, pale face and the smile hanging at the corners of her mouth looked so attractive against the twilight. She went ahead to meet the three girls and put her arm around Xueyan's shoulder. It was hard to imagine anything horrible had ever happened to her.

The four started going back to the west garden. At the door to the garden, they caught a flash of light beside the Taihu Scholar rock behind the peony bed. All four of them saw it, and stopped walking, but no one said anything. Amah Zhao came out of the servants' quarters. Obviously, she had seen the light, too.

She stood there for a while and then ran to light the lamps in the main rooms: "Ladies, come into the room, please. Don't stand in the garden on such a cold day."

When the four entered, Amah Zhao took May's hand and said: "My dear miss, you won't say anything, will you?"

Then she turned to the other three ladies: "When Mrs Zhao burnt joss sticks in the back garden that night, she said she had seen a line of tiny red lanterns hung under the eaves of the building in the back garden. Let's pray that we'll all be blessed by the spirits, fairies, gods and goddesses."

She said the last sentence rather loudly as if that would make the spirits, fairies, gods and goddesses hear her. The three were dumfounded at her words.

May was scared and asked Amah Zhao in a whisper: "Were they fox spirits?"

Amah Zhao reproached her, whispering: "What kid's nonsense!" She meant to tell those spirits, fairies, gods and goddesses not to take offence from a child's innocent talk. May was scared and clammed up.

"So, what's that living in our backyard?" asked Xuan, when she came to herself, laughing. "If they are so capable, why won't they help us fight the Japanese?"

Amah Zhao didn't dare to scold Xuan, but she kept waving her hand in disapproval, begging her young lady to hold her tongue.

Xueyan tried to change the subject of the conversation: "Is there a power cut around Di'anmen city gate here today? We have them on Tuesdays."

"Sometimes we have them twice in a week. Darkness is always followed by evil things," Amah Zhao answered, while lighting the lamps. After checking on the heater and serving hot tea to the ladies, she went on to make the beds in the master bedroom.

"Many things in the world still don't have scientific explanations, such as the origin of life. I have just taken general biology, but I have already been amazed how mysterious life is." These words proved Earl was a bona fide student of biology.

"That's because scientists are incapable of finding explanations!" said Xuan. "Because we Chinese are incapable, giving the enemy the opportunity to feed their insatiable desire, now all of the Chinese have become conquered slaves! We are the conquered, so we have become slaves of the conquerors! For a conquered nation, there are no nobles, no common folk! There are only slaves!"

Xuan and Earl looked at each other. Remembering the moment of humiliation and insult in the afternoon, their eyes brimmed with tears. They had been raised like the apples of their parents. How could they suffer such humiliation if Beiping had not been taken by the Japanese?

"We have been providing for those fox spirits. Why won't they do anything to match what we have offered them?" sneered Xuan.

"It would be too much to ask them to fight the Japanese. Maybe we can ask them for some signs?", suggested Xueyan, raising her head, who had been sitting by the stove with her head bowed on her chest. She didn't believe in such 'supernatural creatures', but she couldn't resist longing for some signs.

Xuan laughed: "So true! Since these fox spirits have such powerful magic, why shouldn't we ask them to give us some signs?"

"How?" asked Earl.

"Can we make up something? There are no set rules, anyway."

Everyone was fascinated. After some discussions, they searched in the room and found some coloured candles, though they were all wondering whether those fox spirits could figure out what they wanted to know via the made-up rules. Each claimed her colour. Xueyan took the white one, Xuan chose the green one, Earl picked the blue one, and May asked for the red one. Each was glad to have got their favourite colour without having to fight with anyone else for it. Earl said those candles should be lit on the Taihu Scholar rock, while Xueyan thought it would work even if they were put in the room. Xuan suggested a compromise between the first two proposals — to put them on the low handrails along the gallery. May didn't have anything to say, but she felt so excited even to look at the other three talking.

Amah Zhao knew well it was none of her business. Besides, Xueyan was already married. How could Amah Zhao interfere with the affairs of a married lady? She just pleaded with them, smiling, before excusing herself and going back to the servants' quarters: "Just be sincere. And be careful not to offend anyone."

The four went to the gallery. A crescent moon was perched just above the tree tops, shedding light on the unmelted snow under the gallery, glittering. The Taihu Scholar rock stood quietly behind the flowerbed against the wall. Xuan took out the candles and lined them up along the handrail. Earl was ready to strike a match to light the candles when someone suddenly entered the garden with quiet, light footsteps and soft laughter: "I heard Aunt Ling is here, so I came to say hello." It was Lü Xiangge.

Xueyan smiled: "Look what fun we are having. Come and join us." They asked Xiangge to take a black candle, and set it on the handrail before Earl was able to light them all one by one. The dim yellow flame from the candles muted the colours. The tiny flames flickered, defying the darkness in the garden, which looked even darker in the beam of light, hurling its fathomless mystery toward the spectators.

The shared wish of the four was to defeat the Japanese and expel them from China! How could one be oneself without one's country and home? They also had other wishes. Xueyan was eager to receive news of Wei Feng; Xuan was thinking about her father who was far away; Earl was thinking about her father and Kiddo. Xuan and Earl respectively had their personal wishes. As a writer, I wouldn't speculate. May wished that all of the wishes of her sister and her cousins would come true. Xiangge was wishing for something quite peculiar. We would come to know what she had wished for some time later.

A chilly breeze passed, pulling the flames along so far that it seemed as if they would drift with the wind into the far distance. The flames gradually regained their shapes when the wind was gone. One flame died without any sign, in a puff of pale smoke which dispersed into the darkness.

It was Xueyan who first realised that was her white candle.

The remaining four kept burning quietly. Another breeze pushed the flames bobbing from left to right. The blue one died. The green one's flame was drawn away as if it were trying to fly away with the wind, then it died, too. Now only the red and black candles were still burning.

"Well, it should be like this. May is the youngest, after all," giggled Xuan, tossing her bright laughter into the darkness.

They kept waiting. The flames of the two flickering candles looked robust. Another breeze. The red one dimmed and then died, leaving a pale trail of smoke in the moonlight. Only the black one was still burning, its flame drawn hither and thither wherever the breeze took it. They all watched breathlessly. It died out a while later.

They all released the breath they had been holding.

Xiangge said: "It was just a fun game. Mine should have died out first a long time ago, but it was the last one. So, it must have been a rather flimsy performance."

Xueyan said: "Fate is not so easy to predict."

Though it was natural for the wind to blow out the candles, they all felt their hearts sinking under a heavy weight. When they were back in the room, they had lost all interest in the proceedings. A game of fun seemed to have turned out to be a burden to bear when the fox spirits gave them the 'sign'.

Amah Liu came to pick up Xuan. She was carrying a lantern, which was painted with two little men carrying a lantern each.

"Madam has ordered a car for the two young ladies to go to school tomorrow." She stood in the gallery, raising the lantern tall and high, shedding light on the five burnt candle stubs on the handrail.

Kiddo was released from the hospital when Chinese New Year's Eve was just around the corner. Only a handful of guests were still staying in the south compound. At the roar of the engine, all of them, led by Lü Guitang, came out of the gate and lined up to welcome Kiddo's return.

Once the car came to a halt, Lü Guitang beat everyone and lifted Kiddo in his arms. Bichu interposed: "Be careful of his stomach!" All the servants from the three families had now gathered at the gate, rubber-necking to see the young master who had escaped death.

"I can walk. I can walk," said Kiddo, smiling and trying to wriggle out of Lü Guitang's arms. His face was fair, tinged with a rosy hue. The crowd walked with them to the second gate and stopped. Jiangchu, Xuan, Earl, May and Wei were already waiting at the second gate.

Jiangchu said: "Kiddo, you have picked the best time! Now you are all well and ready for the new year! All of us can celebrate the coming of the new year with all our hearts."

Upon seeing May and Wei, Kiddo was so happy he started shouting excitedly, grabbing May's hand and swinging it without stopping. He asked to see his grandfather when he reached the master compound.

It was a custom that guests staying in the south compound wouldn't go beyond the second gate, and that the servants working in the front garden couldn't go to the master garden. Only a few were privileged to go to the main rooms in the master compound. Bichu took Kiddo, Wei and May to the main rooms. The spacious rooms were too cold for the old man in winter, so he retreated to the inner rooms in his compound. The old man looked much older than he had barely a month ago. Leaning against the headboard of the bed with quilts piled high behind him, he was coughing hard and loud. Lianxiu was briefing him by the bedside about Kiddo's illness while stroking his back.

"Grandpa, I'm back!" Kiddo declared triumphantly, as if he had just won a battle.

Before the old man could say anything, he was caught in a spasm of coughs, and was unable to answer. He stretched out his hand and waved to Kiddo to sit on the bed after coughing for a while.

"You have recovered now! We owe so much to advances in medical science. Otherwise I can't imagine how we would have dealt with it! Why didn't you tell me earlier?" Bichu didn't tell her father about Kiddo's operation until she was informed of Kiddo's release from the hospital.

The old man asked more about the hospital, and then asked about Wei and May's homework. He picked up an open book from the nightstand, *Wen Xuan* (文选) or *Selections of Refined Literature*.

Pointing at the book, he said to the kids: "Yu Xin's *Lament for the South* sounds so different from when I read it in my youth. 'Li Ling cried for the departure of the wild ducks heading north, and Su Wu sighed at the sight when the lone wild goose flew south.' Both poets had lost the will to live because they had been deprived of the opportunity to return to their motherland before they died."

Bichu talked with Lianxiu in a corner of the room. After some hesitation, Lianxiu decided to tell Bichu. She whispered: "Grandpa is coughing more frequently. Besides, he wakes up with loud sobs in the middle of the night, saying he wants to practice his Shaolin boxing."

Bichu knew her father was suffering due to the fall of Nanjing. His heart was aching. After another fit of coughing, Bichu said goodbye to her father and took the kids away with her. When she reached the door of the room, the old man called her from behind in his croaky voice: "Daughter!"

Bichu stopped immediately and returned to his bedside. The old man continued slowly: "You have lost so much weight. Kiddo is alright now. You need to take more care of yourself." Bichu gave a hurried promise and turned back with downcast eyes.

During Bichu's absence from home, Amah Zhao and Chef Chai thought there might not be any festivities to welcome in the new year, since Earl was not in charge of the household and May was too young to do so. Chef Chai racked his brains to prepare a family reunion dinner according to their usual custom, thinking even during Madam Bichu's absence that the two young ladies would still feel the atmosphere of the Spring Festival. Now that Kiddo had recovered and was back home, the whole residence was bathed in happiness, and the west garden was beaming with merriment. Even Earl was bustling in and out, trying to help, though practically her efforts didn't amount to much.

Among the snacks Bichu brought back from the hospital, May found a can of peanut butter. After confirming with Bichu that it was edible and that she could have it, she happily unscrewed the lid. The sweet smell of roasted peanuts escaped into the air immediately. May was licking the thick layer left on the inside of the lid when Earl spotted it.

"You greedy thing! Why are you licking the lid? Where are your manners?" She scolded her little sister without delay.

May was mad. She didn't want to be greedy. She just couldn't control herself anymore. Besides, her mum had already told her it was OK. How could her sister stand in her way? She decided she would fight back hard against her sister, and then she said: "It's none of your business! If you don't stop meddling, may the Japanese bayonets hover over your head again and again!"

But she regretted it the moment she had said it. Leaving her peanut butter behind, she ran to her sister and threw her arms around her waist. Earl stood still at May's words, but didn't flare up as she normally would. Her pointed chin quivered again.

Bichu was very upset when she discovered what had happed to Earl and Xuan that afternoon. She didn't scold May, but took Earl's hand and said: "Aunt Jiangchu has made a nice arrangement. If we can't leave next semester, you'd better live in the dormitory on campus."

"Is there any hope for us to leave?" The three children asked, anxiously.

"There is always hope," Bichu assured them. "Come! Let's get ready to celebrate the coming of the new year. Cheer up! It will be easier to travel when spring comes."

The prospect of leaving had been so inspiring that they were all deliriously happy when the Spring Festival arrived.

The Meng family followed Fuzhi's family tradition of paying their respects to the family ancestors before the big feast on new year's eve, and the breakfast on new year's day. The ancestral tablets had been packed in cases after they moved into town from Square Teakettle. A table, which functioned as an altar, had been set up in front of the north wall in the reception room in the west garden. An incense burner was put in the middle of the altar, with vessels and candle holders standing on each side. When everything was ready, the ancestral tablet was brought in to be presented on the altar. The pedestal of the tablet was surrounded by delicately carved rails. The upper part was covered in a Phoebe *zhennan* wood (a superior, durable softwood) case. With the case off, one could see the characters engraved on the tablet 'The Mengs of Xiangyang' in emerald-coloured ink.

This tablet was an ancient piece handed down from generation to generation in the Meng family. Fuzhi had one sibling, a younger brother, who worked in the ministry of foreign affairs and had been stationed abroad. Hence he was the one that held the tablet. There were three generations in the family who once served in the Qing dynasty government in a series of positions like modern governors or mayors. A ring of agate and a ring of jade were embedded around the pedestal by different generations, not for their material value but for memorial significance. Those who had adopted a progressive way of living had long since abandoned ancestor worship in the 1930s, but Fuzhi insisted that since they still had the tablet, it was their responsibility to pay their due respects. Bichu, wanting everything to be just as it was when Fuzhi was at home, especially during his absence, carefully saw to it that the salutation to the Meng family ancestors be included in the celebration ceremonies of the new year.

The three children didn't have any new clothes as they used to have when the new year came. Earl was wearing the light-yellow winter gown with a silver sprigged silk surface that she wore last year. It still fit her well. May's pink gown decorated with Rhinestone studs was rather short for her this year. Kiddo was draped merrily in a loose ash-grey cotton-padded gown to protect his wound. The three of them looked fresh and high-spirited. Amah Zhao exclaimed that she had never seen more beautiful kids than those three. She said that every year. When setting the table for lunch, Bichu asked her to put a pair of chopsticks and a bowl where Fuzhi sat. The kids didn't speak as loudly as they did when their father was present.

After lunch, May invited Xiangge to join her for a game of 'catch the marbles'. She spread one of her mother's woollen scarves on a table, tossed five marbles onto it, and then picked them up in various ways. One way was to fling two marbles into the air at once, catch one while letting the other land on the scarved table, and catch the second one after it bounced once on the table. Only on woollen fabrics could the marbles bounce like that.

May's small nimble hands were busy throwing, catching and casting, the colourful marbles bouncing and rolling all over the place. She didn't care much about winning or losing, and she was genuinely happy whenever she or Xiangge won. Xiangge laughed half-heartedly with May.

Kiddo asked if he could join the two of them later, so the game changed into flipping hard roasted broad beans. First, one drew a line with one's index finger between two beans which were first tossed onto the table, then one flung one's bean against the other player's bean on the table. If one's bean touched the other bean, then one won that bean.

Wei came to visit them. He was in his new cotton-padded gown with a navy-blue woollen surface. He joined the game and soon won lots of beans. He shared his beans with the others and they started all over again.

Earl came to have a look, and sneered at the players scornfully: "Were you all born yesterday? What a childish game! What a leisurely and carefree mood!"

No one paid any attention to her, except Xiangge who stood up to offer her his seat.

It was dark even at 5:00pm. Tantai's kitchen in the front asked Xiangge to go over and help, and Wei went back to the front compound, too. The red candles on the altar table were alight. A red rug had been laid on the floor in front of the table to kowtow on. Bichu stood to attention, and took a small bundle of joss sticks.

Kiddo cried out, laughing: "Let me light one! Let me light one!" Last year during the salutation, he begged to be allowed to light the joss sticks and his wish was granted. He wanted to do it this year.

He struck a match twice in vain. Bichu hinted to Earl, hoping that Earl could help her little brother, but Earl turned her head away from her mother. To light up the joss stick was Earl's responsibility, the eldest child in the household. But she didn't want to shoulder such a responsibility since the youngest child considered the ceremony to be a game. Why should she care? In the end, May stepped in and helped Kiddo. May was happy since she was not the eldest, nor a boy, and she didn't have much to lose.

After putting the sticks into the incense burner, Bichu knelt on the rug, and kowtowed three times. Then it was Earl, May and Kiddo's turn. When May knelt, she thought the ancestors looked very affable in the sparkling candle flames.

New year's eve dinners used to be held in every household. Grandpa Lü had never joined the dinner with Jiangchu and her family although they lived in the same residence. Traditionally, married daughters were 'outsiders'. And Grandpa Lü clung to some traditions. But this year, with Bichu present, and in the absence of Tantai Mian and Fuzhi, he decided dinner would be held in the master compound joined by the three households. Bichu and her three children stood in front of the altar for a while to pay their respects, and then left for the master compound.

The light in the main hall was dim and yellow, as if it was about to go out at any second. The giant stove was radiating with heat, and the coal was blazing up. When Bichu and the three kids arrived, Jiangchu and her two children had just gone into the inner rooms.

Xuan was just back from a dance party held in the Grand Hôtel des Wagons-Lits. She looked dazzling in her pea-green woollen dress and white cashmere shawl. Her theory was that even if one didn't dance, the Japanese would not move out of China by themselves. But she kept running into Japanese wherever she went. That upset her very much. The bright colours of the girls' clothes added to the festive atmosphere in the big hall. All spoke loudly to let Grandpa Lü hear what they were talking about. It was boisterous in the master compound.

Snacks and dim sum were brimming over several tea tables specially prepared for the Spring Festival. They used to have a dozen different specialties like hawthorn sticks, sugar-coated roasted peanuts, fruit preserves, and so on, mixed together.

But this year, they were reduced to only a couple of varieties. Lianxiu had put on her dark reddish-purple cotton-padded gown, and was busy dispensing snacks to the youngsters.

Everyone sat around the big round table when it was time to serve dinner. Grandpa Lü was sitting in the host's seat, with Jiangchu and Lianxiu on either side. Bichu sat next to Lianxiu. All the bowls, plates and cups were old ones used for such occasions. The cups for wine were made of white glazed China from the Ding kiln, famous since the Tang dynasty more than a thousand years ago. They looked almost transparent as if they were ready to melt into the air. But the dishes in the plates were quite shabby, marking a sharp contrast with the fine quality of the containers. The four-footed plates with hollowed-out work around the top all contained cabbage dishes: stir fried cabbage and wood ears, sweet and sour cabbage, cabbage mound with mustard (a popular dish among Beiping city folk), and spicy pickled cabbage stems.

Grandpa Lü couldn't make out what the dishes were, so he asked about them one by one. When he was introduced to the four cabbage dishes, he laughed: "I know a lot about chicken cooked in three styles. This sounds even better — vegetables cooked in four styles. I certainly want to have a try."

Lianxiu hurried to serve him the dishes, but Jiangchu said: "They might be too tough for father."

The old man answered: "I'll still have a try however tough they are."

Lü Guitang, who was sitting next to Wei, whispered: "The situation was rather tense a few days ago because, according to what I heard, the Japanese consulate had been bombed, injuring many high-ranking officials and Chinese who worked there."

"Lü Guitang, speak louder," urged Xuan in a loud voice.

Lü Guitang repeated what he had said.

The old man listened attentively. When Lü Guitang had finished, he said: "Say that again! Say it louder!"

Lü Guitang turned his head to take a look at the door of the room, then repeated what he had said loudly. Everyone was radiant with joy. Even the dim yellow light in the room seemed to brighten up a little.

"That is what a Chinese should be doing!" The old man held up his wine cup and drank the wine in one go. Lianxiu looked at him, concerned.

"What a pity that I am senile and useless," he remarked, thumping down the cup and heaving a heavy sigh. The rest of the table fell silent.

Liu Fengcai came to serve food out of a hamper and put a plate of sautéd tofu and steamed fish on the table. When he was done serving, he moved to stand behind Jiangchu and whispered to her: Mrs Zheng, the police have sent a message, saying there are going to be house-to-house checks by the Japanese tonight. He and his people will come to our residence early so as not to disturb Mr Lü's bedtime."

The lively atmosphere was dragged down to its former depressed state after hearing such news. Only Grandpa Lü spoke up since he hadn't heard clearly what Liu Fengcai had been whispering. Jiangchu said it again more loudly. The old man fell silent, too.

After a long while, he demanded: "All the kids go to the ancestral temple and hide there!"

"What about father?"

"I'll sit right here!"

Bichu hurriedly walked up to him: "Father, why don't you go inside and lie down? We don't know whether the Japanese soldiers will be reasonable or not. You just go back and stay there. Don't bother to see them."

She urged Lianxiu to help her take the old man to his bedroom while she continued to try and persuade him. Xuan and the other children, including Xiangge, went to the ancestral temple immediately. Jiangchu asked Liu Fengcai to go and take care of the front compound, while Lü Guitang stayed in the master compound.

She had barely finished her instructions when Chef Chai hurried in, speaking in a muffled voice: "They are coming!" Liu Fengcai hurried out to meet them.

Heavy footsteps came nearer and nearer. Old Zheng's voice, the policeman close to the family, could be heard above the sound of footsteps: "Mr Liu, I am so sorry to stop by on new year's eve!" As he spoke, a group of about ten people comprising Chinese policemen, the community director, Chinese soldiers working for the puppet government and Japanese soldiers came into the hall.

Old Zheng introduced the household to the Japanese soldiers, who were not listening but their eyes were searching all over the hall. When they saw the fish on the table, they sat down and began to eat. The speed with which they ate was astonishing. Fish bones came out of both corners of their mouths as if the bones were being ejected by a machine. The rest of the group was standing still, too shocked to move. The community director poured each one a cup of wine.

When they had finished eating and drinking, they had a look at the household register and asked about Lü Guitang's identity. It took Old Zheng a while to explain it until he put it more simply, saying that Lü Guitang was Grandpa Lü's nephew – only then did the Japanese soldiers nod their consent. They didn't ask what Lü Guitang's job was, nor did they bother to ask where the students on the register were. They looked as if they knew the answers.

The head Japanese soldier gracefully wiped his mouth with a handkerchief and lifted the door curtain to the master bedroom. Seeing the old man lying in bed, he turned and ordered his men to leave. Heavy footsteps thudded out of the master compound, with Liu Fengcai following behind the small group in turmoil, bowing and smiling obsequiously.

"Aren't they afraid that the dishes might be poisoned?" Lü Guitang exclaimed in a whisper.

One Japanese soldier shouted in the garden in his Chinese with a strong Japanese accent: "What a big house!". If they had wanted this house, then it was theirs — but they wouldn't say that, would they?

According to Chinese custom, married daughters pay a visit to their parents on the second day of the Spring Festival. During the years when the Tantai family stayed with Grandpa Lü in the residence, Jiangchu had never set foot in the master compound on new year's day. She would always wait until the second day. But this year she broke with tradition since Bichu was so worried about the old man. She talked to Jiangchu and the two decided to pay their respects to their father on new year's day instead of the customary second day of the new year.

On Chinese New Year's Day in 1938, the Meng family first paid their respects to their ancestors. Then Amah Zhao and Chef Chai presented their new year salutations to Bichu as they always did in the many years they had worked for the family. They kowtowed in front of the altar table to the Meng ancestors, chanting: "We kowtow to his lordship and her ladyship."

Amah Zhao always added some auspicious words

expressing good wishes. The theme of her wishes this year was peace: "I wish we could have a peaceful year free from diseases and disasters and that everyone could be healthy and happy!"

Bichu raised herself slightly from her chair to return the favour and gave them new year gift tips. The gift tips were not much more than they had received the previous year, although they had been doing more chores, but both were happier than ever.

After breakfast, Jiangchu and Bichu took the children to the master apartment to attend a ceremony led by Grandpa Lü to salute the Lü ancestors in the small ancestral temple in the residence. Grandpa Lü himself didn't have any sons, so he paid special attention to the formalities of the ceremony. He put one hand on Kiddo's head, the other holding Wei's hand, and wished in his heart that both would grow to be pillars of the nation.

The inner rooms were quiet. The stove had long since died out and the cold ash had not yet been cleared away. The group tiptoed into the bedroom to find the old man reclining on the bed, staring at a sword with a red tassel hung on the wall, lost in thought. Lianxiu was busy helping him wash his face with a hot, wet towel. Their female servant Amah Wei was cleaning the room.

"Father, you are already up," Jiangchu greeted the old man gently.

The old man turned to face his two daughters. Such a simple action looked to require so much effort from him. His pupils were dilated as if he were considering what he should say. He didn't say anything.

Bichu asked: "Father, would you like to stay in bed? You

don't need to push yourself to get up." She turned to Jiangchu, seeking help.

Jiangchu added: "Bichu is right. Why don't you stay in bed? It's cold in the outer rooms."

"You carry on to the ancestral temple. I'll excuse myself this year," he said, turning to face the wall. The silence in the room was as pure as the wintry blanket outside. It was so silent that the younger kids thought they were breathing too loud.

The two sisters exchanged looks and Jiangchu said: "That's a good plan. Let's present our new year salutation to father first." They all knelt on hearing her words. Lianxiu hurried to get out of their way.

"You all get up! Now!" The old man suddenly sat up straight.

"I don't deserve your salutation! I have achieved nothing for my country but witness the Japanese invaders trespassing in my residence. How can I face all my ancestors and my descendants?" the old man mumbled, jibbering. Jiangchu paid no attention to her father and finished her three kowtows as required by custom.

Bichu's heart sank with sorrow. She uttered a soft "father" and kowtowed.

When the salutation was done, the old man still didn't turn around, so Jiangchu led the team to the ancestral temple. No one asked whether Lianxiu would like to come with them, since she always stayed by Grandpa Lü's side. There were no tablets in the temple. The portraits of Grandpa Lü's grandparents and parents hung on the wall facing the gate with dark-bronze gauze decoration around the frames. Both his grandfather and father were officials once with posts in the capital, so they were in their official robes with their badges of rank. On one of the side walls hung a picture of his first wife, an enlarged photo of Madam Zhang. It was easy to see the family resemblance between Bichu and Jiangchu and their mother.

In past years, the family used to pay their respects in the ancestral temple amid boisterous merriment. The solemnity of the temple was an appropriate balance to that merriment. But this year, this balance had turned into a lead weight adding to the solemnity which had been weighing heavily on the family. It was ghastly and dismal. The biting northern wind blew into the temple through the shredded window paper, lifting the gauze decorations, and freezing the room into an icy cellar. Bichu put her arm around Kiddo while May moved closer to her mum as she felt disturbed at the frightening life-sized picture of her grandmother.

When the children came out of the temple, they didn't go to Xuan and Wei's apartments to play and then have dinner with the Tantais in the front compound, as they would have done in the past.

Wei tugged at May's sleeve, and May turned to him. The two exchanged a look, and then shook their heads at the same time. They went their separate ways, heading silently for their own places.

In the west garden, May turned on the radio to listen to Lian Kuoru's narration of the *Romance of the Eastern Han Dynasty*. It was in the middle of the legendary battle by Jia Fu, a general of the Eastern Han dynasty, who was heavily injured by the enemy general and tried to continue fighting by wrapping his intestines around his waist. When the radio was turned on, Kiddo immediately objected, complaining the story was too terrifying, and begged someone to turn the radio off. They switched instead to reading. Earl just buried her face without getting annoyed with anyone.

Nobody thought anyone would come to present their new year greetings at such a time, but in the afternoon some people from Tantai Mian's company and some colleagues from Meng Fuzhi's university came bearing some information. It was a relief that no one connected with the puppet government showed up, including Miao Donghui.

Things continued smoothly until the fifth day of the Spring Festival. Jiangchu and Bichu assumed that the new officials who were in power might have forgotten about Grandpa Lü, and that the old man might be able to enjoy the rest of his life in the residence, living like a hermit.

CHAPTER V

Part 1

Spring came amidst sandstorms. The frozen surface of Shicha lake was thinning by the day. Then one day, it all melted into a giant spring puddle.

The weeping willows along the dyke woke up in the wind, coating themselves with blurred, tender yellow. The city folk in Beiping had such a poetic name for the spring sandstorms — the tree-wakening breeze, which never fulfilled its function of waking up the trees and kept blowing when the trees were already wide awake. It blew so hard that pedestrians couldn't keep their eyes open, the summit of green Jingshan mountain was lost in a grey haze, and the whole city felt like it was permeated with thick, hazy, choke-inducing waves of smoke from tens of thousands of people starting up their coal-fired stoves at the same time. Then another day, the wind suddenly died down and people found that the spring, which was supposed to be blooming with a riot of colours, was gone. It was already summer.

The spring of 1938 didn't delight people with its blooming colours like it did in the past. People's attention was not only focused on the withering wind outside the window, but on all kinds of messages which no door or wind could shut out. Radio listeners became much more cautious when they listened to the broadcast from the government after the last house-to-house checks. People were still informed about events such as that the troops led by Zhang Zizhong and Pang Binxun had a fierce battle with the Japanese in Shandong province, that the government was determined to fight the Japanese, that the New Fourth Army was heading north to fight the Japanese, and that the Eighth Route Army had launched guerrilla warfare in the plains.

All that news was encouraging. The Chinese army's victory at the battle of Tai'erzhuang came in early April, the best season to enjoy magnolias in bloom. People's hearts were raised from the bottom of the icy pit of winter and were kept warm for a while.

Grandpa Lü had been getting better since the end of the spring. He could get out of his bed and walk around for a while. But his hollow eyes full of indifference made people feel so sad when they saw them.

Wei and May caught a severe cold at the same time. May recovered quickly, but Wei caught another cold just as she was recovering from the first one. That cold then developed into bronchopneumonia. The whole family was on tenterhooks and nursed Wei very carefully. He recovered gradually after ten days or so.

That day, Jiangchu was feeding Wei tangerines in his room. She would hold up each segment against the light to make sure there were no seeds left in them while she listened to Wei reading *Gulliver's Travels* which he had started to read after he finished *Robinson Crusoe*.

Liu Fengcai came to say Secretary Huang was here. Secretary Huang had a low position in the company with a poor salary, so he didn't get any travel allowance to move his big family of old and young to the south. He stayed behind in the company to take care of things, but he didn't have much to take care of and he hadn't paid Jiangchu a visit for a long time.

Jiangchu said to Wei: "Take a break from your reading now. You have only just recovered. Don't tire yourself out."

She got up to go and meet Secretary Huang in the living room. He was rooted to the spot, with his thin, skinny figure worrying where he should place himself. He gave Jiangchu a deep bow upon seeing her.

"What's the matter?" Jiangchu thought he had come to present his regular greetings to her, but now she felt in her heart that something was amiss.

"Yes... yes... There is something," answered Secretary Huang rather hesitantly while he fumbled in his pocket to get out a telegram. "Please don't worry about the general manager. He is safe and sound. It is just, just, that he had a fall and got hurt. Not a serious one." Jiangchu snatched the telegram:

'MR. TANTAI MIAN HAS FALLEN FROM HIS HORSE STOP BROKEN HIS LEG STOP LOOKING FORWARD TO MRS TANTAI'S ARRIVAL STOP'

The telegram was dated one week ago. "Is it true? It's nothing serious?" asked Jiangchu in a trembling voice, her hands trembling, too.

"No, no!" Secretary Huang sympathised with Mrs Tantai, and his face was so contorted, it looked like the harder he tried, the more sympathy he had for her. As Mian's secretary, he was supposed to propose solutions, but he really didn't know what to suggest. He just looked at Jiangchu expectantly, with a pained look on his face and chanted: "No, no."

"Ask Mrs Meng to come over." Jiangchu sent Amah Liu, who was serving tea, for Bichu, and instructed: "Ask Liu Fengcai to pick up Miss Xuan from school."

She went directly to the reading table at the other end of the room and opened a map of China. The location of Xichang city had long been imprinted on her mind when Mian was sent there. Now she had to study the route to the place and check how far the train could take them.

Bichu came in no time. Secretary Huang greeted her: "Mrs Meng, you see, who could have known what would happen."

After he told Bichu the whole story, she tried to comfort her sister: "It's normal that Mian needs someone to take care of him. His broken leg will confine him to bed and cause him a lot of inconvenience. It's very unlikely that something terrible has happened. Anyway, we will all leave in the end. If you leave now, at least your family can be reunited earlier."

They then discussed for a while and agreed that Jiangchu had to go to Wuhan first and then figure out what to do next once she was there. When they were done, they sent Secretary Huang back home. Before he left, it occurred to him that he might go to the company and ask the old employees who had remained whether anyone could go with Jiangchu or if anyone had any good ideas to share.

Bichu pondered: "We'd better lie low and make sure as few people as possible know about the departure. In case anyone tries to stop them, it's very likely that they won't be able to leave at all. It's just my assumption, though. I don't know much about Mian's company, after all."

Jiangchu nodded and said to Huang: "My sister has made a very good point. Yes, you don't need to tell anyone about our departure except the few families who are very close to us. You may also need to check the train tickets for us, too."

Upon those words, the pained expression on Secretary Huang's face eased somewhat, then he bowed and said his goodbyes.

Xuan came back home fast. She ran gracefully up the steps and stood behind her mother once she had entered the room as if she was guarding her. "When are we leaving?" asked Xuan.

Jiangchu felt supported, leaning against Xuan. "Where's Wei? Has he heard the news? Is he well enough to travel with us?" She showered her mother with questions about Wei, comfortable in the assumption that she was sure to be going with her mother.

Jiangchu and Bichu looked at each other and decided to talk about Wei later. Jiangchu sighed: "What a heavy load you are going to shoulder now you must take care of father all by yourself. How should I deliver the news to father?"

"Is there anything that will upset him more? Let's just tell him the truth," Bichu said. "Besides, it's certainly not the best time to travel, and you need to make several transfers, too, so I think you'd better take someone with you to help you out. You can't count on anyone from Mian's company. Liu Fengcai is a good choice in terms of his capability, but he has his family to take care of. It would be improper to ask him to desert his family to accompany ours."

"He won't go with me. I know this man," said Jiangchu.

Xuan said: "I will be mum's first bodyguard. It's OK if we don't have anyone else to help."

Bichu said: "I'm well aware how capable my darling niece Xuan is. I'm thinking about our chef Chai Fali. He has a strong sense of responsibility, and is literate. He has been running the kitchen quite well for the last six years. When you arrive in Nanchang, it'll be a big help for you if he can do the cooking. When you move on, he'll be very helpful all the way."

Jiangchu thought hard: "What are you going to do then? You will leave, too. But who will leave with you if Chef Chai leaves with me this time?"

"We'll see what we can do when we leave. If I leave with father, then we'll have Lü Guitang. If we plan well ahead of time, it shouldn't be a problem. But your situation is urgent. It's better for you to have some help."

Jiangchu fell silent.

"How should we pack? I'll do the packing!" Xuan put the question impatiently, wishing she had wings so that she could fly to her father immediately.

Jiangchu said to Bichu thoughtfully: "Xuan is leaving with me. That's settled. She has to quit school, though. I'm concerned about Wei. He has just recovered and is not strong enough for such a long trip. If the inflammation comes back, where could I find a doctor along the way?"

Bichu proposed, musingly: "If you trust me, leave Wei with me then."

Jiangchu fell silent again. She trusted herself best.

Time was pressing, so Xuan was first asked to go back to her college to apply for her permit to be suspended from school. A couple of peddlers selling snacks were still visible on campus, but instead of the choice of delicacies they used to provide, they only had things such as dried apricot candy bars and crispy sugar-coated walnuts favoured by 17 and 18-year-old girls.

Xuan, perfunctorily dealing with greetings from several classmates, continued to walk through the campus, with mixed feelings of disturbance and excitement in her heart. The application process was quite simple since she only needed an official transcript for a transfer to another college in the future. After she had completed the application, she went back to her dormitory to pack her things. She was told to inform Earl to go back home, too.

Seeing Earl lying lazily in her bed, Xuan jumped at her: "Get up!" yelled Xuan at Earl, thinking to herself: "My hands are so full. How can I spare any time to tell you to go home?"

Earl looked at Xuan rather impatiently, but when she knew what had happened, she jumped out of her bed: "You are leaving first! That's so great!"

"My father has a broken leg. How great is that?"

"I'll help you with your packing." Earl seldom offered to help with anything.

After informing Earl to go home, Xuan turned to her own business. She first said goodbye to her close friends on campus, and then phoned several more when she got home, including Paul, who had asked if he could visit her the following day.

When Paul visited, Xuan was wearing a white frilly apron, and was busy packing her luggage with Xiangge. She wasn't taking much with her, so most of the items were packed. The furniture in the small living room of her apartment was already covered, leaving lots of books scattered on the floor. Her dolls were lined up individually against one wall, with their enormous eyes staring at the room. The Japanese ones had been eradicated from her collection.

Seeing Xuan so serious about her packing, Paul said: "I think this is the best for you. You know, war sometimes throws up so many surprises."

Xuan seated him on a small stool by the piles of furniture and asked the servant to serve tea, but no one replied.

Xiangge rushed to offer her help: "I'll go and get the tea."

"Look how miserable we are — being forced to leave home to meet my father who is thousands of miles away," smiled Xuan. "But I'm really excited about leaving Beiping and being free of the shiny bayonets dangling over my head. It's hard for me to leave the college and the city, though."

"I'm excited for you, too," Paul said. "Whatever happens, how dare those Japanese hover their bayonets over Miss Tantai's head?"

A rosy tint flushed Xuan's fair, tender face. She sneered: "How naïve you are! You don't think it could happen to you because you still have your country standing firmly behind you!"

Paul continued without taking offence: "The Chinese government fought a fine battle at Tai'erzhuang, and the communist party has won battles, too."

"So maybe we're not completely doomed. We may come back one day." Her eyes were fixed on the line of dolls: "They are doomed to hide in a trunk. They are lucky that they won't age though I don't know how many years they will have to stay put."

Xiangge brought tea for Paul. She glanced at Paul, biting her lips in a smile, eyes goggling.

Xuan introduced her as a member of the clan. When Paul said he didn't get it, Xuan explained in English, then Paul realised Xiangge was a distant relative on Xuan's mother's side, but that she could rely on Xuan's family and the extended Lü family.

"What a lot of favours to take care of so many," he said, telling Xuan that he thought this girl was good-looking.

"I'm fed up with Beiping," said Paul, his eyes fixed on Xiangge's back as she was leaving. "Maybe I'll head for the south. But it depends on the world situation. The Japanese invasion of China is just the beginning of a bigger war."

"That would be exciting."

"Certainly it would. We Americans have the responsibility for world peace and safety, so we have to take many things into consideration."

"Oh, my Lord! We Chinese have been considering a lot, too! But unlike you, I can't represent China. You said you are fed up with Beiping, I assume you mean Beiping under the rule of the Japanese? No one would get bored with the real Beiping."

"Have you had any news from Wei Feng?"

"No. Are you going to interrogate me?"

Paul laughed: "Sometimes, I think fate is a strange thing. And the strangest is that I have learned Chinese and have been sent to work in China."

Xuan said rather seriously: "I think fate is strange, too. Why me? Why am I leaving Beiping now, instead of Earl and her family?"

"Will the Meng family leave, too?"

"Of course, they will. Later. Eventually."

The door opened gently, and three heads popped in through the crack, with Wei's on the top, May's in the middle and Kiddo's at the bottom.

The sight made Paul laugh out: "Hello, guys." Xuan instructed them to come in immediately. Paul excused himself after wishing Xuan a safe trip.

May squatted in front of the line of dolls when she entered: "I'm so sorry that they have to be locked up in a case."

"Come, pick one," said Xuan.

"Can I?" She took Shirley into her arms at once: "Cousin Xuan, I know you love Shirley most. I'll take care of her for you."

"You may put a couple more in my luggage," said Wei.

"Your luggage? It's still not sure whether you are going to leave with us at all," said his sister.

"I want to take care of dad, too" said Wei. "It's better you stay, actually."

"I'm sorry, brother, because it's not I who caught bronchopneumonia," said Xuan mischievously, wrapping her hands gently around her brother's shoulders.

No decision was made about whether Wei would stay or not until the day before Jiangchu and Xuan's departure. However reluctant Wei felt, he had enough sense to know he should listen and not add to his mother's worries.

As Jiangchu swallowed her tears and told him of her decision, he was speechless for a while before he agreed. Then he came to soothe Jiangchu instead: "Mum, don't you worry about me. I'm completely recovered and won't be a burden to Aunt Bichu."

Once it was settled that Wei would stay, the first thing they did was to move his room from the master compound to one of the main rooms in the west garden. May and Kiddo were so happy that they bustled in and out, helping carry small items from Wei's room to their garden.

A vacant house might attract attention from the Japanese, so they also decided Secretary Huang and his family should move into Tantai's compound in the front garden to take care of the place, too. The west garden had no room for Wei's large toys and his model plane, so a room in the front garden was specially earmarked as his games room.

Jiangchu was meticulous about things in Wei's new room, from big pieces of furniture to small decorative items. All of the quilts and comforters had been tagged, but she still reminded him again and again that he should remember to change them according to the season.

She emphasized: "Aunt Bichu is family. You should listen to her anytime. You must remember to take your prescription medicine on time. When you are completely recovered, you need to read, and do your boxing and exercise regularly every day. Don't neglect your study or your exercise. Remember you are not allowed to go out of the residence! When you have time, go and see your grandfather as often as possible and keep him entertained." At these words, Wei turned around to wipe his tears with the back of his hands.

He was lucky because he still had May, Kiddo and Henry, his German shepherd dog. Henry had been moved to the west garden, too. Upon seeing his doghouse in the gallery, he went into it without being told. His paws were resting on the small door-sill of his doghouse, his head on his paws. His sad eyes followed Wei as if he were asking him "when are we going to leave?"

Wei told his mother: "Mum, don't treat me like a child anymore. Trust me. I was no longer a child from the day the Japanese entered Beiping." He had grown taller than Jiangchu, a fact which made his words even more convincing.

Jiangchu dabbed her eyes with her handkerchief and forced a smile: "Who is treating you like a child? You are staying because you are a brave and smart grown-up man with a strong sense of responsibility. You are staying to help Aunt Bichu."

Xuan added: "We'll see each other in several days. Don't take such matters to heart."

When Jiangchu and Xuan were leaving, Wei was not allowed to see them off, and he didn't insist, either. May and Kiddo had kept him company from morning until bedtime. Grandpa Lü asked Wei to join him at dinner that evening, and gave him a pure yellow bloodstone with red spots all over it. It was of first-class quality.

When Chef Chai left with Jiangchu, Bichu asked Liu Fengcai to cook and Amah Zhao to do the laundry and house cleaning.

Time passed peacefully. Liu Fengcai had once learnt how to cook, but since he hadn't cooked for a long time, his rudimentary skills were quite rusty. Sometimes the dishes were tasteless, sometimes they were too salty, which amazed everybody. All the kids, except Earl who would complain when she was eating at home, handled this with quite good humour. Wei called Liu Fengcai's cooking a book of jokes published in instalments, which was updated every two days, and that what happened next was going to be told in the next chapter. Liu Fengcai didn't take any offence since those words came from his young master.

Wei grew better and stronger with every passing day. He seemed to grow even taller. These facts made Bichu visibly happy. Another comforting thing for her was that no one had come to bother her father since Beiping had been occupied almost one year ago. Maybe, just maybe, the old man had outgrown his usefulness to the Japanese. Plus, the old man couldn't stand much exhausting long-distance travel. Staying in Beiping seemed to be the best option.

In the still of the night, or when she awoke from her dreams, Bichu would turn this thing over and over in her mind. All previous plans to leave had focused on the old man. A more realistic assessment of these plans revealed how impossible it was to carry them out. To take father with her when she left was almost out of the question. But how could her heart rest in peace if she left the old man behind? Would the Japanese put him under secret surveillance? What upset her most was the old man's strange, dull look with that pair of hollow, wondering eyes peering into the distance, focusing on nothing.

Families with close relationships with the Tantais and the Mengs left one by one. Several days after Jiangchu's departure, Mrs Qin, the wife of President Qin, called Bichu to say goodbye. Li Lian's wife, Jin Shizhen, came to visit Bichu with her children one fine, sunny afternoon in early May.

Mrs Li, Jin Shizhen, was wearing a *qipao* decorated with broad lines in the same colour as the dress. It was hard to discern the style and material, but the colour looked like Indanthrene dye. She was very thin, but not graceful. Her movements were stiff and stick-like.

Holding her only son, Zhiquan, in her hand, she walked into the west garden, commenting loudly: "How come you have such a big house in town! Why are there so many people in the front garden? What a noisy crowd! Does the master of the house live in the back garden? How many people are staying with him? Isn't it horrible to live in such a big house with so few people?"

Her eldest daughter Zhiqin was quietly following behind her, holding her sister Zhiwei by the hand.

Bichu immediately invited her in, asked her to take a seat

and ordered tea to be served for them. She told Earl and May to keep Zhiqin and the other two kids company, saying she'd like to have tea with Mrs Li.

Mrs Li came from a family which belonged to the eight Mongol banners[1], and her family name Jin was said to have been given by one of the Qing emperors, and was of royal lineage. But why the family was given the name remained unknown. The Li family stayed in town most of the time, so Mrs Li didn't have many connections with other professors' wives. Her manners and her accent were both marked with a sort of philistine flavour. She was also known for her eccentric religious beliefs and her mysterious tricks and treatments as well.

"You are so kind to have accepted Wenlian's request to take us along with you to the south. We are all counting on you." Jin Shizhen was direct, her smile languishing in her voice, trying to be elegant by addressing her husband by his courtesy name 'Wenlian'. "Whatever price I'm going to pay, I'll stick around with him. He can't get rid of us. Who knows how long this war will last."

Bichu told her she was welcome to join them. Having made her point, Jin Shizhen then switched the conversation to gossip.

As for the children, Earl came out and greeted her, then went back to her room and stayed there. May took over the job of entertaining the other kids.

---

[1] The Eight banners (八旗 or *baqi*) were administrative and military divisions in the Qing dynasty. All Manchu households were placed into the Eight banners which functioned as armies in wartimes, the elite forces of the Qing military. The banner system was also the basic organizational framework of the Manchu society. Membership of the banners was hereditary, and bannermen were granted land and income by the emperor.

Zhiqin was a very gentle girl with a very ordinary face. With her two long braids hanging down all the way from her head along her chest, she was always framed with a thoughtful but dull look, belying her age.

Upon seeing Kiddo taking out a variety of toys — cars, guns, cannons, trains, and dolls — she couldn't hold back the inclination to exclaim: "How many toys you have!" She picked up a toy train at random: "It's very well made."

Zhiwei stood rather foolishly by her side, while Zhiquan looked up at her elder sister and snatched the train from her, exclaiming: "What are you doing? We are setting up the track to run the train."

May and Kiddo were aghast to witness such rudeness, but they helped Zhiquan with the construction of the track anyway. The train was running around the track in no time. The kids all cheered up.

"You are so happy," Zhiqin forced a smile. "We have never played like this before," she told May.

"What do you do then when you are off school?"

"I do the house chores, take care of my sister and little brother, and do my homework," answered Zhiqin, as if absorbed in thought. She also helped her mum to hold religious rites, or to make a big feast of chicken or goose and suchlike to entertain members of her mother's communion, which she was embarrassed to mention.

"I help with the chores and I take care of Kiddo," said May innocently. "If he gets naughty, I hand him to Amah Zhao."

Zhiqin chuckled: "Why don't you hand him to your elder sister?"

"She's grumpy all the time. But I'm happy all the time,"

said May, tilting her head a little, her expressive eyes brimming with laughter, echoing her statement that she was happy about everything. She looked beautiful.

Zhiqin looked out of the window, lost in thought. Lilac twigs with thick fading blossoms were clustered riotously in front of the window, from which a small bundle of gay colours flew out. "A butterfly!" Zhiqin happily took May's hand and ran out of the room.

"Why are you running about? Where are your manners?" yelled her mother from the inner room. Zhiqin halted at the sound of her voice.

"Shall we let them go out and have a look?" Bichu suggested. "There are some flowers in the garden."

Zhiqin didn't pay any attention to the flowers in the garden. Her eyes were fixed on the butterfly beating its wings up and down.

"Is she happy that she has been accepted by the biology department?" She was going to graduate from high school in a couple of months, but she wasn't asked by anyone what she would like to study in college.

"Who? You mean my sister? I don't see it." May was busy watching the butterfly, too. "You like butterflies? Do you want to go to the biology department, too?"

May guessed right that Zhiqin did want to study biology, simply due to her love of butterflies. She wanted to study butterflies, but now that had turned out to be just an unrequited wish since they had to leave their home and move far away to the disease-ridden southwest. Maybe she would have to quit school and stay at home to do the chores.

"There are many butterflies in Kunming, bigger ones,"

said May. "When my eldest aunt, Aunt Suchu, and her family visited us here in Beiping, Huishu brought many for us. But they were all left behind in Square Teakettle."

Zhiqin had heard of Square Teakettle. Her father Li Lian took her to Minglun University once and told her the name of each building. It was during that time that she saw many butterflies dancing up and down in front of the Leaning-Against-the-Clouds apartment building, over the lawn festooned with flowers in the grass in front of Square Teakettle and Round Rice-Steamer. She sighed softly: "Huishu?"

"Huishu is my cousin, and Square Teakettle is my home. We have lots of fireflies back there. I like fireflies even more than butterflies," May said, disappearing into the flowers.

"Do you want to have this one?" she asked, pointing at one brightly-coloured butterfly. With a nimble pinch of her thumb and forefinger, she had the butterfly between her fingers.

"Oh, no, no. I don't want it," Zhiqin said immediately, waving her hand. She cast a glance at the floral door curtain made of finely sliced bamboo hanging in the doorway to the room where her mother and Bichu were.

"Zhiqin! Why are you mingling with the small kids?" barked Mrs Li. "Come inside."

Zhiqin shot an apologetic smile at May and went back into the room. May felt sorry for her. She set the butterfly in her palm, blew gently on it, and set it free.

She heard Mrs Li saying in the room: "Since our eldest girl is too honest to know things, the four of us will be such a burden to you."

Bichu said: "Is Zhiqin the same age as Earl? But she looks much more mature. I'm sure you won't be a burden to me at all."

"When can we leave? Do you have any set date? This is so annoying. Wenlian has been gone for so long and he has sent us only one single letter," said Mrs Li through clenched teeth as she remembered the solitary letter. "He wants to dump us all. I will never let that happen!"

Bichu tried to calm her: "Professor Li left at the end of last year. It would have taken him such a long time to get there before he could settle down. Besides, you know how unreliable the postal services are nowadays. Anyway, we'll leave Beiping together. That's for sure."

"You and your husband are so trustworthy, that's why we asked if we could join you," said Mrs Li, urging Bichu to accept the two packs of pastry she had brought with her. While her kind offer was being declined, May went into the room with a big bouquet of lilac flowers in her arms. Mrs Li came face to face with May, which led her to exclaim, as if she had only just noticed May: "Oh! Is this Miss May?"

After eyeing May up from head to toe, she uttered: "This girl is destined to marry one of the highest-ranking officials in the country in the future. I'm not joking."

May, neither embarrassed nor annoyed, showed her mother the lilac bouquet and ran into the bedroom. Bichu thought to herself: "Fortunately she was talking about May. If she had been talking about Earl, Earl would have taken huge offence!"

She then noticed Mrs Li's eyes had lost focus, which reminded her of the rumour that Mrs Li had a 'mind-eye' which could see into the future and the past. She decided to interrupt: "Do you have a carriage waiting? We have one or two who know us well and they can come to pick you up now, if that suits you." Her words broke Mrs Li's trance, and as she came around, she got her group together and said goodbye to Bichu.

Having seen Mrs Li and her children off, Bichu felt worn out. Back in the room, she found Wei, who had been with her grandfather, fiddling with a piece of round opaque cream-coloured stone. Wei raised the stone for Bichu to look at, and told her merrily: "Grandfather asked me to carve four characters on this stone. I have been practicing on soap bars."

He handed her a piece of paper with four Chinese characters written in small-seal style, fresh with red ink-paste: 剑吼西风 (*jian hou xi feng*) — 'my sword rages against the biting west wind'.

"*Jian hou xi feng?*" Bichu was stroking the round stone as she uttered these words, lost in thought.

"Yes, *jian hou xi feng*." Grandfather didn't explain to him what the four characters meant, but he could feel the power and grandeur embodied in them. His carving knife in hand, he was scutinising the stone this way and that in high spirits.

> *"How pathetic a veteran I have become,*
> *Who has outgrown his usefulness*
> *To volunteer to fight at the front,*
> *And capture the enemy's commander.*
> *Look! Even my sword is roaring with rage,*
> *Against the biting west wind."*

Bichu hummed several lines from the poem entitled *Song of the Six States: The Hero Trapped* by He Zhu[2] who lived in the early Song dynasty (960-1127). Sadness surged from her heart. She stroked Wei's shoulders like Jiangchu would have, and went into her room.

---

[2] He Zhu: (贺铸) a poet in the Northern Song dynasty who is best known for his witty lyrics (词 *ci*) and poems full of subtlety and feeling.

Part 2

Bichu felt very tired. The responsibilities once shared by the Tantai and Meng couples now rested completely on her shoulders. She not only had to concern herself with day-to-day necessities. Her priority now was how to ensure a safe trip for all the remaining family members to move south, and whether she should take her father with her or leave him behind here in Beiping. The latter was the real headache.

About two weeks after Jiangchu left, Bichu received a letter from Fuzhi. The letter was habitually laconic and general, but Bichu was well aware of what was implied, reading between the lines. Fuzhi said the College of Liberal Arts had been moved to a small county called Guihui, and he was asking her to join him when it was convenient for her to do so. In the postscript, he attached four lines:

> *"My soul is never afraid of any blockade,*
> *Be it mountains or grenades,*
> *It travels back to you and lingers*
> *At Square Teakettle, every night."*

Bichu pressed the letter against her heart for a long time, and then opened it and kept reading at least 20 more times.

She sat in silence for a while, cut the lines off, put the slip of paper into her handbag, and headed for the master compound. When she had almost reached the door to the hall, she paused, thinking it would be better if she informed Lianxiu first. She went back to the west garden, and sent May for Granny Lianxiu.

Lianxiu came in with her regular ingratiating smile: "Time is going fast! Now the peonies are in full bloom. I'm going to ask you to let me have one or two to put into a vase for Grandpa Lü to appreciate."

Bichu looked out of the window and saw how true it was — two white Chinese herbaceous peonies were proudly displaying their complicated petals in crowns as big as saucers, radiating with elegance and luxuriance. She said with genuine admiration: "Only Aunt Lianxiu possesses such tranquillity. I pass the bush many times a day, but I have never noticed the change, the buds or the blossoms."

She handed Lianxiu Fuzhi's letter and said: "It was always the plan to leave. What's father's opinion? Has he ever mentioned it to you?"

Lianxiu answered: "He has never talked about the whole issue with me, but I can guess from the scraps of information he has given. He won't leave Beiping. Miss Bichu, he can't leave. His health won't allow him to travel. This is the first reason. The second reason is that if he stays, he won't attract any attention, but if he leaves it's very likely that no one in the family could leave at all."

Her eyes were shiny like buttons, but both her gaunt face and her eyes were raked with furrows of anxiety. "It looks like he has made up his mind. But I dare not say."

Bichu thought for a while and then went to the master compound with Lianxiu. The old man was sitting in bed with the lower part of his body tucked neatly in a comforter. When he saw Lianxiu, he asked gently: "Where have you been?"

"I've been seeing Miss Bichu." Lianxiu tucked in one corner of the comforter one more time before going to get a towel. She wet the towel in the basin set on the stove which kept the water warm, dried it, and wiped the old man's eyes and whiskers carefully. The old man's eyes followed her wherever she went, attached, docile and somewhat absent-minded. Bichu's heart ached upon seeing the kitten-like look in her father's eyes.

"I assume you are going to leave soon, too?" he asked Bichu quietly. For him, daughters were never meant to be kept at home. from the day they got married, he had never thought of counting on them if he was too old to live alone. Among his three daughters, his favourite had always been Bichu, who was keen, calm and kind. However great a daughter she was, she still had her own family to take care of. He was well satisfied to have had her by his side for all those years in Beiping.

"Father is so far-sighted," said Bichu, forcing a smile. She told him about Fuzhi's letter. "Mrs Zhuang and her children asked us to go with them a long time ago. Now Mrs Li and her children are going to join us. With the three families travelling together, we can take even better care of you, father. We'll transfer to ships when we get to Tianjin. It'll be much more comfortable for you to travel by sea."

The old man shook his head: "I appreciate your love for and devotion to me, but I have run out of strength to travel so far."

"If father can enjoy a peaceful life even if you must conceal your identity, it is not a bad choice to stay. But how can they resist the opportunity to create trouble? Yes, we don't see anything coming yet, but who knows what they will cook up."

"That's why I'm asking you all to leave while you still can!" The old man interrupted his daughter, panting, and immediately had a coughing spasm. His face turned purple, and he kept alternately sneezing and spitting. Lianxiu rushed to clean up the sputum he had coughed up which stained his whiskers, while Bichu rubbed his chest and massaged his back.

When the coughing fit died down, he then said to Bichu: "See? Do you still think I can leave? I will only be a burden to you. You just take the kids and leave. The vigilante committee was set up a long time ago, and no one has come to me or to bother me. I think I have outgrown my usefulness to them. They will tolerate my living here with a concealed identity. I've got Lianxiu here to help me in the residence, and Lü Guitang for the outside world. I can manage."

"But how can I leave if father remains in the tiger's mouth? We are in a time of war!" Bichu was choking with sobs.

The old man said gently: "It is true that if I stay, I am living in the tiger's mouth; but if I leave, I'm dragging you all into the tiger's mouth. If I stay, the jaws of that tiger may not close after all, but if the tiger is annoyed, it will surely take a big bite. Still, we can think it over and see whether we can figure out a better way."

Knowing only too well that there was no other way out, Bichu accepted her father's words of comfort and went back to the west garden. Without anyone she could talk to about it, her heart was pounding, and her stomach felt like it was teeming with a million butterflies.

That night, she kept tossing and turning long after they had gone to bed. May was turning in her small bed, too, and then she whispered to Bichu: "Mummy, can I come into your bed?" With these words, she crawled into the big bed and slipped under Bichu's quilt. "Mummy, I know grandpa can't leave with us, and that that worries you so much. Why don't you take sister and Kiddo with you while I stay here to take care of grandpa?"

Bichu pulled that small bundle of warmth to her side: "My girl! How thoughtful you are! But you are too young to do that. You go back to sleep, now."

"I'm old enough. Whatever you ask me to do, I'll manage." May wanted desperately to leave with her mother. She wanted to see her father, but if her staying behind would ease her mother's pain so that she could help out her grandfather, she would stay. She had never been her grandfather's favourite, though.

"It won't help even if you stay, my girl," said Bichu, patting May on the back, and reached inside the bed to feel Kiddo and make sure he was covered under his quilt. "Granny Lianxiu can take care of grandpa. Anyone who stays will have to handle the Japanese, but they have no protection since Beiping has fallen into the hands of the Japanese."

"When we arrive in the south, we'll have our country and our protection, won't we?" May tried hard to see through the darkness, then she continued: "Will Beiping remain occupied by the Japanese forever?"

Bichu answered immediately: "That won't happen! It all depends on whether we have the capability to beat the Japanese and win it back."

"Then I will study hard and become very capable!" said May. Lying beside her mother, May felt warm and secure. She wanted to say more but she had already fallen asleep.

Stroking May's silk-like hair, Bichu mulled over May's

words and was moved by her kindness, then her heart sank again with heavy bitterness.

Early next morning, Bichu got up to clean the house while the kids were still asleep. Amah Zhao had told Bichu that she would do the cleaning, but Bichu insisted. When she reached the gallery, she saw the two peony flowers brimming with vitality and beauty. She didn't realise she needed a vase until she had cut them off and put them on the table. She was busy rummaging in the cabinet when Lianxiu's voice reached her: "Miss Bichu, Grandpa Lü is here."

Bichu stopped fumbling around and went out to see the old man tottering in, with Lü Guitang and Lianxiu on either side each holding one of his arms, followed by Xiangge carrying a spittoon and some hand towels.

"Father! What brings you here so early?" Bichu hastened to move a recliner for the old man to sit on.

"I need to exercise to get some strength for the trip," the old man answered jubilantly. He looked refreshed in his loose, light damson-coloured morning coat, his long thin silver-grey whiskers flying in front of his chest.

"Father is leaving?" Bichu felt refreshed and surprised at these words.

"I'm telling you this," the old man said in a mysterious tone. "Last night, the guerrillas from Xishan sent someone to me, saying they are going to pick me up to stay with them in the mountains. If I can manage to get out of the city gate, it shouldn't take long to reach the mountains, should it, Guitang? Guitang brought the man in to meet me, didn't you?"

As he was talking to Bichu, he referred to Guitang from time to time, as if to seek confirmation from him. Guitang kept nodding his head, but the uneasiness on his face was too obvious to miss. Lianxiu's face was tear-stained as well, but she dared not dry herself.

Bichu was at a loss, looking at the old man, expecting to learn more. The old man continued: "That guy studied in Minglun, too. He said he knew Wei Feng, and he also knew that I spent my whole life overthrowing the Qing government, participating in the revolution in 1911, and later promoting cooperation between the Nanjing government and the communist party, which succeeded in putting me on Chiang Kai-shek's 'naughty list'. He knew I had only one wish — to see a flourishing and prosperous China. He has invited me to stay in Xishan until they take back Beiping. When we win the war against the Japanese, China will then gain global recognition that we Chinese are a capable member of the world community."

"How are you going to reach Xishan?" asked Bichu.

"When you all leave, they'll come to pick me up. You just go ahead. Don't worry about me. They'll come to get me," the old man said with a forceful nod.

Upon these words, Lianxiu could no longer hold back her tears. It suddenly dawned on Bichu that her father was just trying to comfort her. That was his best way out! Her voice died out in sobs when she muttered: "Father!"

Lü Guitang raised his voice: "It was I who brought the man in to meet Grandpa Lü. They had a very good talk. Aunt Bichu, you and the kids just leave. The guerrillas are very resourceful. They always get what they want with their connections from the bottom to the top. This is so easy for them." The old man heard Lü Guitang very clearly and smiled with satisfaction.

"I know father always tells the truth." Except for the old man's favourite reply, Bichu couldn't think of anything else to say. The old man looked at her closely and solicited a reluctant smile from her.

He was worried that Bichu might cry in front of him, so he patted her on the arm to show that he wanted to get up: "I want to have a look at the kids. Are they still asleep?" Everyone rushed to help him.

Bichu led the old man to Wei's room first. Wei was asleep with his face facing the wall. Half of the thin dark-green silk cover was lying on the floor. He woke and sat up abruptly, staring at his grandfather in confusion.

"Wei, my good boy. You are going to leave now. The country needs you. You must try your best at whatever it is you are going to do. Never let up on anything," said the old man.

Though baffled, Wei immediately jumped out of bed, and answered respectfully: "Yes, I will."

Noticing the round stone on the nightstand, the old man reached for it and brought it close to his eyes.

Wei said: "I have tried three times."

The old man nodded: "Umm. Print it out and show me later."

May and Kiddo were sound asleep. May's face looked rosy. Kiddo was making smacking noises with his mouth in his dream. The old man stood there, waving his hand to tell them not to wake up the kids. His eyes lingered on Kiddo for a long, long time. He sighed softly and went back to the living room.

He asked: "Is Earl home?" Bichu said Earl was on campus. The old man nodded and left the west garden, attended by a small crowd. Bichu walked the old man back, helped him sit on the bed, and then excused herself.

"Aunt Bichu!" Lü Guitang called from behind. He sounded rather hesitant. "Grandpa Lü asked me to say so. It is so real for him. He has been trying hard to help you make up your mind to leave without him. His heart won't rest until he sees you leave with the kids."

"We are all at our wits' end." Bichu's was grief-stricken. "We will leave! But how can I set my heart at ease like this?"

We will leave! That was Bichu's final decision. She set up a meeting with Della immediately. Zhuang Youchen had been in Kunming for a while since finishing his task in Tianjin. After several rounds of discussion, Bichu and Della decided they would go to Tianjin and travel by ship from there. The time of departure was set for early June.

The master compound had become so empty that the old man decided to move into the gallery garden where Xuan used to live, while Lü Guitang and his daughter moved to the south compound. All the non-essential stuff would be left in the west garden. Bichu suggested the moving be done before her departure since more helping hands were still available. It was too much for the handful of them to live in dozens of empty rooms. When the move began, the residence was topsy-turvy. Everything that was left was given to Liu Fengcai, Amah Zhao and Grandpa Lü's cook. The latter was considered as 'non-essential' and was thus dismissed. Some of the guests who once stayed in the south compound came back to ask for things when they heard the news.

Bichu was doing the packing with the help of Amah Zhao but was in such a troubled state of mind. Would she ever come back? Would she ever see her father again? How silly it was for her to want all the family to stay together in such an unstable time of war! She was so lucky that she could still look forward to being reunited. How about those less fortunate ones who had lost their homes and their lives? Sometimes she would blame herself like that, other times she would feel so happy at the thought that she was going to see Fuzhi so soon. The packing went on for several days amid her mood swings.

That day, she remembered she should bring some clothing materials for her eldest sister Suchu. Those pieces of brocade she had didn't look beautiful enough. Besides, she also needed to pack some everyday articles. She decided to go to the Dong'an market. May and Kiddo were raised on the Minglun campus. They seldom went into town, and the trips they made to the Dong'an market were few and far between, so they begged to tag along, and asked Wei to join them, too. Wei said since they were leaving, it was worth paying a visit to the market.

It had been raining continuously for almost a week. It was wet everywhere, complicating the process of moving and cleaning up. Amah Zhao allowed herself a bit of time out from the heavy burden of moving to make a doll in a red coat with a pair of green trousers, holding a broom in its arms, and put it up on the door frame of the hall. She would make such dolls for May, her 'rain sweepers', when it rained a lot.

When people went out or came in, they would all give the doll a poke, urging it to do its rain sweeping. Bichu laughed at Amah Zhao: "You have so much work to do, how did you find time to make this?"

"Miss May loves those small items I make. I just wanted to make one more for her in case I don't have the chance to see her again."

May looked at her and said: "Thank you, Amah." But she didn't pay much attention to Amah Zhao's words because shewas too excited about the prospect of going to the Dong'an market, of taking a big ship to travel to a place that was far, far away where winter-sweet flowers bloomed, and daddy was sitting under one of those blooming trees, reading his book.

It was obvious that the rain sweeper didn't take its responsibility seriously. When they went to the market, it was still drizzling. The top of Jingshan mountain was capped with thick cloud and fog. It looked like the mountain was wearing a giant lousy hat under the gloomy sky. Bichu led the way, holding Kiddo by the hand, followed by May, holding Wei's sleeve, and Wei.

The pavement in the market was quite narrow and uneven with worn out bricks which trapped many puddles of rain, like those old streets in ancient villages. The shops lining the road were brightly lit. The various lovely exhibits in the windows were a fine sight. People on the street could certainly feel the warmth and peace from the light. One store had an elegant display of multicoloured silk; the next one dazzled with sparkling jewellery; another one was full of all kinds of chinaware and hardwood furniture. All these attractive items slowed the pace of their viewers, who were keen to have a careful look at each and every item.

Before they left home, Kiddo had asked his mother to buy him a bowl of chestnut noodles. When he learned chestnut noodles were out of season in spring, he asked for an ice cream instead.

A beautifully printed picture book in the window of an old bookstore caught May's attention. She pressed her face against the glass and figured out it was *Alice in Wonderland*. She had read the Chinese translation, but she had never found such a beautiful picture in that translated version. Wei came to have a look, and commented that the March Hare had such a peculiar look on its face.

Bichu retraced her steps to search for the kids when she found they were not following her. The shop assistant in a long gown came out of the store and invited them to go in and have a look around. "We are running out of time," Bichu frowned.

The shop assistant, beaming, took the book May was looking at and gave it to her, while addressing his words to Bichu: "This is an edition from a well known publisher. You see how much it is? Fifty cents!" Fifty cents could buy half a bag of flour.

May didn't have the faintest idea how much 50 cents was, but she looked up at her mother: "Mummy, I don't want it if it's expensive." Kiddo was on tiptoes, trying to have a good look at the book. He pointed at the March Hare and laughed.

"One book for all three kids! You still think it is not worth the price?" said the shop assistant. Bichu laughed and paid for the book.

"Mummy, can we get one more for Cousin Huishu?" pleaded May, looking up at her mother again.

"Then you'll have to take two. Don't forget your cousin Yingshu," Bichu reminded May.

Yingshu was Huishu's half-brother. It took May a long time to understand the relationship between Huishu and Yingshu later when she had grown up.

May decided to give another copy of Alice in Wonderland to Huishu, while Wei took *Treasure Island* for Yingshu. May carried all three books triumphantly like a winning general.

Then they went into a shop with silks and satin patronised by the family. The shop owner, wearing a skullcap, greeted Bichu happily: "Mrs Meng, I haven't seen you for ages!"

Then he apologized that he couldn't deliver the goods to her door as he used to since he was short-handed for delivery services, otherwise Bichu could just have phoned for what she needed. After she had told them what she wanted, several shop assistants spread out rolls of silks with different colours and patterns on the counter for Bichu to choose from. Some even wrapped the goods around them or on May, so Bichu could have a better look. The shop owner also busied himself offering Bichu his opinion. The silks and satins that had been spread out glowed gracefully in the dim light, filling the shop with a kind of gaiety. Both the buyer and the seller were indulging themselves in the old friendly ambience of the art of trading in Beiping, almost forgetting the fact that the city no longer belonged to them.

Someone opened the door and came in, hurling out some words in Japanese. Everyone in the shop stood rooted to the spot. The shop owner came to his senses first and ran to meet the Japanese, bowing all the way. They were two Japanese officers followed by their orderly.

"Welcome to our humble shop. Please take a seat, gentlemen," said the shop owner, brushing the grand armchairs skilfully with his sleeve. The Japanese cast an arrogant glance around the shop with their bearded jaws held high. May rushed to hide behind her mother. Bichu dragged Wei to her side and jammed her handbag into his hand, telling him to pay immediately, while she hastily pointed at two of the silks and satins.

The orderly went close to Bichu to see what she had got. Bichu, looking neither right nor left, took May and Kiddo to another counter. When Wei was done paying, she signalled to him to lead the way while she acted as the rear guard. Once they were out of the store, they spontaneously picked up their speed in unison. They didn't slow down until they reached the exit of the market. Then they all breathed a sigh of relief.

Everything around Bichu had changed. The gleaming charm had been consumed, so had she. She just wanted to have a good cry. No one mentioned the ice cream. No one wanted to slow down their steps to have a good look at all the goodies. When they were going out of the exit, they ran into several finely dressed Japanese men and women, talking and laughing, bloated with pride and swollen with arrogance. They surveyed Bichu and the kids out of the corners of their eyes. Bichu felt sick. Holding Kiddo with one hand, and Wei with the other, she fled back home.

When Earl jeered at their poor choices later that day, no one said anything.

The day of departure was approaching. Bichu wanted Amah Zhao to leave with her, but Amah Zhao said she was already in her 50s and was worried whether she could make it back alive, so she preferred to stay. She hated to part with May the most. May cried and begged Amah Zhao to go with her, but then she cheered up again. The excitement of travelling was spreading among the kids, who talked over and again about what to pack.

Everyone but Kiddo had a personal case. Earl and Wei each had a real suitcase for their clothes, while May had rather a decorative case for her favourite stuff.

She had already put into it a small round inkwell and a bronze ink box with a lid engraved with four characters '自强不息' (*zi qiang bu xi*), which mean 'heaven rewards those who are industrious'. They were a prize she won in her primary school. She also put two paper weights made in the style of wood filled with a copper core, carved with delicate patterns, and engraved with two lines '少壮不努力，老

大徒伤悲' (*shao zhuang bu nuli, lao da tu shang bei*) — a youngster that doesn't work hard is destined to be a beggar in old age. They were presents from her grandfather. She also packed a beautiful sewing box with a green velvet lining and embroidered with traditional cross-stitching, a present her father bought for her during his visit to Europe. Stuffed in between those items were multicoloured marbles, ribbons and silk hankies.

She only had room left for one doll, so she had to decide which one she would take with her between Shirley, Lilly and Little Pitiful. It was an easy decision to leave Lilly behind, but it was a tough one to choose between Shirley and Little Pitiful. She couldn't leave Shirley behind, not because of her beauty, but because of her promise to Cousin Xuan that she'd take care of Shirley for Xuan. How could she break her promise and leave Shirley behind? But Wei told her it was OK to leave Shirley behind because Xuan might want Shirley to stay with her other dolls and wait for her to come back. That settled May's struggle. She invited Shirley to share her bed for one night, said many affectionate words to her, and then said goodbye.

What worried Wei most was his German shepherd dog Henry because his grandfather had never been a fan of any pets. Little Lion was small and grandfather hardly noticed he existed, so he was left to Lianxiu. But Henry was too big to hide from grandfather. Liu Fengcai offered to take care of Henry in the expectation that he might be able to mooch off the dog's allowance. Bichu wanted to give Henry away at first, but then Wei told her that if Liu Fengcai could keep the dog for him, then Henry would still be his dog. It was then agreed that Liu Fengcai would have a two-yuan monthly allowance from Lianxiu for taking care of Henry.

Henry was very upset upon seeing the messy piles of furniture in the garden. He would dash toward Wei from the garden and rest his jaw on Wei's knees, who would pet him and comfort him. When Wei was having meals, he would sit by him, his head held high to look at Wei, his mouth open wide, panting, but no one would blame him for losing his manners by waiting at the table.

The day of departure eventually came. Grandpa Lü had already ordered the kids not to see him off. He planned to move to the gallery garden when Bichu and the kids left. He looked in good spirits watching people moving things from the master compound to the gallery garden.

Bichu took Earl to say goodbye to the old man the night before their departure since they were leaving very early the next morning. The master compound looked even emptier once all the furniture had been moved out, leaving only the two chairs in their original spot where Grandpa Lü and Lianxiu would sit every day. A freshly cleaned low rosewood couch, which had been stored in the east room, had been moved across the room facing the door. The deceased Lady Zhang Mengjia used to sit or lie in it when she was alive. Grandpa Lü sometimes went to sit on it and meditate. The mother-of-pearl inlay on the carved armrests shone in the light.

"Father, why did you put the couch over here? Do you want it moved to the gallery garden?" asked Bichu gently, taking hold of the low stool handed to her by Lianxiu, and sitting down. Earl leaned against the armrest of the couch and stood up.

"Just leave. Don't bother with anything else," retorted the old man impatiently, but he immediately moderated his tone and asked: "So how is everything? Are you all ready to go?"

Bichu nodded.

Lianxiu said: "Grandpa Lü wants to recite his scriptures here, so we asked them to keep some chairs. It will be convenient whenever he comes."

"That sounds good. It's very quiet here." Bichu assumed it might be because of her father's reluctance to leave the compound, and she stopped asking questions.

The old man once mentioned that Xuan was full of life and energy but she lacked depth. She needed to be more discreet. Now when he looked at Earl, he found he had no knowledge about this granddaughter and he didn't know what advice to give her.

After thinking for a while, he said rather vaguely: "It won't be difficult for you to continue your college in Yunnan as a transfer student. Your sister and brother are still young, so you need to help more at home. Talk to your parents if you encounter any trouble."

Earl answered with a simple "yes".

Bichu opened a small bronze-coloured brocade case she had been carrying in front of Lianxiu. Inside were two gold bracelets, four gold rings, other pieces of jewellery, and a deposit book of 500 yuan she planned to use to cover the daily expenses for her father. Bichu said: "I know father doesn't ask the three of us to support him. He didn't need anything in the past. Now it is different, and no one is certain what will happen. I don't know when I will see father again. Father, I want you to keep these things, so I can leave with fewer worries."

"Though we are going to part in life, it's more likely we will be separated by d…" The old man swallowed the word, and signalled to Lianxiu to take the case.

These things would help Lianxiu to maintain their life for

some time, hoped Bichu. Looking at the sunken face of his youngest and favourite daughter and her red-rimmed eyes, he said slowly: "My friend, knowing you are all safe and sound is the happiest thing for me. A good wife is not a title easily earned. You take better care of yourself."

Seeing Bichu silent, he continued: "We can trust the guerrillas. Let's both take care. I have no more to say."

Bichu handed Lianxiu the case and remained seated on the low stool. Lianxiu went over and took her hand. When did Lianxiu's smooth hands become so rough? Why hadn't Lianxiu mentioned anything about the hardships she had been going through? Father's life would be completely dependent on Lianxiu. Turning these things over in her mind, Bichu's heart was overcome with appreciation and trust, holding the rough hands full of calluses.

"Aunt Lianxiu!" she called and stood up, and then she knelt in front of Lianxiu: "Aunt Lianxiu! Thank you so much for taking care of father for the three of us! Thank you!" She was ready to kowtow, but Lianxiu had knelt in front of her and stopped her in time, their eyes wet with tears.

"Mum! Get up, please!" Earl, who was very unhappy with the situation, went over to Bichu and helped her to stand up. What a disgraceful act her mother had just undertaken when she knelt before Lianxiu!

"You go along," the old man said quietly, closing his eyes.

When Bichu reached the door, it suddenly occurred to her: "Aunt Lianxiu, do you need me to send something back to your relatives in your hometown? Have you written a letter?"

Lianxiu shook her head, forcing a brief smile: "I came from a rather small family. No relatives are left in my hometown. When you see Miss Suchu, please give her my regards."

She picked up a red schoolbag embroidered with lots of flowers of different colours and sizes: "This blessed item is for May. Tell her to take it with her." Only Lianxiu knew the meaning of the word 'blessed'. She put the bag by the incense burner every night when she lit joss sticks to pray. It was steeped with all the blessings from all the sacred spirits.

Bichu left with Earl. It was a warm, sweet summer night, but the two felt everything had left them before they left Beiping. Even the all-embracing dark night had become so remote for them.

PART 3

Many things changed in No. 3 Chestnut Street once Bichu left. Lü Guitang and his daughter moved into the south compound; the kitchen garden was empty once all the formally employed cooks had been dismissed. The front garden was occupied by the big extended family of Secretary Huang, who had meals separately in their own rooms with their smaller families, transforming the compound into one of those typical bustling Beijing common-folk courtyards shared by many households. People dashed in and out of the south compound and the kitchen garden freely. The passage to the master compound, which was empty now, was locked.

Grandpa Lü and Lianxiu stayed in the gallery garden. Behind the closed gate to the gallery, it was another world, where Lianxiu suddenly realized that she had become the one who was completely in charge of things.

It had already been 15 years since she had married Mr Lü at the age of 25. For the past 15 years, she had had only one task — to take good care of him. Jiangchu had always been the true head of the household. When friends and relatives had a favour to ask, they would all go to Jiangchu. When they went to Jiangchu, they would always urge her: "Be careful to serve Mr Lü."

"You should hold him in case he slips."

Some would remind her it was easier to catch a cold in one's head, while others would inform her it was easier to catch a cold in one's feet. They were so eager to order her about this way and that, as if the more orders they gave, the more it demonstrated their concern for him.

She always answered yes to all demands with a compliant smile. She had never thought that one day she would be treated as his equal and as a respected family elder. What she wished for was that Mr Lü's two daughters would be satisfied with her service and wouldn't find fault with her. That would make for a perfect peaceful life for her.

Many of their relatives and friends had left for the south; those who had stayed in Beiping remained quietly at home behind closed doors. In the whole month since Bichu's departure, only Ling Jingyao paid a visit to Mr Lü; the latter became more and more attached to Lianxiu, leaving her in charge of everything and telling her not to worry about other people's opinions.

At the beginning, she felt lost and uneasy, then she came to realise how convenient it was without all those other concerns. Now she even enjoyed making decisions, though she never allowed herself to get carried away. What a guilty sense of pleasure she had now that Beiping was in the grip of the Japanese!

For the last two weeks, the old man had been coughing much less, and he was strong enough to walk the length of the garden from the east end to the west ten times or more. He would count the number of times very seriously and insist on finishing it by himself. When he was done with his walking, he would stand at the west end, facing the door to the gallery, and mutter: "Why is it taking so long for the guerrillas to come?"

He might well have forgotten that the guerrillas were just his own creation on which he pinned all his hopes. When such a moment came, Lianxiu would hurry to ask him about a character she didn't know, or a line from an article she couldn't understand, or just brought up some trivial matter to discuss with him, to distract his attention. The old man would withdraw his longing look and gaze upon her face with much attachment. Her face, which looked so withered in the gloomy master compound, now looked somewhat rosy.

Her button-like eyes looked sparkling with life. In fact, she had never been so tired in the last 15 years because of the absence of Amah Wei, who had promised to serve Grandpa Lü, but had to quit when her son sent for her to go back. She told Lianxiu that her daughter-in-law had died and she had to go back to take care of her young grandson. But she never explained the reason for her daughter-in-law's death. She left with the person that had been sent for her, saying she would come back when things were settled at home. Who knows whether she would be allowed to come back into town once she went out of the city?

Lianxiu hated to lower Grandpa Lü's quality of life. She tried her best to make every meal as good as possible, and insisted on changing his clothes on a daily basis. They had a quiet life, though not materially rich anymore, with Xiangge always ready to lend a hand in the home, and Lü Guitang very adept at handling things outside the home. She was hoping, that maybe, just maybe, if she could keep it up for one or two more years, Grandpa Lü might be able to see his daughters again.

The temperature rose as the days passed with one very

much like another. One evening, Grandpa Lü was sitting in the garden, enjoying himself, when he mentioned that it was time to set up the summer awnings at this time of the year.

Guitang answered: "I can put up the awnings by myself. It won't take much work since the garden is smaller, and we still have those poles and reed mats from last year. I'll sort them out tomorrow and see if I can set it up."

Lianxiu was taking in the clean laundry from a clothesline in the garden where it had been drying in the sun, and she smiled at Lü Guitang's words: "What a capable fellow Guitang is! Shall we ask him to make it up for us?" She was looking at Grandpa Lü, waiting for his consent, while he was smiling at her, obviously waiting for her to decide.

Xiangge went out of the kitchen when she was done with the dishes. She took the clothes from Lianxiu and said: "What high spirits you are both in! Since my father doesn't have much to do and I can help, too, let's build our own awning!" She had recently begun to address Lianxiu with the title 'my lady', although she denied Lianxiu the title in her heart as she always had done.

Knowing how smart and crafty Xiangge was, Lianxiu didn't want to make a fuss about the change. She told Grandpa Lü: "Xiangge always wants to do things better. She recites a lot of classic Chinese prose by herself." She was also learning Japanese from Secretary Huang's eldest son, Ruiqi, but Lianxiu didn't want to bring this up to the old man.

Lü Guitang chuckled: "That is the only proper business she does when she has some time of her own."

The old man nodded approvingly, and said: "Show me one."

Xiangge put down the clean laundry, tossed her long braid back and was ready to recite when they heard a gentle knock on the door connecting the gallery and the garden. Someone came in.

"You have moved into this part," the visitor spoke up.

"It's Mr Miao!" Lianxiu said loudly in the old man's ear.

She was grateful that Miao Donghui hadn't forgotten the old man after all. She tried to support the old man while she reached out to pull up a chair for Miao Donghui, signalling Xiangge to make tea at the same time.

"Mr Miao, please come in and take a seat."

Miao Donghui was his usual self with all his calm demeanour and elegant taste in clothes. He first asked the old man how he was getting on, exchanged pleasantries with Guitang, and talked with Lianxiu about some routine affairs, while he evaluated the furnishings in the room.

There was a set of old sofas against the east wall; there was an old-fashioned square table with seating for eight people against the west wall, cluttered with a duster holder, and containers for sauce, vinegar and sugar. Mr Miao assumed it was the dining table. What modest furniture!

But he only said: "What an uncorrupted way of living you have! No one can match you in that regard!" They politely invited each other to sit down and immediately engaged in cheerful and humorous conversation.

Although they differed in their political viewpoints, the two had known each other so well for many years. Grandpa Lü was sincerely happy to see him knowing that Mr Miao didn't work for the puppet government, had sent medicine to the hospital for Kiddo, and was now paying him a visit. They exchanged information about each other's relatives and friends with whom they were mutually acquainted, discussed some verses of Buddhist scripture, and were enjoying themselves. The topic gradually shifted to the general situation.

Miao Donghui sighed: "The war has been going on for almost one year, and yet we still don't see any hope of winning. We lost Shanghai and Nanjing last year, and now Wuhan is in danger. Any Chinese would be burdened with sorrow at such a turn of events' But isn't it obvious that we are losing the war? What we should prioritise are the lives of millions of civilians and the peaceful life they desire. I'm trying my best to work in this direction, and I'm working with many other patriots who attach due importance to the benefits of the general masses of the people. Things would be much easier to handle if considered from this point of view." Miao had always been a good talker.

The old man, sensing what Mr Miao was insinuating, smiled wanly: "I've been struggling with my illness and senility in this small, humble world of mine behind closed doors, and am quite ignorant about what has been going on outside. If you have any suggestions, please enlighten me."

"Suppose my proposal is not in line with what you have in mind, please think about it from the viewpoint of how it would benefit millions of civilians," Miao Donghui began with utter sincerity. "Since the founding of the North China Provisional Government half a year ago, it has met with a lot of opposition in many forms, including bombing, burning, shooting and leafleting. Such harassment and wrecking activities have done nothing but inflict suffering on the civilian population by providing solid excuses for the Japanese to apply more heavy-handed measures. Some say it is lucky we only lost our country; we would be doomed if we lose our race! I quite agree with such an opinion. If we have a government which could guarantee a peaceful life for the millions of Chinese, and prevent direct rule by the Japanese, that would greatly reduce people's suffering! But such a provisional government needs support from someone who enjoys high prestige and commands universal respect. The position is nominal, and you don't need to do anything. When I read history, I always admire Feng Dao[3]. How much humiliation did he swallow and what a heavy load did he shoulder when he served those different kings in different dynasties? Those who didn't want to go with the flow and chose to die a heroic death or to live in seclusion did earn themselves good reputations. Those who discard fame or blame and are willing to sacrifice for the millions of commoners are the greatest!"

The old man laughed: "I'm adept with neither the pen nor the sword, how dare I be compared with those great people in history?" He paused, looking hard at Miao Donghui: "What a peculiar logic you have. A peaceful life for the civilian population led by what government? Whose government?" He didn't have the strength to rise to his full height and pound the table. Instead, he asked calmly with an inner peace welling up from inside him. That dull look surged up again from the bottom of his eyes.

"I'm putting the interests of the whole nation above everything else — if you don't give your support, what will happen to the people?" Miao Donghui redoubled his efforts to say the last sentence.

The old man raised his tea with a smile, signalling Lianxiu to see the guest out. Suddenly, his hand shook violently, spilling his cup of water. Lianxiu hurried forward, took his cup, and looked at Miao Donghui.

The old man stood up with Lianxiu's help, and spoke with

---

[3] Feng Dao: (冯道 (882-954)) was a Confucian master given credit for the first printing of the Confucian Classics, but later Confucian scholars, who cherished loyalty first, vilified him for serving at least 10 kings and five royal houses during the chaotic Five Dynasties and Ten Kingdoms period (907-979).

a smile on his face: "Mr Miao is a talented learner! When did you learn so eloquently about Su Qin[4]? I'm sorry I'm not interested in your theory of subjugating the nation to save its people. You need to find a more willing ear for your rhetoric."

Miao Donghui had to rise and bowed to take his leave of the old man. When he was in the garden, he told Lianxiu: "Madam Lü, the Japanese have decided to ask Mr Lü to take a position in the provisional government. I came to give you a heads-up in the expectation that he won't confront the tough Japanese with toughness."

Shocked to be addressed as 'Madam Lü", Lianxiu muttered hesitantly: "We are counting on you, Mr Miao, to act as an intermediary with the Japanese. Mr Lü is not as sharp as he used to be on account of his age. I'm afraid it really won't work."

Miao Donghui smiled bitterly: "I have been acting diplomatically among my connections and striving to find the least unpalatable solution. Who knows what I have been through? I'm just doing my best for my country. My best for my country."

As they were talking, they reached the gate where his car was waiting. The driver opened the door for him, but he stood and spoke to Lianxiu: "Things are going to be very tough. You must be more careful."

Lü Guitang greeted Lianxiu in the gallery after Lianxiu had seen Miao Donghui off. Both had the feeling that a great calamity was hovering over them all. They went into the room, thinking they would run into a storm where the old man would give Miao a huge piece of his mind. They were surprised to find the old man lying quietly against the headboard of the

---

[4] Su Qin (380–284 BCE), an influential political strategist during the Warring States period of ancient China.

bed, fingering the sword carved with delicate images of tigers and dragons in the clouds.

Xiangge said coldly: "He asked me to take it off the wall, saying he couldn't see it clearly over there."

The old man seemed to have forgotten who had visited. He lifted the sword and sighed: "What a pity that such a nice sword can only be hung on the wall."

"They don't fight with swords or spears nowadays. They use guns and artillery," Xiangge reminded the old man.

> *"How pathetic a veteran I have become,*
> *Who has outgrown his usefulness*
> *To volunteer to fight at the front,*
> *And capture the enemy's commander.*
> *Look! Even my sword was roaring with rage,*
> *Against the biting west wind!"*

The old man recited those lines with a grieved smile.

That night, the old man kept tossing and turning in bed and asked for a sleeping pill. Lianxiu gave him one pill and a glass of water. The old man asked for one more after he took the first pill, claiming one pill was not enough to put him to sleep.

Lianxiu informed him: "This is Dr Zhu's prescription. It's quite a strong one." But the old man wouldn't listen and insisted on taking one more. When he got his wish, he finally calmed down and went to sleep.

Early the next morning, the old man wanted to go to the master compound. They had left several pieces of furniture there for the old man to recite his Buddhist scriptures, but he hadn't been back since they had been moved to the gallery garden. Lianxiu asked Lü Guitang to go and clean it up first, then later she helped the old man to walk over there slowly.

The master compound had been cleaned up when they moved out. It had only been two weeks since their move, but the grass near the front steps to the hall had grown to knee height. Unidentified wild grass popped up everywhere between the bricks in the courtyard, making the place very unsightly. The freshly cleaned rooms smelled pleasantly cool. The low couch was still lying across the room facing the door. Beside it stood a low, long narrow table neatly arranged with some writing paper, writing brushes, an inkwell and various different scriptures. The old man nodded quietly and sat on the low couch in silence. After a while, he asked for *the Heart Sutra* and began to chant softly.

Lianxiu felt relieved to see the old man resume his old habit of chanting his scriptures in the morning, though it was a pity that he couldn't read his newspapers. Lü Guitang went to the back and checked the building, then he whispered to Lianxiu that there was a leak over the back window and that he would come back to do some maintenance another day.

When the old man reached "Form is emptiness and emptiness itself is form; emptiness does not differ from form, nor does form differ from emptiness, whatever is emptiness, that is form. The same is true of feelings, perceptions, impulses and consciousness", he raised his head and saw Lianxiu and Guitang standing beside each other. His heart flipped: what a matching pair in age and figure!

Lianxiu approached him and asked: "Would you like some lilac scent?"

"Do we still have any?"

"I have saved some."

The bronze burner made in the time of the fifth emperor of the Ming dynasty was set on the table with the other things.

Lianxiu lit the piece of lilac scent, and the faint sweetness of the scent began to fill the room. The old man smiled at Lianxiu and Guitang: "All is settled. You may leave me alone now."

"Madam needs to take care of things at the front of the house. Let me stay with you, Mr Lü," said Guitang.

"You don't have to. I can't have complete inner peace if you stay." The old man took up *the Heart Sutra* again. Seeing the old man calm and settled, Lianxiu and Guitang left him alone.

From that morning on, the old man would go to the master compound to read his scriptures until it was almost lunch time and then return to the gallery garden. Sometimes Guitang would keep him company, transcribing something; sometimes, the old man would go alone. In the endless deep silence, his memories became his best company. Sometimes he even wondered whether all the experiences that featured in his flashbacks were his stories or those of other people.

Fear pricked him again when his thoughts turned back to the prison break. He was already registered as a successful candidate in the imperial examinations at the provincial level in the reign of the Qing dynasty, but he and three of his friends had joined the Chinese Revolutionary Alliance (同盟会 *tongmenghui*) led by Sun Yat-sun, determined to overthrow the Qing government. The four would gather round to discuss the situation and encourage each other, which earned them the title 'the Virtuous Four from Fuyang'. Then the eldest of the four, Liu Zimin, was arrested and detained in the county prison. He and more than 10 other young men raised the money to buy off the prison guard, who asked him during the negotiation: "You already have a reputation, aren't you afraid of losing your wealth and fame?"

"The people are living on the verge of starvation, and the country is running out of peace. The more fame and wealth I have, the more infamy will I gain!" He explained the situation as simply as possible, without educating the man with the concept of revolution, but money was one of the major means of realising such a cause.

When Liu Zimin had boarded the carriage waiting outside the prison accompanied by several friends, he ran off in the opposite direction, and the prison guard caught up with him. He was then expecting a cut-throat fight, but the prison guard slipped a packet of money into his hand: "I'm giving you back half the money. You'll need it."

He didn't know what had happened to that man. He couldn't remember what he looked like now. He rushed to their meeting point, explained what had happened and left the money for Liu Zimin to take care of his wound, while he fled the city by climbing over the city gate in the dead of night. It was lucky for him that the city gate was not very high and that he had friends to help him. They tied a thick rope around his waist and lowered him over the city wall as low as possible, then they let go of the rope for him to drop to the ground with an open umbrella. He landed safely. It was extremely dark that night. He felt he was jumping into a bottomless pit of darkness when he closed his eyes and fell.

It was Mengjia who had come up with the idea of breaking his fall with an umbrella. The old man always remembered Mengjia with such gentle and sacred remorse. He visited places of ill repute, like many others did, but such a feeling was only shared by a married couple.

A married couple! What a beautiful expression! The love between such a pair might be one of the most sacred. But he left his wife behind for his secret cause, leaving her living alone in terror while he went into exile with a concealed identity. What were all his sacrifices for? To help the Japanese maintain their rule and order over his beloved homeland?

His grief and humiliation at being an impotent, senile old man was so all-consuming that he had to turn to his scripture chanting. When he was tormented by his memories, the lines could lull the billowing waves in his mind; but during his chanting, his memories would kidnap him and take him away.

He also read the *Song Dynasty History of Zen Buddhism in China* (1252) and The *Dharmic Treasure Altar - Sutra of the Sixth Patriarch*. He read at random, paying no attention to the content nor the chronology. What he would read aloud was only *the Heart Sutra*. Every time when he reached the lines "Therefore one should know the prajnaparamita is the greatest mantra. It is the clearest mantra, the highest mantra, the soother of all suffering", he would feel a strong aversion: who could achieve the soothing of all sufferings? Then he would ridicule himself for his lack of perception in being a follower of Buddhism, a realisation which would again drown him in his memories.

When the Qing dynasty was overthrown, the first national congress was held on 8 April 1913, and Lü Qingfei, the young Mr Lü, was elected as one of the congress members. The Lü family was staying in a courtyard in the old Ling residence then. When Yuan Shih-kai[5] seized power and cracked down on the KMT, he demanded the arrest of those who opposed him. Qingfei once harboured one of the men most wanted by Yuan Shih-kai in their bedroom for half a month until the man

---

[5] Yuan Shih-kai: (袁世凯 *yuan shikai*) 1859-1916, was a high-ranking Qing military commander and the first formal president of the first Chinese republic from 1912 to 1916. He is also remembered for his short-lived attempt to restore the monarchy in China.

was securely transported to Japan. The whole experience was as gripping as any stage drama.

That day, when the armed police followed the clues, and pursued the man into the courtyard where Qingfei and his family were staying in the Ling residence, they had a visitor sitting in the reception room, who was a wild, unruly character. When the guest saw the armed police, he stood up immediately, shaking all over and claimed in a trembling voice that he was an occasional visitor. When the head of the armed team ignored him, he stuck close to the wall without moving a muscle, trying hard to attract less attention.

The commanding officer told Qingfei what he was after, but before Qingfei could answer, the doors on the west and east wings of the courtyard opened and the teenage Jiangchu and Bichu stood in front of them, simultaneously inviting the group to search their rooms in their melodious voices. The search party was taken by surprise and stood rooted to the spot. Then the door in the middle, between the doors where Jiangchu and Bichu were standing, swung open, and out stepped Madam Lü, Zhang Mengjie, smiling. She said that since they were here, they'd better take the trouble to make a thorough search. With these words, she stepped aside to let the group in.

The commanding officer was hesitating before making his next move when Bichu went over to her mother and said: "Mother, Commander Yan has sent you 10 quality Yunnan hams and 50 cans of pickled leek flowers made from a secret recipe. I've already received it and despatched someone to deal with it."

Bichu's report appropriately reminded the commanding officer of the Lü family's connection with the armed forces in Yunnan province. It also reminded him about the announcement of the engagement between Commander Yan Liangzu and the eldest daughter of Lü Qingfei, Lü Suchu, published recently in the newspapers. Maybe these things made him realise the situation could become problematic when the military forces were involved. Or maybe he believed that it was just better to stay out of trouble where possible. So he explained that he was just on duty and it was nothing but a routine check. He then excused himself immediately. The guest was still pressed against the wall even after the search party had left.

He could still remember the frightened guest huddled against the wall, but he had long lost track of the man's name. Jiangchu and Bichu had both married good men and had happy families, but things were somewhat different for Suchu. It was Yan Liangzu's second marriage when he married Suchu, and he also had a concubine. Although Suchu had given birth to a daughter, Huishu, she might not have had such a happy life. Who knows? Her reticent disposition might have shielded her from such a perception.

How great it would be if everybody was shielded from perception! That would really be the way to 'assuage all suffering'. The Chinese nation had never been short of heroes and heroines. How could it have reached the point where the nation's existence was in peril, and the Chinese people were being trampled on like tiny ants? How could one's heart be at ease? How could one feel inner peace?

Every day, the old man carried out his meditation, with his mind shuttling between the *Heart Sutra* and his history. He seemed to have returned to his daily routine. Another two weeks passed smoothly like this. One evening, when the red setting sun had faded into the horizon and the garden was filled with the chirping of cicadas, Lianxiu busied herself cleaning the old man's whiskers. She first soaked the hairs with a wet towel, then rinsed them in another clean basin of water, and dried them with a clean dry towel until each silver-grey hair shone in the afterglow of the setting sun. The old man combed his whiskers with three of his fingers and asked how Lü Guitang's transcription business was going these days.

"He mentioned that some of the professors at Yiren University are still conducting research, so he still has things to transcribe. But the pay is getting much lower because of the soaring prices," said Lianxiu, looking at the old man while she cleared up the towels and basins. "But that's all he said. He didn't tell me much," added Lianxiu.

"That reminds me of something." The old man seemed undecided. "If you can sort through the poems I wrote, we might find a record for this section of history."

"That would be nice!" Lianxiu answered, immediately. "You can ask Lü Guitang to do the transcription for you, then."

"How's Xiangge? Is she occupied?" asked the old man, after pausing for thought.

"Xiangge is busy with her sewing and mending. She charges less than a tailor does but achieves the same quality." Hurried footsteps reached Lianxiu. It sounded as if several people had entered the door to the gallery.

"Mr Lü, you have visitors!" Secretary Huang's voice could be heard. Upon his announcement, three Chinese swollen with arrogance came in. Two looked like government officials, while the third looked like their attendant. Secretary Huang bowed all the way: "This is Mr Lü, and this is…" he bowed again.

The three ignored him as if he didn't exist. One said to the old man with a poker face: "We have been sent by Mayor Jiang. You have been appointed to serve on the maintenance committee." He handed over the appointment in a giant red hardcover which was at least 20 inches in length. The ornate characters on the cover sparkled in the pale light.

The old man was not disturbed by the presence of the people from the puppet government. He kept combing his whiskers with his fingers and picked up the walking stick leaning against his chair to stop the man who was trying to hand the appointment to him: "Please tell Jiang Chaozong I am a Chinese, and I won't accept any position in the puppet government."

The man seemed unsurprised by the old man's reaction. He didn't argue. Instead, he felt the table to make sure it was clean and put the document down on it. He took out an invitation: "The municipal government is hosting a banquet tomorrow. You are invited. The media will be informed about your appointment and it will be announced in the newspapers in three days. Now, excuse me." He handed the invitation to Lianxiu, turned around and prepared to leave.

"Throw them out! Throw both out!" shouted the old man in a fit of rage, banging the floor with his walking stick. He then dropped his walking stick, grabbed the invitation from Lianxiu and tried to tear it up. But the paper was too tough, so he hurled it against the backs of the three men. But the paper was too light to travel far, and it drifted toward the ground instead.

The man leading the group turned back and sneered: "It will be in the papers in three days."

The old man, seething with anger, straightened his back and jabbed his walking stick toward the man. The stick landed aimlessly on the ground. The door was slammed with a loud bang. Lianxiu rushed to make the old man sit in the chair, helping him to lean slowly against the back of the chair. The old man was panting heavily. Lianxiu kept rubbing his chest and patting him on the back, soothing him gently: "Mr Lü, Mr Lü, don't be mad! Don't be mad!" When Lü Guitang stormed in, followed by Xiangge, she sighed.

Seeing the appointment in the red cover and the furious Mr Lü, Guitang had already guessed what had happened. He was burning inside. When the old man calmed down, he asked Lianxiu: "Should we ask Professor Ling a favour to put off the appointment, at least for a while?"

"You don't need to ask anyone for any favours!" shouted the old man. "I know what to do. You don't need to worry about me!"

Lianxiu and Guitang looked at each other. Lianxiu's look was a mixture of doubt, anxiety, supplication and trust. She thought she had guessed 'what' the old man intended to do, but she didn't dare to think about it.

The old man seemed to read her mind because he grabbed her tightly by the hand and said with determination: "YOU need to keep out of this!" He said the word 'you' with such emphasis that it seemed that the whole world could be involved with his business, but that only 'you' — Lianxiu — couldn't.

Lianxiu was in the habit of obeying. She dropped her eyes and whispered: "How about going back and lying down? Don't think about anything right now." She helped the old man lie down on the bed.

When things were set, Lü Guitang didn't hold him back anymore and said: "I think you'd better talk to Professor

Ling. Mr Lü is so old, and I know nothing about government matters. Madam, do you have any idea?"

Lianxiu tried to speak, but swallowed her words.

Xiangge said: "Is Mr Lü still waiting for the guerrillas?"

"It's all in his imagination! How can you treat that as something real?" Lianxiu's eyes were wet: "Why don't you pay Professor Ling a visit? We don't have anyone else to turn to."

Having asked Xiangge to keep Lianxiu company in the outer room, Guitang hurried to the Lings'.

No one would have expected Guitang to be gone all night. The old man slept for a while before waking up, muttering something indistinctly to himself, and then going back to sleep again. He woke up many times during the night. Lianxiu asked Xiangge to make her a makeshift bed by pulling together several benches and chairs behind the screen door in the room, then she sat by Lord Lü's bedside, waiting for Lü Guitang to come back.

Xiangge woke up in the middle of the night. After finding that her father hadn't come back yet, she sat up and put on her clothes, moaning. Lianxiu wanted to comfort her, but she couldn't find the words. The two sat with each other in the dim light. The still darkness enveloping them seemed to shut out the light and drown everything in its dark embrace.

"Lianxiu! Lianxiu! Where are you?" The old man was calling for her in the inner room. Lianxiu went into the room and sat by his bed. The old man asked gently: "I'm alright. You shouldn't stay up so late."

Lianxiu brushed aside the weight of worries on her mind and braced herself: "I have been by your side for so many years. Now we are facing a crisis. Would you please listen to me just once? Whatever happens, if we survive, we still have a chance. It's very likely that the people the guerrillas send will arrive one of these days."

The old man shook his head: "It's just a dream! A mad man talking in his dreams! You don't need to worry about me. I won't try and kill myself. I'll send Guitang for Ling Jingyao."

Lianxiu didn't dare to tell him she had already sent Guitang to look for Ling Jingyao, so she answered rather ambiguously: "Yes. Maybe Professor Ling can find a way to stop them."

The old man laughed: "So, you go and take a rest. Tomorrow will be a busy day."

Lying in bed, Lianxiu stared hard into the dark night, unwilling to close her eyes. As she was slipping into sleep at daybreak, she heard a yell from Mr Lü: "Out! Get out! You all get out!"

She jumped out of bed and rushed into the old man's bedroom. The old man was still yelling loudly "get out", with one hand pressed against his chest, the other waving wildly in the air as if he was trying to push something away. She lowered herself and asked: "Mr Lü! Mr Lü! What's happening?" The old man struggled several times before opening his terror-stricken eyes. When he saw Lianxiu, he heaved a sigh of relief.

"Did you have a nightmare? Don't be afraid. There, there!" Lianxiu comforted him as if he were a child. The old man shook his head. A tear escaped from the corner of his eye.

"I have to get up," the old man said. "I need to recite my scriptures in the master compound."

"But it is still early! You don't need to do that at such an early hour."

"My time is already fixed. I don't want to miss it." He rose and began to get dressed. When Lianxiu had finished cleaning him, he insisted on going immediately without breakfast. When he was in the outside room, he looked around and asked: "Where is that thing?"

"In the cabinet," said Lianxiu. She knew what he was referring to.

"Return it later," the old man instructed imperturbably. His steps were steady and sure as he walked out of the gallery garden with the aid of his walking stick.

He didn't look back.

The front garden was quiet since Secretary Huang and his big family were still asleep. Lianxiu unlocked the door to the passageway, and the two of them walked into the secluded shade of the wisteria garden.

Lianxiu tried to make the old man talk: "What a natural awning! It's just a little bit gloomy, isn't it?"

The old man ignored her and walked on.

Because of the old man's regular visits to the master compound these days, a path in the master courtyard had been weeded and cleaned up. The remaining weeds growing out of the cracks between the paving bricks were almost knee high. They looked darker in the first rays of the morning sun, the tips of the blades shiny with dew from the night. The old man walked steadily forward without looking sideways, his walking stick tapping the paving bricks briskly, making gentle, echoing, clanking sounds.

The door to the reception hall was open, and the faint rays of the morning sun slanted through the door and lay on the front steps, where several battens lay. Hoping the old man might turn back to see the rays of light, Lianxiu pretended that she had stumbled over the battens and uttered an "oh", then she said: "These battens are good for the awning."

But the old man didn't turn back.

He walked into the hall and stopped by the low couch, his hand stroking the back with its delicate mother-of-pearl inlays.

He looked confident. "You may leave now," he smiled. But he added sternly with knitted eyebrows: "Remember, I don't need anything!"

"You don't need what, my lord?" asked Lianxiu. She helped him sit on the couch and continued arranging the items on the low table. She first put three pieces of lilac incense into the burner, paused, and then took two out. She had to use the incense sparingly. Looking around, she didn't find anything amiss. It might do him good to have some time alone, thought Lianxiu.

"Do you want to meditate or recite scriptures?" She took up the *Heart Sutra* and prepared to hand it to him.

"You may leave," the old man shook his head, his eyes hollow as if they didn't see Lianxiu at all.

Lianxiu put down the Heart Sutra, smoothed the creases in his gown, and said: "I'll come and get you when breakfast is ready."

She turned back when she reached the door, seeing the old man sitting bolt upright, his eyes closed. He looked like he was already meditating. A passionate sadness seized her throat.

She rushed back to the old man: "I want to stay with you, may I?"

The old man answered with the same determination and effort with his eyes closed: "Just leave!"

When he was aware that Lianxiu remained quietly by his side, he opened his eyes and said impatiently: "Leave!"

Not daring to disobey, Lianxiu left. She took a look at her watch, for no particular reason. It was ten to six.

The first thing Lianxiu did when she was back in the gallery garden was to start the cooking stove, which used coal briquettes and had to be started daily since it couldn't be smothered by closing the air vent as they were able to do with the giant heating stove. Xiangge wasn't in the garden. She had probably gone to the south compound or was out looking for some news. Lianxiu busied herself with the fire with a restless heart.

Once the briquette in the stove was burning, Lianxiu had also finished her morning chores. She saw Secretary Huang stick his head around the door to the gallery in the smoke.

"Are you making breakfast already, Madam Lü?", he asked, entering the garden. He lowered his voice: "Would you advise Mr Lü to accept the appointment? They won't ask him to do anything. I guess they just want his name on the committee. We need to protect him."

Lianxiu felt his low voice was drifting away from her, so she spoke up loudly: "You don't need to whisper like this. Mr Lü isn't here."

Secretary Huang was surprised by the information: "Not here? Where is he then?"

"Where is he? Where is he?" Her heart began to pound so madly that she felt it might leap out of her chest.

"Where is he? Where is he?"

She dropped the container she was using to make the cornflour mixture for the breakfast pancakes, ignoring the astounded Secretary Huang, rushed out of the gallery garden and ran toward the master compound.

She gently pushed open the door and saw the old man lying neatly on the low couch. She took a stride forward and stood by the couch. The old man's eyes were loosely closed, his face tranquil. There was no pulse.

"Mr Lü! Mr Lü!" Lianxiu yelled in terror.

She prodded him.

She tried to wake him up, but she wasn't able to.

When she finally realized what had happened, she dropped onto the floor and covered her face in her hands. She didn't dare to look around her. The deathly silence in the room was so suffocating she couldn't breathe. She didn't know how long she remained seated on the floor, but then an idea flashed through her mind: "I need to find a doctor. A doctor might save him!" She jumped to her feet as the idea flashed through her mind,, charged toward the door, and almost ran into Ling Jingyao and Lü Guitang who were striding toward the room. "You are here!" She almost tripped over as she quickly drew a few steps back upon seeing the two men. Lü Guitang caught her just in time. With Xiangge's help, who was running after her father and Professor Ling, they seated her in her old chair by the door. She was shaking all over.

Ling Jingyao was standing by the low couch.

"Mr Lü, I'm sorry I'm late!" he muttered. A sad voice was yelling at him in his head: "What would it matter if you had arrived in time?"

He turned around and asked Lü Guitang to fetch a doctor at once. Guitang rushed out in response to the order.

Jingyao saw a piece of paper on the low table with an empty bottle of sleeping pills on it. There were two lines of characters written in brush strokes the size of dried walnuts:

"My death is more valuable than my breath."

The second line read:

"Send my obituary to the major newspapers to announce my death immediately."

This was the old man's will.

Seeing the will, Jingyao was absolutely certain that the old man had chosen to die rather than to accept the appointment to serve in the puppet government. Tears trickled down his cheeks as a multitude of feelings welled up in his heart. Grief lowered his body. He knelt by the couch, trying hard to stifle his desire to weep loudly by tightly gripping the armrest of the couch .

Lianxiu calmed down when she saw Jingyao crying. Helped by Xiangge, she knelt by his side. She said while she was drying her tears: "Professor Ling, please don't cry. I'm counting on you now to arrange Mr Lü's funeral."

Jingyao ignored Lianxiu and continued sobbing. Only when the doctor arrived, did he stand up. The doctor ran a private clinic on the Di'anmen City Gate Avenue, but the Lüs had never sent for him before. He went through the standard procedure of checking the body for vital signs, and declared it "deceased".

He picked up the bottle and had a sniff, then asked: "Did he take all of them?" Then he cast an enquiring glance at Lü Guitang, as if to imply who should pay him. When he had been paid by Guitang, he instructed that the body be buried as soon as possible since it was getting warmer, it might start to smell and the Japanese would ask questions. Then he left.

Jingyao gathered all his strength and talked with Lianxiu about what to write in the obituary. Guitang went close to the low couch, kowtowed three times, and hurried out. He was going to the newspapers for the obituary to commemorate Mr

Lü's life. Then he realized the obituary hadn't been drafted yet, and he returned.

Lianxiu didn't know the old man's date of birth: "We'll have to ask Madam Jiangchu and Bichu."

Jingyao couldn't reach either of Mr Lü's two daughters, but he decided the simpler the better, so he just wrote down: "Mr Lü Qingfei died on 7 July 1938. His widow Zhao Lianxiu." He asked Guitang and Xiangge to make several copies. Xiangge fetched him water, and when he had cleaned himself up, he and Guitang went to different newspapers to issue the obituary.

Lianxiu tried to cover the body with a white sheet. The sheet shook in her trembling hands when she covered the face. It made her think the old man had come back to life, and that she had to pull it off to check. When she found it was just her trembling hands causing the sheet to move rather than the old man's breath, she put the sheet down but then pulled it off again. She repeated that several times.

Then Secretary Huang and his family, the director of the community, and the police all came, but no one asked how the old man had died. People began making preparations for the funeral.

When it was almost noon, Jingyao and Guitang came back one after the other, both saying the obituary would be in the newspapers the next day.

Jingyao asked Lianxiu to help him lift the sheet, and he tried to close the old man's eyes. The body was already stiff, so he tried three times to 'close' the old man's eyes.

Lianxiu said to herself, her heart choked with grief: "Who was he looking forward to? What was he worried about?" She couldn't answer these questions. She had always felt some distance between herself and the old man, a distance as huge as now — the distance between life and death. She was always aware of all his material needs, but she was never able to share his spiritual burdens. Neither did she understand the thing which had left that shell of a body. She saw the candle of his life each day, but she only saw the candle, she never perceived the flickering flame piercing through the darkness.

If one was rich, things were arranged quickly even in an enemy-occupied city like Beiping. By the afternoon, all the funeral preparations had been completed.

Ling Jingyao thought it would be better to notify people like Miao Donghui once the obituary was in the newspaper. After talking to Lianxiu and Guitang, they agreed that the body should be put in a coffin and that the coffin should be kept in the master compound until Mr Lü's three daughters had been notified and further instructions had been given.

The reception hall in the master compound had been transformed into a mourning hall with the memorial tablet, the incense burner, and candle holders set on the table. The coffin, adorned with blue silk lining with a pillow and a quilt of the same colour and material, was placed in the very centre of the hall. Staring at the lining of the coffin, Jingyao thought it must be comfortable to lie in there.

"Professor Ling, should we put Mr Lü in now?", asked Lü Guitang, in a low, measured voice.

Jingyao cast an enquiring look toward Lianxiu, who was standing there supported by Xiangge. Her button-like eyes were red and swollen. She was thinking now that she was free of her service, and the best way out for her might be her own death. But she immediately reproached herself for such a stupid idea, then she nodded apologetically.

After gesticulating at Xiangge not to follow her, she went

up to the body of the old man. Without the slightest hesitation, she carried the body with Guitang and two other helpers from the funeral parlour and placed it in the coffin.

The old man was carefully tucked in the blue silk quilt, on which lay his neat, carefully cleaned silver-grey whiskers. It looked like he was quite comfortable with the corners of his mouth curving slightly upward, as if he were going to open his eyes to greet someone with that old pet phrase of his "my friend"!

The two helpers from the funeral parlour put the lid on the coffin. No one asked them to hold the lid open for a while so they could have one more look at their beloved. No lament. No cries of anguish. Only dead silence.

The heavy coffin lid was lowered down slowly, but not nailed since the three daughters had not yet been informed. Looking around, Jingyao felt a sense of utter desolation piercing his heart. How many could understand the old man and his death? What was the value of his integrity that he had defended at the cost of his life? How many could understand him, Ling Jingyao? How would he meet his end, then? Sorrow welled up from his heart, as did his tears. Jingyao burst into tears again, sobbing loudly.

Lianxiu knelt quietly, with Lü Guitang and Xiangge kneeling behind her. Jingyao suddenly realized the three were as unrelated as he was to the person lying in the coffin. What a paradox life was! The most important things were always left in the hands of the most irrelevant. So many things would prompt tears besides Mr Lü's death!

Jingyao felt better after the outburst. Guitang came forward, trying hard to stem his tears, and consoled Jingyao: "We share your deepest sympathies, Professor Ling." Then Guitang found he had nothing more to say. Jingyao gradually calmed down and stopped crying. He gave three more deep bows toward the coffin.

People began to leave when the joss sticks were lit, the symbolic paper money burnt, and other rituals performed. Jingyao, Lianxiu, Guitang and Xiangge left the mourning hall slowly. Many of the weeds in the courtyard had been trampled on; those which had not been were still growing jubilantly.

A Soliloquy from Inside the Coffin

Darkness. Endless darkness.

My body lies in a tiny case free from any disturbance. The black case is now protecting me, creating a fence between life and death.

The journey was too long, with too many hardships and dangers. My third leg - a walking stick - has been complaining with its tapping as the bottom hits the floor that it is exhausted by having to support such a senile body. Quit, then. I thought that often.

My very existence had become such a burden to everyone. Deprivation had become the best option. Now I have acquired such deprivation, by my own efforts, which has been rewarded with such endless darkness, which spares nothing. I am finally free from all pretences.

I had been longing for such deprivation for such a long time, but I didn't find the opportunity, or an excuse. Now I have made full use of the act of depriving myself of my life, but also of the intention which tried to make use of my sorry existence. How lucky I am! It is so often said that some deaths weigh more heavily than Mount Tai, some lighter than a feather. My death won't weigh that much, but at least it will weigh more than my 'third leg' does.

I've been preoccupied by the fact that my busy life didn't mean much to my country, that my sword had to be hung on the wall exposed to the biting west wind instead of lunging forward into battle. I didn't expect my last move in life would have quenched the burning pride of the enemy! Lying here, I feel a little bit proud of myself, and I want to cry out loud: "What do you think of my action, my friend?"

Darkness is closing in on me. I feel my body is weighing me down, further down. That fleeting moment of pride and glory has gone. Jingyao, you need to stop crying like a baby. Remember, you are a man with 40-odd years of experience. How's your daughter? Can she survive all the hardships? How will your grandchildren be? Will they grow to be Chinese who bring no shame to their names? How many years will it take for us to be victorious? How many years? I have been living amid worry and anxiety all my life. Will death put an end to my worry and anxiety? Does death change a man's nature?

My body feels weighed down with all the responsibilities I have been shouldering, crammed into such a tiny space in a coffin, crushing me.

How I hate all this! I was never given the opportunity to live to be a worthy, decent man. Instead, humiliation followed me like a shadow. Now I have been forced to lie in such a tiny casket, how can I feel proud of myself?

How I hate all this! I don't hear the weeping, moaning or sighs. How long have I been here?

Time won't stop, and I won't be able to get up again.

How I'd like to be able to manage a scornful grin, but I can't move the corners of my mouth.

Darkness. Endless darkness, again.

CHAPTER VI

PART 1

Though the 'rain sweeper' had been holding its broom 24/7, there was no let up in the rain when Bichu and the kids left Beiping. Mist curled around the green tree tops under the gloomy sky. The grand Tiananmen city gate and Zhengyangmen city gate were dwarfed by the listless wetness. The bustling streams of people at Zhengyangmen city gate train station were strangely quiet. They were so terrified that any unexpected disaster might land on them out of the blue that they strove to attract as little attention as possible. People streamed in and out of the station, without any noise, without any vitality. No one was looking at anyone else around them, as if they were lost in speculation about how the place where they were born and brought up had fallen into the claws of a predator.

It was quite an orderly scene, very different from the stampeed one year ago when the city folk tried to escape the city. The five from the Meng family met the three from the Zhuang family escorted by two of Mrs Zhuang's friends from England, who were busy finding their seats for them in the business section equipped with soft seats. A moment later, the two families were joined by Mrs Li, Jin Shizhen, and her three children. The group of 12 were all quite excited. Kiddo pressed his face against the glass of the window streaked with rain, trying to see through it, but the glass was blurred. He looked patiently at the glass in the window instead.

"Beiping is crying," he cried out loudly.

Bichu, who was sitting across the aisle, stood up immediately and asked Kiddo to sit by her side, but he refused. Pointing at the window, he repeated: "Beiping is crying." All three mothers and the two elder girls frowned at these words, but no one felt it appropriate to scold him. "Beiping is indeed crying." May agreed with Kiddo privately, but she knew better than to say such things on their departure, so she picked up a picture book and asked Kiddo to look at it with her. But Kiddo didn't want to read. His eyes were glued to the window.

Beiping was crying. The time-honoured city of Beiping, a Chinese city steeped in glorious history, was trembling and crying under the iron hoofs of the invading Japanese army. Rain leaked through the station roof. Rainwater trickled down from a ragged sheet-iron roof extension, drop by drop. Tears welled up from every nook and cranny in Beiping, dripping into people's hearts. When would Beiping stop crying? Maybe when we come back, thought May.

The train started to pull out of the station. Everyone in the group of 12 harboured the same expectation: we will come back. Wei whispered to Kiddo:

"We will come back."

Li Zhiqin, who was sitting opposite Wei in the seats to her right, smiled at Wei and said: "We will come back."

The rumbling of the locomotive became louder and faster. No one spoke any more. It rained harder outside. The rumbling and the rain pounded the travellers' hearts like waves, urging those heading for the South: Rush! Hurry! When can you make your way back from the South to the North. It's completely up to you and how much you want to make it happen.

"We will come back," said Wei with solid confidence, patting Kiddo on the shoulder.

"Is the track safe?" Mrs Li asked in a low voice. In the absence of any comment from Della and Bichu, she continued: "I had a dream last night. I dreamt one section of the track was broken." She also saw a flower put on the railing, but she had no intention of sharing such a detail with these earthly companions of hers. Bichu and Della kept smiling but made no comment, since neither of them was inclined to prattle in circumstances lacking privacy. Mrs Li turned to Earl, a pointless exercise since Earl was generally always cold to people.

They stayed in Tianjin overnight and boarded a ship named '*Dongshun*' (东顺 meaning 'Favourable Easterly Breeze'), which held out the prospect of sailing eastward safe and sound. Ships were a brand new experience for the Meng children. How could such an enormous monster of a thing hold so many people on the water? Kiddo literally yelled with delight at his first sight of the ship. May was also excited. Upon seeing Della, the attendant waiting to welcome passengers aboard the ship led them directly upstairs to the first-class cabins. Only when they got to the cabins did he figure out that the group actually had second-class cabins, so he had to lead them back downstairs with the group at his heels, dragging and pulling their luggage.

Earl said to Zhiqin: "I now see why these cabins are also

called the feast-class. You may have a Western-style feast in your cabin. First class — Feast class."

"Or they are just for foreigners," Zhiqin whispered back.

"I am not a foreigner. I am a Chinese!" said Della, who was carrying a leather case in her right hand, her body tilting to the left to balance the weight. She winked jubilantly at Zhiqin with this merry declaration.

They finally settled down in the right cabins. Each cabin had two bunk beds with four bunks flanking the two walls. Bichu and Kiddo shared the lower bunk in one bed while May took the upper bunk. The two kids didn't waste even one second before they pressed their faces against the small round windows at the end of the bunks. Earl and Zhiqin shared the other bed, with Earl on top and Zhiqin underneath, just as Bichu had arranged. Earl, who decided that she wouldn't lower herself to argue for a bottom bunk, was unpacking her things in a sort of sultry silence. Zhiqin smiled at Earl apologetically. When Zhiqin was done with her unpacking, she told Bichu she was going to her mother's cabin.

When she found her mother and her two siblings had taken the two bottom spots, leaving Della and Wucai the top ones, she blamed her mother, whispering:

"How could you have taken both of the two bottom bunks?"

Her mother, Shizhen, laughed: "See? I told you it isn't appropriate. My daughter is blaming me for that."

Della hurried to explain: "It works fine for me. I can go up and down quite easily." Indeed, her figure, which could do justice to any figure-hugging *qipao*, a traditional Chinese close-fitting woman's dress with a high neck and slit skirt, moved up and down with considerable agility.

Seeing her two daughters rooted to the spot, she instructed Zhiqin:

"Take them out and have a look around. Don't stay here and get in the way."

She began to dig into her net-basket.

Della said kindly: "You'd better stay in the cabin. When the ship leaves, you may go out and explore then." So Zhiqin took her two younger siblings to the end of one bunk and began to tell them stories.

Wuyin appeared at the door and knocked. Jin Shizhen said with a laugh:

"What good manners your child has! The door is open, but he still knocks!"

Della asked Wuyin: "How are things in your cabin?"

"Very good," answered Wuyin. "How about you, mum? Do you need any help?"

Jin Shizhen jumped into the conversation: "What a dutiful son! Why are your children so well behaved? They are also so good looking!"

She stared at Wuyin unblinkingly, wondering why he didn't have any trace of his English mother while his sister Wucai looked exactly like a normal person of mixed race.

Wucai, climbing down from her bunk, said: "Mum, I want to go to brother's cabin."

Della told her she would like to go to have a look too, and so they left the cabin to Mrs Li and her children.

Wuyin and Wei shared their cabin with two strange male passengers. Bichu was helping Wei with his package, who was standing by her side racking his brain about what he could do to help. When they were finished, they all went to the Mengs' cabin and sat on the bunks, waiting for the ship to depart.

The number of passengers coming and going carrying parcels of all sizes past their door became fewer and fewer. A while later, the sound of shoes slapping against the deck reached their ears, followed by the noise of chains being dragged.

"They are taking up the anchor to set sail," Wuyin told May. He had been to England with Della, taking a giant ship across the sea.

"Toooooooooot —" the horn blew. The ship was offshore.

When order was restored, the children were given permission to go up on deck. The sun was fully risen and the shore was out of sight, and the ship was churning up waves in the boundless sea. Standing on the deck, May was amazed by the sight. How vast the sea was! If viewed from high up in the sky, the ship must appear to be so lonely in such a boundless expanse of water, thought May. Leaning against the railing, she looked down at the dark water which extended on and on until it became a grey line where the sea and the sky met. The almost black colour under the ship lightened into the distance until it melted into a vast profound blue, so vast that no human eye could ever take it in. How could such a tiny body like hers take in the enormity of the sea? May closed her eyes.

"There are no chairs or sunshades," said Wuyin, who wanted to find a seat for May. This ship was so different from the one he took to England, which had comfortable chairs, bright-coloured sunshades, and fresh flowers all over the deck. He thought May deserved a ship like that.

"Of course there are no such things! We are at war!" said

Wei. He had been to Beidaihe district[1] once for a summer vacation with his parents and he had experienced the beach, but this was a new experience for him to be at sea, instead of by the sea. "All the good ships have gone to war," assumed Wei.

"China doesn't have a navy, and we are not fighting at sea," Wuyin said. Though unwilling to embarrass Wei, he had to tell the truth.

"It's true we don't have a navy and we are not fighting at sea, but all the good ships should have gone to fight in the war. Maybe they have all gone for that," said Wei in an attempt to justify his seemingly contradictory assumption.

Then some gentle music reached their ears from up above. They looked up to see the pointed tops of a couple of brightly coloured sunshades, and the vines of some hanging plants swaying between the rails. Several handsomely dressed foreigners were leaning against the rails, pointing, talking and laughing.

The truth was that all the wonderful things mentioned in the children's conversation were still there. It was just that they didn't have the privilege of enjoying them because they were not travelling first-class.

Wei turned back to the endless sea and kept his head down. Wuyin felt sorry for Wei because he had ventured to tell Wei that the good ships were not fighting in the war, so he gave Wei a compassionate nudge:

"Let's go and have a look at the engine!"

---

[1] Beidaihe district: (北戴河区 *beidaihe qu*) is a district of the city of Qinhuangdao, Hebei province on China's Bohai sea coast. It is a very popular summer beach resort because of its warm, temperate, semi-humid, marine climate characteristics. Forest covers more than 70% of the area, and the average summer temperature is only about 24.5degC.

The two young lads ran off. Kiddo wanted to tag along, but was stopped by May with one grab.

"You are so nice to your brother," Zhiqin said. She was standing by May, but her eyes were fixed on her sister and brother.

"I love my brother," said May. "Kiddo is my doll." The 'doll' pouted at her to show his disapproval.

"I love my brother and sister, too," Zhiqin said, looking at the sea thoughtfully, her hands fondling the ends of the braids hanging on her chest. "But sometimes they are nasty. Very nasty."

It occurred to May that if Kiddo turned nasty, she didn't have Amah Zhao to turn him over to. To show she could handle the situation without Amah Zhao, she took out a handkerchief to dry Kiddo's sweat.

Zhiqin watched her attentively and smiled: "You talk and behave like an understanding adult! Why doesn't your big sister handle these things?"

"She has temper issues, so I have to be more considerate. If she doesn't get annoyed, the rest of us are all very happy."

"If no one got annoyed with me, I would be happy, too," muttered Zhiqin to herself. Then Zhiquan gave his little sister a shove, and both fell onto the floor, howling and refusing to get up by themselves. When Zhiqin went over to pick one of them up, the other immediately fell down on the floor. All the other passengers on deck turned and looked at them. May took Kiddo's hand and they hurried back to their cabin.

That night, each family went to bed early. Around midnight, they heard knocking in the distance mixed with the sounds of people calling out and talking. People were knocking on cabin doors one by one, checking tickets. They stayed in Della's cabin for a long time, asking a lot of questions about how a foreigner had ended up in an economy cabin instead of a first-class cabin. Wuyin rushed to explain to the staff when he heard the commotion. When the staff learned Della was indeed a professor's wife, they let it go. Della shrugged and smiled wryly at Wuyin.

Jin Shizhen said: "You are asking for trouble. If I were you, I would have long since gone back to England."

"One can encounter problems in England, too," answered Della.

When she found Wuyin was still in his pyjamas, she thanked him and rushed him back to his cabin: "You should go back to sleep."

Jin Shizhen commented again: "Oh my! I have never seen a mother thank her son! How courteous you all are!"

Wuyin excused himself, but he had lost all interest in sleep, so he went up on deck. The night looked so dark and heavy that the sea seemed as if it was stifled by the darkness. The churning wake behind the ship seemed to be the only opening where the sea could breathe.

"What lies at the bottom of the sea?" He stood against the railing, exploring the darkness, trying to fish out an answer. The sky, the sea and the dark night had united to form a solid mass in front of him, embodying endless mysteries. He suddenly felt so lonely and tiny. He was no stranger to loneliness, although he had lacked for nothing as a teenager. He also had what other teenagers lacked — an intellectual education which was much more extensive than average, and a cross-cultural education which few shared. They were the gifts from his scientist father and his foreign stepmother. But his heart was lonely and closed, refusing to open up to anyone. It didn't have any desire to open up to anyone, anyway.

The feeling of being so tiny was a new experience, which rather surprised him. He felt he was tiny, as was human beings' capacity. What a sad realisation.

A clatter of feet emerged out of the darkness. Some dark figures were dragging something behind them. When they reached the opposite side of the ship, they whispered in unison "one, two, three", lifted the object up, and threw it into the sea. The noise when it hit the water was muffled by the roar of the engine and the waves.

"What are you doing here?" Several people searched the stern of the ship and found Wei standing against the vast darkness. Wuyin rushed up and stood by Wei's side.

"Are you the kids with that foreigner? Please go back to your cabin." The man had a Guangdong accent. He was more polite when he realised that the two of them were related to a foreign passenger.

The two teenagers were rooted to the spot. Those people were ready to go below to their cabins. One yelled at them: "What's so interesting about a dead body?"

That was a corpse, then! The sadness in Wuyin's heart grew heavier. What lay at the bottom of the sea? A dead body. How helpless the sea was if it had to take whatever was thrown into it. The ship roared on, ploughing a furrow through the sea. Was the sea willing to be ploughed? What was the sea? The sea was something that would take anything. What was a corpse? A corpse was a dead body without life. What was life, then?

Wei felt sorry for the person who was to be devoured by

fish. Who was it? The world no longer had this person. The family would never trace this member and would be grief-stricken. It was horrible. He said out loud: "Death is horrible."

"It is indeed horrible. When life is snuffed out, it leaves no trace, not even in the air," answered Wuyin. Would the sea eliminate that body? He looked hard at the sea in the same vast darkness of the night.

"I think a truly brave person should die in battle," said Wei.

"But people die whether there are wars or not. Chinese people would die anyway, with or without the Japanese invasion, just for different reasons," said Wuyin.

"Then at least they wouldn't die such a hurried worthless death!" Wei said indignantly.

No! Death shouldn't happen in such a hurry and in such a worthless way! Life shouldn't be allowed to succumb to such a fate! What is life? Life is grand, noble and irreplaceable. Why couldn't he sum up all the adjectives that had come to him with a single noun?

During breakfast the next morning in the dining hall, someone whispered that a man had died in steerage and was thrown into the sea because he had sneaked on board without a ticket and was travelling alone. No one enquired about his whereabouts. The accident had to be kept from the Hong Kong police or they might suspect that he had died of a contagious disease and demand that the ship be completely sterilised. Then everyone would be in trouble. Wuyin and Wei exchanged looks and began to talk to May, trying their best to shield her from the news.

When the ship neared Shanghai, this small group underwent another surge of emotions. Since the ship was only going to be docked for a couple of hours, none of the passengers were allowed to disembark. The harbour was crowded with ships of all shapes and sizes; tall buildings towered along the riverbanks. Japanese national flags were visible on ships and buildings all over the city, mixed with flags from other countries. Bichu and the others were standing beside the dock with other passengers on board. Someone in the crowd shouted: "Look!" People looked in the direction they were pointing and found one flag billowing distinctly in the wind silhouetted against the blue sky, drawing the eye to its bright red, blue and white colours. It was the flag of the besieged 1st Battalion, 524th Regiment of the famed 88th Division of the Chinese National Revolutionary Army (NRA), which was raised each day. It was the only Chinese national flag which would be raised every day in Japanese-occupied Shanghai, a symbol of free China that was not subjected to imperial rule!

"The 800 heroes[2]!" Wei uttered a muffled cry. What backed up the 800 heroes stubbornly holding out against the Imperial Japanese Army's Elite 3rd Division at Sihang warehouse was shared by all other Chinese. Bichu's eyes were wet, and Della rubbed Bichu's arm gently. The group led by the two ladies stood silently and respectfully, saluting the flag in the distance on which their eyes were fixed.

At this moment, a small group of Japanese soldiers boarded the ship.

All the passengers dropped their eyes in unison. Bichu,

---

[2] The defence of Sihang warehouse began on 26 October and lasted until 1 November 1937, which marked the end of the Battle of Shanghai in the opening phase of the Chinese People's War of Resistance against Japanese Aggression. It witnessed the heroic defence from the soldiers camped at the warehouse fighting against the elite troops of the Japanese forces to cover the Chinese forces' retreat. The warehouse was located on the opposite bank of the Suzhou river from the Shanghai International Settlement.

Della and Jin Shizhen pulled Earl and Zhiqin behind them. The nervous crowd didn't look at the solders, nor did they dare to look at the defiant flag.

The Japanese thumped toward the stern in their heavy boots, but an officer paused in front of Della, stared at her for a moment, and then marched on. Earl exhaled gently. The sight of these Japanese soldiers reminded her of that horrible experience of bayonets suspended over her head. Strong hatred surged up in her heart, complicated by her pride at having experienced such a thing once. All the complicated emotions transformed into a single one — her loathing for Zhiqin, who grabbed Earl's hand unexpectedly with her sweaty, sticky hand.

Driven by her obsession with hygene, Earl glared at Zhiqin, who was leaning against Earl, and was ready to pull her hand out of Zhiqin's clutch. When Bichu turned her back, she immediately held Zhiqin:

"Zhiqin, what's wrong with you?"

The latter shook her head. Her mother, Jin Shizhen, also came to her, trying to help her to stand still: "What a fuss you are making!"

Della said Zhiqin might faint, so the three mothers, half holding and half carrying, took Zhiqin back to the cabin and let her lie down in her bed. Zhiqin's face had blanched white as a sheet and was wet with sweat. Since Jin Shizhen was in a complete panic, Bichu and Della talked it over and decided to give Zhiqin several sips of water with sugar dissolved in it. They then took out some multivitamins, ground them and had Zhiqin wash them down with water. Some time later, the colour came back to Zhiqin's face.

As Zhiqin's face began to look better, Jin Shizhen's became

worse. When they were at home, she had long been prone to complain, blaming her eldest daughter for not taking good care of herself. How could Zhiqin take care of her siblings and do the chores if she became ill? What a serious neglect of duty!

Zhiqin didn't get out of bed for dinner that night. May went to see her during her meal and brought her an origami crane:

"I know you like butterflies, Sister Li, but I don't know how to make them with paper, so I made you this. You may consider it as a butterfly." While she was talking, she tugged the tail of the paper crane, and the wings moved. May giggled with delight.

Zhiqin took the bird, smiling, gave her small hand a gentle squeeze, and spoke softly: "Go and finish your dinner." May ran off, but soon returned with a small plate of sliced apple. Zhiqin sat up in her bed and felt much better when she had consumed several slices.

Shizhen had finished her dinner and walked into the cabin, wiping her mouth with the small table cloth from the dining room. She made a big fuss at the sight of May: "What a kind girl you are, taking such good care of Zhiqin! Zhiqin, you are such a disappointment! We have been having such a tough time traveling south. How could you let yourself get sick? You shouldn't be so delicate!"

"Sister Li is just a bit seasick. She'll be well soon," said May, in defense of Zhiqin. One corner of Jin Shizhen's mouth twitched involuntarily, indicating her disapproval of May poking her nose into her family's business. May gave Zhiqin a smile and went back to the dining room for her meal. Most of the diners in the dining room had finished, leaving behind messy piles of dirty dishes, bowls and chopsticks.

Bichu asked May gently: "The rice has gone cold. How about some steamed buns?" She handed May a bowl of hot soup which had just been served to them.

May slowly broke the steamed bun into smaller pieces and put them into her soup. She looked up from her soup and asked: "Why are there people like that?"

"The outside world is so different from our Square Teakettle. You'll come to that realisation yourself very soon." Bichu added one of her gentle and encouraging smiles.

Having taken Kiddo for a walk around the deck, Wei came back and sat by May. He told her: "Wuyin is proposing to watch the sunrise early tomorrow morning."

"Kiddo may stay with me. It might be too early for him," Bichu said.

May kept her eyes lowered on the soaked pieces of steamed bun in her bowl. A teardrop fell and disappeared into her soup.

Early next morning, Wuyin, Wucai, Wei and May came up on deck together. Wuyin led them to the starboard side and told them: "This way is east."

The darkness of the night was yielding to the light, revealing a thin pearl-grey haze over the sea, like the gauze on a screen door. As the gauze gradually disappeared, the tranquil sea was presented to observers in all its glory. Even without anything blocking their view, they still found they couldn't see many sections clearly, and however calm it appeared, they could feel the turbulent force under the tranquil appearance, all because it was the great sea, vast, fathomless, and abstruse. These small people were leaning against the ship's railing and looking into the distance with admiration.

"I'm going to study the sea," said Wei softly.

"Aren't you going to fly?" asked Wucai. "How about me studying the sea? When you fly your plane over the sea, I'll call you loudly."

Wuyin asked: "How about you, May?"

Looking into the far distance, May answered: "I'm going to study people and why they are different."

"How about we begin our study on why on earth there exist such things as Japanese devils, and how we can beat them and throw them out of our country?" Wei was looking into the distance, too.

The skyline glowed a magnificent red colour, splashing the sky and the sea with endless rays of red, bestowing a straight golden path decorated with colourful sparks from the skyline onto the sea. The red colours were turning from pink to peach, vermillion, crimson and scarlet to a brash translucent red, redder than a gigantic melting pot pouring out its work. The outer rim of the central shades of red radiated with violet, amaranth and other colours, defying description. All the colours diffused and tinted the sea near the skyline. The kids were beside themselves with excitement. The two boys were rubbernecking and the two girls were on tiptoes. They had to shield their eyes from the blinding rays from time to time.

"It's coming out! The sun is rising!" Wei yelled, excitedly.

May hurried to open her eyes in time to see the red ball of the sun rising from amid the gorgeous kaleidoscope of colours. It bounced, like a ball hit by someone. It bounced again, then it was off the sea, hanging on the horizon, gazing down quietly at the deep ocean. It splashed the resplendent dawn clouds with endless rays of pink, bathing the ship braving the water and the people on the deck with its pink glory.

After the kids had all exhaled with relief, they found Bichu, Della and Earl were actually standing beside them. Kiddo, who had been standing on a stool, ran to May and took her hand, while the two mothers remained where they were, smiling at them. Their big sister Earl, who had been affected by the vitality of nature, composed her face and turned away when she saw them.

Della told Bichu: "This scene reminds me of the lines from a dramatic poem by Lord Byron which describes a sunset, saying the sun is the material god, the centre of all stars, and the supreme lord. What grandeur the sun possesses!"

"Which mak'st our earth

Endurable, and temperest the hues

And hearts of all who walk within thy rays!"

"Sire of the seasons! Monarch of the climes..." added Wei, reciting the next line.

Della was surprised: "You have read *Manfred* already, Wei?"

"Xuan read it once. I joined her sometimes, but I can only remember this line, and I don't know what it means," answered Wei.

Wuyin asked May all of a sudden: "Guess what I am thinking about."

"Will the sun ever die?" answered May, raising her bright and vivid face, jubilant with confidence.

Wuyin smiled at her, appreciatively. It got hot when the sun had fully risen, casting irregular shadows on the deck, changing and moving in synch with their owners.

"We are going to arrive in Hong Kong in the afternoon," someone said.

PART 2

Three days later, Bichu and the others were in second-class cabins on the '*Great Guangdong*' sailing from Hong Kong to Hai Phong, the 3rd largest city in Vietnam. Wei had to share a cabin with a stranger on the upper floor since Wuyin had stayed behind at a summer school in Hong Kong. Bichu was quite concerned about this.

They had been on board for half a day, but she had been upstairs several times. Boarding a ship was no longer a fresh experience for all of them, so they tried to keep themselves entertained. Bichu and Zhiqin were busy with their knitting, Kiddo played with the blocks he had brought with him all the way, Earl was anchored to her bed lost in thought, and May had started reading a novel she had found in the hotel during their stay in Hong Kong. She soon got bored with it and discarded it, indulging herself with flashbacks to their stay in Hong Kong.

"I hate Hong Kong!" This was May's summary of her impression about the place. She could remember clearly the day when they arrived in the boiling hot sun among crowds of elbowing passengers. For some reason, the vessel '*Dongshun*' was not allowed to disembark by the quayside; passengers had to take a small boat to disembark. The boat, which was not small at all, looked more like a mini open hall without any seating. Holding on tightly to the edge of her mother's blouse in one hand, and her small item of luggage and the family's toiletries in the other, May saw nothing but people's backs, and cases and bags of all sizes and shapes. She was suffering in silence with a heavy headache.

Wucai and Della were received by their English friend when they got ashore; the Mengs and the Lis took a bus to a hotel.

Kiddo said: "It's rather strange. The hotel doesn't move."

May shared Kiddo's feelings. She didn't notice the movement when she was aboard the '*Dongshun*'. Not until she was ashore did she notice the difference. The '*Great Guangdong*' sailed so smoothly that she didn't feel much movement aboard it either. Maybe she would when she was ashore again.

The headache she had that day was so crushing that she felt her head was going to explode. Shortly after they reached the hotel, she couldn't hold back any longer and threw up. Her throat was so sore that she couldn't swallow the noodles she had for dinner that evening. She took only sips of the soup served with noodles.

Her conduct was immediately criticised by her big sister: "What a reckless waste of god's good gifts!"

The truth was that Earl herself didn't have any appetite that evening, either. The sun was too harsh for all of them since they had never experienced such a diabolical sun in Beiping. What nice sunshine Beiping had! It would shine through all kinds of things blocking the light and heat, such as those ancient tall Chinese scholar trees and willows, as well as the summer awnings made of reed sheets.

I felt much better the next day and wanted to go shopping with my mother. Earl was saying she wanted to take a ride on the peak tram. But mother wouldn't allow me to go out, so I stayed in the room, walking a little bit and then standing by the window for a while and walking again. The tall buildings I saw outside the room looked so close that I almost felt I could touch them; people down on the streets looked like dolls, busy coming and going. What were they all doing?

I sat down in a gigantic armchair, wishing a burglar or a robber would come in and take me away. What a pity that nobody came for me. Or I could have had so much fun!

Sister Zhiqin paid me a visit. Although she was still not feeling well, she had to take care of the two monsters who were her sister and brother, and me, by the way. Her mother joined my mother and Earl. I was certain that the latter two had no intention of taking Mrs Li along. They were just out of options.

I had fallen asleep in a chair when my mother came back, both her and Earl were carrying loads of things. I had two sets of clothes, one was a white top with a blue skirt, the other was a peach-coloured outfit. One of the boxes was beautiful. I didn't get up to meet them. Mother sat with me in the same chair, holding me in her arms for a while, and checked my temperature by touching her forehead against mine.

She looked exhausted. I felt lucky that no bandits had come to take me away, or mother would be grieving. Kiddo gave all of the candies people had given him to me, but I told him I didn't want any. Then he said he would keep them for me.

On the third day of our stay, Wuyin and Wucai came to take

Wei and me to the top of the peak by car. I saw the sea again. How shiny the water was! Some people were swimming; colourful beach umbrellas were clustered along the beach, with foreigners under each one. Wei said Hong Kong didn't belong to Japan, nor to China.

How busy that snack street was, with all of the tables displayed along both sides! The driver pointed at a building and told us it was a restaurant frequented by foreigners and thus was known as 'the building haunted by *gweilo*' — foreign ghosts — among the locals. Wuyin and I had quite a laugh.

It was very windy at the top of the peak. We leaned against the railing, overlooking this prosperous island, which no longer belonged to China, and which was mentioned in one of my history books.

Wei had come here the day before, but he said he had more fun today. Wuyin said he was going to register for a month-long summer course held by a maths professor from Great Britain. He said maths was the foundation of science, and asked Wei and me to stay with him. The two of them would attend classes, while I could play and enjoy myself, and then when summer was over, the three of us could leave together.

I didn't want to stay here. I wanted to go with mum to join daddy, who was waiting for us in Guihui, Yunnan province. Then the sight-seeing peak tram climbed all the way up the peak, rumbling like a crawling worm. Wucai suggested we take a ride. When all of us were settled in our seats, the person sitting in front of us suddenly turned back and asked:

"Are you the second daughter of the Meng family? Meng Lingji, isn't it? Do you still remember me?"

Ah! It was Zhang Xinlei - Thunderhand. He was dressed quite stylishly and looked rather like a dandy.

He said he had arrived here several months ago from Changsha, and he was staying in Hong Kong instead of going to Kunming. He said during his stay in an empty house in Changsha, he was attacked by some evil spirit and was struck down with a very serious disease. He used to ignore me when we met back in Beiping, but that day he prattled on and on. I couldn't go anywhere else in the cable car and so I tried my best to listen to him as patiently as possible. The peak tram cable car went through the shady green of the woods and was soon at the foot of the mountain.

Thunderhand invited us for ice cream, but we declined. He said he would drop by our hotel in the evening, and then he left with his friends. We first laughed at his name, then the air he put on when he spoke. When the cable car moved uphill again, I saw the sea, retreating backward in slow motion. The sea here was such a bright blue colour, like a sapphire. I had never seen a sapphire, though.

Wuyin bought us ice cream, but the strong wind blew so hard that the ice cream simply spilt on Wucai and me, leaving patches of yellow and white on our clothes. We wanted so much to laugh, but we couldn't breathe smoothly amid the gusts of wind. Nor could we laugh as we wanted.

We then went to where the Zhuangs were staying. All the way, Wuyin had been trying to talk Wei and me into staying in Hong Kong. Aunt Della said if Wei was willing to stay, he would go to the summer school as well; but it was pointless for me to stay. Besides, I would have been left unsupervised when they were at school. Only at that point did Wuyin drop the matter. Wei didn't want to stay either since he wanted to travel with us.

How beautiful those shops were! People said you could find anything in those shops. Indeed, Beiping had all the things which could be found in other places, and things which couldn't be found in other places.

Wucai said she needed pencils, so we went into a small gift shop. I casually looked at the items in the glass display counters. A bracelet lying on a rose-coloured pad caught my eye. It was a milky colour and was the shape of a reed blade bent into a hoop, with the end touching the tip, where two tiny insects glistened with their wings spread out.

"Fireflies!" I cried out, losing control of myself.

Wei said they didn't look like fireflies because the two were much better looking.

It was true that fireflies weren't very good looking, but they shone. The shimmering light from them over the creek could illuminate and awaken any dark memories!

Wuyin said: "If anyone is going to paint a portrait for May, paint her sitting by the creek with a vast swarm of fireflies in the background."

A swarm of fireflies.

"Just like the night on July 7th last year when you and Kiddo were outside Square Teakettle."

"And then this one is Dianna, and this one is Apollo," I said, pointing at the two insects. Wuyin smiled. He seldom smiled, but when he did, he shone like those fireflies.

"We had planned to watch those fireflies near Square Teakettle with you," Wei said with much regret.

Would those tiny shiny things fly over the creek this year?

Both Cousin Wei and I thought Xuan would like Hong Kong very much. It was a pity she was not with us.

May tumbled into her bed, feeling the hull of the ship pitching. This ship was very different from the '*Dongshun*'.

The sky looked to be looming over the sea through the cabin window. The sea looked serene. Maybe the ship had run into a swarm of fish? Kiddo's blocks collapsed. He patiently began to rebuild them.

That evening, Thunderhand did indeed come to our hotel. My sister Earl was very happy because the two shared many acquaintances. He mentioned again his life in Changsha, the bleak residence whose original inhabitants had run for their lives. The Japanese fighter planes that would drop bombs while they were having lessons, and some of the professors would even carry on their work during the air raids. He hated living like that. Here in Hong Kong, he could lead a comfortable life. With the help of his relatives, he could continue his college or start a business. He asked my mother and sister for their opinions.

Mother told him out of politeness: "It's not appropriate for someone like me, who is not your family, to make such a decision for you. Since we are now facing a national calamity, I suppose we should answer the call for united efforts to save our nation."

"Even if you can't answer the call, at least you shouldn't run away from it!" said my sister Earl, putting it rather bluntly.

Thunderhand blushed and pushed at his glasses a couple of times. He then said he might go to Kunming, too, depending on how things turned out here. My sister later said he was too practical to be a Chinese.

Wuyin came to our ship to see us off this morning. Although he was staying behind alone, he was not afraid at all. When we were standing on the deck, he gave me a beautiful carbon box with that firefly bracelet in it.

"Is this for me?" I couldn't believe my eyes.

"It is for you." Wuyin didn't smile. Aunt Della said he was free to spend his allowance however he wished. Everyone said it was a beautiful bracelet. I held it in front of my eyes to look at the sea through it. A milk-white circle against the azure sea. The two fireflies seemed to be glimmering. Other people liked the bracelet, only the four of us knew the significance of the two fireflies.

Kiddo cried. He knew best about the fireflies!

May leaned out of her bed and tried to look at Kiddo who was in the bottom bunk when the ship tilted suddenly and tossed May against the wall. Kiddo's blocks crashed down.

"Mummy!" she and Kiddo cried out at the same time.

The door slammed open with Jin Shizhen standing at the door, yelling: "There is a howling gale, the clouds are pressing. The sea is rising like great mountains, higher than the skyscrapers in Hong Kong!"

Her hair was messy like a nest blown out of a tree in the jungle. An old *qipao* made of indanthrene cloth was wrapped hastily around her with an unbuttoned collar. Her eyes shone with a bizarre light of excitement: "The ox-headed and horse-faced demons in Hades are riding the waves. And the imps and bad spirits, too! I have seen them! I have seen them all!"

Zhiqin jumped out of her bed and asked her mum to sit down, imploring in a whisper: "Stop! You have to stop!"

The ship was still tilting. Jin Shizhen lost her balance and fell right on top of Bichu, who hurriedly stood up and took the opportunity to sit Jin Shizhen down on the bed. Kiddo didn't hesitate to climb up to the top and stayed with May. Della and Wucai came, bringing Jin Shizhen's two smaller children with them.

Waiters came to inform them that all passengers should stay in their cabins to keep things in order. They were not going to serve dinner during a storm since nothing would stay put on the table, but they would provide passengers with bread, which would be delivered to their cabins in a while.

Zhiwei and Zhiquan both insisted on staying with Zhiqin in her cabin. Zhiqin forced a bitter smile: "Mrs Meng and Mrs Zhuang, please don't laugh at us. It's just that my mother has a wild imagination."

Jin Shizhen seemed not to hear this comment, busy with her muttering and mumbling. She pointed her finger frantically toward the outside and said: "I know this man who is holding a knife, but I don't know that one with a rope."

Bichu and Della tried every possible way to persuade Jin Shizhen to go back to her own cabin. She began to quieten down gradually.

Back in Bichu's cabin, Zhiqin began to throw up. She literally buried her face in the basin. Many passengers threw up. Vomiting noises were heard here and there from time to time. Earl said she felt sick, but she managed not to throw up.

A while later, some cold hot dogs were delivered to the cabin, but no one wanted any. Bichu was concerned about Wei who was staying upstairs and wanted to go to check on him. The ship was rolling even worse from side to side. She managed to go forward a few steps before she was thrown back to where she had started. She had to sit on the bed.

"Open the door! Everyone open the door!" The waiter was shouting in Guangdong dialect while he walked through the dining room. He was knocked down, slipped all the way from one end of the room to the other, and fell violently on the floor, crashing against the wall when his workmate crashed into him. He was lucky to be hit by his workmate instead of a dining table, which was originally hooked to the floor, but the hooks had broken loose, sending the table sliding wildly around the room, bumping and thumping against the walls from time to time.

The sea was pitch black. The waves punched into the ship and then retreated and then punched into it again. The ship was rolling violently like a leaf in a storm. Each roll seemed to be over 30 degrees, reaching the tipping point. All the passengers were tumbling in their bunks rhythmically under the onslaught of the waves, listening to the howling of the gale and the torrent of water.

Bichu suggested: "I can't do my knitting, you can't read. How about reciting some poems?" May gave her speedy consent.

> *"In spring the river rises as high as the sea,*
> *And with the river's rise, the bright moon rises.*
> *The rolling waves extend for miles,*
> *Wherever the river flows,*
> *The moon sheds its silver light."*

May's tender voice muffled the sound of the wind and rain outside. The atmosphere inside the cabin was quiet and peaceful with Kiddo's constant interruptions and Bichu's occasional reminders about the lines of the long poem. When May was done reciting '*A Moonlit Night on the Spring River*' by the Tang dynasty poet Zhang Ruoxu, Kiddo began '*A Note Left for an Absent Hermit*' by another Tang poet and monk named Jia Dao:

> *"When I ran into your pupil, under a pine tree,*

> *'My master's gone for herbs, you see,*
> *but toward which corner of the mountain,*
> *How can I tell, through clouds like these?'"*

Bichu, looking at the frame of the upper bunk, shouted her praise for Kiddo amid the roaring noise.

"Mum, let's recite the longest poem," said May, popping her head out from above. Without waiting for her mother's response, she began *'The Everlasting Regret'*. Even Earl contributed a line or two in her indifferent fashion. Zhiqin listened with admiration and envy. She felt limp all over after taking a sea-sickness pill.

Suddenly the light went out. May rolled over as the ship listed, and she and Kiddo bumped into each other, giggling.

"I hate this!" Earl said.

It occurred to Bichu that there must have been some sort of mechanical problem. Fear seized her. After calming herself down, she held the railing of the bed and stood up: "You go on reciting your poems. I must take a look at Wei."

Someone shouted at the other end of the dining room: "Put on your life jackets! Put on your life jackets!" The shaking and terrifying voice echoed all along the passage.

Zhiqin and Earl sat up in their beds while Bichu was busy looking for the life jackets with her flashlight. Each room was equipped with four life jackets. She didn't inform the children about this fact, but handed out one jacket each.

She headed outside: "I have to go upstairs to check on Wei." She whispered in such a low voice it sounded more like she was murmuring to herself.

"Mum, I will go with you." Both Earl and May were ready to get off their beds when the ship tilted, sending them tumbling down onto their beds again.

"You two stay put! You must listen to me. You stay here and take care of Kiddo. I'll be back in no time," pleaded Bichu sternly.

With her flashlight, she first grabbed the bed railing, then the door knob, and then the door handle. The dining room was deserted with only one gas light still working at the other end, casting some light on the moving tables. She watched for a moment before she moved forward, clutching at anything on the wall, avoiding the moving tables as best she could, inching her way toward the staircase.

It didn't take her long to figure out a pattern — when the ship tilted towards her, she would pick up her pace; when the ship tilted away from her, she would clutch onto a handle fixed on the wall and steady herself. The staircase was within reach in front of her. When the ship tilted again, she let go of the handle, slipped and stopped right at the foot of the steps. She climbed up without a second thought. Having lost her footing twice on the soaked, slippery steps, she made it to the top the third time.

What a horrifying scene it was up on deck — mountains of angry waves towered over and smashed down onto the ship in the total darkness like landslides. She was soon drained as the rain slammed into her. Every time the ship jolted to the side, the deck looked like it would be drowned in the sea, and she was so afraid that she would fall into the sea herself. With her stomach gripped by fear, she took a sure grip of the handrail. How lucky she was that Wei's cabin was close to the staircase and she was able to reach it within one jolt.

"Who's out there on deck? Get off, now!" A sailor ran to Bichu with consummate skill, tracking her with his flashlight. He first shouted in Cantonese, then switched to his raw Putonghua: "Have you lost your mind? Go back to your cabin!"

"I want to check on my child in this cabin," Bichu answered, struggling to grip the handrail and pass down the aisle. "Wei! Wei!" she cried, pushing open the door of the cabin.

Wei, anchored in his bed, jumped up. With a flash of lightning, he saw Bichu in her dripping clothes.

"Aunt Bichu!" He took a stride forward, secured Bichu in his arms, and seated her on the bed: "How did you manage to come up all this way?"

Bichu smiled with relief upon seeing him equipped with his life jacket. The passenger who shared the cabin with Wei sat up in his bed: "This is a very rare storm!" His thick Cantonese accent made his Putonghua rather hard to understand. "I have been travelling by this route for almost 20 years and have never seen a storm as violent as this! I am in the business of medicinal herbs."

"Aunt Bichu, why haven't you put on your life jacket?" asked Wei, busy drying Bichu's hair with a towel. Bichu kept smiling without answering his question.

"You need to be very careful when you walk on deck!" warned the medicinal herbs businessman. "Don't worry. Tantai Wei is a good lad. And a very smart one, too."

"Wei," said Bichu, composing herself and taking Wei's hand: "You must take care of yourself. If they are going to transfer us to a lifeboat, board it when it's your turn. Don't worry about us. It won't be a good thing if you worry too much." Wei nodded without much assurance.

Bichu took out a small leather purse from the inside pocket of her blouse, took the only hundred-yuan note, and put it into the pocket of the life vest. She gave the pocket several pats as if that would secure the money inside: "Be sure to bear my words in mind. I am with Aunt Della and two grownup girls, and I don't need anyone to look after me, so don't you get distracted by worrying about me and the others. Take care of yourself!"

The businessman smiled: "We'll be OK. Our ship '*Great Guangdong*' is a big ship. If we were on '*Small Guangdong*', we might have been blown into the sky a long time ago!"

"I do hope so. Could you please give him a hand if he needs help? Thank you!" said Bichu to the businessman, with a small bow.

She then turned to Wei in a firm and stern tone: "I'm going downstairs. Don't follow me. Two people have to watch out for each other, adding much work. I have got the hang of walking in the storm." With these words, she left the cabin with a controlled, skilful movement.

A flash of lightning illuminated the ship's handrail for her. She waited for the jolt toward her. Wei was right at her heels but didn't dare to make a noise. The ship tilted toward her, she walked steadily and reached the staircase. Then down she went.

The towering waves crashed onto the ship amid rolling booms of thunder reverberating around the vessel. The man pulled Wei back into the cabin, muttering: "We will have to wait this out! We'll have to wait this out!"

The trip back was much easier for Bichu. The power was back, too, though the light bulb was still only providing a dim, flickering light, casting a crepuscular glow within the room. She guessed that Della might not have a life jacket either, so she planned to go to room service and ask for two.

When she passed Della's cabin, she overheard Zhiqin talking to Della.

"I thought Mrs Li might be suffering from some old illness, so I fetched Zhiqin," said Della, forcing a smile when she saw Bichu. "She insists on kneeling on the bed. When she fell off onto the floor, she tried to remain in the same kneeling position. See? She has cut her forehead." She had a stronger Beiping accent than Bichu.

Jin Shizhen remained kneeling on the bed, steadying herself by holding the handrails. A bloodstain was distinctly visible on the left corner of her temple. Zhiqin called her, but she didn't respond. Her two smaller kids had tucked themselves into the far corner of the bed, eyes wide with fear.

Zhiqin, obviously having run out of options, spoke up: "My mother has her own way of dealing with things. Aunt Zhuang may just ignore her and let her be."

It was rather surprising that Jin Shizhen actually heard these words, for she jumped off her bed, pulled Zhiqin by her long braids and boxed Zhiqin's ears. The ship jolted, and both fell in a heap, which prompted horrified cries from Zhiwei.

Bichu and Della hurriedly stood up while Zhiqin and her mother remained sitting on the floor. Zhiqin was stupefied for a moment before she stood up and tried to help her mother, who pushed her away and stood up by herself. She pointed at Zhiqin and yelled: "You ungrateful vixen! Others may not know what I am doing. How dare you make out you don't know what I am doing? I am praying for the lives aboard the ship! You asked them to ignore me? All of you may well see what happens if you do that!"

Her words made everyone in the room speechless. It was truly impossible for them to stand, so Bichu spoke up: "Let's forget it. It's already over. How about we go back to the cabins and lie in bed?"

She checked with Della whether she had a life jacket. Della said she was taking a lifebuoy (or ring flotation device), hoping she might have a chance to swim, so she didn't need a life vest. What happened next was stunning. Upon seeing Della's lifebuoy, Jin Shizhen snatched it and put it around her neck, muttering all the time. Bichu and Della decided there was no point in arguing with Jin Shizhen, so they talked about making alternative arrangements and then said good night to each other. Bichu took Zhiqin back to their cabin.

Zhiqin didn't cry. Instead, she explained to Bichu: "My mother is a warm-hearted person. She is a little bit odd because of her obsession with her beliefs."

Bichu said: "Anyone who is obsessed with anything seems somewhat odd. Once one knows about it, they don't seem odd anymore."

Zhiqin looked gratefully at Bichu. Then they lay down in their own beds.

The ship was still rocking rhythmically. It was quiet inside the cabin except for the splashing of the waves and the thumping and clunking of the moving tables hitting the wall. The storm was not over yet, but the panic was, as if people had got used to it.

May and Kiddo were not frightened. They were somewhat lightheaded due to fatigue. Like her younger sister and brother, Earl thought things were quite funny in the storm, but when the little ones laughed, she would scold them. She thought the moving tables hitting the wall were the most hilarious thing. When she saw them sliding this way and that, she almost couldn't hold back her laughter. She would cover her face with a corner of her bedcover to stifle her laughter amid all the rolling and jolting.

Late in the small hours of the night, when Bichu was staring at the dim yellow light, Zhiqin let out a loud groan.

Bichu sat bolt upright and asked: "What's wrong?" Zhiqin carried on groaning without any response. Bichu got off her bed and went to Zhiqin, whose eyes were half closed and her forehead was oozing with cold sweat. Zhiqin was pressing one hand on her chest, while the other was clenched tight, as if she was enduring throbbing pain. It didn't look like seasickness. Bichu felt her pulse, which was weak and fast.

She leaned over and asked: "Do you have pain somewhere?"

Zhiqin pointed at her chest and said through clenched teeth: "It hurts. It hurts so much…"

"Have you had this before when you were at home?" asked Bichu, rushing to take out the emergency kit, and rummaging around for some medicine.

Zhiqin nodded and answered with much effort: "I have heart problems…"

Bichu took out some Snowdrop Bush (Styrax Officinalis) pills, a traditional Chinese medicine designed to induce resuscitation with aromatics. She first thought of going to check with Jin Shizhen; on second thoughts, she decided not to and forced the pills into Zhiqin's mouth: "Chew them and swallow slowly. Don't choke yourself." She gently lifted Zhiqin's head to help her swallow. Earl and May sat up in their beds and looked down at Zhiqin, full of concern.

A while later, Zhiqin quietened down as the pain subsided. All the others in the cabin lay down in bed. But in less than an hour, she was moaning in pain again. Bichu couldn't give Zhiqin another dose of the same medicine at such a short interval, so she decided to go and tell Jin Shizhen after asking Zhiqin to keep a piece of ginseng in her mouth.

As she walked out of the cabin heading for the passage, she found it was much easier to walk and the tables were slipping back before they hit the walls. The ship was sailing much more steadily. The storm was dying away. Realising this relaxed her. She heaved a deep sigh of relief, and leaned against the door without realising what she was doing. How exhausted she was!

"Aunt Bichu! The waves are much smaller. We have survived the storm!" Wei ran all the way down the stairs, obviously unable to restrain his joy. He looked like a junior sailor in his life jacket, thought Bichu.

"My good boy! You may take off your life jacket now, but keep it within reach." Bichu looked at Wei lovingly and gestured to him to go back to his cabin.

She went to Della's cabin to find Jin Shizhen and her two small kids were sound asleep, all snoring evenly and peacefully. Della remained awake. She was standing in the cabin busy calculating in her mind to what extend the jolts had reduced.

Bichu told her about Zhiqin's heart problem. The two talked it over and concluded that there was no use waking up Jin Shizhen. Della went back to Bichu's cabin.

Zhiqin felt much better and was talking to Wei: "Don't know when we can go back to Beiping. But I'm afraid I won't make it back."

Wei answered her reassuringly: "How come you won't make it back? Even if we have to continue fighting for several years, or several decades, we'll all make our way back!" He paused for a moment and then said gently: "As the old saying goes — one who survives a disaster is blessed ever after. Sister Li, you will get better in no time."

A thin smile appeared at the corners of Zhiqin's mouth. A tint of rosiness gradually came back to her face which had been as white as a sheet a while ago. With the piece of ginseng in her mouth, she was regaining her strength. Everyone heaved a second sigh of relief.

The ship sailed more and more steadily. Once the storm had died down, the sun shone. People poured out everywhere, up on deck, along the passageways and into the dining hall. Everyone was smiling.

"My life has been saved!"

"Who should we thank? There's someone on board who has shared their good luck with us!"

News spread around noon that two smaller ships had sunk during the storm the previous night.

What a mysterious and intangible force the sea possessed! No one should be so bold as to challenge it or enrage it! May came up on deck again. As she stood by the handrail, her heart was filled with awe and admiration — the sea could be gentle and enraged, it could be balmy and boiling, all because of the force it embodied, a force so vast and so ever-changing as to defy people's comprehension.

One day later, the ship reached Haiphong, north Vietnam. When the passengers disembarked, they felt how weird and solid the land was under their feet. May and Kiddo swung their bodies, but the ground remained still. Kiddo literally thumped each step he took, as if he were going to make the land tremble, while every footstep of May's was very gentle as if she feared that her weight might be a burden on the ground.

Everyone got used to the stability in no time and turned their attention to the customs clearance in Trung Ky, or Annam. The customs officers opened the pieces of luggage violently and threw them aside when they had finished poking through the contents, ordering the passengers to tidy up the mess themselves. The three families were travelling with quite a number of cases and bags. At the sight of the open cases and bags with clothes and other items scattered all over the place, the three ladies frowned.

They were lucky that Fuzhi had already asked the Chinese consul general to meet them at the customs, so their luggage survived the inspection. Della and Wuyin, who were going to travel directly to Kunming by train, were picked up by a local friend. As they did in Hong Kong, the Mengs and the Lis stayed together in a hotel.

Bichu asked Shizhen once they were settled in the hotel: "Aren't you going to take Zhiqin to the hospital for a check-up and see what is wrong with her?"

Shizhen answered: "This girl of mine has never been short of ailments since her childhood. She is also a natural worrier who keeps things to herself. We have made countless hospital visits. And for the last year, she has had to go to school in the day and help with the chores at home when our servant left. We couldn't afford to hire any help. I know she is worn out." She looked at Zhiqin with love in her eyes as she talked. She had been sane since they had reached the shore. No one asked what had happened to her during the storm.

Zhiqin didn't feel better at all, but she was so used to suffering in silence that she kept the pain to herself. When she heard her mother and Bichu talking about her, she held back her tears and struggled to wash Zhiquan's clothes, although she was so weak that she just wanted to lie in bed. That night, she had very serious diarrhoea. The colour faded from her face. Shizhen was so concerned that Zhiqin might not be able to board the train with such diarrhoea. She asked the hotel to send for a doctor to prescribe some medicine for it.

Early next morning the nine members of the group made up of the Mengs and the Lis, young and old, boarded the train to Yunnan province via Bisezhai railway station where they transferred onto a smaller train to Guihui. It was not crowded in the carriage. Several local Annamese people, who looked like vendors, sat in the seats which formed a circle around the sides of the carriage, leaving space in the centre for luggage.

Earl muttered to herself: "This is not a passenger train. It's a freight train!" Strangely, Shizhen didn't comment on this.

The train started with the door wide open. No one came to close it at all. The strong draught near the door drove people to sit further inside, as far away from the door as possible. May was still in charge of her small case and the family's toiletries, which she had put in among the small items in their large cases.

They had been warned all the way that the thieves in Annam were notorious for their skills and the wide range of things they were interested in targeting — gold, silver, cash, hats, shoes, socks, even handkerchiefs. They stole whatever they set their eyes on. During a meal in Hanoi, all the kids' sunhats went missing. Wei chose to sit near the door to protect their luggage.

The Yunnan-Vietnam railway followed the Song Hong and Red river valleys. The rivers surged between the towering cliffs, winding this way and that, raging in whirlpools so violent that the river looked as if it had lost its direction amid all the spinning and swirling. The train carried on for several hours. Seldom did they find any calm water. It kept rolling and roaring all the way. The mountains were covered with typical subtropical dense and wet green vegetation, glowing with unrestrained vitality.

"Monkeys! Monkeys!" yelled Wei at the door. A troop of monkeys were playing, some bouncing and leaping from branch to branch, some swinging through the high vines with fluid movements of their hands. The kids clapped and cheered.

Just before noon, their excitement was gradually replaced by low spirits induced by fatigue. The seats were so hard that they felt they were pricking into their flesh. The kids were fidgeting with discomfort, sitting or standing, but no one complained. The train pulled into a station in the evening. Representatives from local inns were waiting to tout for customers. Bichu and Shizhen picked one who was neatly dressed and followed him.

When they finally reached the inn after a long walk, they were all exhausted. Some lay down, some sat in the room, and no one wanted to eat. Zhiqin's diarrhoea came back. Having run to the bathroom several times, she was too weak and light-headed to lift her head. Bichu touched her forehead to feel her temperature and found Zhiqin was burning hot. She asked Shizhen whether they should go back to Hanoi where Della was staying and see what Della could do, but Shizhen said confidently:

"It doesn't matter. She can bear it. As soon as we reach Bisezhai, I know how to deal with it. What a troublesome child she has always been!" She went around to Zhiqin and fed her more anti-diarrhoea medicine. When it was done, she sat aside in silence, as if she was practicing her magic.

To give some comfort to Zhiqin, May put her beloved firefly bracelet by her pillow. Zhiqin gave her a faint smile and whispered: "You need to put it away. We don't want it to be stolen."

When May picked up the bracelet, she found two scarlet bugs. She brushed off the bugs and put the bracelet carefully back into her small case. After one more look, she found several more on Zhiqin's pillow and in her bed. They stank. When she asked, Bichu told her they were bed bugs.

"Those bed bugs are beautiful," commented Kiddo.

The next noon, when the train approached the old street at the frontier station, and everyone in the carriage was still half asleep, they heard Bichu shouting suddenly: "Hey! What are you doing?"

They opened their eyes to find an Annamese man in a headcloth had snatched one case in each hand and dropped them off the train. These two fine-looking cases had all Meng's clothing inside. When Bichu yelled, the man grabbed May's small case before leaping out of the railway carriage.

"Thief!"

"Pickpocket!"

"Robber!"

The Mengs and Lis yelled loudly, but the Annamese people in the same carriage remained in their seats quietly, shutting their eyes and turning a deaf ear to what was happening. May ran after the thief, but Wei pulled her back when she was by the door, just as she saw the thief regain his feet and wave at her. The terrain sloped gently in this section so the thief didn't tumble into the deep valley when he jumped out of the railway carriage. It was not hard to conclude that this thief was familiar with the local terrain and had taken full advantage of it.

May cried. Her case containing all her precious memories was now in the hands of a thief!

"Mummy!" She turned around and threw herself into her mother's arms, smearing her tears on her mother's dress.

"Don't cry, my darling! There's no use in crying," said Bichu, stroking May's back to calm her. "Your safety is what's most important. Material things come and go."

Wei came to comfort her, too: "We can always find new souvenirs."

Kiddo added: "That one probably has nothing to eat. He must be starving!"

"The thief has good taste to have picked your cases, which are the best of the lot," said Jin Shizhen, somewhat gloatingly.

Things gradually quietened down in the car. Amid the rumbling of the train, they heard a moaning sound from the corner where Zhiqin was lying.

"What's wrong with you? Why are you whining?" Shizhen pushed away Zhiquan who was leaning against her and walked to the corner.

"I don't feel well…" Zhiqin answered between clenched teeth. "Very dizzy."

"Car-sick? Has your diarrhoea stopped?" Shizhen went back to find some Jintan[3]. May stood up, drying her tears with her mother's handkerchief and grabbing her mother's sleeve, and followed Bichu to Zhiqin's side.

Zhiqin's forehead was soaked with cold sweat again. The collar of her *qipao* made of starched light-blue cotton cloth was drenched. Her face was as white as a sheet and her eyes shut tight. Her nose and her mouth were almost displaced. May was shocked at the sight and hid behind Bichu.

---

[3] Jintan: (人丹 or 仁丹, pronounced *jintan* in Japanese or *rendan* in Chinese pinyin) is a patented Japanese medicine which was originally promoted as a panacea.

"Zhiqin, do you have a pain in your chest?" asked Bichu, lowering herself, unbuttoning Zhiqin's *qipao* and pulling Earl's light shawl up to cover Zhiqin.

Zhiqin nodded weakly in reply and tried to open her eyes to look around. She had felt ill when she boarded the train, but she had been suffering in silence and persevering until she couldn't bear it any longer. She didn't want to hold back any longer.

"Shall we give her some pills for heart-relief?" said Bichu to Shizhen, and asked May to hand over the medicine kit.

The liquid styrax pills were lodged stubbornly in Zhiqin's mouth. It took her a long while to swallow a small portion of the pills but she threw up most of them. She couldn't swallow the sliced ginseng either. Blood trickled out of one corner of her mouth. She might have bitten her tongue because of the pain. Shizhen wiped the blood off. The realisation of how serious the situation had become was freaking her out.

She howled: "You just hold on for a while. We are arriving at Bisezhai. Once we are there, I will find a way to deal with this." She dragged May to her side: "Talk to her! She likes you! Tell her to hang on for a while!"

May wanted to cry, too, but she took Zhiqin's hand and said: "Sister Zhiqin, hang on for a while!" She didn't know what Zhiqin was supposed to wait for, so she added: "You wait for a while and we will catch you some butterflies."

Zhiqin opened her eyes, looked at May, and asked with difficulty: "Where is Tantai Wei?"

Wei hurried up to her and said: "Sister Zhiqin, when we arrive at Guihui, we will go and hunt for the most beautiful butterflies for you."

A thin smile flashed across Zhiqin's face. She gathered her

strength and said: "You are both very nice... very beautiful..." Her grip on May's hand tightened. Bichu wanted to let May step aside, so she stroked Zhiqin gently, but May couldn't release her hand from Zhiqin's grip. She was scared, but she carried on, saying: "Sister Zhiqin, hang on for a while!"

Zhiwei and Zhiqin began to weep.

Zhiqin loosened her grip.

"What are you crying for? Your big sister is so ill that she may die! Shush!" Shizhen yelled at the two kids. Earl pulled the kids back and looked at Shizhen, shaking her head to let Shizhen know she was taking care of the kids and there was no need to yell.

Zhiqin closed her eyes. The pained expression lingered on her face. It would linger forever and would never change. The spot where her emaciated body lay was slowly getting wet with traces of sweat, but the life had gone out of it, leaving her body soulless.

May, leaning close to Bichu, was the one who stayed closest to Zhiqin. She just stared at the body lying lifeless in front of her and her mother. Something hard and tough lay heavy on their chests, that required a lot of effort to melt into burning tears. Not until the tears flowed did Bichu realise she should take May away and sit down with her.

"What? My daughter! Why couldn't you wait for a while? What am I going to tell your father?" Jin Shizhen threw herself at Zhiqin's body, wailing loudly and stamping hard.

"Why couldn't you wait? The holy spirit is waiting in Bisezhai, waiting to save you! Why couldn't your destiny have been more fortunate?" She was stricken with grief. Zhiwei and Zhiquan stumbled over to her, grabbed her dress in terror, and stamped like their mother.

Bichu hugged Kiddo in one arm, and held May's hand with the other while Earl and Wei stood by their side, sobbing softly. Neither the weeping and wailing nor the soft sobs could wake up the girl who had deserted her shell of a body in a railway carriage on a speeding train in the prime of her youth full of happy longing for days yet to come. Zhiqin of the Li family didn't reach the land free from the iron grip of the invader, neither did she reach the butterfly spring in Dali, Yunnan province. How impotent the holy spirit in Bisezhai was when it failed to cover the 100 miles needed to save the life of a young girl!

PART 3

Guihui used to be a prosperous town in southern Yunnan. When the local inhabitants refused to let the Yunnan-Vietnam railroad go through the town, the railroad took a detour and made a grand station in Bisezhai, which enjoyed all the benefits brought by the advantages of an advanced traffic network, leaving Guihui to its tranquillity and time-honoured air of unsophistication.

It was such a small town that if one stood in the centre of it and turned around, all four town gates located at the four points of the compass would be right under one's nose. All four town gates had well maintained, elegant, crenellated parapets. A small lake lay to the south of the town. During the rainy season, the lake presented a vast expanse of misty, rolling water. The town boasted several narrow streets lined with various styles of houses. Some had courtyards in the northern style, some two-storey buildings in the southern style, and there was a deserted French-style bank on the outskirts of town. All were enveloped in green from the trees that were perennially in leaf. The town rippled with refreshing greenness. Even the mist at dusk was tinted with green.

In the misty dusk, Fuzhi, his family and the friend who came along to pick up Bichu and the kids passed the crossroad. Though many strangers had moved to the town since the war, some of the locals still crowded around when newcomers arrived.

"More have come! More have come!" the local kids shouted in Yunnan dialect.

Most of them wore heavy silver-coated necklaces with lock pendants, symbolising their parents' wish to keep their kids locked fast in this world. One embroidered undergarment covered the chest and abdomen, intricate work done by their mothers, and below they were naked, revealing nature in all its glory.

The Lis stayed in Bisezhai for Zhiqin's funeral. The Mengs, having no relief from the shadow of Zhiqin's death, dragged themselves along in gloomy silence. The happy reunion of the family didn't neutralise the terror of absolute helplessness when they were forced to confront death.

It was especially hard for May. All her days in Square Teakettle and Chestnut Street were history, dead like Zhiqin's corpse. She was no longer the same Meng Lingji.

At Bisezhai station, Bichu took her to the bathroom and made her wash her hands with soap several times. It might have helped to wash off the dirt, but it couldn't wash off her experience, her feelings and grief over Zhiqin. She had an urge to have a good cry, seemingly not for Zhiqin but for herself, for her parents, and for everything, although she couldn't explain why.

She didn't cry. Instead, she dropped her head and dried her tears in silence. All the members of the Meng family had strong control over their emotions. Wei stroked her head, and she raised her eyes to look at him. Her ample eyelashes were shining with a half ring of tiny sparkling diamonds.

Wei was very sorry about what had happened. He was also sorry that May was sad. He consoled her, whispering: "Mr Qian, the one who came to pick us up, said that there is a big garden in the foreign bank outside town. I think we may find fireflies there."

How long could the light from the fireflies' mini lanterns last? Wouldn't they wear out? May walked laboriously, lost in thought. They thought they might go by car once they got off the train, or a horse-drawn carriage would be even better. Only when the smiling Mr Qian urged them to move along did they realise they had to go on foot. Who were those people lining the street? Could they happen to have heard of Zhiqin, who was no longer able to walk? May, tugging Wei's sleeve, followed the adults and walked to Kidney-Bean Street step by step, where their home was.

The two-storey courtyard house in Kidney-Bean Street was shaped like a square with one side missing. The Mengs stayed on the ground floor and the Qian couple lived on the first floor.

Mr Qian Mingjing, who was always smiling, was well known for his shrewdness. Some joked that his given name, Mingjing, should be read backward like 'Jingming', which sounded exactly like the Chinese expression for shrewdness. It was he who had hunted down the house. Having settled down several months ago, they had energy to spare to help the Mengs. Assuming Bichu and the kids might not have had lunch on the train, they had prepared snacks upstairs.

The first floor was surrounded by a veranda on the left, right and front side. The walls were made of intricately carved wood. The east room served as the Qians' reception room. The door with four latticework windows was wide open, allowing air to circulate smoothly and the slanting rays of the setting sun to shed their glory on the tastefully laid-out room. In the centre stood a hardwood round table encircled by stools of the same material. All were carved with fine flowers. On the table were warm sweet porridge and pancakes filled with jam.

"You don't look like you are taking refuge here. Where did you find all these lovely things?" Bichu's eyes turned to the two traditional wooden armchairs at both ends of the room with marble backs and arms inlaid with mother-of-pearl. They caught her full attention and she went over for a closer look: "When were they made? Have you traced their origin?"

Mrs Qian, Zheng Huifen, answered: "The furniture all belongs to the owner of the house. When Mingjing found the house, he was so fond of the furniture that he rented the house furnished. This is the only room with several nice pieces of furniture like these. The other rooms are rather empty without much furniture."

"I think this pair of armchairs might have been made during the reign of Emperor Shunzhi in the Qing dynasty, between 1644 and 1661. See how well preserved they are!" Qian Mingjing said proudly. "This town is quite close to the tin mines in Gejiu city. Some of the businessmen in the tin trade have made a fortune and become very rich. Our landlord is one of those men. Most of his best stuff has been shipped to Kunming where he lives now."

"Regarding the furniture, the fewer pieces, the better," said Fuzhi. "It saves time spent on cleaning and maintenance. Especially the fine furniture which requires high maintenance. I don't have that much energy."

"This is virgin land which has never been exploited.

I bet we can dig out some antiques," said Qian Mingjing enthusiastically with his laconic smile.

"How could you be in such a good mood?" said Huifen reproachfully.

They talked and sat down to eat their porridge. Mingjing explained: "There is a store known by the townsfolk for its sweet porridge. Since the owner's family name is Lei, it is called Lei's Porridge. Try it. It's very different from what we used to have in Beiping."

They all tried it and agreed it was quite good, but no one had much appetite.

Seeing the kids in low spirits, Mingjing tried to cheer them up: "Although Guihui is a small town, it used to be the site for customs clearance of the goods along the Yunnan-Vietnam railway. The place was teeming with businessmen. It once had a very big foreign bank, which is closed now. Our university has been set up right in its garden. It has a racetrack for horses, too. I'll show you around in a few days."

"I have never ridden a horse before," said Kiddo, who was sipping porridge from his bowl. He leaned backward, forgetting he was sitting on a stool instead of the chair he used to sit on at home in Beiping, and fell down on the floor with a thump. Bichu rushed toward him to try and pick him up, and the others all lept to their feet. Kiddo wanted to cry because of the pain, but he struggled to hold back the tears, realising that all the attention was on him.

"Meng Heji is very brave," said Mingjing, looking at Kiddo.

"How do you know my name?" asked Kiddo, wriggling out of Bichu's arms. He returned to his stool and sat down properly.

"I have seen you and your sisters at Square Teakettle on more than occasion," Mingjing answered with a smile. "But I have never met Tantai Wei." Mingjing addressed the kids formally with their full names, which made them very happy. He turned to Wei: "I have met your father, just once, though."

"My father has fully recovered. They are going to move to Kunming soon," answered Wei, tucking the letter from his parents delivered by Fuzhi in his pocket. He was planning to read it carefully once he was alone.

"Where is Madam Liu now?" Bichu asked.

"She is now in Kunming. Very likely she will be moving to Chongqing," Huifen answered.

"Which Madam Liu are you talking about?" asked Earl, who was not very talkative when she was with a large group of people. "Madam Liu the singer?"

"Yes, that's her. She is Mrs Qian's sister," answered Bichu. She then turned to Huifen again: "All my kids have a passion for music, but not a gift for it."

"When I was in Kunming for a meeting last week, I heard that Huiyuan couldn't find a piano. It was Ziwei who helped her to borrow one from a church," added Fuzhi.

When Earl learned that Qian-Zheng Huifen was Liu-Zheng Huiyuan's sister, she couldn't help but cast several more looks at her. Huifen was wearing a dark blue *qipao* made of cotton cloth with floral patterns on the seams. Her face was a perfect oval shape and she had crystal-clear eyes. Not like Liu-Zheng Huiyuan, who was full of feminine charms, she looked rather handsome.

Feeling Earl's gaze upon her, Huifen smiled: "I was a painter and learned to play some musical instruments, too, but now I am a housewife looking after our daily livelihood needs for the two of us." She nodded at Mingjing with a smile and turned to Bichu: "Living expenses inland are much lower. Ham is about 20 cents for one pound. You can buy 100 eggs for 10 cents. It's not hard to survive at all."

"Look! What a grocery expert she has become! She definitely excels as a housewife! But it is academically underdeveloped here, and people are somewhat narrow-minded. Few books are available. I paid a visit to the county library where I found no books at all."

Fuzhi said: "Most of the university's books have been shipped to Kunming. We can't keep the university here for long. We'll have to move to Kunming soon."

He smiled apologetically at Bichu: "You see, you have just arrived and I'm already talking about moving. We won't move right now. It will take at least a few months."

"Compared with the trouble our nation is facing, moving a few times doesn't count for anything," answered Bichu.

"I have found you a servant. Here they call servants helpers. She'll be here soon," Huifen told Bichu.

While they were talking, the Qian couple's helper, Sister Wang, brought a married woman to meet them, saying the woman's family name was Zhang and they could call her Sister Zhang. Bichu talked to Sister Zhang for a moment and told her to stay. The Meng family then all went downstairs.

The main room downstairs was empty except for a makeshift bed comprising several boards pieced together. Fuzhi was staying in the room in the west wing. A wobbly campbed was visible in the room with an unpainted whitewood table piled with manuscripts. Everyone was amazed at the two rows of bowls of all sizes neatly stacked along the wall.

"What are these for?" asked Bichu, smiling. "Are we going to open up a diner?"

"Since you are here, you all need bowls for meals," replied Fuzhi, confidently.

When she took a second look at the bowls, Bichu noticed that all the bowls were being used without having been properly cleaned. She stifled a laugh and assigned everyone their tasks to help with the clean-up, saying: "It's much better than I expected. I thought we might end up in a hut."

"The thing is we can't have meals or study without a table," noted Earl, coolly. "Are we going to sit on the floor?"

"It is already remarkable for your dad to have thought about preparing the beds and the bowls," said Bichu. "We'll buy the other necessities gradually. There's no hurry."

"Let's stick to the basics in times of war," said Wei. He had just finished reading the *New Yunnan Daily* and noticed that the wedding announcements all shared the same line — "Let's stick to the basics in times of war."

Earl shot him a dirty look and said nothing more.

Later in life when the Meng family recalled their stay at Guihui, they all felt it had been a short, tranquil and gentle section in the rapids, which offered a window of time for them to loosen the iron grip that clutched their hearts. The feeling of freedom with the land under their feet which belonged to them, and without the bayonets hanging over their heads, only resonated with those who had been subjected to the experience of being a 'conquered people'. They did suffer the same melancholy as those who had to leave their hometowns, and the frustrations because of different dialects and customs, but the rich ethnic colours of this small town, the pastoral scenery, and the family reunion brought so much more pleasure and happiness to the Mengs.

Strangers were much better off economically as one yuan

in the legal currency issued by the central bank was equal to 10 yuan in the new local Yunnan currency, and 100 yuan in the old Yunnan currency. Some shop keepers for food such as poultry and vegetables accepted only the old Yunnan currency, so the cash the strangers had suddenly became 100 times more valuable than before. That explained why Qian Mingjing was so enthusiastic about searching for antiques.

Of course, such an economic benefit didn't negate other inconveniences. In Bichu's case, her biggest inconvenience was that she couldn't find a capable servant, which meant she had to worry about everything herself. Fuzhi and Earl were so used to being the master and the mistress of the house that it never occurred to them that they should help. When it did occur to them, they didn't. Only May and Wei would often ask: "Mummy, can I help?"

"Aunt Bichu, can I do anything?"

But the two couldn't help much, either, despite their willingness to do so.

For the kids, life in Guihui opened up a new world for them. Here they didn't have the campus like at Minglun University or the tall walls around No. 3 Chestnut Street to block out the outside world. Life in the courtyard house in Kidney-Bean Street and life in Guihui town were intertwined.

On market day, street vendors filled the streets, crying out the names of all sorts of goods and wares for sale from fruit and vegetables to bamboo wares and artefacts made from straw. The kids were exposed to the authentic Yunnan dialect. At the very beginning, the kids were amazed at how close these cries were, then on further reflection, they realised it was really easy to walk around such a small town. Several steps would take them out of their home onto the open street instead of the layers of gardens they had to traverse in the residence before they could reach the street in Chestnut Street.

What an experience of hide-and-seek when all the streets which were supposed to be hidden just popped out in front of them! A handful of shops selling a variety of items could be found along the streets, and they were genuine fun for the kids.

They had long since become acquainted with the owner of Porridge Lei. Each time he saw the kids, he would invite them to come to his store: "Come! Sit! One bowl for free!" The porridge in the big cauldron was sizzling and bubbling away, transparent and sticky. It always looked so appealing. But they always declined the invitation with a polite "thank you", which always gained the owner's loud and heartfelt praise: "Professors' kids! Good manners!"

The shop that drew them like a magnet was the bookstore next to Porridge Lei, which sold and rented books. Most of the books were novels and stories involving kung-fu masters, detectives, and judges handling complicated criminal cases, such as *Thirteen Heroes with Seven Swords, The 19 Heroes of Mount Qingcheng, The Adventures of Sherlock Holmes, The Adventures of Arsène Lupin, The Cases of Judge Shi Shilun,* and *The Cases of Judge Peng Peng*. Most of the readers were town dwellers who harboured the same admiration for the professors who had moved to Guihui with the university, as those of Hutai county for the people who taught in universities. They always smiled at Wei and May and told them self-deprecatingly: "We don't read much."

Once Wei decided by himself to rent a book entitled *King Yue's Sword*, and later he also rented its sequel *The Phoenix's Sword*. Both had themes combining kung fu and romance where the heroes gave their rare swords as love tokens to their loved ones. May was so into the books that she would keep reading at night in the dim light from the kerosene lamp.

"May, what have you been reading?" Holding the clean laundry she had been folding in one hand, she took hold of May's book in the other.

"What's this about? Sword masters and gallant knights?" Bichu lost her temper more easily these days, but she was aware of her shorter fuse and tried her best to control it. She put down the laundry, paused a while before she took hold of the book and had a quick scan. She gave the book back to May, patted her shiny black hair, and said: "Now it's time for bed. You put the light out yourself."

The following day, Bichu declared that Wei and May should follow Fuzhi to the university to do their lessons there. Wei and May locked eyes. Wei shrugged at May, who blinked back. Both were happy with the decision since they were so used to having their lives governed by routine and the steady acquisition of knowledge. They felt their brains might rot without regular work.

"What should I do? Mummy, I want to go to school, too!" Kiddo tugged the edge of his mother's blouse.

"You? Will it be OK for you to walk to and from school?" Bichu stroked his hand and looked down at Kiddo for his confirmation.

May immediately came to Kiddo's aid: "Let him go, mum. I'll take care of him. Besides, we have Cousin Wei."

Bichu smiled apologetically at Wei: "You'll have to keep an eye on Kiddo. Alright, you are the commanding general." The general stood to attention upon hearing of the appointment. Kiddo burst into loud chuckles.

Minglun University had been laying emphasis on physical

education, and tried to make it part of its tradition. Such an emphasis had led to the university's more active and earlier involvement with military training and morning exercise than other universities. When it was moved to Guihui, the flag-raising ceremony and morning runs had become a regular part of the physical education course, which was coached and supervised by a captain from among the local troops. Many students complained bitterly about having to wake up so early. Fuzhi, who was an early bird, always came to join the flag-raising ceremony. He loved to watch the brightly-coloured national flag rising slowly against the blue sky to welcome the new day, to appreciate the hopeful morning breeze and the rosy morning glow, and to enjoy the not very tidy footsteps of the students echoing the vitality of youth and the power of the country.

The three kids were seen among the young people on campus. Sometimes they arrived early with Fuzhi, but they never went to the playground. Most of the time they just watched in the distance. The first time when they saw the national flag rising through the green trees, Wei jumped with joy but then stopped and stood solemnly. Once the flag reached the top of the pole, he yelled: "I see it again! I see it again!" May and Kiddo also clapped their hands to show their happiness. Once they had had to burn their national flag, now they saw it rising again!

In the entangled lush greenery in the big garden stood a single-storey house with rooms lined up in a row, one of which was Fuzhi's office. Under the window stood a long unpainted whitewood table. The three kids would crowd around the table for their study. Fuzhi had asked a professor of logic to teach Wei maths, while May and Kiddo worked on their recitation of classical poetry, learnt some simple English, and practiced writing Chinese characters in large and small print.

In the afternoons when they were dismissed from study, they went to explore the campus. At first, they followed the wide path paved with slate. They would go past a rose arbour which extended over an area of about 50 metres, and then went around the main building until they reached a narrow path covered with thick plants. There they would return without venturing off the beaten track. But as they became bolder with each passing day, they explored all the narrow lanes and squeezed through all the openings they could manage.

Once they followed a zigzag lane to low-lying ground, oblivious of all the twigs and vines that covered the lane. Their eyes lit up when they encountered a kaleidoscope of bouncing colours from the wild flowers in the centre of the low-lying land surrounded by a wall of green. Bustling among the flowers were thousands of butterflies of all sizes.

The kids stood there in amazement, staring at the flowers and the butterflies. The colours of the butterflies constantly changed as they fluttered in the sunshine, like layers of scudding clouds, casting kaleidoscopic reflections on the flowers. The surrounding serene green served as a solid backdrop for the flickering colours as if it to say: "Oh come and have a good look! Few have seen this before!" It seemed that the kids had heard the call and were all thinking about Zhiqin: how happy she would have been if she could have been here to see this! No one spoke the words out loud, though.

After they had stood there for a while, Wei spotted a half-hidden lane extending all the way up the hill. He led the way to the hilltop, with May and Kiddo tagging along behind. When they parted the thick blanket of twigs, they were aghast at what confronted them. They were standing high on a cliff edge over a big irregular-shaped pond. The water looked an abysmally dark green. The trees grew in a gloomy tangle around the pond. From the dark water, something mysterious seemed to be ready to spring out at any second.

"I'm scared!" Kiddo whispered to Wei while he took Wei's hand. He was already shocked by the flowers and butterflies, but the sight of this pond made his hair stand on end.

May was scared, though she didn't tell anyone. She felt as if Zhiqin were dwelling in the pond, now rising slowly from the bottom. Zhiqin shouldn't have been scary, alive or dead, but May was scared anyway.

"What a creepy atmosphere..." muttered Wei. "Let's go back!" He led his army in flight back the way they had come.

They didn't roam in the garden after the pond adventure for several days. Kiddo was under the weather, so he didn't go to school with Wei and May. May had dreamed of Zhiqin standing by the pond surrounded by flying butterflies for several nights in a row, but Wei wanted to take advantage of Kiddo's absence and go back to the pond and have a better look at it. Although Bichu had been warning them not to get themselves into trouble, Wei managed to persuade May to follow him on one more exploration.

They made sure they didn't take the lane full of butterflies this time, and took a different one. It was a very narrow path lined with big, tall trees. After they walked along a small section of it, the path seemed to plunge into a forest. The path began to go downhill and became wetter and wetter. May, grasping the back of Wei's coat, was trembling with fear: "Cousin Wei, do you think we might run into some snakes?" The garden was renowned for its popularity with snakes, but they had never come across one.

"I don't know, but since we have never encountered one, we can just forget about it," Wei answered, picking up a big stick from the side of the path. They soon entered a mini canyon with earth mounds on either side overgrown with towering trees blocking out the sunshine. Many roots were exposed in the air looking like strong muscles and tendons.

The path went further down. They took a turn at the exit of the 'canyon' and unexpectedly sprawled in front of them was that pond of mysterious dark water.

This time their feet were low and in close proximity to the pond. The water was creepy and still as if a giant dragon head or something would leap out of it the next second. The plants growing on the mounds around the pond formed a thick wall around them. They stood there still, holding their breath, until they heard a rustling noise on the opposite side of the pond.

"Snakes!" May shrieked with a muffled yell.

Wei thought: "If it was just snakes we might be better off." He was afraid it might be something they had never seen, and he was also wishing it could be something they had never seen. They fixed their eyes in the direction where the noise came from and didn't move a muscle.

"Ah-ee… Ah-ee-ah…" With a hissing whistle a man walked out of the lush plants. Wei didn't recognise it was a human at first. He wanted to drag May and run away together, but his feet were rooted to the spot. After a second look, he realised it was Professor Li Lian.

"All mortals must die! All mortals must die!" Li Lian walked toward the kids, talking to himself loudly. His clothes were rather sloppy and he looked worn out. When he saw them, he asked: "Why have you come here? Exploring?"

"Why are you here? For Sister Zhiqin?" May almost blurted out the words, but she swallowed them and looked up at Wei, who then said: "We just came to have some fun. Sorry if we have disturbed you."

"It's a fun place indeed. This is called Black Dragon pond. I named it," smiled Li Lian. "I come to hide out sometimes to get some peace and to stay close to nature, too. Some students come here to read. But it's the first time I've seen kids around here."

"Snakes! Snakes!" yelled May. In the tall grass near the pond, two snakes were visible with the upper half of their bodies sticking straight up from the ground, then they darted toward the other side of the pond and disappeared into the tall grass again.

"Don't be afraid. There are no poisonous snakes in the garden. At least that's what they say," opined Li Lian, in an attempt to calm May. "Well, it's quite alright to be afraid of things. It's not the worst feeling at all."

"What's the worst feeling then?" Wei asked out of pure curiosity. "Hatred? Or grief?"

"The worst feeling is one which makes you suffer," said Li Lian, as if he was still pondering his answer. He continued slowly: "I think it's disgust."

He suddenly cheered up and spoke twice as fast: "There are other ponds, smaller than this one, such as the Yellow Dragon pond and the White Dragon pond. But you should go home now. I'll show you around next time." He nodded farewell, vigorously climbed up the mound he had come from and disappeared into the woods in no time.

"He's looking for the butterflies," May said, trying to figure out which direction they should go.

The Black Dragon pond no longer seemed so mysterious. Beams of sunshine squeezing through the canopy of trees made the place less gloomy. But something weighed heavily on their hearts as the two of them hurriedly left the place.

The Mengs, who abided by the wisdom of Confucius that "when eating, he did not converse; when in bed, he did not speak", did not allow the kids to talk during meals. They had to wait until they had finished eating their supper and were all sitting together to enjoy some leisure time before they were allowed to speak to their heart's content.

That evening after dinner, May talked about their adventure at Black Dragon pond and imitated the way Li Lian talked.

Fuzhi said to Bichu: "Professor Li has been blaming himself for not going to Hai Phong to meet his family. He is thinking that if he had been there, things might have been different."

Bichu answered: "No one is to blame but the Japanese devils. If they hadn't invaded us, how could Zhiqin have ended up like this?" She paused for a while before continuing in very low spirits: "I should be blamed for not insisting on staying in Hai Phong to give Zhiqin proper treatment."

Fuzhi shook his head: "How could you have insisted on that in the presence of Mrs Li?"

"A lonely soul wandering alone in a strange place thousands of miles away! What a horrible thing!" Wei muttered. The gloomy Black Dragon pond reminded him of the desolate ancient forest and the souls wondering among the trees. He felt so sorry for Zhiqin and was concerned that she might be scared, too.

"Xiao Cheng has written in his letter that he's arriving this week to discuss moving the university to Kunming," Fuzhi told Bichu. "We are going to hold an exam for the students applying for a transfer to our university in mid-July. I think it would be nice if Earl could go to Kunming with Xiao Cheng."

Bichu thought for a while before she responded: "My

sister Jiangchu and her family are arriving in Kunming at the end of July, so maybe Wei could tag along with Earl and Xiao Cheng. Wei and Earl could stay with our elder sister Suchu before Jiangchu and the others arrive."

When Bichu and the kids first arrived in Guihui, Suchu sent a man to greet them and wanted to pick up the kids for a visit, but the kids were reluctant to go.

Wei said: "Can I leave later?" He was still thinking about exploring the many other mysterious places in that giant garden.

"I have never been to the race course," protested Kiddo.

"We'll come back to this later," said Bichu.

Earl kept quiet the whole time.

A couple of days later, Xiao Cheng, who was in his fine clothes and looked handsome as usual, arrived in Guihui. He joined the Mengs for dinner that evening. As soon as he arrived, he went to the kitchen to greet Bichu, praising "what a capable helper" Earl was as she picked and cleaned pea shoots, then giving candies to May and Kiddo, and a brief introduction of the airplane factory in Kunming to Wei. All the children were literally shouting "Uncle Cheng" with great excitement. Earl, who was boisterously happy inside, even offered to make a dish with the pea shoots she had cleaned. Bichu agreed with a smile lingering on her face.

However, the most important news Xiao Cheng brought was the central government's progressive evacuation of Wuhan, Hubei province. To stop the enemy's further advance, the central government had destroyed the dike by using explosives in June at Huayuankou, Zhengzhou city, on the south bank of the Yellow river, flooding 17 counties of all sizes and driving several million villagers from their homes. But the government didn't release the news until very recently. For the past year, Chinese had witnessed many evacuations and gained more real knowledge about how tough and resilient the resistance against the Japanese was. Still, the evacuation of the central government, the core of the leadership for the war against the Japanese, was something of supreme significance, a heavy load upon every Chinese heart.

Fuzhi pondered for a moment before commenting: "The Chinese art of war includes the application of fire or water, but such an application is always carried out with caution. For example, if one wants to set fire to the enemy fleet, one had better be sure to wait for the eastern wind which helps keep the fire away from one's own fleet, while destroying the enemy's."

"And there's this thing about you," said Xiao Cheng, continuing to pace back and forth across the room, with his hands clasped behind his back.

Fuzhi lifted his glasses with thick lenses and fixed his gaze on the slender figure of Xiao Cheng.

"It's also about me," Xiao Cheng paused, hesitantly. "There is talk of you being connected to THAT side, or at least of you being a leftist sympathiser with that side. You heard of such talk long ago. Now it's about someone in your family who is connected to that side. It is said that your father-in-law has been heading to that side. How did they ever cook up such a tale?"

"Guilt by association is an old Chinese custom. We shouldn't lend any credence to such talk," laughed Fuzhi. "My thoughts are tied up with my work and are above-board and beyond reproach. Indeed, it's not wrong to say I am a leftist. Left or right, I attach the utmost importance to the country and the nation. What I wish for is a prosperous, independent and powerful country, and a fair and just society.

If socialism can achieve such goals, I'll give it my support. I'm afraid there is still a dire shortage of experts in this field. Anyway, colleges are places to pass on that knowledge and to promote academic research, so I have never had any intention of getting involved in politics on campus. A college should tolerate all kinds of 'isms' while keeping its distance from them. We have shared such a standpoint for many years."

Xiao Cheng nodded: "The principal function of a college is to teach and to learn. Without an encyclopaedic knowledge to teach and freedom to learn, not many of the students will outdo their teachers. Now speaking of the talk about me, someone proposed that I be the dean of teaching when the university moves to Kunming and that I be stationed there with assistance from the Ministry of Education for the establishment. What a ridiculous proposal!"

Hearing the proposal, Fuzhi felt somewhat offended because of the mistrust against him. He smiled faintly at the thought. If Youchen were here, his eyes would have widened in total disbelief, wondering how one's stand could affect the cooperation between the KMT and the CPC. Confrontation and struggle were omnipresent, indeed. It was just that both Youchen and I were nerds, to some degree. Xiao Cheng, resourceful, observant, and with a good sense of propriety, was the better option. Turning all these things over in his mind, he answered sincerely: "I agree with this proposal."

"I don't agree," Xiao Cheng said resolutely. "I'm not like you. You are earnest and serious about your work. You are devoted, while I want to listen to music, and I want to play bridge. President Qin insists that you are the best candidate. We should back him up. Minglun is going to face lots of challenges, but with your seniority and your reputation, it will be easier for you to cope with the work."

"You would manage such work in between your laughing and joking," said Fuzhi, laughing. "You will get things done during the breaks between your music and your singing. It's a rare case for Minglun to have attracted so many of the best brains. What is of prime importance is how to guarantee them the freedom to create and inspire."

Xiao Cheng sighed softly: "I have heard that some local parents don't allow their children to apply for Minglun, saying Minglun is ill-equipped, but the younger generation has been keen to apply. The applications for Minglun outnumbered those for the local colleges and universities. It's all because of these brains."

He remembered how he had joked at Fuzhi's encyclopaedic knowledge and memory retention, saying that Fuzhi was a walking library of Beiping. He then remembered the academic magnets in other departments. The talk about Professor Jiang Fang came to mind: "People are talking about Professor Jiang Fang, too, saying he is copying Lu Xun[4], but not so talented."

"Outrageous!" Fuzhi shouted, but took control of his emotions and lowered his voice. "I know Jiang Fang. He does have Lu Xun's iron backbone, but he doesn't want to copy anyone. His romance and innocence are completely different from Lu Xun's style. I don't approve of many of Lu Xun's literary works with people cursing. They are too crude for me."

He raised his glasses with their thick lenses. His slender, long fingers looked somewhat transparent in the slanting rays

---

[4] Lu Xun (鲁迅) was the pen name of Zhou Shuren (周树人) (25 September 1881 – 19 October 1936), commonly considered the greatest writer in 20th-century Chinese literature, known for his sharp insight into the traditions of old China and the conditions of modern China. He was also a short story writer, poet, editor, translator, literary critic and essayist.

of the setting sun. He continued slowly: "We boast the best brains and the best minds."

"But we still need to survive before we can make a difference," reminded Xiao Cheng.

"How pathetic Chinese intellectuals are!" sighed Fuzhi.

Their eyes met and both fell silent.

Late that night, Fuzhi told Bichu what he had heard from Xiao Cheng.

Bichu, who was making the bed, turned round and asked: "Indeed, what has happened to father? He used to imagine the guerillas coming to pick him up. Is it possible that the guerillas really did pick him up?"

"Not very likely," answered Fuzhi, pensively.

Bichu sank into a long silence before she spoke again: "It's nice of Xiao Cheng to be so honest. You should relieve yourself from your administrative duties. As you age, I'm afraid you might not be able to handle it like you used to." She had made the bed and lay down on it.

"My ambition is to do my research and achieve something in education as well. That's why I have spent so much time on administrative affairs these past years. When we move to Kunming, I will resign from my position. The best thing so far is that I'm wrapping up my book." As he was talking, he went to see Bichu, thinking how unusual it was for her to go to bed so early. When he got closer, he could see she was in low spirits and her face was pale without any colour.

He tried to comfort her: "It's not a big deal. People always talk."

"I'm not worried about people talking. I, I feel disaster is looming — what has happened to father?" Bichu's voice was low and soft.

"Don't upset yourself by making wild guesses. Nothing will go wrong with father. Dinner tonight was great. Thank you for all the hard work! Such a tough life is wearing you out."

"Bitter days are yet to come." Two tear drops rolled down her pale, sunken cheeks.

PART 4

About two weeks later, Earl went to Kunming with Xiao Cheng. The following month, Fuzhi finished his voluminous 400,000-character book *Exploring Chinese History*. He felt blessed to have wrapped up such a work during such hard times, and while having been displaced and deprived of a home.

Early that morning he had been reading through the last chapter. Around 10 o'clock, when he had finished reading the very last sentence of the book, he put down his pen and drew a deep breath. Excitement, appreciation and a strong sense of relief surged up in his heart. The book was Meng Fuzhi's testament, a historian's insight into history, society and life, the comprehensive and profound thinking which had been brewing in one of the best heads for years. Now the thoughts had been solidly committed to paper. He owed thanks to all who had supported him. He owed most to Bichu.

"I have finished it!" He wanted to jump up and shout, but he didn't. As Bichu was passing the window, he knocked on the glass. Bichu turned her head toward him and smiled, the light from the tender, brightly coloured Yunnan bitter vegetables in her hands reflected against her pale and exhausted face. She didn't pause on her way to the kitchen.

"She's worn out," thought Fuzhi. He felt very sorry for her. He wanted to tell her this but wasn't in the habit of visiting the kitchen. Qian Mingjing once saw a couplet that he thought would be very appropriate to put in the Mengs' kitchen: "A gentleman keeps at a safe distance from the kitchen, where a lady might find her confidence."

Arrangements for the printing and publishing of this book had long since been made with Qian Mingjing's introduction. It was quite beyond Fuzhi's expectation that there might be a lithographic printing workshop hidden among the shops lining the two main streets crossing the town centre. It had been agreed that once Fuzhi finished writing it, he would send the manuscript to the workshop.

Sister Zhang appeared in the courtyard. Fuzhi knocked at the window and asked: "Please ask madam to come over."

Bichu came into the room in a while.

"You work too hard — I'm done," he whispered.

"You are done?" A blush of excitement danced across her pale cheeks. Her husband's achievement was hers, and the family's as well.

"I'm alright, but it hasn't been easy for you!"

She smiled at Fuzhi's words. Her smooth arms were on the plain whitewood table, adding a touch of glamour to the withered wood.

What touched Fuzhi most was the fact that she was genuinely happy at her husband's achievement despite the fact she was snowed under with work of her own and worn out by her arduous chores. He tucked a loose strand of dark hair behind her ear and said: "I want to deliver it to the workshop now."

"I need to wrap it up properly for you before you take it. Oh, if Kiddo were big enough, you wouldn't need to go yourself," said Bichu.

She quickly found some old newspaper and two cloth wrappers. The manuscript was divided into two neatly wrapped packages in her smart, capable hands. When she had finished her packing, Fuzhi put on his long gown. He weighed one package in each hand.

Bichu chuckled: "You look so much like a poor private adviser paying a visit to your rich relative in town."

"I should take something else with me instead of my manuscript, then," nodded Fuzhi. He left with the two packages in his hands.

The workshop was on the low land by the east town gate. The weeds ran riot along the road leading to it. Anyone without any inside information wouldn't believe such a workshop would have any printing equipment.

When the owner saw Fuzhi, it seemed he had seen god himself. He cleaned the desk and the chair several times before inviting Fuzhi to sit down, then he ordered his apprentice to boil water in the kettle on the stove. When the water was ready and he made tea, he then started talking: "Everyone in Guihui knows you, Professor Meng! We are so lucky your university has moved to Guihui. Otherwise how could we ever have seen a university here in our life time?"

He made more arrangements to welcome Fuzhi before he settled down to listen to him. When he learned the reason for Fuzhi's visit, he was gripped with excitement again: "What a great honour! What a great honour!" It didn't take much time for the two to agree to print 200 copies at a price of 30 yuan in total.

When the owner told Fuzhi the copies would be ready in two months, Fuzhi asked him whether he could finish the work in one month since the university was going to move to Kunming in one month.

"Your book must have priority! We'll do it faster!" Out of his pure admiration for knowledge, the owner seemed to be very determined not to let any difficulty get in his way.

Things went smoothly as expected. Fuzhi gave the owner the manuscripts which he took from him respectfully with both hands. They talked more about the local customs and practices in Yunnan province.

When Fuzhi was ready to leave, the owner suddenly asked: "One more moment, please. I have this item I would like Professor Meng to take a look at."

He turned to fetch a case in a green velvet cover. He put it on the table and lifted off the cover. It was an inkstone case painted scarlet. The colour of the paint was dark, smooth and lustrous with some cracks down the sides. When the case was opened, an oval-shaped inkstone was revealed. The stone had a very fine pattern; one end of the inkstone was carved in a decorative belt shape; on the other end was a spot of ivory with an azure blue dot in the centre. Several flowing clouds were carved out of the stone near the ivory spot. A shallow well to store water was carved out beneath the clouds. The inkstone was smooth to the touch like a baby's skin. An inkstick ground in such an inkstone would yield ink as smooth as silk.

"What a beautiful quality inkstone!" Holding it in both hands, Fuzhi was struck with admiration.

"It is indeed a rare one," agreed the owner. "It's called 'the Moon Hidden in the Clouds'. Please see the inscriptions here."

Fuzhi turned over the inkstone to find several lines of inscriptions in small graceful handwriting, which claimed that the inkstone was as valuable as precious jade – valuable enough to buy several cities. It was engraved with the words 'Inscribed by Dragon's Door for Mr Lian Shen'. Mr Lian Shen must have been the former owner but then who was 'Dragon's Door'?

Fuzhi thought for a while in silence and then he remembered that it was the alias of Wang Maohong, a successful candidate in the highest imperial examinations during the reign of Emperor Kangxi of the Qing dynasty who was well known back then for his poetry and calligraphy. No wonder the inscriptions looked so graceful and unrestrained. So, the inkstone must have been more than 300 years old.

He turned his attention to the inkstone case and found four medium-size Chinese characters inscribed with regular script: 'Dragon's Door inscribed here', and three unofficial personal seals reading: 'Samadhi' (a sankrit word denoting the achievement of a state of trance in Buddhist meditation), 'Snow Serendipity' and 'Supreme Quality'. There was a line in small print: "I don't know who Mr Lian Shen is, but when I got this inkstone in Kunming, I was amazed by its smoothness and supreme quality, which inspired me to name it 'the Moon Hidden in the Clouds'". It was signed 'Zou Qing'. Fuzhi guessed that when Zou Qing acquired the inkstone, he made a case to protect it.

When Fuzhi had finished studying the inkstone, he sighed: "How did such a cherished treasure end up like this?"

The workshop owner said: "The owner of the inkstone has

now fallen on hard times and wants to find a better owner, someone who can appreciate its value. It is just like a good sword that should go to a good knight."

"Who is the owner?"

"He doesn't want to reveal his identity."

Fuzhi knew he shouldn't ask more questions. After some discussion, he offered 50 yuan for the inkstone, which was a big amount of money then. The workshop owner was very happy with the deal and told Fuzhi he would come to collect the money the next day. Fuzhi then wrapped up the inkstone in his cloth wrapper and took his time to walk back home.

When Fuzhi entered the courtyard, he saw Li Lian coming out of the reception room, telling him in an unsettled tone: "Five students have caught malaria, two of whom have fever. The university clinic is running out of quinine. Some people are saying our students have got malaria, and others have suggested inviting my wife, Shizhen, to exorcise the malaria spirit. I am not in a position to stop Shizhen."

It was not hard for Fuzhi to tell that Li Lian had already tried to stop Shizhen and had gone through a tough fight in the family already, which obviously hadn't ended well for Li Lian.

"Our students don't believe in such things," said Fuzhi, hastily putting down the inkstone and striding toward the school with Li Lian. He wanted so much to send Li Lian to ask his wife why she didn't try to exorcise the evil spirit and save Zhiqin on the train to Guihui. Was it because they were in unfamiliar territory where the evil spirits were beyond her reach?

"She was asked by the old man who is taking care of the garden. I don't know how she has so many connections with the local folk," Li Lian lamented.

"Has Mrs Li been to the students' dormitory already?" asked Fuzhi.

"No, she hasn't. I forbade her to go. I have made sure if she does, the students would drive her out." Sure enough, Li Lian had tried to stop his wife.

It had taken such a long time to move, which had resulted in a very short summer vacation. The dorm was crowded. Three students were completely overcome with malaria with one shuddering with chills, two in a coma due to a high fever, one moaning involuntarily, and one suffering in silence. Two had still not reached the stage of having a fit, but both were lying in bed, leaning against the headboards. One was holding an exercise book on calculus.

"Professor Meng! Professor Li!" The doctor from the school clinic and the students who were watching over the sick were all happy to see them. The doctor, who was a local, reported immediately that he couldn't do anything with the shortage of medicine. He had already tried some herbal medicine prescriptions but they didn't work. The three students had fits anyway.

All the students turned their eyes toward Fuzhi, their young faces full of trust. The one who was silently suffering from fever had once taken one of Fuzhi's courses. Fuzhi thought his family name might have been 'Sun', or something like that. He was not sure. He was a good-looking lad with a smart head. His face was now crimson with a high temperature. Everything on his face looked swollen with heat. Fuzhi almost cried out: "My dear boy!" But he just stroked his head and asked Li Lian:

"Lian, do you mind going to Kunming to get some medicine?"

"Of course I don't!" Li Lian braced up. "I will go! I want to go!"

Qian Mingjing was Fuzhi's first choice because of his connections, but now Li Lian was eager to go. He might be able to run away from a family drama. Thinking of this, Fuzhi said: "Then there is no time to be lost. Have we missed the last train?"

"It will arrive in half an hour. I can make it. I will stay overnight at Bisezhai," said Li Lian vigorously. "I'm not going back home since I have enough money on me to buy the tickets." He then asked the doctor to write him a prescription.

The doctor was affected by Li Lian's vigour and said: "We still have time. A couple of shivering fits won't be fatal." He finished writing his prescription in no time. Li Lian left in a hurry.

Fuzhi felt the students' thin, stiff quilts. Their mosquito nets were perforated with holes of all sizes offering lots of opportunities for the mosquitoes to enter. He remembered he had once paid a visit to this dormitory when the university had just moved from Changsha to Guihui. He witnessed a fight between two dorm mates over a spot near the window; they were busy insulting each other with sharp words. He gave each of them a piece of his mind on the spot. Later Qian Mingjing told him the two students had stopped fighting and followed Fuzhi's advice, which showed the respect they had for Fuzhi. Mingjing confessed that he would never get himself involved in this kind of thing, but Fuzhi thought these students were of a similar age to Earl, and they were all far away from their parents. This was a far cry from the close supervision they used to get from the dormitory managers and janitors back in Beiping. He never paid any visit to the dorms back in Beiping, either, but now he couldn't believe what he was seeing.

"These mosquito nets need mending, so the mosquitoes

can't get in." He had never touched needles and threads, but he assumed his students might be more experienced than he was.

"We are leaving Guihui, so we'll make do with the nets for a couple more days," the one with a childish face answered. He was immersed in studying a thick foreign-language book by his bedside.

"Professor Meng," said the one who looked more mature, coming up to Fuzhi. "We have graduated and will be leaving the campus next week. Could we ask for your autograph for our classbooks?"

"Certainly," said Fuzhi. "Have you found a job?"

"Some will go to Chongqing and others to Kunming. I'm going to work with the battlefield service regiment," he answered with a smile. "I have graduated," he repeated emphatically.

In Changsha, some students from Minglun decided to drop their studies to join the battlefield service regiment in the belief that "how can one remain in college, when the nation is in the iron grip of the invader?". Fuzhi once gave a talk during the morning exercise, trying to persuade them to stay and finish college.

"I'm not going to try and persuade you to stay this time," said Fuzhi with a smile on his face.

"We might be sent back to serve in northern China, where hands are needed most," the student continued calmly. Northern China was the most dangerous place with the toughest work, for sure. "My name is Wu Jiagu." He had been to Square Teakettle many times since his younger sister Wu Jiaxin was a friend of Earl, but Fuzhi didn't remember him.

Fuzhi kept silent for a moment and then nodded: "You may

come to my office to get your classbooks back in a couple of days."

He turned to the rest of the dormitory: "Although you are leaving, you still need to take your mosquito nets with you. The mosquitoes belong to Guihui, while the mosquito nets don't. Hopefully, the mosquitoes here in Guihui won't share information with those in Kunming." Everybody laughed. Even the one shuddering with chills grinned.

Fuzhi went to other dormitories to take a look before leaving the campus. At the gate, he asked the old doorman to tell Mrs Li about her husband's trip to Kunming.

It was already high noon. Lining the road leading to town were luxuriantly green bushes without trees, leaving no shade from the sun to shelter anyone walking along the road. Fuzhi took off his long gown and quickened his pace. He just wanted to be home again.

When he was near the town gate, he spotted a tall, thin, stick-like woman walking unsteadily toward him, carrying a big heavy wooden bucket with great difficulty.

The woman stared at him for a moment and then laughed: "Isn't this Professor Meng? I hardly recognise you without your long gown."

Fuzhi gave her a closer look and guessed it must be Li Lian's wife, who had never paid a visit to the Mengs since their arrival in Guihui.

"I have sent someone to inform Mrs Li that Professor Li has gone to Kunming for some medicine. He'll be back in a couple of days." Fuzhi was somewhat nervous. What if Mrs Li flew into a rage upon seeing him and blamed him for her husband's absence?

"That's quite alright! He's busy doing things in his own way. I'll do things my way," said Mrs Li without changing either her tone or her expression. "I made this bucket of potion with herbs to cure malaria. It can prevent malaria from spreading, too."

She then put the bucket down in front of Fuzhi. A lotus leaf covered the surface of the potion. A mud-coloured froth gathered along the edge of the leaf.

"Mrs Li, what do you…" Fuzhi couldn't guess her intention.

"I'm taking this for the students," explained Shizhen with some pride. "I saw in a book in Beiping that such herbs cure malaria. The local folks know this, too. I found it at the foot of the town gate." She picked up the bucket and prepared to move on.

Fuzhi had no choice but to follow her, turning over in his mind that witchcraft actually had a connection with medication. It was nice of Mrs Li to try to help the students, but would the potion be poisonous? How could he let the students try something like that?

When they reached the university gate, he asked Shizhen to have a rest and sent the gateman to fetch the doctor.

The doctor came in a while. When he saw the muddy fluid, his eyebrows furrowed: "I have tried several herbs and none worked. Yours might be…"

Shizhen didn't wait for him to finish his sentence. She snatched a bowl from somewhere, scooped up half a bowl of her potion, and consumed it without hesitation. "Poisonous? I just had a bowl of it!"

Fuzhi instantly admired her courage. The potion was at least not poisonous. He turned to discuss with the doctor whether they could ask the students to have a try.

"Better be quick. The malaria demon hates the smell of the herb." Shizhen tried to carry the bucket into the dormitory.

Upon hearing of 'the malaria demon', neither Fuzhi nor the doctor wanted to try the potion at all.

Fuzhi began: "Thank you so much, Mrs Li, for all your trouble to make and deliver the potion to the students. All the wives of the faculty should learn from you. Please leave the potion here. Doctor Zhao will give it out to the students."

His tone, though mild and tactful, was determined. Before Shizhen began to argue, he continued: "Your young kids need your attention back home. We have Doctor Zhao here to take charge. Please don't worry."

"Then you hurry up and let the sick drink it." Shizhen didn't try to argue. Maybe she thought that once she had delivered the potion to the university gate, she had done her bit in terms of saving lives. She willingly left to go home.

Fuzhi and the doctor carried the bucket to a less frequented corner and poured the potion onto the grass. A sudden loud rattling noise startled the two. Three or four snakes hidden in a place far from the grass slithered into the far distance when the potion touched the grass.

"I don't smell anything odd," the doctor said.

"Maybe the malaria demon does," replied Fuzhi.

Three days later, Li Lian came back from Kunming with lots of medicine to beat the malaria demon. The next Monday, Fuzhi went to the university for the flag-raising ceremony.

Time passed, but not many students were to be seen on the playground. Those that were there were not lined up. The young physical education teacher went up and explained that the new military instructor who had taken up the position several days ago was always late for duty. Whjle they were talking, the military instructor dawdled onto the playground with his collar unbuttoned and his cap not properly placed on his head. He was holding the national flag in one hand, and a hookah (or shisha pipe), which could only be found here in Yunnan, in the other. He walked listlessly to the flag pole.

How irresponsible! Fuzhi was boiling inside. He couldn't help snapping at the guy in a whisper: "You are late."

"What did you say?" The soldier, who might have been tipsy, at once dropped his head and tossed the national flag onto the floor. "I don't give a damn who you are."

Fuzhi was overcome with rage. He bellowed: "You are neglecting your duty! How could you throw the national flag onto the floor? Do you still remember you are an instructor?"

"I have been sent by my captain. I am a Second Lieutenant! I'm Second Lieutenant Chen! So what? You should be grateful that I have taken in you damn refugees!" The guy cursed and waved his long pipe wildly, which almost hit Fuzhi on the shoulder.

Some students stood between the man and Fuzhi to protect the latter. Several professors came close. Fuzhi ignored the man and asked him to raise the flag. All those present stood solemnly.

When the ceremony was done, more students who were late tiptoed into the lines in succession. Fuzhi began his speech:

"The war has been going on for more than a year. The enemy initially expected a quick fix and wanted to take over China in three months. But they failed because our nation has awakened, and realised the importance of unity before all are engaged in the common cause to fight against foreign aggression. This war should serve as the turning point for our nation! This war should be our chance for survival!

"My dear students, I know you have all heard the story about chopsticks. It is so easy to break a single chopstick, but it is impossible to break a bundle of chopsticks. If everyone shoulders their responsibility and dedicates their power, however minuscule that might be, when all these individual powers are bundled and united, we will be unstoppable.

"Not long ago, some of you were ill, but luckily you have all fully recovered. When I visited the dormitories, I was so touched to find those who were seriously ill were still working on their books. Without any desk to work on, one student even sat on the floor beside his bed and put his foreign-language book on the bed so he could read and take notes.

"You have overcome so many hardships and undertaken many long journeys to come here to learn, so we teachers will not flinch from risking our old lives to do our best to teach you. No matter how many hardships we must endure, we will try our best to run our university well.

"Mencius once said, whenever heaven is about to place a great responsibility on a great man, it always exercises his mind with frustration, and his body with hardship and starvation. My dear students, now you have gone through so many tribulations, I am confident that you will be competent to shoulder the responsibility of saving the nation at such a critical moment of survival or extinction!"

He then announced the university's decision to move to Kunming and the relevant details of the movement.

He concluded: "The opportunity to continue the school has been won by the men fighting on the front line. It is not an exaggeration to say that every minute you enjoy in class is a trade-off for the blood of our men at the front. We shouldn't forget the front when we study in the classroom. When we are needed to go to the front to fight the enemy, we'll be ready to go. Now our university is striving to cultivate specialised personnel in all fields of endeavour for the country, which is what our nation needs most. I hope everyone here will work hard to achieve this goal."

After Fuzhi's pep talk, the students went about their regular activities. Since Fuzhi had no intention of being pestered by that second lieutenant, he headed directly for his office. He heard shoes slapping against the ground. Before he knew what had happened, the man had caught up with Fuzhi and planted himself in front of him. Not knowing what the man wanted, Fuzhi stopped and looked at the ferocious face calmly, thinking: "This man might have fought, or will soon fight, in a cruel battle. He might fight bravely on the battlefield. He might not be able to understand the metaphorical significance of the national flag, or the significance of education. But one thing that is for sure is that we don't know each other."

"Aha! You are Professor Meng! The Professor Meng!" Quite unexpectedly, the second lieutenant's countenance changed and became wreathed in ingratiating smiles.

He tried to button up his collar while he talked on: "I have been told now. You are related to Commander Yan!"

He handed over his shisha pipe: "May I have the honour of asking you to share my pipe? May I ask you to put in a good word for me with Commander Yan?"

If the man had struck him with his pipe, Fuzhi wouldn't have felt so hurt; but he felt so insulted due to having been identified as a relative of Commander Yan.

"I am not!" he said, enunciating each word clearly and forcefully, pushing away the pipe stuck in front of him, and he strode forward.

The man was stunned for a moment, yelled something, turned and left.

The rosy dawn clouds cast a bright red reflection on the lake to the south of the town, a mixture of placidness and merriment. The weeping willows and dense bushes standing firmly alongside the dike looked like a green silk strip around the lake. Several wild ducks tried to skim over the water, the noise of their flapping wings spreading far and wide. They didn't fly far or high, and soon landed in the water again. Looking around, Fuzhi felt so sad and lonely.

The students began to sing in the distance.

> *"Guns on our shoulders,*
> *Blood boiling in our chests.*
> *We are defending our motherland,*
> *We are going to the battlefield!"*

It was a song the students sang often, but it sounded extremely heroic and tragic to Fuzhi that morning.

Once he had finished the official business in his office and drawn his salary, Fuzhi found it was almost lunch time. He began to head home. When he was close to the rose arbour, he heard someone asking, "how much would you like to donate". It seemed like there was some fundraising going on.

A small blackboard was hung on the branch of a tree, under which stood a desk. A big sign stood by the desk that read: 'Dear teachers and fellow students: Please help our men at the front by lending them a helping hand with money for medicine."

Several students were busy collecting donations and writing receipts. Wu Jiagu was one of them.

"It is said that when Jiujiang fell, many soldiers were sick. Even though they fought as best they could, it didn't make much difference." Some wanted to make a donation and began conversing with the students

"It was hot and the soldiers suffered from malnutrition and disease. How could they fight well even if they were willing to?" said two professors from the Chinese department, each of whom gave 20 yuan. Wu Jiagu wrote down their names on the small blackboard, which had rows of different names on it.

Fuzhi watched in silence for a while, smiling and nodding at everyone, and took 20 yuan out of his wallet. More people gathered around the desk. One member of staff, who had just received his salary, gave 50 yuan without a trace of hesitation.

Wu Jiagu was so moved by his action, but he didn't hesitate to remind him: "You may donate less and save some for your family."

"My family is not here," smiled the staff member.

Fuzhi had already left, but when he heard these words, he turned to find the name of that staff member. "Maybe I should drop the plan to buy the inkstone," he thought. He returned to the donation desk, and took out 150 yuan from his wallet, which was the greater part of his salary. Wu Jiagu and other students didn't try to ask him to save some for his family, assuming that Professor Meng should donate much more than anyone else. Seeing the number on the blackboard, Fuzhi felt relieved. He was not thinking about the men at the front. Instead, he was more concerned whether he was worthy of his name.

When Fuzhi left again, Wu Jiagu caught up with him, and asked: "Professor Meng, are you going home?"

"This is the script you asked for before." Fuzhi opened the checked blue cloth wrapper he had been carrying with him all the time, took out his calligraphy work, and gave it to Wu Jiagu. He didn't just 'sign' the classbooks as Wu Jiagu had asked. "Jiujiang and Huangmei have both been lost. The army is even evacuating Wuhan. Are you still determined to go that way?"

"The battlefield service regiment has actually recruited us to go to the front," answered Wu Jiagu, casting his eyes on the lush green plants on campus. "Life is tough these days, but it's a precious part of one's life. I assume life will be even harder in the days to come. If I can do something for my country, I feel my life won't have been in vain. We will never forget our alma mater."

"Great! Take care of yourself for your country's sake," said Fuzhi. He continued on a few steps before turning around and asking: "Which department are you from?"

"I used to be in the biology department, but I transferred to the Chinese department when we moved to Changsha." Wu Jiagu gave a deep respectful bow to Fuzhi. He opened the scroll, on which Fuzhi had written: "Nothing ventured, nothing gained."

May and Kiddo ran out of the grove and stood close by their father's side. The lush summer plants tinted their thin clothes and clear eyes with their green dye.

"Is he leaving?" asked May.

"We are leaving, too," answered Fuzhi, looking lovingly at his two kids.

CHAPTER VII

PART 1

The amiable, warm plateau climate in the southwest, where the trees remained clothed in green and flowers bloomed in a riot of colours even in mid-October, was quite unlike Beiping, with its four distinct seasons which caused people to be amazed by the orderly precision of the passage of the seasons. When autumn arrived, the 13th solar term, the summer heat turned into a subdued 'autumn-tiger heat', which was even more tricky because some coolness would always manage to mingle with the dominant heat. Hard on the heels of the beginning of autumn was the 'stopping of the heat', meaning that the summer heat would now come to an end and the coolness of autumn would reign supreme. When it reached the 'cold dew', ripples of autumn wind would blow the green leaves of summer in the city into layers of gold, copper and caramel. City folks then clearly got the message in the wind that it was time to prepare their winter jackets.

Two days after Grandpa Lü passed away, the city administration came and took the body for cremation against the will of all the relatives. Lianxiu had been bed-ridden for two months since that day. She didn't want to lie in bed, but neither did she have the strength to get out of bed. The loneliness and guilt were crushing. Where could she go when the tree she had been relying on had been felled? Her life had lost its purpose and focus once she no longer needed to take care of the old man and prepare his meals. She blamed herself because she felt she had failed Bichu. Her self-accusation was so unbearable that numbness was an easier choice than living. When Lü Guitang or Xiangge brought her food and drink, she ate and drank as she was told with no other responses.

Time is always the best cure for pain, and Lianxiu didn't need a big dose. The autumn blasts gradually lifted the shrouds covering her mind. Some breezes slithered into the room through the cracked openings in the weather-beaten paper window blinds, lingering in mini swirls. She confined herself to her bed. At first, she didn't feel anything; then she began to feel the draught brushing against her shoulders and the newspapers on the nightstand.

On the nightstand were the newspapers with the old man's obituary she had saved. The top one had gathered a thin layer of dust. Lianxiu had no knowledge of the sympathy and discussion sparked by his obituary. People who knew the old man passed the news to one another with awe and admiration for his loyalty and integrity. Neither did she know that four days after the old man's death, the newspapers had carried another announcement:

The Beiping municipal government intended to invite Lü Qingfei to sit on the committee, but unfortunately Lü had a sudden cardiac failure and died before dawn on July 7.

The news dawned on those who had never known the old man that his death might have had something to do with the puppet government's 'invitation'. Word on the street was that the old man was murdered by the Japanese with detailed accounts of how the Japanese forced the old man to take poison.

On the third day after the old man's death, the Japanese did come. But they came for a thorough inspection. To do that, they opened the coffin. It seemed that such a deed was too horrible for Lianxiu to witness, hence she willingly allowed herself to slip into an abyss of numbness to forget the pain.

Four came that day. Two Japanese and two Chinese accompanied by Miao Donghui. They asked for the death certificate, and went to the funeral parlour to inspect the corpse. Miao Donghui whispered something to them. One of the Japanese asked in his shoddy Chinese: "What's inside the coffin?"

Lianxiu was speechless at such a question.

"What's inside the coffin?" repeated the Japanese man, raising his voice.

"Nothing," answered Lianxiu.

"She means there is Grandpa Lü's body and nothing else," explained Lü Guitang, who was standing behind Lianxiu, and felt the need to intervene urgently.

The Japanese eyed Lianxiu dubiously and then said something to Miao Donghui, who managed a bitter smile at Lianxiu and Guitang. "They're asking for the coffin to be opened," he said.

At these words, Lianxiu's head went into a spin that left her reeling in astonishment. How dare they disturb the old man resting in peace? Grandpa, forgive Lianxiu! She was powerless to stop the four of them, who had already put on the surgical masks they had brought with them. How well prepared they were!

When the two Chinese removed the lid of the coffin, a pungent odour wafted out of it, suffocating everyone in the room. Even Miao Donghui, who was fully and elegantly dressed as usual, completely lost his composure. He stumbled hurriedly away from the coffin until he reached the low couch. He held onto the back of the couch to support himself, and fumbled in his pocket to get out his silk handkerchief to cover his nose and mouth.

The two Japanese took out a picture, went forward, and compared it carefully with the face of the man lying in the coffin. They nodded in confirmation.

Lianxiu thought she might have seen the old man's sparkling whiskers and the bleak sneer frozen on his face.

Guitang took several quick steps to get hold of the walking stick hung on the back of the low couch, and handed it to her.

"It's all Lianxiu's fault letting those people disturb your peace!" Lianxiu couldn't forgive herself. Not knowing what kind of karma she would suffer for such a blunder, she leaned on the old man's walking stick, quivering with terror.

When the two Chinese put the lid back on the coffin, they conveyed the order from the Japanese that it was not hygenic to keep the body in a coffin like this and that the body had to be cremated immediately.

Miao Donghui seemed to agree with this and repeatedly nodded his approval. He told Lianxiu attentively: "Mrs Lü, it's not right to keep the body like this. It'll cause trouble."

When those people left, Lianxiu talked with Lü Guitang. Both agreed that they couldn't let them cremate the body since the old man's three daughters still hadn't been informed of their father's death. They hadn't bade farewell to him. When they left, they had left the old man for Lianxiu and Guitang to take care of. Now they were no longer capable of giving them back their father. How could they have the heart to give the three daughters nothing but the old man's ashes? They decided they had to tell Ling Jingyao about what had happened in the afternoon. But a truck came at noon with some soldiers from the puppet army led by the local security head. They declared they were taking the coffin to the crematorium.

"You can't move it!" Lianxiu threw herself at the coffin, spreading her limbs to protect it. "Grandpa Lü's daughters haven't been informed!"

"What daughters?" the head of the small gang asked. "Who are you?"

Lianxiu didn't know how to answer the question and was speechless again, but she didn't let go of the coffin. Lü Guitang told the security head: "You may take it away. Mrs Lü has given you permission."

Xiangge came into the room, followed by Secretary Huang's family. They all had a hard time pulling Lianxiu away from the coffin.

The reception hall in the funeral parlour descended into a deathly silence once the nails had been hammered into the lid.

They began to move the coffin. Lianxiu was rooted to the spot because she had exhausted her energy in her struggle to protect the coffin. Seeing the coffin being carried out of the hall, she took a step forward and threw herself onto the floor and knelt there. Everything she held dear was taken away from her with that coffin.

"It is all Lianxiu's fault that Grandpa Lü will be unable to rest in peace." Lianxiu's thoughts came back to reality in the rustling autumn wind. What came to her mind was still this realisation after all those days of numbness. Glancing around the room with the same layout, she realised, too, that she was living a life which would never again include Grandpa Lü.

Xiangge lifted the door curtain and came in with a bowl of porridge in her hand. She didn't put the bowl down when she reached Lianxiu's bedside. Hard on Xiangge's heels was Lü Guitang, who brought the chill wind in with him which set the lower hem of his winter gown swinging. The lining of the gown was already worn out, revealing a loose patch of cloth.

The day the coffin was taken away, he had followed the group with the intention of bringing back Grandpa Lü's ashes. But once they were outside the gate of the residence, the security head had ordered him to go back. So Guitang came away empty-handed.

"Cold hands?" he asked her daughter caringly. "How are you feeling today?" He asked Lianxiu caringly, too.

Lianxiu wasn't feeling much today, but she did notice the loose patch of cloth dangling from the hem of Guitang's winter gown. She also noticed that Xiangge was wearing a violet sweater. When Xiangge put down the bowl, she kept rubbing her hands. How could she have failed to notice that both the father and daughter needed more proper winter clothing?

Grandpa Lü had left behind several light cotton-padded jackets, which could be of some use to Lü Guitang. The brass-coloured one with a floral-pattern silk cover looked rather old-fashioned for his age. The camel-coloured one would suit him better. And a pair of winter trousers, too. Which one would be better? The dark blue one or the dark grey one? Turning those choices over in her mind, she felt she was strong enough to get out of bed. When she sat up, she leaned back again in horror. How could she think like that? Who had authorised her to give away Grandpa Lü's things during his daughters' absence?

"Xiangge, I thank you and your father for taking care of me!" she said, gently. To express her gratitude was certainly the right thing for her to do.

"The main thing is that you are getting better," said Guitang with genuine happiness. He delivered the bowl of porridge to Lianxiu, who accepted it with much appreciation. She was the one who used to stand by and take care of the old man lying in bed. Now she was the one lying in bed and being taken care of. Would she suffer any consequences from being treated well like this?

"What's it like today?" she asked, rather casually, after taking a sip of the porridge.

"It's frosty," answered Guitang.

That explained why it was getting so cold! It was already frosty. Seeing Lianxiu trying to get out of bed, Guitang excused himself and went outside.

Xiangge asked tentatively: "Do you want to get out now? Are you feeling dizzy?"

Lianxiu waved her hand dismissively, got out of her bed, walked slowly to the table in the room, and sat down. She was quite sure she had never seen Xiangge wear such a sweater before, so she asked: "Did you make a new sweater for yourself?" Xiangge didn't answer.

Later when Xiangge left, Guitang said: "She knitted it herself with woollen yarn given to her by the Huang family. She has been spending a lot of time with Huang Ruiqi, Secretary Huang's eldest son. The lad is lending a helping hand at a grocery store owned by a relative. He can certainly support his family. The Huang family has been good to Xiangge, too. From Mrs Huang's expression and implications, I think Huang Ruiqi wants to propose to Xiangge."

The whole thing sounded so strange, just like Xiangge's new sweater which looked so strange in Lianxiu's eyes. Instinctively, she turned around and saw the statue of Guanyin[1] sitting right in the middle of the tea table. It took her a long while to recall that it was she who had moved the statue from the corner to the table when Grandpa Lü had passed away. It had been her only consolation. Grandpa Lü loved to recite and chant scripts, but he loathed all kinds of praying, so she had to hide away all her sacred statues from him.

"I haven't offered any incense for such a long time. Please forgive my negligence", prayed Lianxiu, silently. She stood up and tried to offer some incense to the statue. Guitang stretched his hands out, trying to help her to stand, but quickly withdrew midway. Lianxiu didn't notice Guitang's weird behaviour, but she did notice how wobbly her legs were. She fell back into her chair.

"You take your time and take it easy," said Guitang, his eyes looking elsewhere, then he soon excused himself.

"Dad, why did you mention the Huangs? They have to ask whether I'm willing or not before they make any moves!" Xiangge complained in a soft, high-pitched voice.

"Are you willing or not? I think it is quite a nice thing. When you are settled, my heart will be settled, too," Guitang's voice was deep and resonant.

Xiangge answered her father with a sneer. The sneer was so different from her usual ingratiating, cloying smiles that Lianxiu was so familiar with. But now she immediately noticed the change and wondered why she had never been aware that Xiangge was capable of sneering like that.

"Give me some cash. I need to buy pickles," Xiangge said.

"Get some fresh vegetables today in addition to the pickles.

Mrs Lü is getting better so she should have something fresh to eat."

Xiangge sneered again. Her sneer extended all the way out. Lianxiu guessed she was probably leaving for the grocery store.

It sounded so weird, though Lianxiu couldn't figure out why. She rose slowly again before carefully cleaning the statue and then going back to lie on her bed.

A couple of days later, Lianxiu felt much better. She was eager to achieve one thing: to pray to all kinds of deities, including the fox fairies, in the back garden for Grandpa Lü to rest in peace in the afterlife.

The rooms got very quiet in the evening during Xiangge's absence. Where had she got to? After the clock struck nine, Lianxiu decided to go to the back garden by herself. She didn't need any excuse to pray in the back garden like she used to when Grandpa was alive. Now she was free to go anywhere anytime, and to stay as long as she wished. Was she enjoying such freedom? This was even harder to forgive than the complacency she had felt several months ago when Grandpa Lü and she had just moved out of the master compound to the gallery garden.

It took a lot of effort on Lianxiu's part to track down a large thick scarf from the trunk. She took the scarf and went to the mirror to wrap herself up. Before she was able to see herself in the mirror, she jumped: how could she even think about looking at herself in a mirror? She apprehensively stumbled several steps back until she reached the door and kept her distance from the mirror.

She heard a couple of people's footsteps outside the door. She was sure Guitang's was not one of them.

"Don't worry. Madam Lü is asleep." It was Xiangge's voice. Why could she always hear Xiangge's voice?

"Honestly, I hate this place. I hate Beiping! I hate my dad and Madam Lü!" Xiangge's voice was low but sharp. Piercingly sharp. Xiangge had changed a lot since Grandpa Lü passed away.

"I hate whatever and whoever you hate," Huang Ruiqi chimed indulgently. "I'm willing to do whatever you want to do."

"I want to leave. I'm willing to go anywhere but here. I want to leave as soon as possible. I want to leave tomorrow!" Xiangge chuckled.

"As long as I can stay with you, I'm willing to go even as far as Japan!"

"It sounds as if you have been invited to go to Japan! Just consider how little Japanese you have learnt. Aren't you aware how lousy it is? You mentioned last time we met that a troupe is recruiting actors and actresses, and a radio station is looking for singers. You said they would send those who excel to go and study in Japan. If I can make the cut, I will certainly go."

"Is it alright to work for the Japanese?" Huang Ruiqi had learned Japanese in his last year of high school before graduation. It never occurred to him that he might make a living with his Japanese.

"I'm well aware I am Chinese. But Chinese have to eat and live, too. Not like the young ladies from the Meng or Tantai families, who have had everything arranged for them. I have to work hard to survive. Weren't you an obedient citizen when you accepted the position in that grocery store which is run according to the new policies issued by the new government? Ouch!"

It sounded as if Huang Ruiqi had given Xiangge a poke. She paused shortly and continued: "I'm going to ask Professor Ling for a favour. He has so many connections in art circles."

"Your dad won't let you do that."

"I won't worry about that. If he doesn't agree, he may at least try to send me to the rear area under KMT rule. He's enjoying himself here. Haven't you noticed that he and Madam Lü have quite a close bond?"

Xiangge's high-pitched voice directly stabbed Lianxiu's heart, which sank into a hubbub of anger, shame and resentment. She wanted to argue. She wanted to confront Xiangge. But she was too shocked to do anything with her two jelly-like legs. Propping herself against her ancient wooden chair, she found she didn't even have the strength to tremble.

Xiangge lifted the door curtain and walked into the room. Noticing Lianxiu had got out of bed, she pouted, the corners of her two thin rosy lips giving one downward twitch.

"Madam, have you got up? Brother Ruiqi has come to fetch something." She tossed the door curtain behind her, and asked Huang Ruiqi to follow her to the room at the back. Huang Ruiqi glanced apologetically at Lianxiu and followed Xiangge inside.

Lianxiu straightened her back, snatched the key to the door in the passageway leading to the back garden from behind the door, and shot out of the room. A wave of hearty laughter rang out behind her.

She stumbled out of the gallery garden, forcing herself to hold back her tears and calm down.

"Thank heaven! I can still pray to Guanyin. Guanyin bless

me," she said to herself, but her thoughts were broken like her voice. She picked up her pace and walked hastily across the layers of buildings toward the back garden. When she reached the passageway, she found the door had been smashed open. Not in the mood to figure out why it was open, she scurried through and plunged into the garden, leaning on the first tree she saw, and cried.

The old building, which was dimly silhouetted against the bleak light from the waning crescent moon, appeared to be even older than it had been the previous year, surrounded by tall wild grass in the garden. The familiarity in the air was soothing to Lianxiu.

She kept on crying for a while until she was interrupted by the noise of a stray cat leaping up the wall from nowhere and disappearing into the darkness. Through her misty eyes, she saw a red spot of light on in the building. It grew into several rows of bright red lights hanging neatly under the eaves of the building. All of the lights then wavered and swayed into one. Did she actually see that? She dried her tears and had a good look, but all she saw was the dim building.

"Thank you, holy spirit, for not forgetting a poor soul like me!" Lianxiu was not scared by what she thought she might have seen, instead, she felt less lonely in such a big world. Honestly, how could she be so concerned about two children's gossip? How delicate she had become after all those years by Grandpa Lü's side! With these thoughts, she walked slowly to the boulder where she used to burn incense and pray. She fumbled in a hollow under the rock and was happy to feel the incense burner she had hidden.

She had been in such a hurry that she had forgotten to take any incense or matches with her. After brooding silently for a while, she set up the empty incense burner, but was again at a loss what to pray for. What should she pray for? She pondered. In the end, she prayed for Grandpa Lü, wishing that he would rest in peace, and then she prayed for the health and safety of his three daughters and their families. She would pray for her health when Grandpa Lü was still alive so that she could carry out her duty of taking good care of the old man if she was healthy. But now? She had no reason to ask for such a favour from the holy spirits. Should she pray for her judgement instead?

That thought reminded her of the note Grandpa Lü had slipped into The Heart Sutra, on which he had written "Lianxiu, you are not allowed to mourn for me. Meet a suitable man and get married."

Professor Ling knew about the note, too. She was grateful for the arrangements Grandpa Lü had made for her even in the last moments of his life. She should try her utmost to do something worthy of their marriage. He had died for the country and she shouldn't do anything to tarnish that. Grandpa Lü had always said that Lü Guitang was honest, trustworthy and intelligent, in an unobtrusive way. Why did she think of Lü Guitang? She was scared by the turmoil in her mind.

Sudden footsteps behind her almost made her jump to her feet.

"It's me, madam," came Lü Guitang's voice. He approached from the direction of the old building.

Lianxiu almost shot up on hearing the voice. To be sure, Lü Guitang was the last person she wanted to meet right now, but why was it also comforting to know it was him?

Guitang stood by the other side of the boulder and said: "I shouldn't have disturbed your praying, but you were out so long, it worried me. I'll wait by the door to the passageway. When you are done, I'll walk you back."

Lianxiu wanted to say: "You don't need to wait for me. Leave me alone." But she said nothing when she saw him, his head drooping and his eyes fixed to the ground. He was not very tall, but still much taller than she was. Though not muscularly strong, he looked so reliable. Her heart fluttered again — he might be the only person in the world who actually cared for her.

The cold dim moon shed light on the two figures standing on either side of the boulder.

Lü Guitang's heart was roaring in his chest: "What a demon I have become! How could I be unworthy of Grandpa Lü to harbour such feelings? But how can I cheat myself and deny such a feeling? Besides, look what chaos we are now in and she looks so lonely." He was not lonely himself, though, because he had a letter, which seemingly weighed a ton, in one of the pockets in his worn-out light winter-gown.

"If I had never been married to Grandpa Lü, it would have been such a blessing to run into a man like Lü Guitang. But now I can't let others talk behind my back and bring disgrace to Grandpa Lü's name!" Lianxiu felt both scared and unfairly wronged, moving her to tears. She leaned against her side of the boulder and wept.

"You should have a good cry. Don't keep it all to yourself," Guitang said, walking over to her. His heart was filled with pity at the sight of her tiny bony shoulders wrapped in her big scarf. How much he longed to hold her in his arms and keep both of them warm in the depths of such a chilly night! Why not? Really, why not? He took one step forward, but then quickly drew himself back with the rude realisation that he was crossing the line.

"Or should I go back first?" he asked after a pause.

That would be alright. Lianxiu wanted to tell him but she couldn't voice the words. How much she wanted to lean against his shoulder and have a good cry! He and she were equals. She would never have thought of leaning on Grandpa Lü's shoulder to cry!

She slowly raised her head, trying her best to control her sobs, and dried her tears. She thought she saw in her misty eyes a row of red lights dangling in the old building, but when she took a harder look, they were gone.

Noticing her gazing at the building, Guitang gave a sudden tug at her arm: "Let's go back."

Lianxiu froze at that gentle tug. She wished she could go with him anywhere, just as Xiangge had said, but her feet were rooted to the ground.

"I mean, it's getting cold deep into the night," Guitang explained apologetically, letting go of her hand. That tinge of tender feeling of his had evaporated into a ruthless reality with hard edges and corners.

Both fell into an awkward silence. Only the chilly autumn wind moaned on, swinging the tassels on the scarf and the bottom edge of the worn-out winter-gown.

"Xiangge and Ruiqi just talked about leaving Beiping," Lianxiu stammered, remembering what Xiangge had said about her. "She said she would go to see Professor Ling."

"I have to pay a visit to Professor Ling myself," said Guitang, who seemed to cheer up a little bit. "To be honest, madam, I want to leave, too, although I would have had to stay here to mourn for Grandpa Lü if his body and coffin had remained here. But now I have nothing to mourn for, so I'm thinking of going to the rear area. I'm not a fighter, but I can make myself useful being a copy clerk or something."

Lianxiu gave him a quick glance, her eyes sparkling like buttons in the darkness.

"Shouldn't you think about leaving, too? You could go and join Madam Bichu. She's now in your hometown."

The sparkle in those buttons dimmed. Lianxiu shook her head: "That would be great when you all leave." She hesitated, turning over what Xiangge wanted, but decided not to mention it. She was not in the habit of gossiping.

"But I can't leave. I have to stay here. This is where Grandpa Lü once lived and I have to watch over his things."

"Grandpa Lü was such a good instructor to have brought the best out of her," sighed Guitang to himself with admiration for Grandpa Lü. Their eyes drifted apart from each other. The solid wall of the deceased Grandpa Lü stood firmly between the two living beings.

A gust of autumn wind passed, swinging the tassles of the scarf and on the lower edge of the worn-out winter-gown. The wild grass bowed, wrinkled and sighed.

Part 2

Many things had changed in the Ling residence located in East Zongbu Lane during the last two months. The mighty torrent of life flooded the place, shattering their comfortable and privileged life, along with Ling Jingyao's body and mind. Those shattered tiny pieces would never bring back the same Ling Jingyao.

When Miao Donghui was informed that the Japanese wanted to open Grandpa Lü's coffin for inspection, Miao had proposed taking Ling Jingyao with him, but the Japanese rejected his proposal. When he came back from the Japanese, he immediately sent his wife to tell Yue Hengfen to be cautious and not to annoy the Japanese.

"Did you hear that?" Yue Hengfen said to Ling Jingyao the moment Mrs Miao left.

"Didn't I tell you that it was not appropriate to go to the Lü's? It is true we are on friendly terms with the Lüs, but Grandpa Lü was too much involved in politics. Besides, all three of his sons-in-law are important figures in different fields. Even someone like me can see how much attention they can attract. How can you have failed to see that?"

"Do you mean to say that I should have walked away and let Zhao Lianxiu take care of things after Grandpa Lü's death?" Jingyao asked coldly.

"Are the Lüs short of relatives and friends? What are we to them?" retorted Hengfen. The word 'relatives' naturally evoked her memory of Wei Feng, who naturally diverted her attention and anger.

"The one who left without saying goodbye hasn't revealed his whereabouts yet. Does this look like proper behaviour becoming a well-bred gentleman? Heaven knows! He might bring disaster on us!" When she said this, of course, she didn't foresee like a diviner what disaster would befall them one day. She was convinced that the destiny of people like her was always to be favoured by fate, and that calamity would automatically be transformed into blessings.

In mid-July, a car parked outside the Ling residence. Out came a couple of people, asking Ling Jingyao to go to the police station.

Jingyao was quite calm when he got in the car because his brain was already numbed. Neither knowledge nor experience counted for anything in such circumstances. All that rang in his head, over and over again, was the old saying "what will be, will be".

The Japanese officer Yōji Karasugi, who could speak both Chinese and French, had met Jingyao once at the Miao's, where the two engaged in a heated discussion about Prosper Mérimée and Charles Pierre Baudelaire. Jingyao was impressed that this Japanese officer actually displayed quite some knowledge about the two French literary giants. When Jingyao saw Yōji Karasugi again, Jingyao felt so sorry for the two French writers.

Karasugi asked Jingyao three questions with a deadpan face: the cause of Grandpa Lü's death, the whereabouts of Wei Feng and his anti-Japanese activities. Jingyao thought it was hilarious. How could any investigation into anti-Japanese activities implicate anyone like him? He almost blurted out that he truly wanted to rise up against the Japanese, but actions? No.

As if knowing what Jingyao was thinking, Karasugi took out a photo. It was a poster of a play, *The Field*, directed by him in 1932. Standing in the dark gloomy forest was a milestone with three numbers '9.18'.

Jingyao froze. Back then, the whole cast was so excited about the milestone in the setting because it embodied something unmentionable. The numbers were bright red, but not so on the picture Karasugi had.

"We needed a milestone in the forest," Jingyao answered after thinking for a while.

"It is not mentioned in the script."

"The script didn't include any stage design."

"Why is it '9.18', and not any other number?"

"How should I know? It was done by someone in charge of the stage design." Fortunately, they had long since left Beiping.

"You are a professor and a director. You should direct your life better than this," said Karasugi calmly and coldly, and signalled that he was free to go. At first, Jingyao thought he was going to be sent to prison, but was surprised to find out that he was being sent back home.

Tears were certainly shed when the three were reunited. Jingyao knew this was just a prelude of more to come. He wanted to tell Hengfen she should save some of her tears for what was yet to come, but he didn't have the heart to let Xueyan know what was coming.

Xueyan was much calmer, in contrast to her mother's reaction. She asked, uncertainly: "We should be categorised as 'good citizens', why did they arrest you?" She hesitated further, before adding: "Is it because of Wei Feng?"

"It's not about him," said Jingyao, smiling at his daughter. "Lots of people have left these universities in Beiping. I told the Japanese Wei Feng had left with others in his faculty, and they didn't ask any more questions."

"Then what are they after?" Two pairs of eyes, which shared such similarity, were fixed on him.

"I can hardly imagine the reason," Jingyao said. "Because we are the conquered."

Then a couple of days later, everything became clear when Yōji Karasugi came to the Ling residence accompanied by two of his men to ask Jingyao to preside over the North China Arts Federation.

"I can't," Jingyao answered without hesitation.

"Lots of people want the position, but we think only you are qualified."

"I can't!" Having restrained his impulse to say "I won't", he repeated instead: "I can't."

Not a single muscle moved on Karasugi's face. He made a small gesture, and the two men flanking him instantly took out a pair of handcuffs and put them on Jingyao's wrists. "Vous avez été arrêté," he said, issuing the command to arrest Jingyao in French.

That was easier than crushing a caterpillar! I really should have left Beiping! How could I have entertained the fantasy that the fallen city of Beiping would be a place for me to remain? Too late! It was too late! Jingyao's heart groaned with the miserable realisation.

"I will inform Mrs Ling and Miss Ling of your arrest," said Karasugi, smiling.

That smile from a Japanese officer sent Jingyao directly to the First Model Prison of Beiping.

How could a prison earn a title like 'model'? Jingyao was quite interested in it.

His first interrogation was rather simple. During Yōji Karasugi's absence, another Japanese officer went through the motions in the same military uniform. Jingyao answered the generic questions automatically.

At his second interrogation, Karasugi was present. He said, also in French, that they had evidence showing that Jingyao had stayed in Beiping because he was on a secret mission from the KMT.

"I don't even have a clue who works for the KMT," said Jingyao, who was shocked at such an accusation.

"Have you ever noticed who is working for the CPC, then?"

"This question is irrelevant." Jingyao thought how incredible this question was.

"But it's easy to make it relevant. If you accept our offer, then we can let bygones be bygones."

"I won't accept it!" Jingyao said indignantly.

Karasugi gave Jingyao a sympathetic look and raised his hand.

How can one's soul remain intact if it has been tormented in hell? Let those who think they can handle it come and try!

Before Jingyao was tortured for the first time, he was

furious. The worst thing that could happen to him was that he might die. And how horrible would that be? He threw an enormous temper tantrum, stomped on the floor and cursed like a sailor.

Several big, muscular guys punched and kicked him in an effort to subdue him. Something red and hot flashed in front of his eyes. Before he could recognise it was a blazing searing iron, his knee caps were burnt with a sharp pain. The smell of barbecued meat immediately filled the room. His flesh! What came to mind was that he would never be able to walk again, and would no longer need to walk.

When he came out of his coma, he found himself lying on dry hay in a cell. His first thought was to kill himself. How smart Lü Qingfei was to arrange his own death before he could be killed! Now the only way he could kill himself was to dash himself hard against the wall, but he didn't have the strength. Besides, the walls in the cell were so filthy.

His thoughts drifted back to the walls at home. Different rooms had walls with different patterns, reflecting the smiling radiance of his wife and daughter. Were his wife and daughter, who had both been raised in affluent circumstances with all the material comforts, crying their eyes out? Oh, Xueyan! She was so young, and she didn't deserve so many tears. But he was no longer able to take care of them.

His temporary sobriety was squeezed out by another bout of coma. He felt as if he were stumbling in an endless dark, tight tunnel scraping past swords and knives on the walls, being stabbed from every direction. Although the pain was excruciating, he still wanted to go through the tunnel because here and there in the darkness, the shining and smooth faces of his wife and his daughter would pop up. He drifted in and out of consciousness: "I can't give up." "I can't do this anymore."

What a horrible darkness! How can I get through it? How can I get rid of it?

A couple of days later, he was subjected to a second torture session which involved lots of water. He was taken to a big barrel filled with filthy, bloody water. He almost threw up at the filth, wondering what they were going to do to him. All of a sudden, his nose was clamped with a pair of clips and he was pushed into the barrel headfirst.

When he felt he was almost drowning, he was dragged out of the water and thrown onto the floor. Several pairs of leather boots stomped ruthlessly on his back, squeezing water and blood out of him. Then they did it all over again: throwing him into the water, dragging him out and stomping on his back. Jingyao was hanging onto his consciousness by a thread, bringing him to the realisation that he was no longer human. Indeed, he was not sure what he was at that point.

He couldn't think for a couple of days after the water torture. The dark tunnel seemed to be tightening, smothering him. He had to get through it! When his consciousness returned, he wailed noisily, feeling so sorry for himself.

Who could imagine the suffering he had been through? Who could have pity on him?

He tried to die a fast death. Anyway, he wouldn't eat the mixture of roots of greens and whatever type of grain they put in his 'food'. Two days after his fast, he was given a shot before he was taken to the gate of a big building.

The gate was opened from the inside. He was confronted by a dozen giant, fierce dogs running about wildly inside the barbed wire, ripping at each other. At the noise of the door opening, they fixed their bloodshot eyes upon Jingyao. Clearly, they were smart enough to locate the prisoner who was their prey.

I was not afraid of death, but I was terrified at the prospect of the moment when my body would be butchered and shredded to pieces! I was not afraid of death, but I was terrified of the fangs and the claws! I was not afraid of death, but I... I was terrified!

"We're helping you out!" The Chinese escort officer said.

All of the dogs crowded at the opening of the barbed wire fence, their long red tongues hanging hungrily out of their mouths. Someone gave Jingyao a shove on the back.

"Je me rends!" Jingyao shouted his surrender in French, automatically putting up his hands at the same time.

Yōji Karasugi arrived promptly, with the same pity lingering in his eyes when he looked at Jingyao. He asked Jingyao, in French, whether he would follow the order from the imperial Japanese army to work for the Greater East Asia Co-Prosperity Sphere.

Jingyao kept nodding in reflex, his body trembling. He stumbled back, as far away as possible from the fierce animals, and then passed out.

He was not sent back to his cell, or home. He was sent to a poorly equipped infirmary to treat his wounds. Miao Donghui visited him once and whispered to him: "I didn't expect you would be the first one. I thought I would be." First or second, did that matter? Jingyao looked at Miao Donghui numbly, imagining what would become of Miao's fine clothes as they were torn by the canine fangs and claws.

During his stay in the infirmary, he thought a lot about the tomb of Charles Pierre Baudelaire in the Cimetière de

Montparnasse, Paris. The poet's bust was set on a tall stone pedestal planted where his head lay, his chin cupped in his hands, gazing down at his own grave, where his dead body lay, eyes closed. Jingyao used to wander time and again there, pondering over life and death with a heavy heart. The image of the tomb floated in his mind with an image of his own dead body torn into thousands of tiny pieces. If no one would recognise Jingyao from that mess, how could anyone carve a bust for him? Maybe someone could still manage.

He gradually recovered. When he regained his strength, he was accorded the privilege of having home-cooked meals. He winced at the sight of his favourite squid stew. His body had managed to go through the dark tunnel and out the other side, but his heart never did; it was trapped there forever. When he took one sip of the delicious stew, which tasted wonderful with its perfect blend of gentle sour and hot flavours, he reckoned that it had all been worthwhile after all. Of course, he was extremely ashamed of such a thought afterwards.

When it reached the point of 'cold dew' on the Chinese calendar, Jingyao was released from the infirmary and was allowed to go back home. Unsurprisingly, he was drenched in Hengfen's and Xueyan's tears. What a pity! Even the entire Cocytus river (a river in Greek mythology leading to Hades, the abode of the dead) couldn't wash away the stains on his body, nor the pain weighing on his mind.

Having clammed up for several days, he eventually told Hengfen what had happened one night. It appeared as though his confession didn't shock Hengfen since her first question was how could they break the news to their only daughter..

The reading on the thermometer dropped more with the intensifying autumn wind, which carpeted the ground with fallen leaves from wall upon wall of Virginia creepers. The lawns were transformed into different shades of yellow.

The three members of the Ling family would spend every evening together in the living room attached to Jingyao and Hengfen's bedroom, listening to the rustling footsteps of the wind.

One night, Xueyan observed that her father might be strong enough, so she delicately raised her question, cautious of her tone and her diction.

"Dad," she called. "What did you promise?" She was not crying when she posed the question, but when she stopped, her tears began to flow. "Dad, let's leave! Let's leave, now!" She said between her tears.

"What did I promise?" Jingyao thought. "I promised to lock up my soul in a pitch-black endless tunnel! Why would you ask me that?"

Feeling wronged and annoyed, Jingyao cut loose his restraint and snapped: "Daydreams! Nonsense!" His heart was crammed with pain and humiliation from the torture he was subjected to in prison. He deserved an outlet!

"Sarcasm!" he added.

"Dad, don't be mad! It's all my fault!" Having never been snapped at by her father, Xueyan was shocked, and then she began to blame herself for such a rash deed. She lowered herself into a kneeling position by the low couch, stroking Jingyao's knees. She could feel her mother's tears dropping on her head. Knowing the reason behind her father's rage, she didn't blame him. Her poor father! With all the bruises inside and outside his body! *Your Xueyan is ready and willing to shoulder all your pain and suffering! But what did you promise? What did you promise?"*

Her look was gentle, but her eyes were persistent. A gentle personality is often accompanied by persistence. She was well aware of the price her father had to pay for his survival.

"Xueyan," Hengfen gave her daughter a tug, drying her puffy red eyes. "Don't ask. Your dad will tell you later."

Jingyao's eyes were fastened on his wife, full of gratitude. The previous week following his release, for the first time in all their years of marriage, Hengfen hadn't uttered a word of blame or complaint, which made him realise his wife really loved him. Unfortunately, he now deserved no love at all.

He wanted to pat Xueyan on the head as he always used to do, but he didn't even have the courage to stroke her hand. Staring at his wife, he gathered whatever strength he had left after his trauma and said:

"Get me my opium lamp!"

Taking the stunned Xueyan into her arms, Hengfen whispered: "We won't keep this from you. Your father has internal injuries, and he needs to kill the pain. Besides, smoking opium is in keeping with the intentions of the Japanese."

The maid Ah Sheng delivered the opium tray to the room quickly. The shiny glass lampshade and the cloisonné pipe embedded with a fine piece of jasper tinted Jingyao's gloomy face with a thin shimmer of colour. A wry smile curled up at the corners of his mouth. It seemed he had found his source of energy and inner peace. Reaching out for the pipe, he uttered: "It has been a long time!"

Not daring to look at such an abhorrent sight, Xueyan first covered her eyes with her hands. Then she exploded with emotion. Lunging over and grabbing the pipe, she cried:

"Dad, why are you hurting yourself like this? Have you

forgotten how much pain you went through when you decided to quit the drug? Why are you taking it up again?"

Jingyao lost his composure again. *This is the only thing I am in control of! I will protect my freedom of choice! Even my daughter has no say in it! I don't need anyone to tell me what to do and what not to do. I don't need anyone to care about me!* Roaring inside, he slowly sat up, only to encounter the lovely pair of eyes sparkling with tears, fixed on his, as if asking: "What did you promise? What did you promise?"

"Xueyan, you stay out of my business." His voice was gentle, but his tone was antagonistic. "Your father doesn't deserve your concern anymore."

What should I do if my father doesn't deserve my concern? The words were like the whimpering of a faint voice trapped deep down in a dark pit.

Hengfen put the pipe back onto the tray, held Xueyan's head, and moaned: "You've got me. You've still got your mum, my dear daughter!"

"Show her the newspaper!" Jingyao's trembling finger pointed at a nightstand inlaid with mother-of-pearl. Hengfen hesitated before going over and taking the newspaper. She handed the paper to Xueyan, which was shaking in her trembling hand.

Ling Jingyao, professor of French literature, renowned dramatist, has been appointed as chairman of the North China Arts Association.

Each Chinese character was like a bullet shooting directly into Xueyan's eyes when she saw the announcement. The sparks in her eyes and her brain were desperately trying to connect the dots but, instead, were just causing a short circuit.

Her brain formulated no thoughts other than to register that she was shocked. But she soon regained control and said calmly: "Yes, I just want to know the truth."

"Now you have been told." Jingyao reached out for the pipe, but his hand kept trembling, losing its grip.

Xueyan quietly sat on a cushion on the floor, her eyes fixed on the pipe.

"Look at you! Why don't you hold it like this?" Hengfen was back to her complaining ways.

The pipe was finally in the grip of that bony hand with blue veins standing out like cords. Xueyan realised things were back on their normal track at the Ling residence. Where was her track? She was certain she could no longer find it here in the residence. Anyway, tradition required that a married daughter should move out of her parents' home.

The three fell silent, but the air was tenser in the room than it might have been amid any loud, noisy fighting. Ah Sheng came in and reported that Lü Guitang and his daughter were here.

How dare someone come to visit? How could someone want to come and visit?

"Are you sure you want to receive visitors now? It's the Lüs, again!" said Hengfen. The pipe in Jingyao's hand shook.

"Bring them in here," Xueyan ordered, resolutely. She had never given orders to servants in her parents' presence, assuming it was their business, but now she had to take a stand.

In the absence of any orders to the contrary, Ah Sheng excused herself and then took the father and the daughter into the living room, who brought in a chilling gust with them.

"Mr and Mrs Ling, I'm sorry but I had to come," said

Guitang with a deep bow. Xiangge muttered some words of greeting behind her father and she stood by Xueyan's side, glancing around the room with great curiosity, taking in the three people who were their host and hostesses. Xueyan quietly passed the newspaper to Guitang.

Guitang read the paper, rubbed his eyes, read it again, then rubbed his eyes again. *Professor Ling is a knowledgable scholar. He is a nice person, too. But has he...? Is he...? What is this place indeed?* Guitang was suddenly scared and regretful. Why had he dragged Xiangge along with him?

"I don't know what has happened. I was thinking, thinking about going to the rear area with you…" Before he could finish his sentence, he already regretted it. How inappropriate! He stopped and then continued, falteringly: "I meant… Guitang meant…" He actually didn't know what he meant. Instinctively, he felt for the pocket in his gown where an important letter was secured. How could he deliver the letter to the receiver on hearing this new information?

"That's alright," the pipe in Jingyao's hand was still shaking. "I won't tell on you."

No one responded. Jingyao took some time to calm down. He pointed at the chair with his pipe, gesturing Guitang to sit down. "How's Mrs Lü? Did anything happen later?"

"No… nothing. She's well. Everyone is well," answered Guitang, blushing.

Hengfen looked suspiciously at Guitang. The phone rang. It was from Yōji Karasugi. When Jingyao took the receiver, he automatically switched into an obedient tone. Karasugi first asked how he was feeling and then suggested Jingyao host a tea party, inviting some noted figures in cultural circles. He then told Jingyao the good news that Jingyao had been invited to visit Japan.

"Japan?" Jingyao repeated in disbelief.

"Just a sightseeing tour. You know, to enhance mutual understanding. Nothing more. How about next month?"

"Votre horaire est mon horaire," Jingyao agreed in French.

"Did you hear that? I've been invited to visit Japan!" Jingyao was overcome with exhaustion when he put the phone down. He laughed: "You are all going to the rear, and I am heading to Japan!"

"If you need someone to serve you, please take me along," said Xiangge, bracing herself. When she realised that everyone else in the room was staring at her in astonishment, she hurriedly added: "I'm willing to go to the rear, and to Japan, too. I just don't want to stay here in Beiping." The luxuriously furnished room and the delicate display gave Xiangge a perfect incentive to break the bonds of the gallery garden and to establish her own world where she would be the mistress.

"For me, Beiping is very nice. Do you think I want to go to Japan?" said Jingyao, turning to Hengfen with a hollow laugh.

Guitang was too embarrassed to know what to say. How rash Xiangge was to say things like that! He looked at Xueyan pleadingly, but wasn't sure how to address her. Should he go with Miss Ling or Mrs Wei? He was even more lost after he saw the sadness permeating Xueyan's delicate face, which had the power to melt any compassionate heart.

"Let's go to the reception hall downstairs," Xueyan said.

Guitang felt the opportunity was beckoning. He felt for his pocket again. He glanced at Jingyao and then Hengfen, bowed, but stayed, not knowing whether he should leave as Xueyan had suggested, or stay, as Jingyao and Hengfen hadn't yet dismissed him. When Jingyao waved at him impatiently to go, he then took Xiangge and left with Xueyan.

The massive glass doors closed gently from outside. The opium lamp inside the doors was lit. The flame in the cover beamed peacefully and cosily, waiting to heat up the drug.

Part 3

Xueyan, do you hate me? A hoarse voice asked, wafting from the top of the opium lamp.

Xueyan, come and join me! A distant but determined voice asked, carrying across thousands of miles of land and water.

Xueyan was sitting in that ancient chair in the gallery garden the following night, with two voices echoing in her ears. One of her hands in the pockets of her thin pale-lilac cashmere coat was caressing the crumpled envelope that had been delivered by Lü Guitang during his visit the night before. Written on the envelope was her name in that darling handwriting. The sight of the handwriting immediately dissipated the gloom of her world and provided her with solid support. Inside the envelope was a slip of paper with only five words: "Xueyan, come and join me."

Xueyan, come and join me!

She had been called. She was going to answer the call despite all the hardships and dangers lurking ahead of her. She was going to go. Her feet in her black medium-heel leather shoes, which were ready to cover thousands of miles, moved involuntarily with her roving thoughts. Her feet touched the small blue suitcase she had been carrying. She finally took it with her and left. For the last year, she had been packing this suitcase over and over again. The clothes packed inside had been rotated several times according to the change of the seasons. How many times had she put the case down in front of her father, ready to leave with him? She had long since lost count, but she remembered the same ending. Each time, she ended up taking the case back to her room and weeping silently. Now the suitcase was leaving with her, but she was leaving her parents behind, who were trapped beyond any call.

Xueyan, come and join me!

The call had come too late. Besides the letter, Lü Guitang had also brought her a message, asking her to meet Li Yuming, the best man at their wedding, and leave with him. If the letter had arrived earlier, maybe her father would have escaped such a dreadful fate? But now? She couldn't tell them she was leaving, and had to keep her whereabouts from them, too.

That night after Lü Guitang left, she had been wandering around outside her parents' rooms, wanting to take one more look at them, or at least have one more fight with them. But in the end, she didn't knock at the door. When Hengfen came to her room and she told her mother she wanted to pay a visit to Lianxiu, Hengfen agreed to it and was even willing to let Xueyan stay overnight, assuming that she wanted something to take her mind off things.

It was not hard to notice that her mother had been cheered up to some degree in anticipation of the same old routine of hosting a houseful of guests. How pathetic it was that her mother's life revolved around those dinner parties and other social activities! She was so used to socialising with those ladies and gentlemen of high rank, ordering servants around, and everything else that was part of her upbringing. She couldn't leave, but her daughter was leaving.

When Ah Sheng came to inform Xueyan that her father had asked to see her, she was finalising her packing of that little blue suitcase, her heart burning with conflicting thoughts of grief and anticipation.

The opium lamp had been lit, but no opium was being heated over it. Jingyao was staring into the flame when Xueyan opened the door. He raised his eyes to meet hers and forced that same bitter smile: "Xueyan, do you hate me?"

Xueyan, do you hate me?

That sounded like words of farewell. That sounded so much like the last question from a dying man on his deathbed.

Xueyan didn't answer. She walked over to Jingyao and stroked his bony hand instead. She couldn't judge her father. How could she judge her father who used to be so absent-minded, but now looked like an innocent baby lying beside the lamp? How could she leave him to all his overwhelming pain and anxieties, which were beyond her mother's comprehension or capacity to bear?

She had a strange urge to cuddle him in her arms and take him away with her.

"I am so sorry, but we are occupied at the moment." *Yes, he had to go downstairs and take orders. Yes, he was occupied with being bullied and slaughtered.*

"I'm afraid I won't have the chance to see you again. Xueyan, do you hate me?"

His fair face was enveloped in a dark cloud of gloom on which smiles had long been absent. When she left, who would take her place to bridge the gap between her parents, who were like two foreigners who spoke different languages? Who would be able to bring out that knowing smile of his? Honestly, even if she stayed, she wouldn't be able to do that anymore. The identity of a conquered nation was already crushing and suffocating, even if it wasn't killing yet.

Father knew what I was doing, and he knew we didn't have much time together. He didn't need to guess where I was heading. Xueyan wanted to tell him: "How can I hate you! You are my father!" But she lost her voice amid her sobbing spasms.

Jingyao slowly rose from his low couch, patted her on the head, took hold of the cane leaning against the couch, and walked out of the room. He had lost so much weight that his alpaca gown was swinging. He wobbled. Xueyan rushed over to try to steady him, but halted on hearing Ah Sheng's voice telling him to mind his step. The glass doors closed, but her father's hoarse voice lingered on in the room.

Xueyan, do you hate me?

Xueyan was well aware who she should hate, but she wasn't capable of an emotion like hatred. Carrying her blue suitcase, she took the servant's passage downstairs. When she reached the gate of the residence, she swerved and ran into a storeroom behind the reception hall. She wanted to see her mother one last time, and bid her farewell.

The three enormous chandeliers were all on, shedding light on dozens of delicately arranged, potted chrysanthemums. The reception hall was radiant with the splendour of the light, the flowers and hosts of guests. Xueyan spotted her mother at once. Hengfen was in her brilliant blue thin cashmere *qipao* with a fine white linear pattern. The supreme quality of the cashmere made her look like she was enveloped in sheer gauze. Her blue-and-white-striped sweater complemented her face wreathed in smiles. In her favourite posture, leaning against the piano, although she didn't play the piano at all, she seemed to be quite enjoying herself in conversation with some figures from the art circles.

Xueyan was willing her mother to turn around and look in her direction, but Hengfen turned away and hurried to the hall gate, where several Japanese were entering, casting their eyes around the hall. Xueyan covered her eyes when she noticed the ingratiating attitude mixed in her mother's controlled, graceful smile.

She looked for her father, who might have been hiding in some tight corner in the hall. People applauded. With the applause, her father appeared from among the pots of chrysanthemums, hesitantly and cowardly, with his slumped shoulders and slouched back. The couple stood in front of a Japanese as if they were confessing in front of a priest, or as if they were getting married again, being witnessed by the man, or as if they were a pair of poor mice that had been captured and caged.

Xueyan, do you hate me?

Xueyan's tears gushed out. She turned away from the hall and almost ran out of the back gate. Once she was in the car, she kept turning back to look at the place where she had spent her last 23 years and which now she felt no ties to. The house was still the same old house, but the home was dissolving, like those buildings fading into the mist out of her sight.

A spasm of coughs from Lianxiu pulled Xueyan's thoughts back to reality, and to Lianxiu's ancient chair where she was now seated. Lianxiu felt so sorry about what Xueyan was going through, her heart torn between the people she cared most about in two different locations, and that she had left Xueyan alone in a trance after they had exchanged pleasantries. She had refreshed Xueyan's tea twice, unnoticed by her guest.

"Just another example of a wife going far and wide in search of her husband!" thought Lianxiu, her heart filled with a mixture of envy and sorrow. Her face turned scarlet with the fitful coughing.

"Where is Xiangge? Isn't she here?" asked Xueyan, gently stroking Lianxiu's back.

"I guess she is hanging out with that kid Ruiqi from the Huangs," answered Lianxiu. She thought it was nice that Xiangge might have found the right man to settle down with. "He's a nice enough kid in such hard times."

Xueyan didn't know Huang Ruiqi, so she refrained from making any comment. No matter how much stress and strain the war had caused, people still needed to survive and to move on, thought Xueyan, but she kept that thought to herself, and asked instead: "Why are you coughing? Have you taken any medicine?"

"Guitang has bought... he has asked Xiangge to buy me some medicine... but I haven't taken any," said Lianxiu, emabarrassed, her voice faltering as if she were tripping over her own tongue.

Xueyan didn't know what to say, so she fell silent again in her chair. The sun had long gone, and it was quite late in the evening. The autumn wind rustled over the fallen leaves on the ground, wafting waves of chill into the room.

Two voices in Xueyan's head were wrestling with each other. One chanted "Xueyan, do you hate me?", and the other cooed "Xueyan, come and join me!" The sorrow embodied in the chanting voice ruthlessly pierced through the happiness carried in the cooing voice, shattering it into millions of pieces.

Lianxiu tried her best to be hospitable to Xueyan. She would check Xueyan's clothes to see if she was warm enough, or touch the tea cup to make sure Xueyan's tea was always hot. Each movement triggered another coughing fit.

Xueyan decided she had to ask: What's taking Lü Guitang so long?"

"I don't know. He stays in the south compound and he doesn't come if he has no business here," answered Lianxiu, turning her head toward the gate, just as Lü Guitang popped in.

Xueyan stood up, pleasantly surprised at the sight of Lü Guitang. They didn't talk much before Guitang took Xueyan through the layers of courtyards all the way to the back garden, which had now been overrun by dead weeds and trees with bare branches.

Guitang whispered to her mysteriously: "You have never been here, have you, Miss Ling? But Mr Li Yuming has stayed here several times already."

They went past the tree where they saw that the door to the old building was tightly closed, with no sign of life. Guitang walked up to the door and gave three soft rhythmic knocks.

The door opened gently at his knocking, and out walked a young businessman, holding something in his hand.

"Li Yuming!" Xueyan cried out.

It was indeed quite dark inside the old building, but in Xueyan's eyes, Li Yuming was illuminating. He came from Wei Feng's side! That was illuminating enough!

"Wei Feng's quite alright." Li Yuming didn't start by greeting her. This simple sentence instantly brought tears to Xueyan's eyes. She had so many questions to ask about Wei Feng.

Yuming then continued that they knew what she was now going through and asked her to leave as early as possible. Two days later, they were going to deliver some drug products. If she could offer her assistance and go along with the team, it would kill two birds with one stone. They knew it was risky to transport drugs in such times, but they were confident they could do it.

"Do you know…" said Yuming, looking at her mischievously, tossing the object in his hand into the air and then catching it. It was a tennis ball he had picked up by the steps leading to the old building. "We used to call you the 'Virgin Mary', so you should go through all those things safe and sound, just like the Virgin Mary."

"I am not afraid of danger," Xueyan said, smiling hesitantly. It was great to start her journey toward Wei Feng; it would be even better if she could do something to help them! At least that would atone, to some degree, for what her father had done. "But, won't you judge me? My father…"

Li Yuming laughed confidently, sure of his knowledge about the rules and policies: "You are you, and Ling Jingyao is Ling Jingyao."

Xueyan noticed the way Yuming talked about her father, referring to him without any respectful title. She blushed with the sharp realisation of this fact.

Yuming noticed Xueyan's blushing and her uneasiness, too, but apart from feeling sorry for Xueyan, he had no other option. He put down the tennis ball, went over the details of the trip, and told Xueyan to meet him at Qianmen station the next morning. He would be wearing a marine blue silk gown with a black leather case in his hand. He reminded Xueyan to follow him but keep her distance so that no one would notice they were travelling together.

Lü Guitang said he wanted Xiangge to tag along with Xueyan as her travel companion.

"Xiangge?" Xueyan could picture Xiangge's smart face in her mind, and also her remarks about her willingness to leave Beiping even if she had to go to Japan. Xueyan felt uneasy at Xiangge's remarks, but then she blamed herself for being selfish. She turned to Guitang and said apologetically: "She might be thrilled that she can finally leave Beiping. She has always wanted to leave Beiping."

"She'll need your training all the way. When she's ready, she can go to Aunt Bichu," answered Guitang, keeping a respectful distance from Xueyan.

"You haven't asked about our destination," reminded Yuming, looking at Xueyan's pale, delicate face.

"We will be heading to where Wei Feng is," answered Xueyan, without thinking, her marble-smooth face turning rosy, adding a glimmer of hazy glamour to the dim room. Yes, what mattered to her was the fact that she was heading to where Wei Feng was. The geographical location didn't matter.

"Our first stop is Anci county in Hebei province, where Wei Feng may pick you up. Remember, you are going back to your hometown to visit your sick mother. If anything happens to me, you need to ignore it and keep going," said Yuming.

Xueyan hurriedly knocked three times on the dusty wooden table. It was a popular custom among the female students in Beiping, who believed that if one said one was not afraid of something horrible, something horrible would surely happen to the speaker, but three knocks on any piece of wooden furniture would cure the curse.

Yuming knew the 'custom' and was grateful for what Xueyan had just done for his sake. He mused for a while and said: "I hate to say this, but I think you need to publish an announcement renouncing your father."

"Is that really necessary?" said Xueyan, her voice trembling.

"Yes, it is. It is necessary for you, for Wei Feng and for Ling Jingyao." When he saw that Xueyan remained silent, he continued: "The medicine is now stored in the residence. You just need to take several packs."

"Xiangge can take some with her," said Guitang, wishing to add that he wanted to leave, too, and to help transport the drugs, but he was hesitant about whether it was proper for him to say so. He couldn't fight, nor could he formulate strategy. What he could do was too limited to be helpful. Instead of being helpful, he might be a hindrance to them.

Yuming happily shook hands with Guitang, as if he were a representative of a superpower, and said in a domineering and commanding tone: "Thank you. You may deliver the announcement to the Lings and let them publish it. I owe my thanks to Young Liu, a good judge of character." Young Liu had met Lü Guitang once when he had delivered a letter for him. He was so confident Guitang could be trusted that he later suggested Li Yuming go to Guitang for help.

At the command, Guitang decided to say nothing.

Li Yuming walked with Xueyan out of the back garden. He felt relieved. Asking Xueyan to transport the drugs reminded him of the time when he had asked Mrs Meng to destroy the document he had hidden in the garden of the Meng's house. Ah! These Virgin Maries! Mrs Meng's gentleness and peacefulness were so soothing. That was why he dared to hide the document in her garden. And Xueyan, who was now standing in front of him, displayed the true definition of female virtue: delicate yet defiant. Her fine taste in clothing was both satisfying and disturbing. The fuzzy pale lilac colour of her cashmere coat seemed to have awoken his long-lost dreams. This was THE woman, the better half of a man's life.

"Have you heard from Tantai Xuan?" asked Yuming, thinking in a jocular way that since the bride and bridegroom were separated, so were the best man and the maid of honour.

"Before Aunt Bichu left, she mentioned that the Tantais were heading for Kunming, too. I don't know where they ended up. But I guess Aunt Bichu and her family have already made it to Kunming."

Li Yuming turned round to look at the small old building whose fragility was masked by the darkness of the night.

"This old building is very nice but, you know, I didn't venture to go upstairs. I want to come back to have a good look at Shicha lake when the war is over and we are victorious." He squatted down and scooped up some soil covered beneath the fallen leaves. He inhaled the soil deeply: "So fresh! Such a good smell! Ultimately, everything reverts to dust."

Xueyan could sense how exhausted he was, and guessed Wei Feng might be feeling the same way. "Xueyan, come and join me!" The words lingered on and on in her heart. She was on her way! For the last year, she had been like an abandoned child wandering in the endless, ruthless desert, waiting, hoping to find some direction, some way out. Now she could see the way out, she could see tomorrow. Tomorrow, she would board the train which would take her to Wei Feng. She would be able to comfort him, guard him, cradle his head in her arms, and mesmerise him with her lullabies. Let her assume his fatigue, his ailments, his risks. Let her! Her face shone with these thoughts.

Li Yuming was moved by the aura Xueyan's face was bathed in.

Back in the gallery garden, Xueyan found Xiangge was already packing, her beautiful rosy cheeks resonating with joy and delight. When did she get the good news that she was leaving? Was she saying goodbye to the Huang kid just now? How come Lianxiu knew nothing while Xiangge was already packing? Xueyan was mystified.

"Miss Xueyan," Xiangge's voice rang like a bell. "If your case can't hold all your clothes, you may put some into my net basket." She was taking a half-empty net basket with her. Guitang came with 10 packs of medicine in his hands, such as quinine and aspirin, and was ready to put them into Xiangge's basket.

"Hey! It won't work like this. Who would put drugs in a net basket?" Xiangge laughed, took the drugs from her father, and handed them all over to Xueyan.

Xueyan took the drugs and gave Guitang a puzzled look, but it didn't take her long to understand Xiangge's intention of taking precautions to keep herself out of trouble by carrying drugs in her basket.

"Five packs for each!" Guitang said resolutely.

"That's alright. I'll put them all in my suitcase," Xueyan said, hurriedly. "My suitcase has an inner section where I can put the drugs. Besides, it is reasonable for someone who is visiting her sick mother to take some medical products with her." She was heading to Wei Feng, and Xiangge was just tagging along. She should shoulder all the risks since Xiangge had given up so much to leave the Huang kid behind.

Xiangge smugly took the clothes that Xueyan had taken out of her suitcase, and examined each item. She couldn't help feeling disappointed at the mediocre quality, but folded them carefully and put them into her basket. When she was done with the basket, she packed some smaller items into her cotton cloth wrapper with printed patterns. When she had finished, she eyed Xueyan: "Do you need a hand, Miss Xueyan?"

"I'm okay. I can manage," affirmed Xueyan, who was already closing her suitcase. She put two more packs of drugs into her handbag since she couldn't fit all 10 packs in her suitcase.

"Your handbag is indeed the safest place to hide them. Huang Ruiqi had once said that people seldom look in a woman's handbag," said Xiangge with a complacent smile, totally ignoring her father's sulking face.

"That will do then," said Xueyan. "Will your friend leave for you soon?"

"Him?" Xiangge twitched her lips, as was her habit. Her twitch was cute, adorable, and it suited her personality. "He's free to go anywhere he likes."

The words "I don't get it" were written all over Xueyan's gentle face.

"Neither of us is tied to the other. We are still young," explained Xiangge jubilantly.

"We are still young!" How blessed Xiangge was, thought Xueyan.

"You are not committed, are you?" asked Xueyan.

"You'll get to know me better later. No one ever really knows me. My dad is worried that I might become a turncoat, and that explains why he is in such a hurry to send me away. I know you are concerned about the safety of your father, Professor Ling, but I am not concerned about mine. He has someone to be concerned for him." Xiangge's eyes were not set on anything. Instead, they shifted with vitality here and there. Her tone already sounded unbridled.

Xueyan felt uneasy at Xiangge's behaviour. There seemed to be two layers in Xiangge's eyes, with the top layer docile like a pet dog, and the bottom defiant like a wolf. The ferocity was veiled under a superficial obedience. Xueyan didn't dare to look into that pair of eyes, nor did she think much about them. She didn't have much time because she had to draft her announcement to denounce her father.

During her last night in Beiping, how had things become so strange? Even the rustling from the leaves outside in the gallery garden was different from the rustling outside the windows of her room. What would happen in the future? Whatever happened, it wouldn't matter that much to her as long as she had the call, the cooing from her darling, calling her to join him in the land of the free. She laboured with every character she wrote down:

Announcement from Ling Xueyan: Ling Xueyan has forever renounced her relationship as a daughter to her father Ling Jingyao.

This didn't quite feel right, so she drafted another version:

Ling Jingyao has renounced his relationship as the father of his daughter Ling Xueyan.

This might help her father, but since they were no longer father and daughter, what did it matter?

Staring at the two pieces of paper, Xueyan felt nauseated. She imagined she could see an enormous opium lamp in the dim yellow light, radiating with a milky shimmer. Her father's gaunt face emerged from the light, looking at her with those sad eyes.

Xueyan, do you hate me?

No! No! No! I don't hate you! But I have to make the announcement to denounce you. You were too weak at the beginning, my dear father! The fire has reached you. Be careful! You should get away from it! Mama, come and help dad! Help!

Xueyan stretched her hand out in panic, trying to remove the lamp from her father, but a cold sweat flooded over her and her body slumped like jelly, too soft to move a limb.

The lamp was gone. Lianxiu was by her side, one hand grabbing hers and the other pinching her upper lip, trying to wake her up. Lianxiu was still coughing fitfully, and her apologetic smile lingered at the corners of her mouth. Her button-like eyes sparkled with tears.

"Alright! Alright! You really need to stop torturing yourself like this. I think it will be fine if you don't make the announcement," advised Lianxiu, full of sympathy and understanding.

It took Xueyan a while to respond. She leaned against the headboard, and checked her watch, which read 2:00am. "Why are you still up? It's so late."

"I just finished making five pancakes for you to take with you. They are made of pure flour." It took all the flour she had to make the five pancakes.

"Forgive me for being direct, but Miss Xueyan, you are so blessed to have a place to go, and to have so many people to worry about," sighed Lianxiu.

Xueyan, come and join me!

I'm coming!

How true it was that to have the option to leave was a blessing for many Chinese. All that was left behind of the city of Beiping was just a husk; the same was true of Ling Jingyao. Under the shining bayonets, by the mesmerising opium lamp, would more poor guys be bamboozled into baking their souls over the lamp fire when this ancient, enormous husk was coated with a veneer of 'culture'?

Xueyan took up her pen again and resolutely wrote for the third time:

Announcement by Ling Xueyan: Ling Xueyan forever renounces her relationship as the daughter of her father Ling Jingyao.

Having bolded up the word 'forever' twice for emphasis, she put the paper into an envelope and put the envelope on the nightstand. Staring at the envelope, she let her streams of tears roll down her cheeks.

A gurgle rose from the room in the back. It was Xiangge laughing in her dreams. It was a bright and bubbly sound, rippling through the darkness with its plump echoes.

When the gurgling stopped, the sobbing was gone, too. Even the fitful coughs paused. Darkness took over and devoured everything in one gulp.

At dawn the next day, in the warm glow of the early morning rays of the sun reflected on the white screen-wall of the front gate of No. 3 Chestnut Street, two slim figures walked out of the gate toward the rising sun. Gusts of wind funnelled the fallen leaves on the ground caked in dust into mini whirlpools, flapping and fluttering.

INTERLUDE

[AT THE END OF DEPARTURE FOR THE SOUTH]

Fallen leaves fluttered on the ground, coated with dust,
The grand, once bustling street lay still, bleak and deserted.
A crushing sadness emanated from
the plain white screen-wall,
While the sun's morning glory
blinded the travellers' eyes.
I deplored the passing of a whole year,
As I mourned for the home I left behind, old and dear.
Chilly autumn winds, I challenge you.
How dare you blow into the eyes of travellers,
And make them cry.
Mountains, rivers, blockades,
Shabby clothes, thin figures, longing hearts.
How many dedicated their hearts and youth
To the nation they loved so profoundly?
The travellers hastened on their way,
Leaving their souls buried in the dust of their hometown.
Were they destined ever to return?

AUTHOR'S NOTE

The original Chinese version of this book was started on 5 April 1985 and finished on 26 December 1987.

By the end of 1987, it felt like for the previous two years, 'struggle' had been the prevailing theme of my life.

For someone like me, who bargains with death on a daily basis, who can't fight with a sword, nor do I have the talent to fight with a pen, and who was stubbornly determined to complete an enormous task like *Wild Gourd Overture,* a four-book series (or possibly five, if I find time to write a fifth one), I totally deserve all the suffering engendered by such audacity.

My struggle derived from the fact that I was torn between the imaginary world of wild bottle gourds and reality. The best-case scenario was that when I wrote, I forgot about reality, concentrating on and indulging myself in the world of wild bottle gourds. Simple in theory but not in practice.

I tried my best to reduce my life to the bare minimum, but I couldn't avoid such duties as taking care of my parents and my children. Besides, my brain wouldn't have survived extended periods of highly stressful work while I was writing.

If I didn't want to burn myself out, I had to take breaks, some of which ended up being really long. It was painful to drag myself away from the world of wild bottle gourds; it was also an ordeal to stay in the real world knowing I hadn't finished my work in that world, and I still owed so much to that period of history, and to the characters in the book, too. Then I would feel even more sorry when I ignored the real people in the real world — my relatives, my friends — and treated them with unfair half-heartedness because of my focus on my writing.

For the previous two years, I seldom experienced enjoyment or pleasure of any kind.

So much for my struggle. What I am trying to say is that I would like to express my sincere gratitude to those who cared about this book, my parents' friends and my family, who generously offered their help. Without their precious insight, this period of history would have been blurred, as if narrated by a child. I would also like to thank the Foreign Literature Research Centre, China Academy of Social Sciences, where I worked, for their understanding and support, which saved me an enormous amount of struggle.

The first chapter of this novel entitled 'The Fireflies at Square Teakettle' was published in the May 1987 issue of *People's Literature*, a monthly magazine published by the China Writers Association, and the second chapter entitled 'Tears Shed in Square Teakettle' was published in June that year. I originally planned to call the four-book series *A Snow Tale of Two Cities*, which was not well received by my friends, so I changed it to *Wild Gourd Overture*, which was indeed the first title that came to mind when I conceived the series. It seems that things have come full circle. Just like the Chinese proverb 'what has he got in his bottle gourds', when asking someone what their true intentions are, one doesn't know what is inside someone else's bottle gourd. Moreover, it's just a 'tale' that relies on you, dear reader, to interpret it.

As another year came to an end, I was relieved to have wrapped up the draft of the first of the four-book series, *Departure for the South*. But the realisation that it was only the first of four, and that it might be just a waste of paper and the beginning of a disastrous journey for my editors and my readers, weighed heavily on my mind.

Whatever happens, I have to struggle on.

Fast-forward to the present - April 2018, three decades after publication of the Chinese edition – and I am about to publish this English edition of *Departure for the South*, to be followed soon by English editions of the other books in the series.